New Insights in Crop Monitoring and Management Using Remote Sensing Data

New Insights in Crop Monitoring and Management Using Remote Sensing Data

Guest Editors

Jonghan Ko
Wei Xue
Xinwei Li

MDPI

Basel • Beijing • Wuhan • Barcelona • Belgrade • Novi Sad • Cluj • Manchester

Guest Editors
Jonghan Ko
Applied Plant Science
Chonnam National
University
Gwangju
Korea

Wei Xue
College of Ecology and
Environment
Xinjiang University
Urumqi
China

Xinwei Li
College of Resource and
Environment
Anhui Science and
Technology University
Fengyang
China

Editorial Office
MDPI AG
Grosspeteranlage 5
4052 Basel, Switzerland

This is a reprint of the Special Issue, published open access by the journal *Remote Sensing* (ISSN 2072-4292), freely accessible at: https://www.mdpi.com/journal/remotesensing/special_issues/2DP2TL8I58.

For citation purposes, cite each article independently as indicated on the article page online and as indicated below:

Lastname, A.A.; Lastname, B.B. Article Title. *Journal Name* **Year**, *Volume Number*, Page Range.

ISBN 978-3-7258-5869-9 (Hbk)
ISBN 978-3-7258-5870-5 (PDF)
https://doi.org/10.3390/books978-3-7258-5870-5

Contents

About the Editors

Jonghan Ko

Jonghan Ko (ORCID: 0000-0001-7974-3808) is an ecological agronomy researcher serving as a Professor of Applied Plant Science, at Chonnam National University, Gwangju, South Korea. His research focuses on agricultural remote sensing and crop modeling to develop and deliver efficient crop growth and productivity monitoring practices for various aspects and scenarios and different geographical regions.

Wei Xue

Wei Xue (ORCID: 0000-0003-3257-7755) is currently an Associate Professor at the College of Ecology and Environment, Xinjiang University. His research is focused on understanding the ecophysiological responses of crops and desert plants to global environmental changes and underlying mechanisms by using mathematical models and remote sensing techniques. Dr. Xue has produced over 20 peer-viewed publications. Significant scientific achievements have been made in the principles of photosynthetic efficiency, the reconstruction of crop growth trajectories by new remote sensing algorithms, and the evolution of soil quality during the reclamation of sandy farmland. He obtained his PhD in plant ecology from the University of Bayreuth (Germany) (2012-2016) and used to work at Chonnam National University as a post-doctoral researcher.

Xinwei Li

Xinwei Li is an Associate Professor in the School of Resources and Environment at Anhui Science and Technology University. Dr. Li's research specializes in the integrated use of satellite, aerial, and ground-based remote sensing for agricultural condition monitoring. His work is primarily focused on the precision diagnosis of crop nitrogen status and the development of variable-rate fertilization control strategies. In addition to his academic role, where he teaches in the Geographic Information Science (GIS) program, Dr. Li serves as the Vice Director of the University's Office of Scientific Research. He also leads the Agricultural Remote Sensing Innovation Team within the School of Resources and Environment.

Preface

Remote sensing is promising for the monitoring and evaluation of crop growth, soil, water, and nutritional conditions and other associated agricultural indicators. This technology, combined with various analytical tools such as artificial intelligence and process-based crop models, can be utilized to collect within-season and spatial data to derive information on crop growth and eco-physiological conditions. Remote sensing with multiple sensors on diverse platforms can generate big data, posing severe challenges in data processing, analysis, and assimilation for the practical application of such data in agricultural production. On the other hand, technological developments in data fusion, machine learning, and artificial intelligence provide opportunities to generate big data and derive new information. The integration of remote sensing with advanced data processing techniques has the potential to revolutionize agricultural management. By leveraging multi-sensor data from satellites, drones, and ground-based sensors, farmers can obtain real-time insights into crop health, water stress, and nutrient deficiencies, allowing for the optimization of crop production at unprecedented spatial and temporal scales. This enables precise interventions, such as targeted irrigation and fertilization, reducing resource waste and environmental impacts. Furthermore, the fusion of remote sensing data with crop growth models and AI-driven analytics facilitates predictive farming, where crop yields and potential issues can be forecasted with high accuracy. Such advancements not only enhance productivity but also contribute to sustainable agricultural practices by optimizing resource use and minimizing ecological footprints.

Research topics included in this Reprint cover crop growth trajectory reconstruction, the retrieval of biophysical traits of leaves and crop canopies, crop aboveground biomass and yield prediction, and field irrigation amount estimation. Specifically, innovative remote sensing and image analysis tools or methods for the enhanced quantification of biophysical and biochemical variables of crops and soils were proposed. To improve the reconstruction accuracy of Landsat 5/7 EVI time series over cloud-prone, fragmented, and mosaic agricultural landscapes, Xue et al. developed a 'Light- and Temperature-Driven Growth Model and Double Logistic Function Fusion Algorithm' (LTDG-DL). The current version and its derivative offer avenues to rebuild large-scale crop growth dynamics over the decades. To retrieve wheat canopy, height, and aboveground biomass data, Muzalevskiy et al. explored the advantages of the joint use of MHz- and GHz-frequency band impulses when employing contactless ground penetration radar (GPR), and Zhu et al. developed a new three-dimensional conceptual model (n3DCM). Muzalevskiy's work validated the plausibility of the sub-nanosecond impulses in GPR loaded on the UAV platform to measure wheat height. The superiority of the n3DCM over the traditional vegetation index model and the traditional multi-feature combination model relies on the fusion of the plant height, leaf area index, and spike number to minimize the spectral saturation effects. Falcioni et al. integrated non-imaging hyperspectral sensors with chlorophyll fluorescence techniques, identifying specific spectral bands that are strongly correlated with chlorophyll a fluorescence to qualitatively estimate seventeen leaf biochemical and biophysical parameters in Tradescantia plants. For plant nitrogen concentrations, Zhou et al. estimated in-season cotton nitrogen contents using multi-angle hyperspectral data and machine learning models. However, most in-orbit satellites and drones equipped with sensors provide only visible and near-infrared (VNIR) bands. Çimtay's work demonstrated that when visible and near-infrared (VNIR)-only indexes are chosen and combined properly as the input for a deep neural network, it is possible to establish a high correlation between the Normalized Difference Nitrogen Index (NDNI) and NIR-only indexes. In this way, by using a VNIR-only band multispectral/hyperspectral camera and/or satellite, it is possible to estimate the nitrogen content of the plant progressively with high accuracy.

The optimization of crop planting density is a high priority in order to achieve substantial crop production. Timely seedling inspection and replenishment at the seedling stage are essential for late crop production management and yield formation. Feng et al. conducted a case study of cotton seedling detection using UAV multispectral images and deep learning methods and found that the UAV multispectral images acquired approximately 23 days after cotton sowing with the YOLOv7 algorithm achieved rapid and accurate seedling detection and counting throughout the cotton seedling stage. Another critical aspect of ensuring food security and irrigation scheduling is effectively monitoring crop growth, with the view of maximizing yield during the cultivation period. Bhusan Dhal et al. tested the performance of machine learning models (i.e., long short-term memory and auto-regressive integrated moving average models) for the in-season forecasting of canopy cover (CC) in cotton crops in Driscoll, Texas, in 2020 and 2021. To predict the daily CC of cotton in different regions, care is necessary when applying these methods. Additionally, the prediction of the entire seasonal CC with a daily resolution still requires data-driven training and the fine-tuning of the ML models in order to match different phases of the growth stage. The inclusion of multiple key growth traits into a 3D canopy model, such as the incorporation of the number of spikes into the n3DCM proposed by Zhu et al. (in this book), may offer an alternative method for effectively predicting in-season crop growth throughout the whole growth period without complex data training and parameter settings.

The precision management of agricultural fields relies on timely and efficient expert decision systems, which in turn are strongly dependent on bulk high-quality data collected by various devices and their corresponding techniques. The real-time and accurate acquisition of spatial soil moisture information at a field scale is beneficial for the timely adjustment of crop irrigation strategies and the refinement of irrigation schemes in local areas, which is helpful for promoting crop growth and improving yields. There are four conventional methods for determining the soil water content in fields: the gravimetric method, the hydrometric method, the electrical method, and dielectric techniques. Han et al. evaluated the performance of a EM38-MK2 geodesic conductivity meter for the inversion of water contents of soil profiles in arid regions where the spatial heterogeneity of the soil water and salt is high. In their results, the spatial heterogeneity of the soil profile's water content and salinity significantly influenced inversion results. The water content inversion accuracy is higher in root zones with low salinity than in non-root zones with high salinity. They also compared the inversion accuracy of the full-period model and the single-period model. Kobe et al. presented a technical approach for cost-effective, non-invasive, and time-lapse crop monitoring that automates the process of deriving further plant parameters, such as biomass, from 3D object information obtained via stereo images in the red, green, and blue (RGB) color spaces. The novelty of their research lies in the automated workflow, which includes a reliable automated data pipeline for 3D point cloud reconstruction from dynamic scenes of RGB images with high spatio-temporal resolutions.

The original contributions in this Reprint further broaden relevant applications in diverse agricultural environments using the latest remote sensing technologies, supporting field management decisions for improved resource use efficiency and sustainable production. We believe this Reprint will be of particular interest for stakeholders in agricultural policy areas, including climate change adaptation, digital agriculture, and modern farming techniques. Moreover, it serves as a valuable resource for researchers, academics, and practitioners seeking to stay abreast of cutting-edge developments in agricultural remote sensing. The in-depth analysis and practical case studies presented can inspire new research directions and innovative approaches in the field. By bridging the gap between theory and practice, this Reprint foster a more collaborative and informed community, working towards the common goal of enhancing agricultural productivity while safeguarding the environment.

Jonghan Ko, Wei Xue, and Xinwei Li
Guest Editors

remote sensing

MDPI

Article

Improving Reliability in Reconstruction of Landsat EVI Seasonal Trajectory over Cloud-Prone, Fragmented, and Mosaic Agricultural Landscapes

Wei Xue [1,2,*], Jonghan Ko [3], Ruyin Cao [4] and Zhiguo Yu [5]

1 Key Laboratory of Oasis Ecology of Education Ministry, College of Ecology and Environment, Xinjiang University, Urumqi 830049, China
2 Xinjiang Jinghe Observation and Research Station of Temperate Desert Ecosystem, Ministry of Education, Jinghe 833300, China
3 Department of Applied Plant Science, Chonnam National University, Gwangju 61186, Republic of Korea; jonghan.ko@jnu.ac.kr
4 School of Resources and Environment, University of Electronic Science and Technology of China, 2006 Xiyuan Avenue, Chengdu 611731, China; cao.ruyin@uestc.edu.cn
5 School of Hydrology and Water Resources, Nanjing University of Information Science and Technology, Nanjing 210044, China; zhiguo.yu@nuist.edu.cn
* Correspondence: xuewei@lzu.edu.cn; Tel.: +86-0931-8912560

Abstract: Although the Landsat 30 m Enhanced Vegetation Index (EVI) products are important input variables in land surface models, recurring Landsat 5/7 EVI time series over cloud-prone, fragmented, and mosaic agricultural landscapes is still a great challenge. In this study, we put forward a simple, but effective "Light and Temperature-Driven Growth model and Double Logistic function fusion algorithm" (LTDG_DL). The empirical basis of the LTDG_DL algorithm was traced from the de Wit crop growth simulation model and the commonly observed nonlinear correlation between the EVI and the Leaf Area Index (LAI). It assimilates the ground daily solar radiation and air temperature to generate seasonal profiles of the empirical LAI and EVI and conducts the within-season calibration of the empirical EVI by adjusting crop growth using cloud-free Landsat EVI observations. The initial date of seedling emergence (DOY_{ini}) and the accumulated Growing Degree Days for completion of the vegetative and Flowering stage (FGDDs) were variables to which the algorithm's accuracy was most sensitive. The variable-constrained optimization of the LTDG_DL algorithm was performed by loading the seedling emergence calendar of local prevailing crops and establishing an FGDD lookup table with an exhaustive sampling without replication method. Compared to temporal interpolation functions and Landsat–MODIS spatiotemporal fusion algorithms, the LTDG_DL algorithm had superior performance in the predictions of the EVI increment slope at the vegetative growth stage, the timing of the peak EVI, and the protection of key Landsat EVI observations over cloud-contaminated and complex landscape agricultural systems. Finally, the advantages and limitations of the LTDG_DL algorithm are discussed.

Keywords: Landsat EVI; time series; EVI reconstruction; agricultural landscapes

1. Introduction

In the 2000s, land holdings per family in China were recorded at 0.53 ha [1]. In Korea, approximately 69% of farms have small land parcels measuring less than 1.0 ha [2]. The majority of agricultural landscapes in East Asia consist of small land parcels (<1.5 ha, approximately 120 × 120 m) [3–5], which are significantly smaller than the average holding size of 19.3 ha in the USA [6]. Additionally, most patchy and fragmented agricultural landscapes in East Asia practice multi-crop planting [7,8]. One common atmospheric characteristic in East Asia monsoon areas is the regular occurrence of precipitation during the summer season, when crop growth accelerates [9,10]. However, the use of open-access high-temporal-resolution products from the Moderate-Resolution Imaging Spectroradiometer (MODIS) in highly fragmented and mosaic agricultural landscapes has been limited due to their coarse spatial resolution [7]. On the other hand, satellite products provided by the Landsat series, which are free to the public, offer an improved spatial resolution of 30 m and the longest continuous record of land surface reflectance since 1984 This includes Landsat 5 (1984–2013), Landsat 7 (1999–present), and Landsat 8 (2013–present) [11]. These data make it possible to analyze historical changes in land use and land cover change in the agricultural sector and detect crop types in certain areas [6,12–14]. However, research on the quality of Landsat data has shown that obtaining at least three high-quality observations from Landsat 5–7 within a single crop growing season is not feasible on a large scale due to issues such as cloud coverage, selective scene acquisition, sensor malfunction, and other factors [15–17]. Therefore, monitoring crop growth in cloud-prone and complex landscape regions is still a significant challenge, especially when using retrospective Landsat VI data from Landsat 5/7.

The contemporary methods for reconstructing Landsat VI can be classified into two groups based on the reconstruction algorithms: those that use auxiliary information to infer the reflectance or VI of ground objects and those that do not [18,19]. The first group includes VI/reflectance temporal interpolation functions, while the second group consists of Landsat–MODIS VI/reflectance spatiotemporal fusion methods. While some reconstruction algorithms provide calibrated reflectance estimates, most of the algorithms in the literature focus on VI as the outcome [20]. The VI temporal interpolation function is specifically designed for Landsat VI data. Two commonly used global temporal interpolation functions, namely Savitzky–Golay (SG) and Double-Logistic (DL), have been successfully applied to single-year continuous MODIS VI time series [21–24]. They have also been used for aggregating multi-year cloud-free Landsat Enhanced Vegetation Index (EVI) data [25]. Harmonic time series models, which utilize sines and cosines, have shown good performance in fitting single-year temporally rich Landsat Normalized Difference Vegetation Index (NDVI) data, with the Root-Mean-Squared Error (RMSE) ranging from 0.05 to 0.08 [26]. However, reliable NDVI reconstruction is challenging when fitting single-year coarse Landsat observations, resulting in higher RMSE values (RMSE $\geq$ 0.12) [27]. The coefficient estimations of the global temporal interpolation functions are highly sensitive to the range of dates and the density of Landsat VI observations. These functions also lack flexibility [28]. Although long-term mean changes in Landsat VI can be detected, they cannot adequately represent inter-annual variability in the land cover and land use in the agricultural sector.

In Landsat–MODIS VI spatiotemporal fusion methods, the first step is to perform gap-filling of missing Landsat values in order to obtain more cloud-free satellite data, then one or two smoothing functions are applied [5,19,29–32]. The Landsat–MODIS fusion method predicts Landsat VI data at daily or consistent time steps. It is trained using a medium number of cloud-free Landsat and MODIS NDVI image pairs on base dates, and then, it predicts Landsat images on prediction dates along with corresponding cloud-free MODIS NDVI image. Various Landsat–MODIS fusion methods with different algorithm structures have been developed. Examples include the Gap-Filling and Savitzky–Golay filtering method (GF-SG) [32], the Spatial and Temporal Adaptive Reflectance Fusion Model (STARFM) [33] and its derivatives [19,34], and the Flexible Spatiotemporal DAta Fusion (FSDAF) [35]. The GF-SG/STARFM/FSDAF method involves a key step, which is the generation of a synthesized NDVI time series. This is achieved by fusing MODIS NDVI time series data at 250/500 m resolution with cloud-free Landsat observations (referred to as Landsat observations unless otherwise indicated). In order to improve the fusion accuracy, algorithms have progressed from directly merging multiple satellite photos on distinct forecast dates to the weighted fusion of partially cloud-free images [32,36,37]. However, there are four critical issues that these fusion methods encounter, which need to be addressed: (1) The EVI, which can reduce the saturating effects of dense canopy as much as possible, performs better than the NDVI [38]. (2) The spatial resolution of MODIS pixels

(500/250 m) covers fragmented land parcels with multi-crop planting systems, resulting in week spatial autocorrelation between the MODIS and Landsat VI temporal shapes. This leads to incorrect quantification of the land surface crop phenology under certain conditions. (3) The reliability of these methods depends on a medium number of consistently gap-filled high-quality Landsat data on dates close to the prediction dates, which cannot be guaranteed in cloud-prone areas wherein the whole Landsat scene is contaminated by clouds at several acquisition dates. (4) These methods cannot be applied to regions or years where/when MODIS observations are not available. Consequently, there may be inadequate reconstruction in Landsat EVI time series in certain areas. For example, this can occur with fast-growing crops that have continuous missing MODIS/Landsat EVI values or in fragmented agricultural ecosystems, where crops with diverse phenological features grow adjacent to each other.

Although numerous methods for Landsat EVI reconstruction have been proposed, the question of how to reduce uncertainty in the daily series reconstruction for small land parcels during periods without MODIS data such as the 1990s and 2000s remains unanswered. This study addressed this question by introducing a novel algorithm, Light- and Temperature-Driven Growth and Double-Logistic fusion (LTDG_DL), which uses daily ground meteorological data and Landsat EVI observations to generate daily 30 m EVI profiles for the crop growing seasons. Section 2 provides a detailed description of the conceptual framework of LTDG_DL and its bivariable co-strained optimization solutions (Section 2). Section 3 discusses the validation objects, including four farming parcels in the Republic of Korea, China, and the USA where the crop types, Landsat, and field EVI observations were known and available; the cloud-prone Haean basin in the Republic of Korea, which features fragmented and mosaic agricultural landscapes with a known crop phenology; and the cloud-prone Shandong Province in China, where the crop types in double-cropped agricultural systems are unknown. The Sections 4 and 5 present the results and discussion, respectively.

2. Development of the LTDG_DL Algorithm

The LTDG_DL algorithm is executed on a daily basis for reconstructing one-season EVI. It consists of two interconnected sub-models (Figure 1): the DL function and the LTDG model. While LTDG_DL does not require site calibration at the per-pixel level, it is still necessary to refine exclusive parameters for different agroclimatic zones. Two structural parameters must be constrained in order to obtain satisfactory daily Landsat EVI data. The algorithm principles of LTDG_DL and its structural parameters are explained in Section 2.1, followed by Section 2.2, which presents the bivariable-constrained optimization solutions.

2.1. Algorithm Principles

2.1.1. The DL Function

The SG and DL functions are commonly used statistical measures for preparing satellite VI time series. The SG function is primarily utilized to smooth consecutive VI time series by applying a weighted moving average with a polynomial of a certain degree [39]. The degree of the smoothing polynomial is determined by the time window size and the number of data points within that window. However, the SG function has limitations when dealing with irregularly distributed observations and continuously missing data points over an extended period. This is due to the fact that rare satellite observations can be considered as "sudden/spike points" and are either removed or flattened [28]. Previous studies have proposed the use of the DL function to fit MODIS NDVI observations from a single season, which allows for less homogeneity in the temporal distribution while preserving important cloud-free observations [23,24]. In this study, we applied the DL model to fit Landsat EVI observations for one season using Equation (1), resulting in the generation of daily EVI data ($dEVI_{DL}$) (as shown in Figure 1).

$$f(t, x_1, x_2, x_3, x_4) = \frac{1}{1 + \exp\left(\frac{x_1 - t}{x_2}\right)} - \frac{1}{1 + \exp\left(\frac{x_3 - t}{x_4}\right)} \quad (1)$$

where x_1 and x_3 are the locations of the left (the increasing phase) and right (the decreasing phase) inflection points, respectively; x_2 and x_4 determine the rate of change at these points; t is the day of the year. x_1 and x_3 are defined as the date when the crop growth rate is maximized and the date when the crop senescence rate is maximized, respectively. The ranges of x_2 and x_4 are limited to [8.8, 40.9] and [8.8, 40.9], respectively. The DL model, which incorporates constrained values for x_2 and x_4, has shown the ability to accurately predict VI time series data for temperate crops [24]. It should be noted that the range of x_2 and x_4 may differ between temperate and tropical crops.

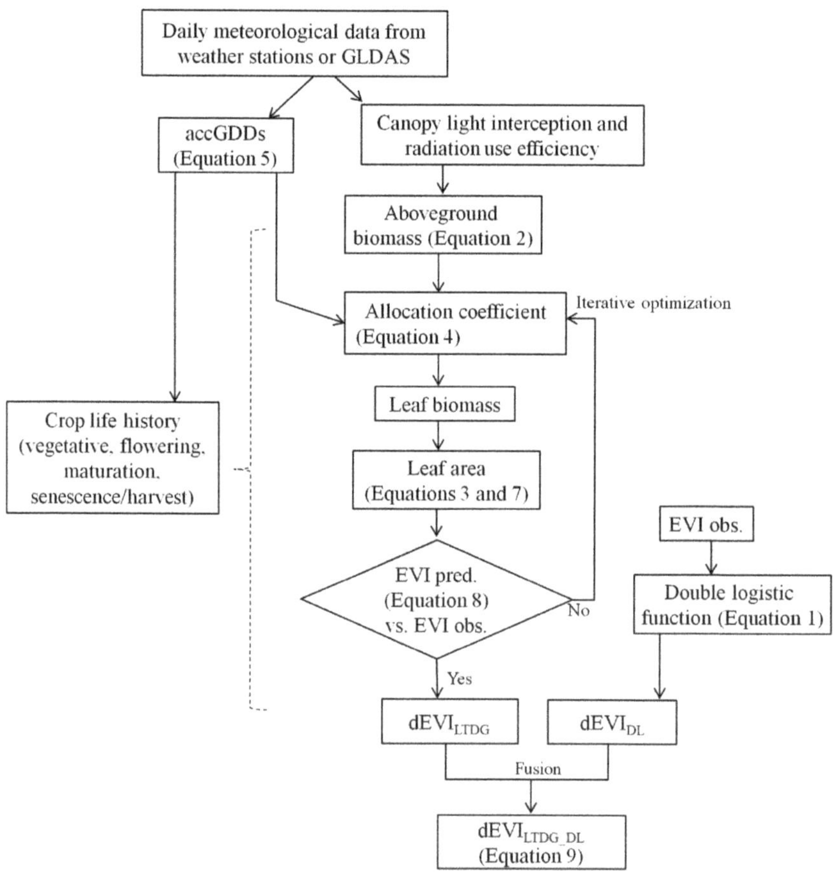

Figure 1. Schematic illustration of the LTDG_DL algorithm to reconstruct one-season daily Landsat EVI data in complex landscape agricultural systems. accGDDs: accumulated Growing Degree Days; EVI: Enhanced Vegetation Index; LTDG_DL: Light- and Temperature-Driven Growth (LTDG) model and Double-Logistic (DL) function fusion algorithm; dEVI$_{LTDG}$: daily EVI data reconstructed by the LTDG; dEVI$_{DL}$: daily EVI data reconstructed by the DL; pred.: prediction; obs.: observation; GLDAS: the Global Land Data Assimilation System; canopy light interception: the amount of solar radiation intercepted by plant canopies.

2.1.2. The LTDG Model

The LTDG model explores the principles of the "School of de Wit" crop growth simulation models [40,41]. It operates under the assumptions that the crop growth and development potentials are primarily influenced by the interception of sunlight by the canopy (i.e., the amount of solar radiation intercepted by the canopy) and the accumulation of Growing Degree Days (accGDDs) [42]. The variations observed in satellite EVI measurements throughout the seasons are attributed to changes in crop growth dynamics, specifically alterations in canopy size in irrigated and rainfed fields [38,43–45]. In the LTDG model, the daily aboveground biomass production is estimated using a radiation use efficiency model, which is then multiplied by canopy light interception and radiation use efficiency [46]. Canopy light interception is typically determined using Beer's law, which calculates it as the product of the green Leaf Area Index (LAI) and light extinction coefficient (k) [47]. The increase in aboveground biomass on the ith day after seedling emergence or transplanting ($\Delta M_{AGB,i}$, units: g) is represented by the following equation:

$$\Delta M_{AGB,i} = \varepsilon \times \beta \times R_{s,i} \downarrow \times (1.0 - \exp(-k \times LAI_i)) \tag{2}$$

where ε is the radiation use efficiency (default 3.5 g MJ^{-1}); β is the fraction of total solar radiation that is photosynthetically active radiation (default 0.45); $R_{s,i}\downarrow$ is the daily incident solar irradiance on the ith day (MJ day^{-1}); k is light extinction coefficient (default 0.5); LAI_i is the green Leaf Area Index on the ith day (m^2 m^{-2}).

The expansion of the canopy area during the vegetative growth and flowering stages, as well as its decline during the maturation stage are regulated by a biomass allocation coefficient (ρ) (Equation (3)). The ρ value indicates whether there is positive or negative growth and senescence in the canopy. This coefficient, expressed as a function of accGDDs in Equation (4), determines the amount of daily increase in aboveground biomass allocated to leaves.

$$\Delta LA_i = \rho_i \times \Delta M_{AGB,i} \times SLA \tag{3}$$

$$\rho_i = 1.0 - a_i \times \exp(b_i \times accGDDs_i) \tag{4}$$

where ρ_i is the allocation coefficient of $\Delta M_{AGB,i}$ to leaves on the ith day; SLA is the Specific Leaf Area (default 0.024 m^2 g^{-1}); ΔLA_i is the daily increase in canopy Leaf Area on the ith day (m^2 m^{-2}); $accGDDs_i$ is the accGDDs on the ith day; a_i and b_i are model coefficients on the ith day. The GDD on the ith + 1 d (GDD_{i+1}, °C) is computed by the daily air temperature and base temperature as follows:

$$accGDDs_{i+1} = accGDDs_i + GDD_{i+1} \tag{5}$$

$$GDD_{i+1} = \max[T_{air,i+1} - T_{base}, 0] \tag{6}$$

where $T_{air,i+1}$ is the daily air temperature on the ith + 1 d (°C) and T_{base} is the base temperature below which crop growth ceases (default 5 °C for crops in temperate regions). The accGDDs on the initial date of seedling emergence/transplanting (DOY_{ini}) are equal to GDD_1. The accumulated leaf area on the ith + 1 d is a product of the LAI on the ith day plus the daily increase in leaf area on the ith day (Equation (7)), and the empirical EVI on the ith + 1 d is generated by using a generic EVI-LAI equation (Equation (8)).

$$LAI_{i+1} = \Delta LA_i + LAI_i \tag{7}$$

$$EVI_{i+1} = e \times LAI_{i+1}^{f} \tag{8}$$

where e and f are model coefficients (defaults 0.39 and 0.51, respectively) [41].

The empirical EVI can deviate significantly from the actual Landsat EVI observation on the same date due to the seasonal impacts of environmental factors, such as prolonged drought or nutrient deficiency, affecting crop growth. The LTDG method utilizes Landsat EVI observations to calibrate the empirical EVI within a season. To ensure that the adjusted EVI simulations match the Landsat EVI observations on all observation dates, the daily ρ and initial conditions of the LAI (LAI_{ini}, default 0.002 m^2 m^{-2}) at seedling emergence/the transplanting date are dynamically adjusted using an iterative numerical procedure. In this iterative process, two statistics, E^+ and E^-, are used to quantify the difference between the simulation and the observation values. E^+ represents the sum of the positive errors between the simulation and the observation values; likewise, E^- represents the absolute value of the sum of the negative errors. The total error, E, is calculated as the sum of E^+ and E^-. A satisfactory fit between the simulation and observation EVI values occurs when E^+ is equal to E^-. To determine the LAI_{ini} that achieves the best fit, the secant method developed by Conte and de Boor [48] is employed. Once the fit involving LAI_{ini} is obtained, daily ρ is adjusted using the parameters a_i and b_i through parabolic interpolation [49] to minimize the value of E.

The life history of annual and perennial crops is traditionally divided into four phenological phases: vegetative, flowering, grain/fruit maturation, and senescence/harvest phases. The development of the crop phenology closely follows the accumulation of GDDs throughout its lifespan. The accGDDs required to transition from one phenological stage to the next are relatively consistent within crops, but vary greatly among different crop types [42,50]. In this study, the total number of accGDDs needed to complete each phenological phases is represented by VGDDs, FGDDs, MGDDs, and HGDDs, respectively. In determinate crops, the plant stops growing beyond the point where the flowers have bloomed. Conversely, morphologically indeterminate crops such as cotton exhibit simultaneous growth and flower setting, which differs from the determinate crops, such as paddy rice. Considering the use of the LTDG in multi-crop planting systems that include both indeterminate and determinate crops, the VGDDs and FGDDs for the vegetative and flowering phases are combined (hereinafter referred to as FGDDs). Differences in crop phenological development between early-maturing and late-maturating varieties mainly stem from variations in the FGDDs [50]. The FGDDs can be considered the primary variable that differs considerably among crop types.

For agricultural pixels with infrequent Landsat EVI observations over prolonged periods of time, the daily EVI data reconstructed by LTDG ($dEVI_{LTDG}$) may yield higher or lower values than the $dEVI_{DL}$ on certain observation dates. Therefore, an average of the $dEVI_{DL}$ and $dEVI_{LTDG}$ without weighted coefficients is used as the resulting output ($dEVI_{LTDG\_DL}$). This calculation is performed as follows:

$$dEVI_{i,LTDG\_DL} = \sum_{i=1} (dEVI_{i,LTDG} + dEVI_{i,DL})/2.0 \tag{9}$$

2.2. Bivariable-Constrained Optimization Solutions

Although LTDG_DL includes numerous parameters, the reconstruction of daily EVI data can be achieved satisfactorily by utilizing constrained configurations of two specific parameters: DOY_{ini} and the FGDDs.

2.2.1. Constrained Configurations of DOY_{ini}

DOY_{ini} can vary greatly across different agroclimatic zones due to variations in personal preference for seeding date and choice of crop [24]. In agricultural landscapes within agroclimatic zones where the crop types are unknown, a landscape-level DOY_{ini} setting was establishing by incorporating the seedling emergence calendar of locally predominant crops. To configure the landscape-level DOY_{ini}, satellite EVI observations from a specific number of agricultural pixels were merged to generate an endmember ensemble of Landsat EVI observation time series (see Figure S1 in the Supporting Information, Section S1). The onset of the consistent increase phase in the seasonal EVI curves included in the endmember EVI ensemble can be used to determine the landscape-level DOY_{ini} more easily.

2.2.2. Constrained Configurations of the FGDDs

Uncertainty in the FGDDs may significantly impact Landsat EVI reconstruction accuracy [41]. In a case study of the paddy rice crop, there were six Landsat EVI observations from DOY_{ini} until the end of the growing seasons (Figure 2a). Reconstructed daily EVI data that well-captured the Landsat EVI observations were obtained using FGDDs = 900 °C. However, when only four Landsat EVI observations were available over the rice growing seasons (two mid-season EVI observations in Figure 2a were masked in Figure 2c), a better reconstruction of the daily EVI profile was achieved using FGDDs = 750 °C. The FGDDs at 750 °C in the case with only three available Landsat EVI observations (three data points in Figure 2a were masked in Figure 2e) generated a superior daily EVI curve compared to other FGDDs (Figure 2e). These results indicate that the satisfactory generation of daily Landsat EVI data using FGDDs is dependent on the number of available Landsat EVI observations. Given the sensitivity of the LDTG_DL modeling performance to the density of Landsat EVI observations, incorporating more EVI data points into LTDG_DL may help improve EVI reconstruction accuracy.

Landsat EVI observations from DOY_{ini} to the end of the crop growing seasons (around mid-October in Northeast Asia) were utilized to generate various combinations of EVI observations. An exhaustive sampling without replication method was employed to develop these groups of EVI observation combinations, resulting in *m* groups of EVI observation combinations, as shown in Figure 3. Each of these *m* groups was then input into LTDG_DL to produce an equal number of $dEVI_{LTDG\_DL}$ outputs. By averaging the *m* groups of $dEVI_{LTDG\_DL}$, a single seasonal EVI profile was obtained (see $\overline{dEVI_{LTDG\_DL}}$ in Figure 3). Notably, it was observed that EVI combination groups with a least three Landsat EVI observations performed better than those with only one or two observations. If there were fewer than three Landsat EVI observations available over the crop growing seasons, no EVI combination groups could be generated. Figure 2b illustrates the generation of twenty EVI combination groups using the exhaustive sampling method with six Landsat EVI observations ($C_6^3 = 20$). Interestingly, the results showed no significant differences in reconstructed daily EVI data when comparing the FGDDs of 750, 800, 850, and 900 °C, which contrasts with the finding presented in Figure 2a. Furthermore, Figure 2d exhibits the superior performance of the FGDDs = 750 °C compared to Figure 2c when four groups of EVI combinations ($C_4^3 = 4$) were used to drive the LTDG_DL model. This is evidenced by the reconstructed maximum EVI closely aligning with the maximum EVI observation shown in Figure 2a. In Figure 2b,d,e, it is apparent that the FGDDs of 750 °C yielded the best results in reconstructing daily EVI data. These findings suggest that the exhaustive sampling without replication method improved the accuracy of EVI reconstruction in crop pixels with low Landsat EVI observation density.

A set of FGDDs produces the same number of $\overline{dEVI_{LTDG\_DL}}$, which were used to create a reference database called $LEVI_{reference,n}$ (refer to Figure 3). The appropriate FGDDs for each agricultural pixel can be determined by comparing them with Landsat EVI observations on various observation dates and selecting the one in the $LEVI_{reference,n}$ database that shows the best agreement with the Landsat EVI observations (i.e., the smallest RMSE), considered as the optimized $dEVI_{LTDG\_DL}$ (see Figure 3). Additionally, a lookup table was established, which comprises *n* groups of FGDDs, MGDDs, and HGDDs (Figure 3). The FGDD lookup table, accompanied by an exhaustive sampling method without replication, plays a vital role in generating the optimized $dEVI_{LTDG\_DL}$.

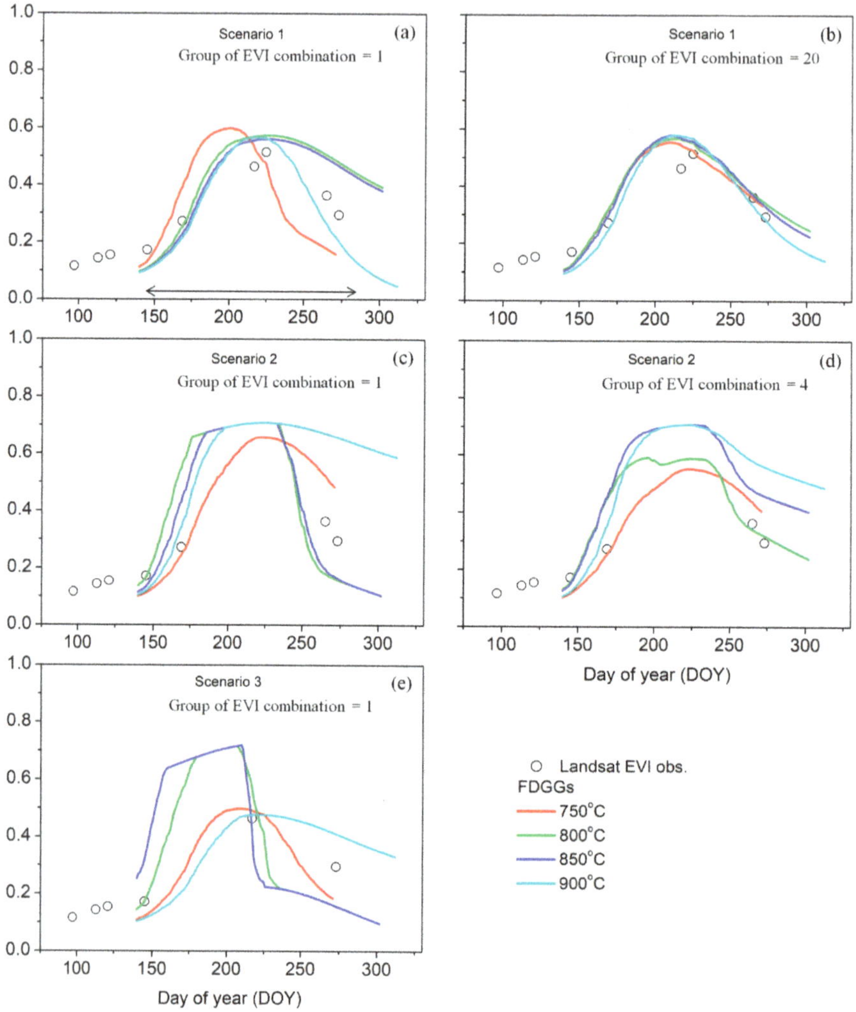

Figure 2. Effects of varying FGGDs values (750, 800, 850, and 900 °C, (**a**,**c**,**e**)) and the group number of Landsat EVI observation combinations (**b**,**d**) on Landsat EVI reconstruction. Crop growing seasons are indicated by the double-arrow line in (**a**). Six, four, and three Landsat EVI observations from DOY_{ini} to the end of the crop growing seasons are available in Scenarios 1, 2, and 3, respectively. The group of EVI observation combination = 1 in (**a**,**c**,**e**) represents that all EVI observations of the crop growing seasons were grouped into one EVI observation combination. For the case of six EVI observations over the crop growing seasons, the exhaustive sampling method without replication helped yield 20 groups of EVI observation combinations, wherein each group had at least three EVI observations ($C_6^3 = 20$, (**b**)). Using this procedure, four EVI observations over the crop growing seasons yielded four groups of EVI observation combinations ($C_4^3 = 4$, (**d**)), and three EVI observations over crop growing seasons had only one group of EVI observation combination ($C_3^3 = 1$, (**e**)). FGDDs: the accumulated Growing Degree Days for completion of the vegetative and Flowering stage; EVI: Enhanced Vegetative Index; DOY_{ini}: the initial seedling emergence/transplanting date; LTDG_DL: Light- and Temperature-Driven Growth model and Double-Logistic function fusion algorithm; obs.: observation.

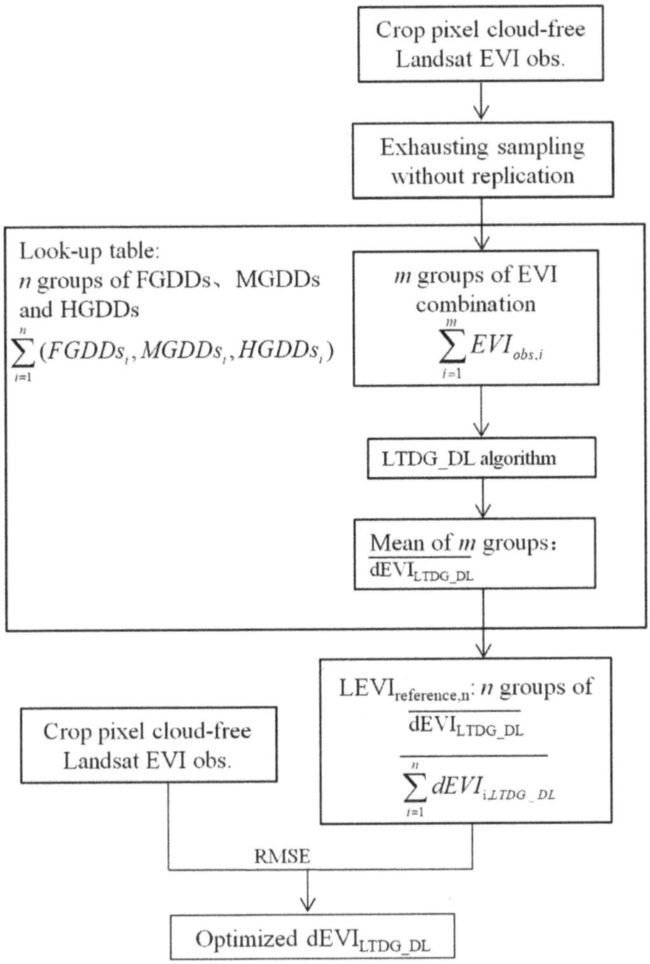

Figure 3. Data-processing roadmap of the FGDD-constrained optimization solution involved in the LTDG_DL algorithm. obs.: observation; GDDs: Growing Degree Days; EVI: Enhanced Vegetation Index; RMSE: root mean square error; LTDG_DL: a parameter-constrained Light- and Temperature-Driven Growth (LTDG) model and Double-Logistic (DL) function fusion algorithm; FGDDs: the accumulated GDDs required to complete the vegetative growth and Flowering stage; MGDDs: the accumulated GDDs for completion of the Maturation stage; HGDDs: the accumulated GDDs for completion of the Harvest stage; $\overline{dEVI_{LTDG\_DL}}$: the mean of daily EVI data reconstructed by m groups of EVI observation combinations.

In this study, a lookup table for the FGDDs was established, encompassing a temperature range of 600 to 1200 °C with a sampling interval of 50 °C (i.e., 600, 650, 700, ..., 1200). For each crop pixel, a total of fourteen $dEVI_{LTDG\_DL}$ datasets were generated. These fourteen datasets were then clustered to create the $LEVI_{reference,n}$, denoted as n ($n \in 14$). The optimized daily Landsat EVI profile, referred to as $LEVI_{optimized}$, was determined by evaluating its RMSE against Landsat EVI observations on all observation dates, as follows:

$$LEVI_{optimized} \approx \min\left(\sum_{j=1}^{n} LEVI_{reference,j}, Landsat_{obs}\right) \tag{10}$$

The development of the FGDD lookup table adhered to the following criteria: (1) FGDDs > MGDDs > HGDDs; (2) the sum of FGDDs, MGDDs, and HGDDs should be equal to or less than the total accGDDs of the crop growing seasons. Crop growing seasons are defined as the period starting on DOY_{ini} and ending on the first autumn date when the daily air temperature falls below T_{base}.

3. Algorithm Validations

Validations of the LTDG_DL were conducted using three independent datasets. The first dataset consisted of three experimental fields; the second dataset included agricultural landscapes in the Haean basin; the third dataset encompassed regional agricultural landscapes in Shandong Province. These datasets presented various climate types, different crop types in distinct cropping systems, and varied densities of Landsat EVI observations throughout the crop growing seasons in each agricultural system. The Haean basin and Shandong Province are characterized by fragmented and mosaic agricultural landscapes, which aligned well with the selection of the validation objects pertaining to our research question. Additionally, auxiliary information regarding crop phenology and weather station data was accessible in the Haean basin.

Four variables were used to assess the accuracy of EVI reconstruction with consideration given to the crop growth trajectory. These variables included the EVI increment slope, the EVI decline slope, the absolute EVI, and the timing of peak EVI (T_{peak_EVI}). It should be noted that the T_{peak_EVI} derived from the crop pixels with a low density of Landsat EVI observations may not accurately represent the field conditions. For the validation of the DL, LTDG, and LTDG_DL methods, crop pixels in the Haean basin that had a peak EVI reasonably close to the flowering stage were selected. To obtain detailed information on crop phenology in the Haean basin, the study by Lindner et al. [3] was consulted. The RMSE and R^2 were calculated as indictors of modeling accuracy.

3.1. Introduction of the Three Experimental Fields and Parameter Settings of the LTDG_DL

Four crops were selected for algorithm validation in well-managed experimental fields located in Yanhu in China (34°27′03″N, 117°07′11″E), Nebraska in the USA (41°10′46.8″N, 96°26′22.7″W), and Gimje in the Republic of Korea (35°45′N, 126°56′E) [51–53]. The DOY_{ini} settings were determined based on the onset of the consistent increase phase of Landsat EVI observations. Portable multi-spectral sensors were used to extract field EVI measurements from these studies. The EVI increment slope, which represents the increase in the EVI per day during the vegetative growth stage, and the EVI decline slope, which represents the decrease in the EVI per day during the senescence stage, derived from the field EVI measurements were considered as benchmarks to evaluate the performances of the DL, LTDG, and LTDG_DL methods. The calculation modes of the EVI increment and decline slopes are illustrated in the inset of Figure 5h.

The Landsat EVI observations of the growing season were categorized into two scenarios, as shown in Figure 5a–d. The first scenario, labeled S1 manipulation, represented the situation where the EVI observations were intentionally excluded during the periods of rapid green-up and senescence. This is depicted by small triangles. The second scenario, labeled S2 manipulation, depicted the condition where the EVI observations were purposely omitted around the date of the maximum EVI. This is represented by big circles. The S1 and S2 scenarios exemplified the instances of low-density Landsat EVI observation and irregular seasonal distributions, which are commonly observed at larger spatial scales [15,16]. For the validation of the DL, LTDG, and LTDG_DL methods, all Landsat EVI observations during the crop growing seasons were utilized.

The year-round daily meteorological data (T_{air} and R_s; see Supporting Information S2) were obtained from the Global Land Data Assimilation System Version 2 products (GLDAS2.0) at the same location and year. These data are available at a daily resolution with a spatial resolution of 0.25° × 0.25° (https://disc.gsfc.nasa.gov/datasets?keywords=GLDAS) (accessed on 5 March 2023). The year-round Landsat 5/7/8 surface reflectance images, centered on the farming lands, were downloaded from the U.S. Geological Survey (USGS) Earth Explorer on 5 July 2022. These images underwent radiometric and atmospheric corrections using the radCor function of the RStoolbox package in the R language (R Core Team, 2021) [54]. Since Landsat 5 and 7 exhibit a good and consistent match in surface reflectance [55], no further adjustments were necessary regarding sensor geometry. However, the Landsat 5/7 surface reflectance was adjusted to be compatible with Landsat 8 using the band-specific surface reflectance linear regression parameters provided by Roy et al. [56]. Data points with poor Quality Assurance (QA) or blue reflectance of $\geq$0.2 were considered outliers due to contamination from clouds or aerosols [24]. Reflectance data in the blue (ρ_{blue}, 450–520 nm), red (ρ_{red}, 630–690 nm), and near-infrared (ρ_{nir}, 760–900 nm) bands were used to calculate the EVI [38]. It should be noted that the radCor processing applied to remove cloud and shadow pixels for atmospheric corrections was not perfect [54]. As a result, residual clouds and shadows may appear as distinct outliers in the EVI time series. Due to the irregular observations and low density of observation during the crop growing seasons, reliable outlier detection could not be performed [26]. Therefore, outlier detection techniques were not used to evaluate the radCor-processed Landsat 5/7/8 EVI images.

3.2. Introduction of Agricultural Landscapes in Haean Basin and Parameter Settings of LTDG_DL

The Haean basin (128°5′–128°11′E, 38°13′–38°20′N, 297 lines × 385 rows) is located in Yanggu county in Gangwon Province, the Republic of Korea. The topography of the basin resembles a "punch-bowl" shape, with a north–south length of 10.5 km and an east–west width of 6.7 km. Within the Haean basin, a single-cropping system is implemented. Based on field census data from 2009 and 2010 [7], the average parcel area for different crops in the Haean basin is as follows: paddy rice 0.91 ha, potato 0.69 ha, orchard 0.81 ha, bean 0.47 ha, cabbage 0.73 ha, radish 0.69 ha, and ginseng 0.80 ha. The mean parcel area of all croplands is 0.72 ± 0.13 ha (mean ± standard deviation). The land use and cover change in the Haean basin during the years 2009 and 2010 are presented in Supporting Information S3.

Field EVI measurements in the Haean basin were not initiated. Surface reflectance images from Landsat 5/7 were downloaded from the Earth Explorer on 26 September 2021 for the years 2009 and 2010. Figure 4 illustrates EVI observational images throughout the crop growing seasons. In 2009, less than 50% of the basin pixels had a fraction of growing season Landsat EVI observations of approximately 91%. In 2010, approximately 87% of the basin pixels had a rate of 61%. A significant proportion had a low fraction of growing season EVI observations (20–40%) in 2009. With the exception of cloud-free data during the early and late growth stages, most pixels had only one or two to three cloud-free EVI observations within the rapid and peak growing seasons.

The landscape-level DOY_{ini} for the onset of vegetation growth (120 DOY) was determined by analyzing the seasonal EVI curves collected from fifty crop pixels. To quantify the landscape-level MGDDs and HGDDs, a meta-analysis of published data on crops grown in the Haean basin was conducted, resulting in values of 300 and 150 °C for the MGDDs and HGDDs, respectively. Two standard weather stations were established in the agricultural lands, one in paddy rice and the other in the dry field zone on an east-facing slope. These stations recorded half-hourly meteorological factors such as incident solar radiation, air temperature, wind speed and direction, relative humidity, and rainfall. Previous research conducted from July to December 2009 revealed insignificant variations in incident solar radiation and daily maximum and minimum air temperatures between the two standard weather stations [3]. Based on these findings, it can be reasonably assumed that all sampled crops in the agricultural landscape developed under similar climate conditions.

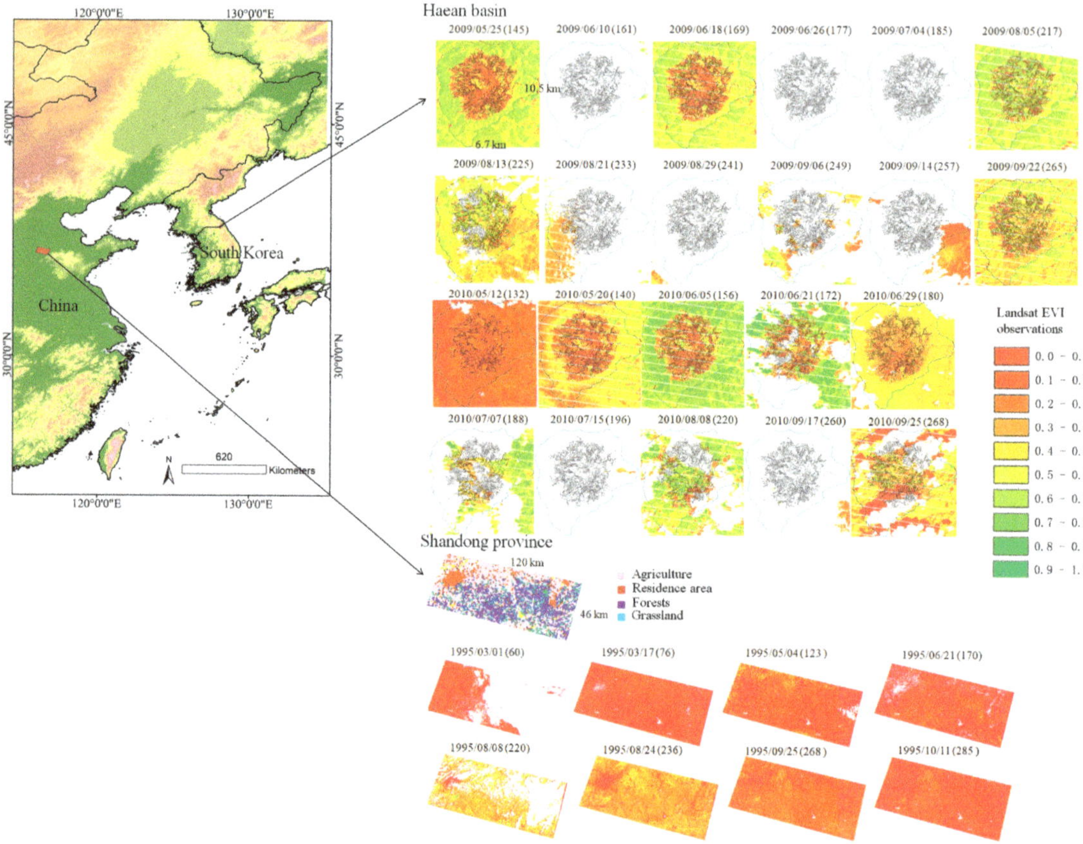

Figure 4. Spatial distributions of the Landsat 5/7 EVI observations from May to October in Haean basin in 2019 and 2010 and from March to October in Shandong Province in 1995. The agricultural land use shapefile was stacked on the Landsat 5–7 EVI images in the Haean basin (gray areas). Observation dates are displayed as year/month/day (day of the year). EVI: Enhanced Vegetation Index.

3.3. Introduction of Regional Agricultural Landscapes in Shandong Province and Parameter Settings of LTDG_DL

This was a double-cropping system, with a rotation of spring and summer crops, in the regional agricultural landscapes of Shandong Province of China (114°19′–122°43′E, 34°22′–38°23′N). The area covered a length of 120km and a width of 46km, consisting of 3993 lines and 2229 rows. The land use and cover data layer, with Level-2 classification information (i.e., paddy fields and upland fields), at a resolution of 30 m in 1995, was obtained from the Resource and Environmental Science and Data Center (https://www.resdc.cn/) (accessed on 15 December 2022). The crop types present in each pixel were unknown, and field EVI measurements were not available in Shandong Province. Only Landsat 5 TM surface reflectance images were available in 1995. Landsat observational images were classified into four land cover types for the period between March and October in Shandong (Figure 4). For spring crops, only four observational images were available from February to mid-June. Among these, two were acquired at 60 and 76 DOY when crop growth was at a high momentum. Another image was obtained on 170 DOY (the end of June) during the harvest stage of the spring crops. The most-valuable Landsat image was acquired on 123 DOY, corresponding to the flourishing growth stage of the spring crops. Regarding the summer crops, four Landsat observational images were available. One image was acquired on 220 DOY, capturing the vigorous growth of summer crops, although a significant portion was contaminated by clouds. The observational images acquired on 236, 268, and 285 DOY had minimal cloud contamination, but only the image acquired on 236 DOY was considered valuable due to the likely maximum canopy size of the summer crops. The density of Landsat EVI observations for the spring and summer crops was very low.

The DOY_{ini} values for the spring and summer crops at the landscape level were determined based on the onset of the consistent increase phase of seasonal EVI observations in fifty randomly selected pixels. This approach was consistent with the DOY_{ini} determination in the Haean basin. Prior knowledge of the life cycles of locally prevalent crops in Shandong Province aided in determining the landscape-level DOY_{ini}. The landscape-level DOY_{ini} values are displayed in Table 1. The GLDAS2.0 daily meteorological products for the entire year in the same area were resampled to a 30 m resolution.

Table 1. Settings of the landscape-level DOY_{ini} in crop pixels in Shandong Province. DOY_{ini}: the initial date of seedling emergence/transplanting.

Site	Crop Types	Life Cycle Classification	Edaphic Classification	Years	DOY_{ini}
Shandong Province	Paddy or upland crops (unknown crop types)	Unknown	Paddy/upland field	1995	55 for spring crops; 170 for summer crops

4. Results

4.1. Performance of the LTDG_DL Algorithm in Experimental Fields

Overestimation of the EVI around the date of peak EVI was observed in the LTDG S1 and S2 simulations (Figure 5a–d). The DL S1 simulation in Nebraska and the DL S1 and S2 simulations in Gimje significantly underestimated the EVI values around the date of the maximum EVI. Satisfactory performances were observed in the LTDG_DL S1 and S2 simulations, with R^2 and RMSE values of 0.71 and 0.09 and 0.84 and 0.07, respectively (Figure 5g). The EVI reconstruction accuracy of LTDG_DL S2 was superior to that of LTDG_DL S1, suggesting the importance of having Landsat EVI observations during periods of rapid green-up and senescence for daily EVI reconstruction.

For the S1 scenario, the simulated EVI increment slope decreased from LTDG and LTDG_DL to DL (Figure 5h). There were no significant differences in the EVI increment slope between the field observation and the LTDG simulation. The deviation amplitude of the DL simulation in the EVI increment slope decreased from 74% to 48% in the LTDG_DL simulation. The EVI decline slope simulated by LTDG_DL was 48% lower than that of the DL simulation, while being closer to the field observation. The improved prediction accuracy of the EVI increment slope in the S2 scenario was also achieved by LTDG_DL (Figure 5i).

4.2. Performance of the LTDG_DL Algorithm in Agricultural Landscapes of Haean Basin

The Landsat EVI observations and simulations in the Haean basin are displayed in Figure 6, using the LTDG_DL, LTDG, and DL methods. A case study examining paddy rice demonstrated that the $dEVI_{DL}$ preserved the Landsat EVI observations of the rice growing seasons (Figure 6a), with the simulated T_{peak_EVI} occurring on 245 DOY. The LTDG method, on the other hand, simulated a T_{peak_EVI} of 210 DOY, which was close to the observed T_{peak_EVI} of 220 DOY. The LTDG_DL method simulated a T_{peak_EVI} of 220 DOY, falling between the $dEVI_{LTDG}$ and $dEVI_{DL}$ T_{peak_EVI} simulations. However, the $dEVI_{LTDG}$ was significantly higher than the $dEVI_{DL}$ at the maturation stage (after 250 DOY). At this stage, the LTDG_DL method effectively captured the EVI's steady declining trend compared to LTDG. The DL method failed to capture Landsat observations during the EVI peak stage in potato (170 DOY) (Figure 6b). The T_{peak_EVI} values for $dEVI_{DL}$, $dEVI_{LTDG}$, and

$dEVI_{LTDG\_DL}$ were 210, 175, and 175 DOY, respectively. In 2009 and 2010, the LTDG_DL method achieved better reconstructions of the seasonal EVI tendency and amplitude in crops such as bean, cabbage, radish, orchard, ginseng, and codonopsis (Figure 6c–p).

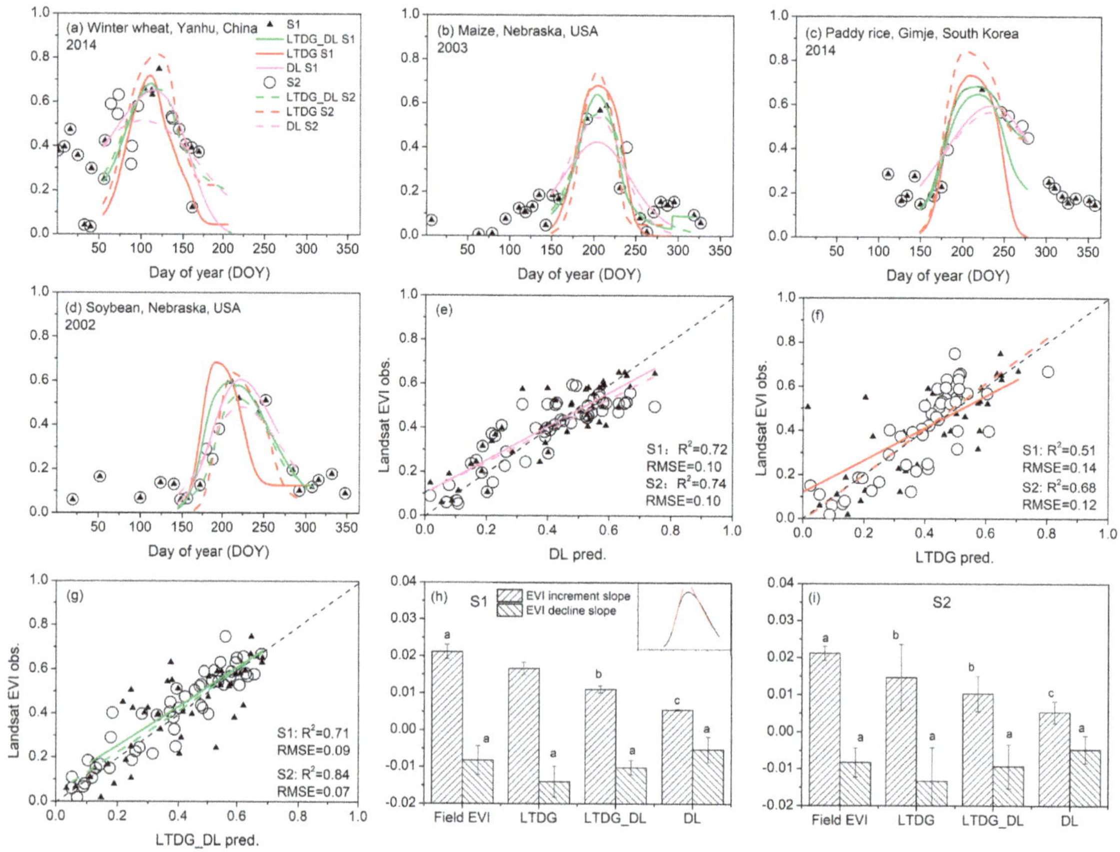

Figure 5. Evaluations of the EVI reconstruction accuracy of the DL, LTDG, and LTDG_DL methods in experimental fields in Yanhu, China (**a**), Nebraska in the USA (**b**,**d**), and Gimje in the Republic of Korea (**c**). The S1 manipulation scenario (small triangles) represented the condition of artificially masked EVI observations during the rapid green-up and senescing periods; the S2 manipulation scenario (big circles) represented the case with missing EVI observations around the date of the maximum EVI. All growing season Landsat EVI observations were applied to evaluate algorithm accuracy (**e**,**f**,**g**). Different letters in (**h**,**i**) indicate that, at the 0.05 level, the difference of the population means was significantly different with the null hypothesis (mean1 − mean2 = 0, one-way ANOVA). The 95% error bars were added to the LTDG_DL S1 and S2 simulations. The inset in (**h**) shows the calculation modes of the EVI increment and decline slopes. EVI: Enhanced Vegetation Index; obs.: observation; pred.: prediction; LTDG: the Light- and Temperature-Driven Growth model; DL: the Double-Logistic function; LTDG_DL: the LTDG and DL fusion algorithm.

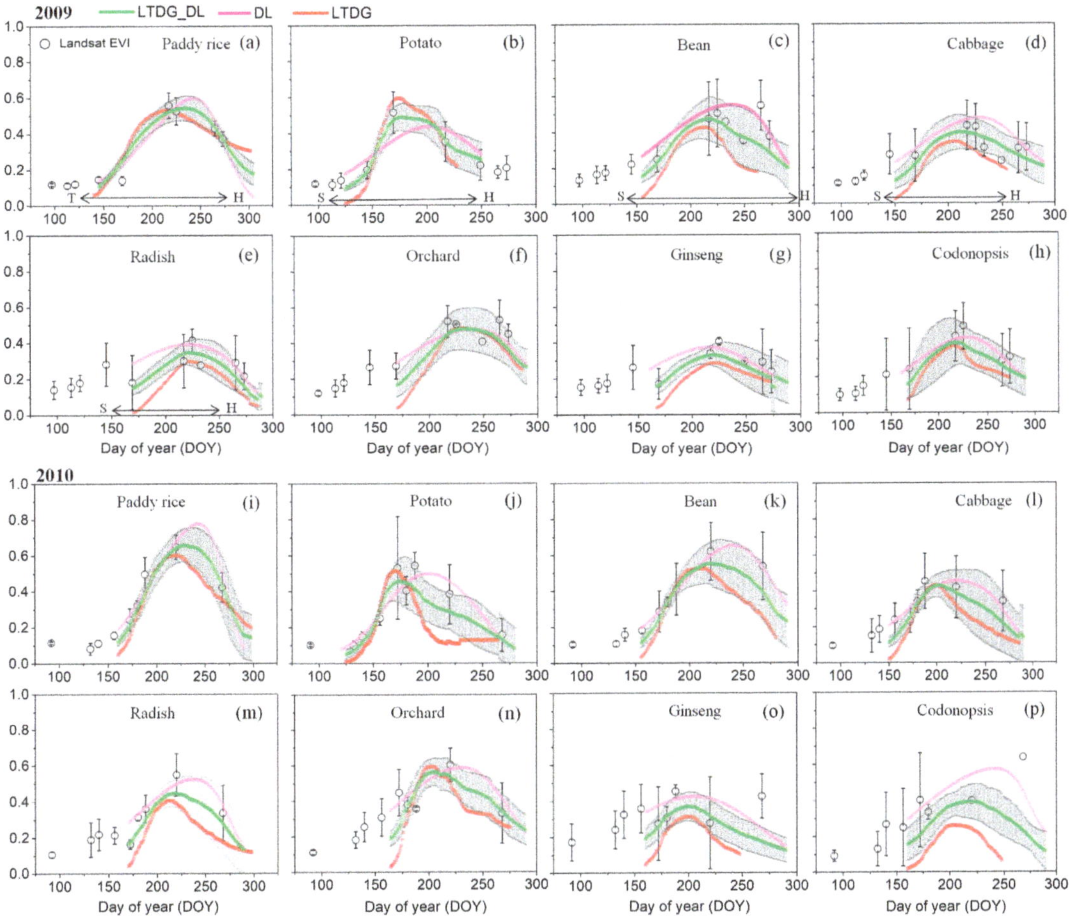

Figure 6. Reconstruction of daily Landsat EVI data using the LTDG, DL, and LTDG_DL methods in paddy rice (**a**,**i**), potato (**b**,**j**), bean (**c**,**k**), cabbage (**d**,**l**), radish (**e**,**m**), orchard (**f**,**n**), ginseng (**g**,**o**), and codonopsis (**h**,**p**) in the Haean basin. EVI: Enhanced Vegetation Index; T: date of seedling Transplanting; S: Seedling emergence date; H: Harvest date; LTDG: the Light- and Temperature-Driven Growth model; DL: the Double-Logistic function; LTDG_DL: the LTDG and DL fusion algorithm. The 95% error bars indicted by grey areas were added to the LTDG_DL simulations.

The comparisons of Landsat EVI observations and simulations revealed that the RMSE values for DL, LTDG, and LTDG_DL were 0.12, 0.07, and 0.07, respectively (Figure 7a–c). The corresponding R^2 values were 0.67, 0.75, and 0.75, respectively. In the T_{peak_EVI} estimation, the RMSE and R^2 values were 4.9 d and 0.53 for DL, 2.68 d and 0.68 for LTDG, and 2.03 d and 0.76 for LTDG_DL (Figure 7d). In 2009, the average EVI increment slope across eight crop types in the LTDG_DL simulations was approximately 0.007, which was 85% higher than that of the DL simulations (Figure 7e), consistent with the findings shown in Figure 5h,i. There were no significant differences in the EVI decline slope between the two methods. Similarly, in 2010, the LTDG_DL yielded an EVI increment slope that was 72% higher than that of the DL method (Figure 7f).

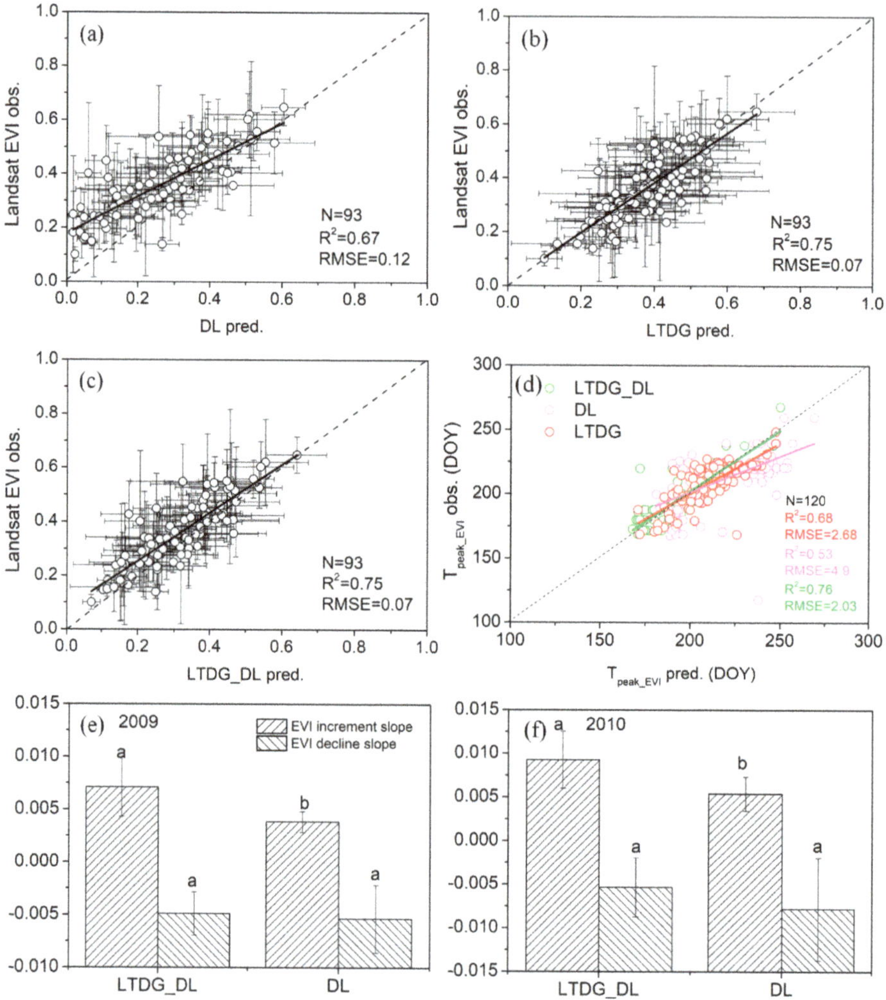

Figure 7. Comparisons between Landsat EVI observations and predictions using the DL (**a**), LTDG (**b**), and LTDG_DL (**c**) methods in randomly selected crop pixels in the Haean basin. Evaluations in estimation of T_{peak_EVI} by the three methods are presented in plot (**d**). Different letters in (**e**,**f**) indicate that, at the 0.05 level, the difference of the population means was significantly different with the null hypothesis (mean1 − mean2 = 0, one-way ANOVA). The dashed line was the 1:1 line (**a**–**c**) and the solid lines were the linear regression fits. LTDG: the Light- and Temperature-Driven Growth model; DL: Double-Logistic function; LTDG_DL: the LTDG and DL fusion algorithm; pred.: prediction; obs.: observation; EVI: Enhanced Vegetative Index; T_{peak_EVI}: the timing of peak EVI.

Figure 8 displays the reconstructed EVI images on the Landsat EVI observation dates in the Haean basin by LTDG_DL. During the period from 145 to 169 DOY in 2009 and 2010, most agricultural lands were dry, while some fields were flooded and prepared for rice seedling transplantation. Seeding emergence did not occur before 160 DOY, causing most agricultural pixels on 132, 140/145, and 156/161 DOY in 2009 and 2010 to appear red (indicating low EVI). On 161 and 169 DOY in 2009, light green pixels were noticeable at the western part of the Haean valley, which are cultivated lands for potato. Potato pixels became deep green on 185 DOY and returned to light green again on 225 DOY, matching the potato field phenology [3]. Orange dominated the paddy pixels on 177 DOY, then shifted to light yellow on 185 DOY and, finally, turned green on 225 DOY. On 257 DOY, light green and yellow colors indicated senescing canopies. Green colors were observed in upland fields around 217 DOY, which corresponded to the date of maximum canopy growth potential. The LTDG_DL well preserved the spatial details in the EVI time series of various crops in 2010.

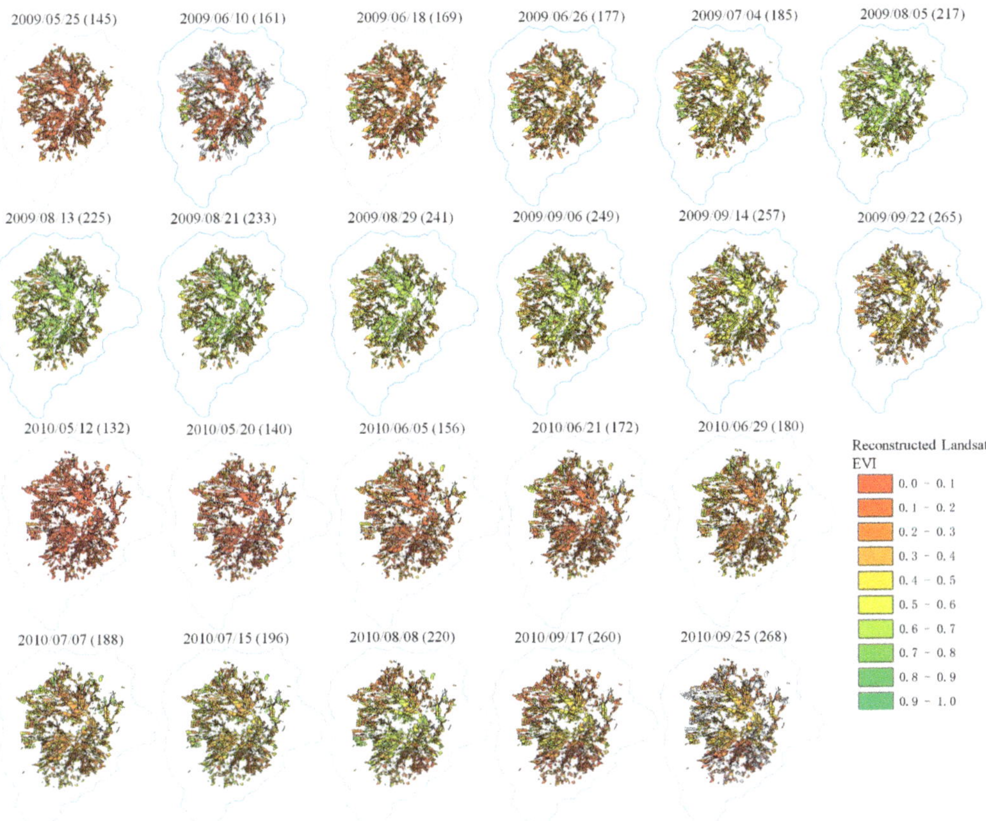

Figure 8. Spatial mapping of reconstructed per-pixel EVI on the Landsat EVI observation dates in the Haean basin in 2009 and 2010. The cropland data layer was stacked on the Landsat EVI maps. EVI: Enhanced Vegetation Index; LTDG_DL: the Light- and Temperature-Driven Growth model and the Double-Logistic function fusion algorithm.

4.3. Performance of the LTDG_DL Algorithm in Regional Agricultural Landscapes of Shandong Province

Seasonal trajectories of the reconstructed Landsat EVI in four representative fields in Shandong are displayed in Figure 9a–d. The DL method successfully captured the Landsat EVI observations during the spring and summer seasons, demonstrating a high R^2 of 0.92 and a low RMSE of 0.05, as depicted in Figure 9e. Similar results were obtained with the LTDG_DL method, as shown in Figure 9g. However, the prediction accuracy declined when using the LTDG simulations, as evidenced in Figure 9f. For the summer crops, the EVI increment slope for the LTDG_DL method was approximately 0.008, while it was around 0.006 for the DL simulation, as indicated in Figure 9h. Statistical analysis revealed significant differences in the EVI increment slope between the LTDG_DL and DL methods, consistent with the findings in Figures 5h,i and 7e,f. Notably, the LTDG_DL simulation exhibited a higher value in the EVI increment slope of approximately 57% than the DL simulation of the spring crops, as illustrated in Figure 9i. However, no significant differences were observed in the EVI decline slope between the two methods in either the spring or summer crops. In comparison to the DL method, the LTDG_DL method accurately captured the growth pattern of the EVI during the vegetative stage of the spring/summer crops and produced consistent seasonal EVI trajectories (Figure 9a–d). This can be attributed to the superior performance of the LTDG_DL method in estimating the EVI increment slope and its ability to combine the advantages of the DL and LTDG methods.

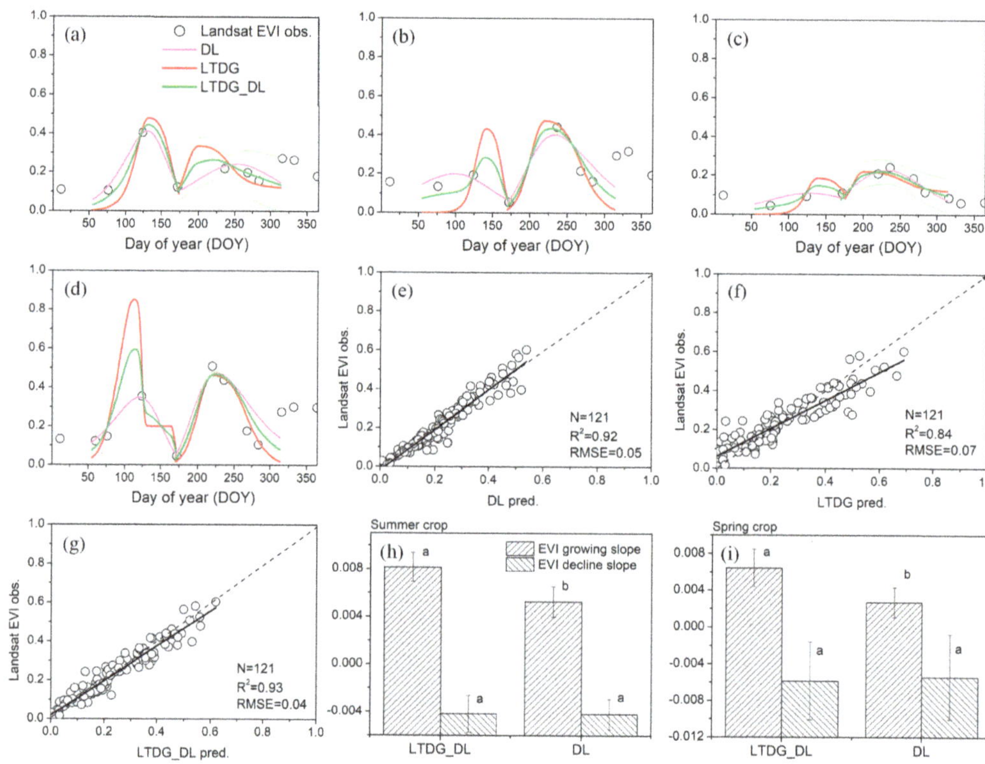

Figure 9. Comparisons in the reconstruction accuracy of daily Landsat EVI data among the DL, LTDG, and LTDG_DL methods in randomly selected crop pixels (**a–d**) in Shandong Province. Comparisons in EVI observation and predictions by the three methods are presented in plots (**e–g**). Different letters in (**h**,**i**) indicate that, at the 0.05 level, the difference of the population means was significantly different with the null hypothesis (mean1 − mean2 = 0, one-way ANOVA). The dashed line was the 1:1 line (**e–g**) and the solid lines were the linear regression fits. LTDG: the Light- and Temperature-Driven Growth model; DL: Double-Logistic function; LTDG_DL: the LTDG and DL fusion algorithm; pred.: prediction; obs.: observation; EVI: Enhanced Vegetative Index.

The results of the LTDG_DL EVI reconstruction in Shandong, where crops were grown under various environmental conditions including rainfed, irrigation, fertilization, and no fertilization, yielded a relatively small RMSE of 0.03 ± 0.02 (mean ± SD) for the spring crops (reversed funnel boxplot in Figure 10) and an RMSE of 0.06 ± 0.02 for the summer crops (small waist gourd boxplot in Figure 10). Approximately 75% of the spring crop pixels had an RMSE less than 0.05. The RMSE range of the summer crops exhibited a distribution shaped like a small-waisted gourd, with 50% of crop pixels having an RMSE less than 0.05 and 25% of pixels having an RMSE ranging from 0.05 to 0.09. The relatively large RMSE in the 25% of pixels was primarily due to the abnormal EVI observational values (approximately 0.01) on 220 DOY of those pixels when the crops grew vigorously. The abnormal low EVI values were not considered outliers and were not removed during the process of calculating the pixel RMSE. LTDG_DL effectively captured the crop seasonal EVI trajectories and spatial features in the double-cropping systems (Figure 10).

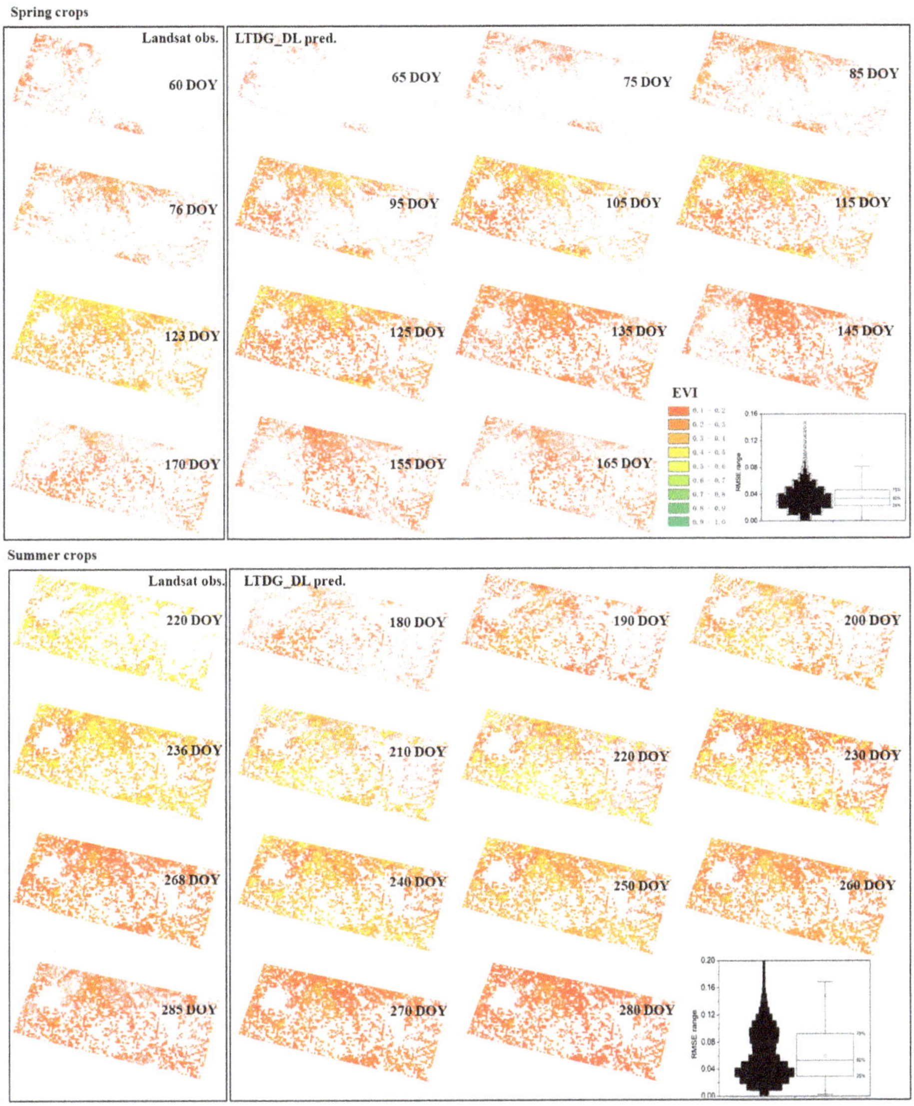

Figure 10. Spatial mapping of daily Landsat EVI reconstructed by LTDG_DL in the spring crop + summer crop rotation systems in Shandong Province. Reconstructed Landsat EVI maps are displayed at 10 d intervals. EVI: Enhanced Vegetation Index; LTDG: the Light- and Temperature-Driven Growth model; DL: the Double-Logistic function; LTDG_DL: the LTDG and DL fusion algorithm; DOY: Day Of Year; RMSE: Root-Mean-Squared Error; obs.: observation; pred.: prediction.

5. Discussion

The predictive capability of the DL model varied depending on the quantity and temporal distribution patterns of the Landsat EVI. The DL model performed poorly in protecting key Landsat EVI observations in experimental fields with irregular temporal distributions. The DL model was sensitive to noise data in the Landsat EVI observations, confirming the previous findings by Liu et al. [28]. The EVI slope during the rapid expansion of the crop canopies in the vegetative growth stage was significantly lower than the expected conditions, indicating a mismatch between the DL-reconstructed Landsat EVI time series and the crop growth trajectory.

The GF-SG is widely recognized for its superior performance in reconstructing the Landsat EVI compared to previous Landsat–MODIS fusion algorithms [32]. Our study revealed that a significant proportion of agricultural pixels, ranging from 10% to 45%, were identified as invalid due to low $Cor_{j\_(x,y)}$ values (see Figure S4a,b in the Supporting Information S4). This issue is particularly prevalent in highly fragmented landscapes, where there is spatiotemporal incompatibility between the EVI time series of the targeted Landsat pixel and neighboring re-sampled MODIS pixels. The spectral response of the near-infrared wavelength band, which varies across different landscapes, was identified as a critical factor influencing MODIS–Landsat spatiotemporal comparability [57]. Recently, Sun et al. [5] proposed a crop-type-based Crop Reference Curve (CRC) approach, wherein they extracted NDVI time series from MODIS 250 m pure crop pixels identified using the Cropland Data Layer (CDL), and used these data to fit Landsat-like observations. Specifically, they selected MODIS candidate curves within a given crop type to match the Landsat observations in pixels where the same crop type was grown. However, it is important to note that land use and land cover data layers in most countries and regions do not accurately register the spatial distributions of crop types. Additionally, the Landsat–MODIS fusion algorithms cannot be applied in years and areas where MODIS products are unavailable. Therefore, there is a pressing need to develop a new algorithm that can address these limitations and enhance the reliability of reconstructed daily Landsat EVI data in mosaic and fragmented agricultural landscapes.

5.1. Superiority of the LTDG_DL Algorithm

The LTDG_DL algorithm differs from the Landsat–MODIS spatiotemporal fusion methods. These fusion algorithms are commonly employed to extract valuable auxiliary information from MODIS data and to align MODIS time series with Landsat observations [5,32]. The primary auxiliary information utilized by LTDG_DL is the daily ground meteorological factors R_s and T_{air}. Global gridded daily data for R_s and T_{air} throughout the year can be freely obtained from satellite-derived products such as GLDAS and the Modern-Era Retrospective analysis for Research and Applications (MERRA) datasets. The foundation of the LTDG_DL algorithm is based on the biophysical mechanisms of growth driven by light and temperature [42,46], which comprehensively consider climatic factors that influence crop growth and development trajectory on a daily basis. It was assumed that changes in the Landsat EVI during different seasons were related the growth of the crop canopy, which is strongly regulated by ambient light, temperature, and soil water content, as sensed by the plants. This assumption is supported by the close correlation between the LAI and EVI, with the EVI capturing more than 80% of the seasonal variations in the LAI [43,45]. Numerous studies have been conducted utilizing VI time series curves derived from remotely sensed data for detecting crop phenology. Satellite EVI time series curves have been found to be closely linked to crop phenology [58], with small RSME values ranging from 1.6 (silking stage) to 5.6 (dent stage) d for maize and from 2.5 (beginning of maturity) to 5.3 (beginning of seedling emergence) d for soybean [59], 10.0 d in the estimation of the paddy rice establishment date in Italy, India, and the Philippine [60], 8.1–14.7 d in the estimation of the Start of Season (SoS) in single rice, early rice, late rice, spring wheat, and summer maize, and 7.9–13.9 d in the estimation of the End of Season (EoS) among those crops [61]. The start of the growing season identified by the satellite EVI time series typically lagged behind the actual conditions by approximately 10 d, while there was a notable correspondence in the timing of the flowering stage between the satellite results and field observations. This suggests that the EVI growing slope derived from the satellite EVI time series should be sufficiently high in order to obtain better estimations of the timing of the flowering stage. The algorithm validations through field experiments, as well as in the Haean basin and Shandong Province, indicated that the LTDG_DL algorithm outperformed in predicting the EVI growth slope and T_{peak_EVI} and safeguarding the Landsat EVI observations. The results demonstrated that the LTDG_DL algorithm, integrating the advantages of a process-based crop model and Landsat EVI observational data, effectively reconstructed the daily Landsat EVI trajectory to align with the crop growth trajectory as closely as possible.

Roy and Yan [26] conducted a study in the Great Plains of North America, analyzing Landsat NDVI data with a rich temporal information (6–9 observations over major crop growing seasons). They found that harmonic models were able to fit the annual time series with RMSE values ranging from 0.05 to 0.08. In another study focusing on the Delmarva Peninsula of the USA, where daily Landsat NDVI reconstruction was performed using 5–9 Landsat observations over major crop growing seasons, the RMSE of the CRC method was found to be 0.07 [5]. However, when attempting to fit coarse Landsat NDVI observations with fewer than three observations within ±20 d using the harmonic modeling method, the resulting RMSE was significantly larger, equal to or greater than 0.12 [27]. The performance of the LTDG_DL algorithm in capturing the seasonal evolution of various crops in the Haean basin was evaluated, and its RMSE value was determined to be 0.07 (Figure 7c). The algorithm successfully represented the non-symmetrical EVI waveform characteristics of paddy rice, winter/spring wheat, maize, and other upland crops (Figure 6). On the other hand, the GF-SG failed to rebuild daily Landsat EVI data in 10–45% of agricultural pixels in complex landscape areas. However, LTDG_DL was able to recreate the daily Landsat EVI profile in those pixels (Figures S4 and S5 in Supporting Information S4). Furthermore, the LTDG_DL algorithm exhibited high accuracy in reconstructing the spring crop EVI in Shandong Province in 1995, as indicated by an RMSE of 0.03. The algorithm proved to be robust against noise and irregular Landsat EVI observations over time, enabling the modeling of rapid canopy changes during the vegetative growth and maturation stages (acceleration/deceleration). Additionally, The LTDG_DL algorithm demonstrated its capability to reconstruct daily Landsat EVI data with relatively high accuracy in crop pixels where crop types were unknown and the Landsat EVI observation density was low at regional scales. To enhance the reconstruction of Landsat data over cloud-prone, fragmented, and mosaic landscapes, as well as for the years prior to 2000, LTDG_DL can utilize auxiliary information from GLDAS2.0 meteorological data and GLC_FCS30 1984–2019 global annual 30 m land use classification products [62]. This integration is expected to improve the accuracy of the reconstructed Landsat EVI data.

5.2. Limitations of the LTDG_DL Algorithm

The LTDG_DL algorithm, constrained by Landsat EVI observations, exhibited imperfections. It was concerning that, although our approach had advantages in reconstructing daily Landsat EVI data, it also had some potential drawbacks. The LTDG_DL algorithm demonstrated high modeling accuracy in rainfed fields in Shandong in 1995, capturing the constrained EVI trajectory over a prolonged period of stress. Crop growth, affected by various environmental factors, exhibits inconsistent responses among different crop types [63]. For instance, the current LTDG_DL algorithm is unlikely to capture sudden changes in crop status (such as a heatwave). Short-term stress typically has the most-significant impact on crop physiology, leading to a depression in canopy reflectance signals in the red waveband [64], which subsequently affects satellite EVI observations. Crops experiencing short-term heat stress usually revert to their initial physiological states once the stress is alleviated [65]. In situations where the Landsat EVI observation density is extremely low, as indicated in Figure 9d, and EVI observations are absent during the flowering stage, LTDG_DL without considering soil water content and drought effects may overestimate the EVI if drought impacts are substantial. Moreover, the current LTDG_DL algorithm does not account for radiation transfer mechanisms, thus failing to capture non-biological singles in canopy reflectance in the red and near-infrared wavebands due to seasonal variations in the solar zenith angle.

Determining the landscape-level DOY_{ini} was the only parameter that needed to be determined. The landscape-level DOY_{ini} can be defined using either the statistical plant phenology extraction method or the endmember EVI ensemble combined with prior knowledge method. Previous studies have shown that the seasonal onset, which is equivalent to DOY_{ini}, is often defined as the date when the relatively flat and low EVI phase intersects with the continuously increasing phase of Landsat EVI observations [21,60,66]. The landscape-level DOY_{ini} setting can be determined in crop pixels by identifying the first date of the minimum EVI during a continuously increasing phase of Landsat EVI observations. However, accurately determining DOY_{ini} using the statistical phenology extraction method was not possible in pixels with a very low density of Landsat EVI observations. The combination of the endmember EVI library and the prior knowledge method assists in visually interpreting the landscape-level DOY_{ini} based on the beginning of the consistent increase phase in the seasonal EVI curves obtained from various crop pixels across a research zone (Figure S1 in Supporting Information S1). The seasonal EVI observations obtained from crop pixels were combined to create an endmember EVI library. Knowledge of the crop growth history of predominant local crops aided in determining the landscape-level DOY_{ini}. The improved reconstruction of Landsat EVI data in Shandong Province and the Haean basin indicated that the semi-empirical determination of the landscape-level DOY_{ini} using the seedling emergence date of local prevailing crops was highly beneficial. The local seeding calendar within the specific agroclimatic zone was relatively consistent over long periods, as indicated by [67,68]. Determining the climate zone suitable for applying the LTDG_DL method involves a balance between zonal size and the consistency of the local seedling emergence calendar, which is more feasible at the state/province level where agroclimatic conditions are comparable.

6. Conclusions

Agricultural ecosystems play a critical role in regulating seasonal variations in carbon and water fluxes at regional and global scales [69]. The EVI time series data are crucial input parameters in numerous land surface models developed to simulate vegetation carbon and water fluxes between the land surface and the atmosphere. Therefore, it is necessary to improve the reliability of Landsat EVI reconstruction for intensive agricultural landscapes. In this study, we developed a parameter-constrained LTDG_DL algorithm and made evaluations in a large range of agricultural systems associated with planting culture, crop types, and field management. The results suggested that LTDG_DL was superior in the predictions of the EVI growing slope and the timing of peak EVI and in the protection of key points in crop pixels with irregular Landsat EVI observations over time. The parameterization of LTDG_DL can be readily set up at a regional scale.

Supplementary Materials: The following Supporting Information can be downloaded at: https://www.mdpi.com/article/10.3390/rs15194673/s1, Figure S1. The DOY_{ini} setting by empirically loading the onset of the consistent increase phase of Landsat EVI observations in crop pixels. DOY_{ini}: the initial date of seedling emergence/transplanting; obs.: observation. Figure S2. Daily incident solar radiation and air temperature profiles in Yanhu, China, in 2014, Gimje in the Republic of Korea in 2014, and Nebraska in the USA in 2002 and 2003. Data were extracted from the Global Land Data Assimilation System Version 2 (GLDAS2.0). Figure S3. Land use and land change in the Haean basin in 2009 and 2010. Figure S4. Accumulated percentage of invalid pixels that cannot be identified by the GF-SG in eight crops and other upland crops in the Haean basin in 2009 and 2010 (Subplots a and b). Subplots c and d show comparisons of the reconstructed daily Landsat EVI data by the LTDG_DL and GF-SG algorithms for potato and cabbage pixels. Two potato and cabbage pixels that can be detected as valid pixels using the GF-SG algorithm were used in Subplots c and d. $Cor_{j\_(x,y)}$: correlation coefficient between the Landsat pixel (x, y) and the neighboring pixels in the local window of 40 × 40 px centered at pixel (x, y) (j = 1:1600) (Chen et al., 2021 [32]). EVI: Enhanced Vegetative Index; LTDG: the Light- and Temperature-Driven Growth model; DL: the Double-Logistic function; LTDG_DL: the LTDG and DL fusing algorithm; GF-SG: the Gap-Filling and Savitzky–Golay filtering method. Figure S5. Daily Landsat EVI data reconstructed by the LTDG_DL algorithm for crop pixels where applications of the GF-SG were hindered in the Haean basin. $Cor_{j\_(x,y)}$: correlation coefficient between the Landsat pixel (x, y) and the neighboring pixels in a local window of 40 × 40 px centered at pixel (x, y). EVI: Enhanced Vegetative Index; LTDG: the Light- and Temperature-Driven Growth model; DL: the Double-Logistic function; LTDG_DL: the LTDG and DL fusion algorithm; GF-SG: the Gap-Filling and Savitzky–Golay filtering method.

Author Contributions: Conceptualization and investigation, methodology, supervision, visualization, and writing—original draft: W.X.; writing—review and editing: J.K., R.C., Z.Y. and W.X. All authors have read and agreed to the published version of the manuscript.

Funding: This work was financially supported by the National Natural Science Foundation of China (32001129) and the Open Funding from CAS Key Laboratory of Tropical Forest Ecology (22-CAS-TFE-03).

Data Availability Statement: Code script of the LTDG_DL algorithm is available in the online materials.

Conflicts of Interest: The authors declare no conflict of interest.

References

1. Lin, M.-L.; Shiu, Y.-S.; Chu, T.-H.; Huang, C.-H. Mapping paddy rice agriculture in a highly fragmented area using a geographic information system object-based post classification process. *J. Appl. Remote Sens.* **2012**, *6*, 063526. [CrossRef]
2. Statistics Korea. 2017. Available online: http://kostat.go.kr/portal/eng/index.action (accessed on 25 January 2022).
3. Lindner, S.; Otieno, D.; Lee, B.; Xue, W.; Arnhold, S.; Kwon, H.; Huwe, B.; Tenhunen, J. Carbon dioxide exchange and its regulation in the main agro-ecosystems of Haean catchment in South Korea. *Agric. Ecosyst. Environ.* **2015**, *199*, 132–145. [CrossRef]
4. Lowder, S.K.; Skoet, J.; Raney, T. The number, size, and distribution of farms, smallholder farms, and family farms worldwide. *World Dev.* **2016**, *87*, 16–29. [CrossRef]
5. Sun, L.; Gao, F.; Xie, D.; Anderson, M.; Chen, R.; Yang, Y.; Yang, Y.; Chen, Z. Reconstructing daily 30 m NDVI over complex agricultural landscapes using a crop reference curve approach. *Remote Sens. Environ.* **2021**, *253*, 112156. [CrossRef]
6. Yan, L.; Roy, D. Conterminous United States crop field size quantification from multi-temporal Landsat data. *Remote Sens. Environ.* **2016**, *172*, 67–86. [CrossRef]
7. Seo, B.; Bogner, C.; Poppenborg, P.; Martin, E.; Hoffmeister, M.; Jun, M.; Koellner, T.; Reineking, B.; Shope, C.L.; Tenhunen, J. Deriving a per-field land use and land cover map in an agricultural mosaic catchment. *Earth Syst. Sci. Data* **2014**, *6*, 339–352. [CrossRef]
8. You, N.; Dong, J.; Huang, J.; Du, G.; Zhang, G.; He, Y.; Yang, T.; Di, Y.; Xiao, X. The 10-m crop type maps in Northeast China during 2017–2019. *Sci. Data* **2021**, *8*, 41. [CrossRef]
9. Kwon, H.; Kim, J.; Hong, J.; Lim, J.-H. Influence of the Asian monsoon on net ecosystem carbon exchange in two major ecosystems in Korea. *Biogeosciences* **2010**, *7*, 1493–1504. [CrossRef]
10. Lee, J.-Y.; Raza, M.; Kwon, K.D. Land use and land cover changes in the Haean Basin of Korea: Impacts on soil erosion. *Episodes* **2019**, *42*, 17–32. [CrossRef]
11. Loveland, T.R.; Irons, J.R. Landsat 8: The plans, the reality, and the legacy. *Remote Sens. Environ.* **2016**, *185*, 1–6. [CrossRef]
12. Lenney, M.P.; Woodcock, C.E.; Collins, J.B.; Hamdi, H. The status of agricultural lands in Egypt: The use of multitemporal NDVI features derived from landsat TM. *Remote Sens. Environ.* **1996**, *56*, 8–20. [CrossRef]
13. Graesser, J.; Ramankutty, N. Detection of cropland field parcels from Landsat imagery. *Remote Sens. Environ.* **2017**, *201*, 165–180. [CrossRef]
14. Song, X.-P.; Potapov, P.V.; Krylov, A.; King, L.; Di Bella, C.M.; Hudson, A.; Khan, A.; Adusei, B.; Stehman, S.V.; Hansen, M.C. National-scale soybean mapping and area estimation in the United States using medium resolution satellite imagery and field survey. *Remote Sens. Environ.* **2017**, *190*, 383–395. [CrossRef]
15. Ju, J.; Roy, D.P. The availability of cloud-free Landsat ETM+ data over the conterminous United States and globally. *Remote Sens. Environ.* **2008**, *112*, 1196–1211. [CrossRef]
16. Kovalskyy, V.; Roy, D. The global availability of Landsat 5 TM and Landsat 7 ETM+ land surface observations and implications for global 30m Landsat data product generation. *Remote Sens. Environ.* **2013**, *130*, 280–293. [CrossRef]
17. Egorov, A.V.; Roy, D.P.; Zhang, H.K.; Li, Z.; Yan, L.; Huang, H. Landsat 4, 5 and 7 (1982 to 2017) analysis ready data (ARD) observation coverage over the conterminous United States and implications for terrestrial monitoring. *Remote Sens.* **2019**, *11*, 447. [CrossRef]

18. Chen, B.; Huang, B.; Chen, L.; Xu, B. Spatially and temporally weighted regression: A novel method to produce continuous cloud-free Landsat imagery. *IEEE Trans. Geosci. Remote Sens.* **2017**, *55*, 27–37. [CrossRef]
19. Moreno-Martínez, Á; Izquierdo-Verdiguier, E.; Maneta, M.P.; Camps-Valls, G.; Robinson, N.; Muñoz-Marí, J.; Sedano, F.; Clinton, N.; Running, S.W. Multispectral high resolution sensor fusion for smoothing and gap-filling in the cloud. *Remote Sens. Environ.* **2020**, *247*, 111901. [CrossRef]
20. Li, S.; Xu, L.; Jing, Y.; Yin, H.; Li, X.; Guan, X. High-quality vegetation index product generation: A review of NDVI time series reconstruction techniques. *Int. J. Appl. Earth Obs. Geoinform.* **2021**, *105*, 102640. [CrossRef]
21. Jonsson, P.; Eklundh, L. Seasonality extraction by function fitting to time-series of satellite sensor data. *IEEE Trans. Geosci. Remote Sens.* **2002**, *40*, 1824–1832. [CrossRef]
22. Chen, J.; Jönsson, P.; Tamura, M.; Gu, Z.; Matsushita, B.; Eklundh, L. A simple method for reconstructing a high-quality NDVI time-series data set based on the Savitzky–Golay filter. *Remote Sens. Environ.* **2004**, *91*, 332–344. [CrossRef]
23. Wu, C.; Gonsamo, A.; Gough, C.M.; Chen, J.M.; Xu, S. Modeling growing season phenology in North American forests using seasonal mean vegetation indices from MODIS. *Remote Sens. Environ.* **2014**, *147*, 79–88. [CrossRef]
24. Xue, W.; Jeong, S.; Ko, J.; Yeom, J.-M. Contribution of biophysical factors to regional variations of evapotranspiration and seasonal cooling effects in paddy rice in South Korea. *Remote Sens.* **2021**, *13*, 3992. [CrossRef]
25. Melaas, E.K.; Friedl, M.A.; Zhu, Z. Detecting interannual variation in deciduous broadleaf forest phenology using Landsat TM/ETM+ data. *Remote Sens. Environ.* **2013**, *132*, 176–185. [CrossRef]
26. Roy, D.; Yan, L. Robust Landsat-based crop time series modelling. *Remote Sens. Environ.* **2020**, *238*, 110810. [CrossRef]
27. Pouliot, D.; Latifovic, R. Reconstruction of Landsat time series in the presence of irregular and sparse observations: Development and assessment in north-eastern Alberta, Canada. *Remote Sens. Environ.* **2018**, *204*, 979–996. [CrossRef]
28. Liu, R.; Shang, R.; Liu, Y.; Lu, X. Global evaluation of gap-filling approaches for seasonal NDVI with considering vegetation growth trajectory, protection of key point, noise resistance and curve stability. *Remote Sens. Environ.* **2017**, *189*, 164–179. [CrossRef]
29. Cao, R.; Chen, Y.; Shen, M.; Chen, J.; Zhou, J.; Wang, C.; Yang, W. A simple method to improve the quality of NDVI time-series data by integrating spatiotemporal information with the Savitzky-Golay filter. *Remote Sens. Environ.* **2018**, *217*, 244–257. [CrossRef]
30. Chen, Y.; Cao, R.Y.; Chen, J.; Zhu, X.L.; Zhou, J.; Wang, G.P.; Shen, M.G.; Chen, X.H.; Yang, W. A new cross-fusion method to automatically determine the optimal input image pairs for NDVI spatiotemporal data fusion. *IEEE Trans. Geosci. Remote Sens.* **2020**, *58*, 5179–5194. [CrossRef]
31. Wang, Q.; Tang, Y.; Tong, X.; Atkinson, P.M. Virtual image pair-based spatio-temporal fusion. *Remote Sens. Environ.* **2020**, *249*, 112009. [CrossRef]
32. Chen, Y.; Cao, R.; Chen, J.; Liu, L.; Matsushita, B. A practical approach to reconstruct high-quality Landsat NDVI time-series data by gap filling and the Savitzky–Golay filter. *ISPRS J. Photogramm. Remote Sens.* **2021**, *180*, 174–190. [CrossRef]
33. Gao, F.; Masek, J.; Schwaller, M.; Hall, F. On the blending of the Landsat and MODIS surface reflectance: Predicting daily Landsat surface reflectance. *IEEE Trans. Geosci. Remote Sens.* **2006**, *44*, 2207–2218. [CrossRef]
34. Zhu, X.; Chen, J.; Gao, F.; Chen, X.; Masek, J.G. An enhanced spatial and temporal adaptive reflectance fusion model for complex heterogeneous regions. *Remote Sens. Environ.* **2010**, *114*, 2610–2623. [CrossRef]
35. Zhu, X.; Helmer, E.H.; Gao, F.; Liu, D.; Chen, J.; Lefsky, M.A. A flexible spatiotemporal method for fusing satellite images with different resolutions. *Remote Sens. Environ.* **2016**, *172*, 165–177. [CrossRef]
36. Luo, Y.; Guan, K.; Peng, J. STAIR: A generic and fully-automated method to fuse multiple sources of optical satellite data to generate a high-resolution, daily and cloud-/gap-free surface reflectance product. *Remote Sens. Environ.* **2018**, *214*, 87–99. [CrossRef]
37. Liu, M.; Yang, W.; Zhu, X.L.; Chen, J.; Chen, X.H.; Yang, L.Q.; Helmer, E.H. An Improved Flexible Spatiotemporal DAta Fusion (IFSDAF) method for producing high spatiotemporal resolution normalized difference vegetation index time series. *Remote Sens. Environ.* **2019**, *227*, 74–89. [CrossRef]
38. Huete, A.; Didan, K.; Miura, T.; Rodriguez, E.P.; Gao, X.; Ferreira, L.G. Overview of the radiometric and biophysical performance of the MODIS vegetation indices. *Remote Sens. Environ.* **2002**, *83*, 195–213. [CrossRef]
39. Savitzky, A.; Golay, M.J.E. Smoothing and differentiation of data by simplified least squares procedures. *Anal. Chem.* **1964**, *36*, 1627–1639. [CrossRef]
40. Bouman, B.A.M.; van Keulen, H.; van Laar, H.H.; Rabbinge, R. The 'School of de Wit' crop growth simulation models: A pedigree and historical overview. *Agric. Syst.* **1996**, *52*, 171–198. [CrossRef]
41. Xue, W.; Ko, J. Radiation estimation and crop growth trajectory reconstruction by novel algorithms improve MOD16 evapotranspiration predictability for global multi-site paddy rice ecosystems. *J. Hydrol.* **2022**, *612*, 128204. [CrossRef]
42. Connor, D.J.; Loomis, R.S.; Cassman, K.G. Development. In *Crop Ecology: Productivity and Management in Agricultural Systems*; Cambridge University Press: Cambridge, UK, 2011; pp. 96–122. [CrossRef]
43. Zhu, Z.; Bi, J.; Pan, Y.; Ganguly, S.; Anav, A.; Xu, L.; Samanta, A.; Piao, S.; Nemani, R.R.; Myneni, R.B. Global Data sets of vegetation leaf area index (LAI)3g and fraction of photosynthetically active radiation (FPAR)3g derived from global inventory modeling and mapping studies (GIMMS) normalized difference vegetation index (NDVI3g) for the period 1981 to 2011. *Remote Sens.* **2013**, *5*, 927–948. [CrossRef]
44. Fang, H.; Liang, S.; Hoogenboom, G. Integration of MODIS LAI and vegetation index products with the CSM–CERES–Maize model for corn yield estimation. *Int. J. Remote Sens.* **2011**, *32*, 1039–1065. [CrossRef]

45. Fang, H.; Baret, F.; Plummer, S.; Schaepman-Strub, G. An overview of global leaf area index (LAI): Methods, products, validation, and applications. *Rev. Geophys.* **2019**, *57*, 739–799. [CrossRef]
46. Monteith, J.L. Climate and the efficiency of crop production in Britain. *Philos. Trans. R. Soc. Lond. Ser. B* **1977**, *281*, 277–294.
47. Russell, G.; Jarvis, P.; Monteith, J. Absorption of radiation by canopies and stand growth. In *Plant Canopies: Their Growth, Form and Function*; Cambridge University Press: Cambridge, UK, 1989; pp. 21–39. [CrossRef]
48. Conte, S.D.; de Boor, C. *Elementary Numerical Analysis: An Algorithmic Approach*; McGraw-Hill: New York, NY, USA, 1965; p. 32.
49. Press, W.H.; Teukolsky, S.A.; Vetterling, W.T.; Flannery, B.P. *Numerical Recipes in Fortran: The Art of Scientific Computing*, 2nd ed.; Cambridge University Press: New York, NY, USA, 1992; p. 283.
50. Yoshida, S. *Rice Crop Science*; The International Rice Research Institute: Manila, Philippines, 1981; p. 279.
51. Guo, C.; Tang, Y.; Lu, J.; Zhu, Y.; Cao, W.; Cheng, T.; Zhang, L.; Tian, Y. Predicting wheat productivity: Integrating time series of vegetation indices into crop modeling via sequential assimilation. *Agric. For. Meteorol.* **2019**, *272–273*, 69–80. [CrossRef]
52. Swain, S.; Wardlow, B.D.; Narumalani, S.; Rundquist, D.C.; Hayes, M.J. Relationships between vegetation indices and root zone soil moisture under maize and soybean canopies in the US Corn Belt: A comparative study using a close-range sensing approach. *Int. J. Remote Sens.* **2013**, *34*, 2814–2828. [CrossRef]
53. Jeong, S.; Ko, J.; Choi, J.; Xue, W.; Yeom, J.-M. Application of an unmanned aerial system for monitoring paddy productivity using the GRAMI-rice model. *Int. J. Remote Sens.* **2018**, *39*, 2441–2462. [CrossRef]
54. Goslee, S. Analyzing remote sensing data in R: The landsat package. *J. Stat. Softw.* **2011**, *43*, 4. [CrossRef]
55. Claverie, M.; Vermote, E.F.; Franch, B.; Masek, J.G. Evaluation of the Landsat-5 TM and Landsat-7 ETM+ surface reflectance products. *Remote Sens. Environ.* **2015**, *169*, 390–403. [CrossRef]
56. Roy, D.P.; Kovalskyy, V.; Zhang, H.K.; Vermote, E.F.; Yan, L.; Kumar, S.S.; Egorov, A. Characterization of Landsat-7 to Landsat-8 reflective wavelength and normalized difference vegetation index continuity. *Remote Sens. Environ.* **2016**, *185*, 57–70. [CrossRef]
57. Chen, B.; Huang, B.; Xu, B. Comparison of spatiotemporal fusion models: A review. *Remote Sens.* **2015**, *7*, 1798–1835. [CrossRef]
58. Zhang, J.; Feng, L.; Yao, F. Improved maize cultivated area estimation over a large scale combining MODIS–EVI time series data and crop phenological information. *ISPRS J. Photogramm. Remote Sens.* **2014**, *94*, 102–113. [CrossRef]
59. Sakamoto, T.; Wardlow, B.D.; Gitelson, A.A.; Verma, S.B.; Suyker, A.E.; Arkebauer, T.J. A Two-Step Filtering approach for detecting maize and soybean phenology with time-series MODIS data. *Remote Sens. Environ.* **2010**, *114*, 2146–2159. [CrossRef]
60. Boschetti, M.; Busetto, L.; Manfron, G.; Laborte, A.; Asilo, S.; Pazhanivelan, S.; Nelson, A. PhenoRice: A method for automatic extraction of spatio-temporal information on rice crops using satellite data time series. *Remote Sens. Environ.* **2017**, *194*, 347–365. [CrossRef]
61. Huang, X.; Liu, J.; Zhu, W.; Atzberger, C.; Liu, Q. The optimal threshold and vegetation index time series for retrieving crop phenology based on a modified dynamic threshold method. *Remote Sens.* **2019**, *11*, 2725. [CrossRef]
62. Zhang, X.; Liu, L.; Chen, X.; Gao, Y.; Xie, S.; Mi, J. GLC_FCS30: Global land-cover product with fine classification system at 30 m using time-series Landsat imagery. *Earth Syst. Sci. Data* **2021**, *13*, 2753–2776. [CrossRef]
63. Ramirez-Villegas, J.; Koehler, A.-K.; Challinor, A.J. Assessing uncertainty and complexity in regional-scale crop model simulations. *Eur. J. Agron.* **2017**, *88*, 84–95. [CrossRef]
64. Melandri, G.; Thorp, K.R.; Broeckling, C.; Thompson, A.L.; Hinze, L.; Pauli, D. Assessing drought and heat stress-induced changes in the cotton leaf metabolome and their relationship with hyperspectral reflectance. *Front. Plant Sci.* **2021**, *12*, 751868. [CrossRef]
65. Xue, W.; Ko, J.; Werner, C.; Tenhunen, J. A spatially hierarchical integration of close-range remote sensing, leaf structure and physiology assists in diagnosing spatiotemporal dimensions of field-scale ecosystem photosynthetic productivity. *Agric. For. Meteorol.* **2017**, *247*, 503–519. [CrossRef]
66. Araya, S.; Ostendorf, B.; Lyle, G.; Lewis, M. CropPhenology: An R package for extracting crop phenology from time series remotely sensed vegetation index imagery. *Ecol. Inform.* **2018**, *46*, 45–56. [CrossRef]
67. van Wart, J.; van Bussel, L.G.J.; Wolf, J.; Licker, R.; Grassini, P.; Nelson, A.; Boogaard, H.; Gerber, J.; Mueller, N.D.; Claessens, L.; et al. Use of agro-climatic zones to upscale simulated crop yield potential. *Field Crop. Res.* **2013**, *143*, 44–55. [CrossRef]
68. Tao, F.; Zhang, L.; Zhang, Z.; Chen, Y. Climate warming outweighed agricultural managements in affecting wheat phenology across China during 1981–2018. *Agric. For. Meteorol.* **2022**, *316*, 108865. [CrossRef]
69. Zeng, N.; Zhao, F.; Collatz, G.J.; Kalnay, E.; Salawitch, R.J.; West, T.O.; Guanter, L. Agricultural Green Revolution as a driver of increasing atmospheric CO_2 seasonal amplitude. *Nature* **2014**, *515*, 394–397. [CrossRef] [PubMed]

remote sensing

MDPI

Article

Measuring Biophysical Parameters of Wheat Canopy with MHz- and GHz-Frequency Range Impulses Employing Contactless GPR

Konstantin Muzalevskiy [1,*], Sergey Fomin [1,†], Andrey Karavayskiy [1,†], Julia Leskova [1], Alexey Lipshin [2] and Vasily Romanov [2]

[1] Laboratory of Radiophysics of the Earth Remote Sensing, Kirensky Institute of Physics, Federal Research Center, KSC Siberian Branch Russian Academy of Science, Krasnoyarsk 660036, Russia; rsd@ksc.krasn.ru (S.F.); rsdak@ksc.krasn.ru (A.K.); leskovajulia.jl@gmail.com (J.L.)

[2] Krasnoyarsk Research Institute of Agriculture Federal Research Center, KSC Siberian Branch Russian Academy of Science, Krasnoyarsk 630090, Russia; alipshin@mail.ru (A.L.); romanov1948@yandex.ru (V.R.)

* Correspondence: rsdkm@ksc.krasn.ru

† These authors contributed equally to this work.

Abstract: In this paper, the advantages of the joint use of MHz- and GHz-frequency band impulses when employing contactless ground penetration radar (GPR) for the remote sensing of biomass, the height of the wheat canopy, and underlying soil moisture were experimentally investigated. A MHz-frequency band nanosecond impulse with a duration of 1.2 ns (average frequency of 750 MHz and spectrum bandwidth of 580 MHz, at a level of –6 dB) was emitted and received by a GPR OKO-3 equipped with an AB-900 M3 antenna unit. A GHz-frequency band sub-nanosecond impulse with a duration of 0.5 ns (average frequency of 3.2 GHz and spectral bandwidth of 1.36 GHz, at a level of −6 dB) was generated using a horn antenna and a Keysight FieldFox N9917B 18 GHz vector network analyzer. It has been shown that changes in the relative amplitudes and time delays of nanosecond impulses, reflected from a soil surface covered with wheat at a height from 0 to 87 cm and fresh above-ground biomass (AGB) from 0 to 1.5 kg/m^2, do not exceed 6% and 0.09 ns, respectively. GPR nanosecond impulses reflected/scattered by the wheat canopy have not been detected. In this research, sub-nanosecond impulses reflected/scattered by the wheat canopy have been confidently identified and make it possible to measure the wheat height (fresh AGB up to 2.3 kg/m^2 and height up to 104 cm) with a determination coefficient (R^2) of ~0.99 and a bias of ~−7 cm, as well as fresh AGB where R^2 = 0.97, with a bias = −0.09 kg/m^2, and a root-mean-square error of 0.1 kg/m^2. The joint use of impulses in two different MHz- and GHz-frequency bands will, in the future, make it possible to create UAV-based reflectometers for simultaneously mapping the soil moisture, height, and biomass of vegetation for precision farming systems.

Keywords: above-ground biomass (AGB); canopy height; soil moisture under vegetation; soil roughness; ground-penetrating radar (GPR); unmanned aerial vehicle (UAV); precision agriculture

1. Introduction

In the near future, the entire cycle of field agricultural work will be carried out without physical human labor, instead using machines and aircraft platforms within the framework of precision agriculture [1–3]. Above-ground biomass (AGB), vegetation canopy height, and soil moisture under vegetation are the most important biophysical parameters that are necessary for crop management in precision agriculture. The use of unmanned aerial vehicles (UAVs) equipped with high spatial resolution sensors over large areas appears to be the most promising cost-effective remote-sensing technology for monitoring these biophysical parameters in the robotic systems of precision agriculture [2,3]. To measure AGB and vegetation canopy height, digital RGB [3], cameras taking multispectral (hyper-spectral) images from the visible to infrared spectrum ranges [4,5], light detection and ranging (LiDAR) technology [6,7], combinations of the above sensors [8–11], and ultrasonic sensors [12] have been used on UAVs. The bare soil's moisture, due to a significant correlation with the brightness of images, can be measured in the optical range (by combining multispectral and infrared bands, the accuracy increases) [13–15]. It seems that in the case of dense vegetation cover, microwave methods have no equal for the UAV-based remote sensing of soil moisture [16–20].

Optical methods for estimating vegetation biomass are based on establishing empirical modeling relationships between AGB, measured in situ, with various vegetation indices and specific spectral bands, including the use of multiple linear (nonlinear) regression methods and machine learning [4,5,21,22]. Such empirical relationships are specific to different types of crops, with the variation of the coefficient of determination (R^2) ranging from 0.3 to 0.7. The accuracy of AGB estimation increases to R^2 = 0.8–0.93 [22–25], when vegetation height (or textural features) is included in these empirical models. In optical methods, the height of vegetation is determined by the photogrammetric method [4,10,24]. In the absence of bare soil as a reference surface, the height of vegetation is apparently impossible to determine since the measurement error will increase unacceptably. The use of LiDAR [6,7,25,26] for a wide variety of agriculture crops makes it possible to successfully estimate not only their height, with R^2~0.7–0.88 [6,26], but also fresh AGB with R^2~0.68–0.82 [6]. However, in the case of densely planted potato crops, due to the very small number of scattered points under the canopy, LiDAR 3D point cloud-based methods lead to a degradation in both estimation of height (R^2 = 0.50, RMSE = 12 cm) and biomass (R^2 = 0.24, RMSE = 22.1 g/m^2) [6], where RMSE stands for the root-mean-square error. Note that when using LiDAR, biomass is determined from empirical relationships with the density of point clouds, scattered by the canopy, or with the canopy height [6,26]. Ultrasonic sensors have a short range, and poor repeatability of canopy height measuring; therefore, they are less widely used for monitoring crop height with UAVs.

At the same time, contactless ground penetrating radar (GPR) methods have the potential to measure not only bare soil moisture [27–32] but also the height and biomass of vegetation [33], as well as soil moisture under the canopy [34–38]. The significant interaction (scattering and attenuation) of GHz-frequency range impulses with plant parts allows us to propose methodologies to retrieve the biophysical parameters of the vegetation canopy. Thus, in Ref. [33], empirical linear regression equations were obtained, linking the height and biomass of the canopy with the time delay between radio impulses (duration of 2 ns and central frequency of 10 GHz), reflected from the upper and lower boundaries of the canopy (with a slope of 20 m/ns and 60.9 $\times$ 10^2 m^2/(kg ns), respectively, and zero *y*-intercepts). These empirical dependencies were further used to estimate the relative complex permittivity (RCP) of the canopy, with Carlson's dielectric model of vegetation [39] used in the approximation of the canopy as a dielectrically homogeneous layer. The average errors when measuring the height and biomass of the vegetation canopy were 8.9% and 18%, respectively. These estimates were obtained for ground-based (UAZ vehicle), aircraft (AN-2), and helicopter (Ka-26) remote measurements of 14 fields with oats, wheat, barley, and rye crops (height from 74 to 132 cm, biomass from 1.46 to 5.34 kg/m^2, and vegetation moisture content from 56% to 81%).

In the sub-GHz range, lower-frequency sensing impulses, reflecting from the soil surface, will interact less with the canopy (in relation to impulses in the GHz range), which makes it possible to propose simple methods for soil moisture retrieval [34–38]. These methods require an a priori determination of the canopy's biophysical parameters to achieve practically significant accuracy in soil moisture retrieval. Without taking into account the influence of vegetation in Refs. [34,35] using ultra-wide-band (UWB) impulses (duration ~2 ns and central frequency of ~1 GHz) makes it possible to retrieve volumetric soil moisture values under a wheat canopy (up to 40 cm in height, with a leaf area index up to ~6.9–9.7 m^2 leaves/m^2) with RMSE values of ~8–12% (maximum bias = −20% for a fully developed canopy) relative to the time domain reflectometry data (depth 2 cm). The RMSE of soil moisture retrieval was reduced to 3% [35] when GPR impulse attenuation in the canopy was described using the Beer–Lambert model (the canopy leaf area index should be known) and the linear dielectric model of a canopy in the form of an additive mixture of air and fresh water was used. In this approach, soil moisture was retrieved by measuring the propagation time of an impulse reflected from a subsurface reflector, or by measuring the modulus of the reflection coefficient (at the central frequency of the GPR impulse) using an empirical dielectric model [40]. In Ref. [41], the empirical calibration of the refractive index and the normalized attenuation coefficient of the canopy (tea plantation with a plant height of 60–90 cm), considered as a dielectric-homogeneous layer, made it possible to reduce the RMSE of volumetric soil moisture retrieval from ~4.5% to 1.3% (soil dielectric model [42]). These estimates were obtained for ground-based remote sensing experiments with the UWB impulse (spectrum width from ~500 MHz to 3 GHz). In other studies [37,38], the field soil moisture value under spring wheat (~27 cm high) was retrieved with off-ground GPR (impulses in the frequency range of 0.2–2 GHz) using the canopy layer model (accounting for scattering) and laboratory-derived data for both the scattering parameter and canopy water content. Without taking the canopy correction parameters into account, the error in soil moisture retrieval increased from ~5% to ~11%. Moreover, as shown in Refs. [37,38], the vegetation parameters and soil moisture cannot be simultaneously retrieved from the inversion of GPR signals of the sub-GHz range. The conducted studies indicate the need for further shifting the frequencies of sensing impulses to the MHz range for the remote sensing of soil moisture, reducing the impulse scattering effect of plant elements and soil surface roughness ([43]: see Figure 4a and discussion in section III.A, where the amplitude and phase spectrum of Green's function are significantly less distorted in the MHz-frequency range of <0.8 GHz; [44]: Figure 9a,b). Note that for the Gaussian height distribution of soil surface roughness, GPR signals reflected from the soil surface can be described using the Fresnel reflection coefficient for a smooth surface with an attenuation factor of $exp\left(-2k_0^2\sigma_r^2cos^2\theta^i\right)$ (coherent model) [45–47], where θ^i is the wave incidence angle, $k_0 = 2\pi/\lambda = 2\pi f/c$ is the wavenumber in free space, λ is the wavelength in free space, c is the velocity of light in a vacuum, σ_r is the root means square (RMS) height of the soil surface roughness, and f is the frequency in the spectrum of GPR impulse.

Unlike existing approaches, this article proposes utilizing a combination of UWB impulses in the GHz-frequency range for vegetation parameter retrieval and in the MHz-frequency range for soil moisture retrieval. Despite the recorded negative experiences associated with the simultaneous retrieval of soil moisture and vegetation biophysical parameters, this article attempts to further investigate this possibility using impulses in the MHz-frequency range. The next aim of the article is to investigate the possibilities of UWB impulses in the GHz-frequency range for measuring the vertical distribution of fresh AGB and canopy height. On the one hand, it is proposed to select the optimal average frequency and spectrum width of the sensing impulse, which would significantly interact with the canopy. On the other hand, for the purpose of measuring the canopy height by time delay, the sensing impulses must be reliably received after being scattered by the air–canopy and canopy–soil interfaces. In contrast to previous articles where the tomographic method [48–50] was proposed for the assessment of the vertical heterogeneity (density) of plants in the canopy, based on multi-angle observations of reflected signals, the methods developed in this investigation must be designed for use with a single UAV performing nadir sensing. Additionally, unlike previous investigations [34,35,37,38,48–50], in this work, the retrieved parameters of canopy biomass and those measured under field conditions will be compared over a wide range of variation values (0–2.3 kg/m^2).

2. Methodology of In Situ and Remote Sensing Measurement

2.1. Test Field and In Situ Measurement

A wheat field during the heading–ripening period was chosen as a test site (an area of several hectares). The field was located on the territory of the Experimental Production Farm "Minino" of the Federal Research Center KSC SB RAS, located in the area of the Minino village, Emelyanov district, Krasnoyarsk region, in the Russian Federation

(56.0641N, 92.6976E). The test field was randomly sown with four kinds of wheat: Krasnoyarskaya no. 12, Beyskaya (osistaya), and Novosibirskaya no. 31 and no. 15. The location of the test field is shown in Figure 1.

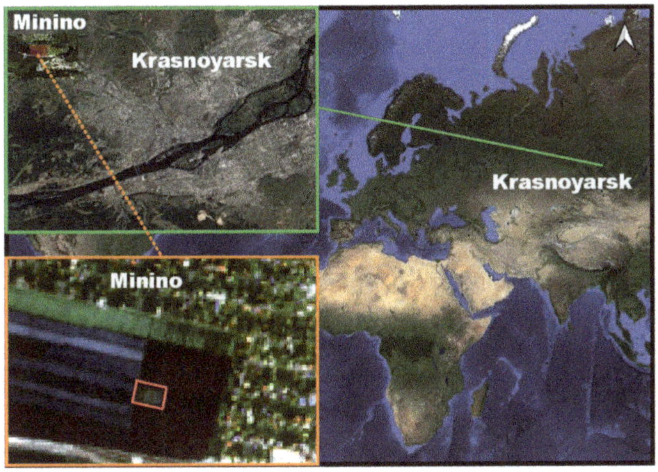

Figure 1. Geographic location of the test field (red rectangle).

The topsoil of the test field is represented by clay loam soils with a clay content of 37–39%. The characteristics of the soil horizons are given in Table 1.

Table 1. Soil characteristics of the test field.

Soil Horizon **	Depth [cm]	Organic Carbon [%]	Dry Bulk Density [g/cm^3]	Soil Texture by Weight [%]		Clay Content by Weight [%] *
				<0.001 mm	<0.01 mm	
A1	0–10	6.9	1.0	35	54	39
A2	10–22	4.8	1.1	34	50	37
AB	22–42	4.8	1.17	32	47	35

* The United States Department of Agriculture (USDA) texture definition. ** $A_{1,2}$ is the mineral horizon containing ≤30% organic matter by weight, and AB is the transitional layer between A and B (the infiltration–illuvial) horizons.

Two cycles of measurements in the MHz- and GHz-frequency ranges were carried out on 25 August and 3 September 2023, respectively, in neighboring plots (2 × 2 m) of the test field. The following parameters were measured at each plot: RMS height and correlation length of soil surface roughness (after the complete cutting of plants), soil moisture, fresh and dry AGB, and canopy height. Roughness parameters were calculated from a digital elevation model (DEM) over five different linear profiles (length of ~1 m) drawn along the soil surface with different azimuths. The DEMs of the plots were constructed using the photogrammetric method (photographing with AIR 2S (DJI, Shenzhen, China) from a height of 2 m at various azimuthal angles). Local coordinates were assigned by a three-dimensional scale ruler (made of mutually perpendicular wooden blocks with a length of 40 cm and 1 m, with a cross-section of 19 × 40 mm) placed on the soil surface. The error in measuring soil surface roughness (<0.4 cm) was estimated as the RMS height along two linear profiles, drawn along the absolutely flat top surfaces of a wooden scale ruler. Soil moisture was measured at ~30 points in each plot using a GS3 (Decagon, San Francisco, CA, USA) sensor (sensor rods piercing the soil surface vertically, down to a depth of 5 cm). The effective thickness of the layer for moisture measurement was ~6–7 cm. The factory calibration of the GS3 sensor for mineral soils was used. Vegetation AGB was measured over entire plots using the thermostat-weight method. Canopy height was measured with a ruler at 10 points on each field plot.

2.2. Methodology of Remote Sensing Measurement

During the long process of vegetation growth, the soil's surface roughness and moisture levels change. These changes constitute additional, uncertain variables that complicate the analysis of remote sensing data. In this paper, both sets of one-day experiments on the contactless GPR remote sensing of wheat were carried out while the moisture and roughness of the soil surface remained unchanged. At the same time, the sequential cutting-down of the wheat canopy (from the top to the soil surface in small layers of 10–20 cm) provided an opportunity to study the distortion of time shapes (amplitudes), propagation delay times, and spectral amplitude (reflection coefficient) of GPR impulses, depending on the height and biomass of the canopy. A monostatic nadir radar scheme was used for remote sensing in the MHz- and GHz-frequency ranges. The OKO-3 GPR with an AB-900M3 antenna unit (Geotech LLC, Moscow, Russia) was used as the source and receiver of impulses in the MHz-frequency range [51]. Continuous-time operating mode of OKO-3 GPR was used, with 1024 as the number of samples per scan and a time range of 32 ns. To generate impulses in the GHz-frequency range, a P6-59 horn antenna (JSC "NNRPA n.a. M.V. Frunze", Nizhny Novgorod, Russia) [52] and a FieldFox N9917B 18GHz (Keysight, Colorado Springs, CO, USA) vector network analyzer (VNA) were used, adopting the method described in Refs. [53–55]. The VNA was initialized with the following presets: start and stop scan frequencies—0.5 GHz and 7.0 GHz, IF bandwidth—3 kHz, sweep resolution—4001 points, and output power—high (5 dBm). Before measurement, calibration of the VNA was performed with a standard mechanical calkit (Full 1-port Cal, 85518A, Type-N-50 Ohm) after a 15-minute warm-up time. The antennas were hung over the soil at fixed heights of 1.15 m (OKO-3 GPR) and 1.57 m (VNA), respectively, during the experiments. The progress of the experiments is shown in Figures 2 and 3.

Figure 2. (**a–d**) The process used in the experiment on the remote sensing of the wheat canopy in the MHz-frequency range with an OKO-3 GPR (23 August 2023); (**d**) measurement over a metal screen. Free space calibration is not shown.

(a) (b) (c) (d)

Figure 3. (**a**–**d**) The process used in the experiment on the remote sensing of the wheat canopy in the GHz-frequency range with a horn antenna (3 September 2023); (**d**) measurement over a metal screen. Free space calibration is not shown.

Calibration relative to a metal screen (brass mesh), performed according to the method used in Refs. [53–55], made it possible to carry out absolute measurement of the GPR impulse amplitudes and the reflection coefficient. In the case of a horn antenna, based on the spectral measurements of the reflection coefficient $S_{11}(f)$ at the antenna terminals by VNA, the GPR impulse was synthesized based on the following formulas:

$$\dot{s}_{sv,\ ref,0}(t) = 2\int_{f_{min}}^{f_{max}} df S_{sv,ref,0}(f)e^{-2\pi ift}, \quad (1)$$

$$s_{sv}(t) = \frac{Re\,\dot{s}_{sv}(t)}{\left|\dot{s}_{ref}(t)\right|_{max}},\ s_{ref}(t) = Re\,\dot{s}_{ref}(t), \quad (2)$$

where t is the time, $S_{sv,ref}(f) = K_\alpha(f)S_{11}(f)$, the smoothing Gaussian spectral window function was chosen as $K_\alpha(f) = \exp(-0.5[(f - f_0)/\alpha]^2)$, $\alpha = \Delta f/\sqrt{-2ln0.5}$, f_{min} and f_{max} are the frequency limits of $S_{11}(f)$ measurement; $\dot{s}_{sv,ref}(t)$ and $\left|\dot{s}_{sv,ref}(t)\right|$ are the analytical signal and envelope of the impulse $s_{sv,ref}(t)$, reflected from the layered structure of vegetation–soil cover (*sv*) and a metal screen (*ref.*); index «0» corresponds to the free space measurements; $\left|\dot{s}_{ref}(t)\right|_{max}$ is the maximum of the impulse envelope, reflected from a metal screen. The average frequency and spectrum half-bandwidth of the window function were set as equal to f_0 = 3.0 GHz and Δf = 1.15 GHz, respectively (the choice of such parameters is justified at the end of this paper). To reduce the influence of the direct wave, the spectrum $S_0(f)$ was measured with the antennas oriented to the zenith (free-space calibration), and it was then subtracted from the spectra $S_{sv,ref}(f)$. In the case of the OKO-3 GPR antenna used, an inverse Fourier transform was performed, the spectrum of the GPR impulses $S_{sv,ref,0}(f)$ was found, and then a similar calibration method to (1)–(2) was performed.

The complex reflection coefficient from the layered structure of vegetation–soil cover was calculated in the spectral region as $R_{sv}(f) = S_{sv}(f)/S_{ref}(f)$. The modules of the reflection coefficient from the layered structure of vegetation–soil cover were calculated at the average frequency of the GPR impulses $|R_{sv}(f_0)| = |\dot{s}_{sv}(t)|_{max}/|\dot{s}_{ref}(t)|_{max}$ and in the time domain $|R_{sv}(t)| = |\dot{s}_{sv}(t)|/|\dot{s}_{ref}(t)|_{max}$.

2.3. Model of the Reflection Coefficient and Dielectric Model of the Canopy

The spectrum of the complex reflection coefficient of a plane wave that is normally incident to the soil surface, which is covered with vegetation, can be written in the following form:

$$R_{sv}^{th}(f) = R_{ac} + \left(1 - R_{ac}^2\right) \cdot exp[2i\sqrt{\varepsilon_{can}}k_0 h_{can}] \cdot R_{cs}(\varepsilon_s) \cdot exp\left[-2\,(k_0\sigma_r)^2\right], \quad (3)$$

where R_{ac} and R_{cs} are the Fresnel reflection coefficients from the air–canopy and canopy–soil interfaces, respectively; $i = \sqrt{-1}$; ε_{can} is the RCP of the vegetation canopy; h_{can} is the height of the canopy; ε_s is the RCP of soil. In model (3), the phenomena of wave scattering on individual elements of plants, as well as multiple wave reflections between the air–canopy and canopy–soil interfaces were neglected. The RCP of soil is $\varepsilon_s = \varepsilon_s(f, W, \rho_d, C)$, where W is the volumetric water content, ρ_d is the dry bulk density, and C is the clay fraction by weight, which was calculated using the Mironov model [56]. The two-relaxation Mironov dielectric model is created based on the RCP data for 6 types of mineral soil samples, measured in the frequency range of 0.04–26.5 GHz. The clay, sand, and silt fractions in these soil samples varied from 7% to 76%, from 0% to 55%, and from 11% to 93%, respectively.

The RCP of the canopy is calculated based on the refractive mixing dielectric model [37,57,58] of air and vegetation [59,60]:

$$\begin{aligned} n_{can}(f) &= 1 + (n_v(f) - 1)v_v, \\ \kappa_{can}(f) &= \kappa_v(f)v_v, \end{aligned} \quad (4)$$

where $\sqrt{\varepsilon_{can,v}} = n_{can,v} + i\,\kappa_{can,v}$, $n_{can,v}$ and $\kappa_{can,v}$ are the refractive index and normalized attenuation coefficient of the canopy (can) and vegetation material (v), and v_v is the volume fraction of vegetation material in the canopy. The RCP of vegetation $\varepsilon_v = \varepsilon_v(f, m_v, m_{salt})$, as a function of frequency, salinity (m_{salt}), and the weight (m_v) of plant fluid, was calculated based on the dielectric model [61]. The volumetric fraction of vegetation material in the canopy is given by the equation:

$$v_v = \frac{V_v}{V} = \frac{m_v}{\rho_v V} = \frac{B}{\rho_v h_{can}}, \quad (5)$$

where V_v and V are the volume of vegetation material and the test volume of the canopy, $V = A \cdot h_{can}$, ρ_v is the density of wet vegetation material, A is the area under the test canopy, and B in [kg/m^2] is the fresh AGB. Gravimetric moisture content in the canopy is given by the equation $m_v = \left(m_{wet} - m_{dry}\right)/m_{wet}$, where m_{wet} and m_{dry} are the weights of wet and dry plants.

The validity of the refractive mixing model (4) for assessing the vegetation b-factor depending on frequency was checked. The b_{refr}-factor was estimated based on model (4) from the optical thickness equation $\tau_{refr} = b_{refr} \cdot B = 2 \cdot k_0 \cdot h_{can} \cdot \kappa_{can}(f)$, using experimental data [62,63] on height, water content, and fresh plant biomass. Conversely, the values of b_{rad}-factor were taken from radiometric-based measurements of the optical thickness of vegetation cover with different AGB values [60,64–66]. Figure 4 shows that the dispersion of the b_{rad}-factor decreases with increasing wave-length, which is a consequence of the predominant wave's attenuation prevails over the scattering phenomenon in the vegetation cover. In general, good agreement between the theoretical estimates of the b-factor based on the refractive model (4) and the experimentally measured ones [60,64–66] can be observed. Furthermore, model (4) will be used to estimate the fresh AGB of the vegetation canopy.

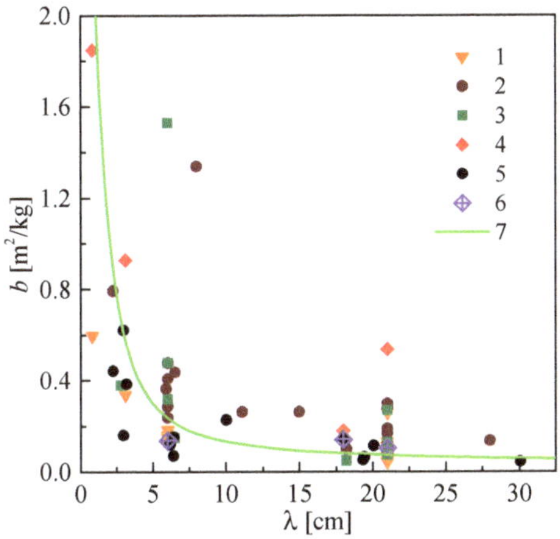

Figure 4. Lambda dependency of the *b*-factors: 1—corn [64,65], 2—soybean [64–67], 3—wheat [64,65], 4—alfalfa [64,65], 5—wheat grains [60], 6—cereals, and sorghum [66] are b_{rad}-factors, estimated based on radiometric measurements, and the 7–b_{refr}-factor, calculated based on the refractive mixing model (4).

2.4. Algorithm for Measuring Soil Moisture and Surface Roughness, Canopy Height, and Biomass

Two algorithms for retrieving soil geophysical and vegetation biometric parameters are considered in the MHz- and GHz-frequency ranges. In the first algorithm, based on OKO-3 measured GPR impulses in MHz-frequency range, (a) soil surface moisture and roughness, and (b) fresh AGB are retrieved from the informative criterion of $|R_{sv}(f)|$ and $arg\ R_{sv}(f)$, respectively (see Figure 5). The inverse problem of soil moisture and soil surface roughness retrieval can be formulated as:

$$\{W_{retr}, \sigma_{r,retr}\}_B = \left[\left|R_{sv}(f, B)\right| - \left|R^{th}_{sv}(f,\ \rho_d, C, W_{retr}, \sigma_{r,retr})\right| \right]^2 \Big|_{min}, \quad (6)$$

where $|R_{sv}(f, B)|$ and $R^{th}_{sv}(f,\ \rho_d, C, W_{retr}, \sigma_{r,retr})\Big|$ are the measured and calculated spectra of the module of reflection coefficient for a given AGB.

The influence of canopy on the attenuation of an impulse, reflected from the soil surface, is neglected; it will be assumed in model (3), where $R_{ac} = 0$ and $h_{can} = 0$ m. The soil dry density and clay content are set as equal to $\rho_d = 1.1\ g/cm^3$ and $C = 39\%$, respectively (see Table 1). The vegetation biomass can be found by minimizing the functional:

$$B_{retr} = \left[arg\ R_{sv}(f, B) - arg\ R^{th}_{sv}(f, B_{retr}) \right]^2 \Big|_{min}, \quad (7)$$

where $arg\ R^{th}_{sv}(f, B_{retr}) = 2k_0 h_{can}\left(Re\sqrt{\varepsilon_{can}(B_{retr},\ m_{salt}, \rho_v, h_{can})} - 1 \right)$, and the phases of the reflection coefficients $R_{ac}(f)$ and $R_{cs}(f)$ in Formula (3) will be neglected. The density of fresh vegetation material is significantly determined by the water content; thus, we will assume that $\rho_v \cong \rho_w \cdot m_v$, where $\rho_w \approx 10^3 kg/m^3$ is the water density in normal conditions. The gravimetric moisture content in the vegetation during the experiment was approximately equal to $m_v \approx 80\%$, with a salinity of $m_{salt} = 10‰$. Also, when solving Formula (7), we assume that h_{can} is a known value (either measured experimentally, or this value was obtained during minimization (6)). The inverse problems (6) and (7) were solved using the Levenberg–Marquardt algorithm [68].

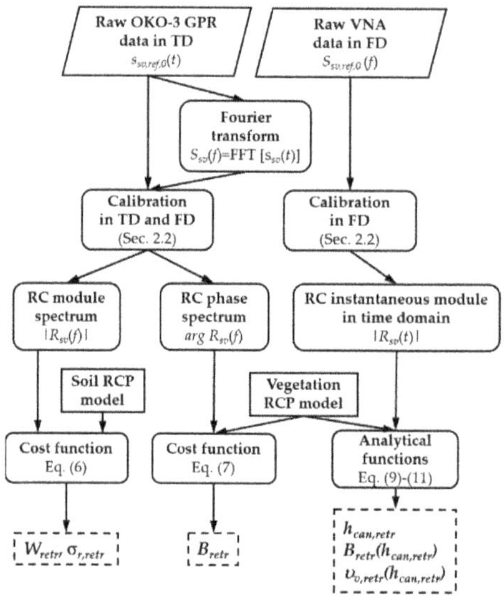

Figure 5. Flowchart of algorithms used for soil geophysical and canopy biometric parameters, based on the measured OKO-3 GPR data in the time domain (TD) and VNA data in the frequency domain (FD).

In the second algorithm, based on the VNA spectral measurements in the GHz-frequency ranges (see Figure 5), neglecting the influence of the reflected wave from the soil surface (see Formula (3) at $R_{cs}\equiv0$), it is possible to estimate the instantaneous values of the refractive index in the internal structure of the canopy $n_{can,retr}(t)$, based on the Fresnel equation:

$$n_{can,retr}(t) = \frac{1+|R_{sv}(t)|}{1-|R_{sv}(t)|}, \tag{8}$$

where $|R_{sv}(t)|$ can be interpreted as the instantaneous value of the module of the reflection coefficient (see the definition at the end of Section 2.2). Note that Formula (3) does not take into account the scattering phenomenon, which can lead to an overestimation of $n_{can,retr}(t)$, calculated using Formula (8). Then, using Formulas (4) and (8), the volumetric content of the vegetation elements $\Delta v_{v,retr}(t)$ in the canopy at time t can be estimated:

$$\Delta v_{v,retr}(t) = \frac{n_{can,retr}(t)-1}{n_v(f_0)-1}, \tag{9}$$

where $n_v(f_0)$ is the refractive index of the vegetation material at the central frequency of the GPR impulse. The time scale t (arrival impulses) can be recalculated into the absolute values of the vertical coordinate z, using the known values of $n_{can,retr}(t)$:

$$z = \frac{1}{2}\frac{(t-t_0)\cdot c}{n_{can}(t)}, \tag{10}$$

where z = 0 m corresponds to the soil surface; t_0 is the arrival time of the maximum impulse envelope, reflected from the metal screen. Based on the measured arrival time of the first impulse, t_{ac}, reflected from the air–canopy interface, the height of the canopy can be estimated from Formula (10) as $z_{max}(t = t_{ac})\Rightarrow h_{can,retr}$. Note that based on Formula (10), the instantaneous values of the refractive index and the volumetric content of vegetation elements can be expressed as a function of the vertical coordinate z or $h_{can,retr}$. Then, using the integral representation of Equation (5), the profile $B(z)$ of fresh AGB can be estimated:

$$B_{retr}(z) = \rho_v \int_0^z dz v_{v,retr}(z), \tag{11}$$

where, as before, it is assumed that $\rho_v \cong \rho_w \cdot m_v$ ($m_v \approx 80\%$).

3. Results

3.1. Experiment in the MHz-Frequency Range

During the experiment conducted on 23 August 2023, an impulse with a duration of $\Delta\tau_{MHz}$ = 1.2 ns (at the 0.5 level of the maximum envelope), with a spectrum bandwidth from 428 MHz to 1.33 GHz (at a level of −6 dB) and a central frequency of 750 MHz, was used for remote sensing of the wheat canopy. The normalized time shape of the GPR impulse, reflected from the metal screen $s_{ref}(t)$ (brass mesh 2 × 2 m), together with the normalized envelope of the analytical signal $\left|\dot{s}_{ref}(t)\right|$, is shown in Figure 6a (see the solid and dashed gray curves, respectively). Following the methodology, the amplitude of the GPR impulses, reflected from the vegetation–soil cover, was normalized by the maximum envelope of the GPR impulse, reflected from the metal screen $\left|\dot{s}_{ref}(t)\right|_{max}$. The measured time shapes of the impulses $s_{sv}(t)$ for the cut-down canopy, calculated layer by layer from the top to the soil surface, are shown in Figure 6a (see the colored curves). The modules of the normalized spectra of GPR impulses, reflected from the metal screen $|S_{ref}(f)|$, and the vegetation–soil cover $|S_{sv}(f)|$ are shown in Figure 6b. As the wheat is cut down layer by layer, the maximum variations in the measured modulus of the reflection coefficient $|R_{sv}(f_0)|$ relative to the average value do not exceed ~6% (see Figure 6c).

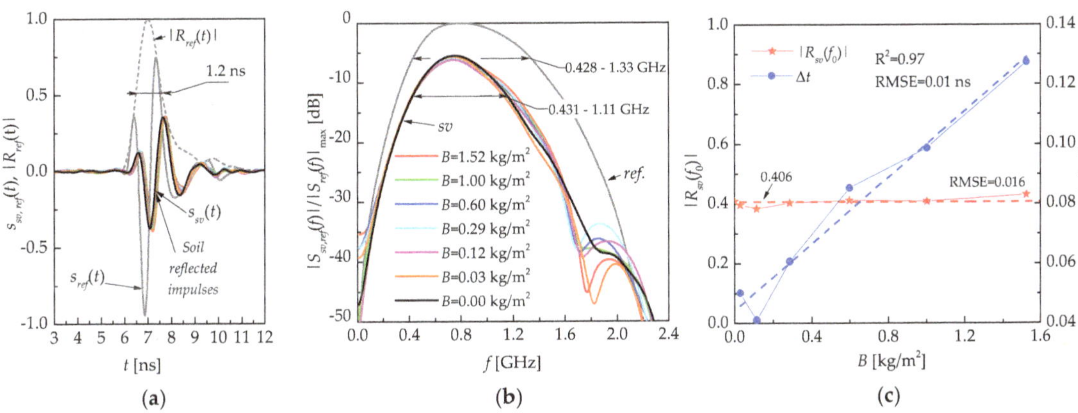

Figure 6. (**a**) Time shapes of the GPR impulse MHz-frequency range, reflected from the vegetation–soil cover $s_{sv}(t)$ (color lines) and metal reflector $s_{ref}(t)$ (gray solid line), with the normalized envelope of impulse, reflected from the metal screen $|R_{ref}(t)| = \left|\dot{s}_{ref}(t)\right| / \left|\dot{s}_{ref}(t)\right|_{max}$ (gray dashed line); (**b**) the corresponding normalized module of the impulse spectrum $|S_{sv,ref}(f)|$; (**c**) the module of the reflection coefficient $|R_{sv}(f_0)|$ and the delay time Δt (calculated from the maximum envelopes) of GPR impulses (see Figure 6a), depending on the measured fresh AGB value calculated by the thermostat-weight method.

It can be seen that against the background of the GPR impulses, which are reflected from the soil surface, the impulses reflected (scattered) by the vegetation cover are not identified. The delay time when the GPR impulses pass twice through the canopy increases from ~0.04 ns to ~0.13 ns as the fresh AGB value increases from 0 kg/m^2 to 1.52 kg/m^2 (see Figure 6c). The time delay of the impulses was calculated as the difference between the arrival times of the impulse's envelopes' maxima, as reflected from the metal screen and the soil surface. The impulse time delay of 0.04 ns at zero for fresh AGB (see Figure 6c) was caused by a calibration error because the metal screen lay on soil with a roughness slightly higher than the average level of the air–soil interface.

The data presented in Figure 6c shows an unambiguous linear correlation between the time delay Δt of the impulse reflected from the soil surface and the fresh AGB of the wheat. Moreover, both the time shapes and the amplitudes of the reflected impulses from the soil surface are practically independent of fresh AGB (up to 1.52 kg/m^2) and a canopy height up to 87 cm. In contrast to the module of reflection coefficient $|R_{sv}(f_0)|$ (see Figure 6c), measured from the maximum of the envelopes' reflected impulses (see Figure 6a), the spectrum of the complex reflection coefficient $R_{sv}(f)$ contains a frequency-dependent relationship with soil surface roughness and vegetation biomass.

Taking advantage of the first algorithm (see Section 2.4, Equations (6) and (7)), the canopy biomass, as well as soil moisture and roughness, were retrieved from the measured complex reflection coefficient. The measured and calculated spectra $|R_{sv}(f,B)|$, $arg\ R_{sv}(f,B)$ with the optimally established parameters are shown in Figure 7a. The retrieved fresh AGB values relative to the measured ones are shown in Figure 7b. The retrieved value of volumetric soil moisture W_{retr} = 23.4 ± 2.6%, with an absolute error of 3.3% (relative error 16.4%), coincides with the measured in situ value of 20.1 ± 3.7% by the Decagon GS3 sensor in 0–6 cm of topsoil on the test plot. The retrieved value of $\sigma_{r,retr}$= 1.4 ± 0.3 cm is, on average, overestimated by 0.5 cm relative to the measured in situ value of 0.9 ± 0.4 cm, due to the fact that model (3) does not take into account the wave-scattering phenomenon found on plant elements in the canopy.

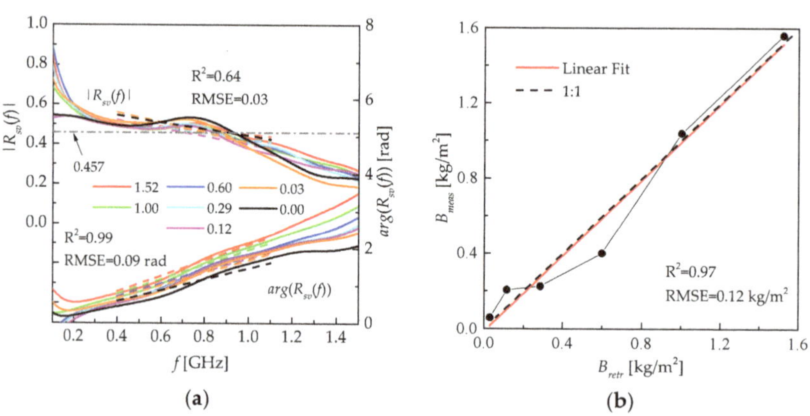

Figure 7. (**a**) The measured (solid lines) and retrieved (dash lines) modules $|R_{sv}(f,B)|$ and arguments $arg\ R_{sv}(f,B)$ of the spectrum of reflection coefficients; (**b**) the correlation between measured and retrieved fresh AGB values. The optimally found parameters while solving the inverse problem (6) were W_{retr} = 23.4 ± 2.6% and $\sigma_{r,retr}$= 1.4 ± 0.3 cm. The color scheme of solid and dashed color lines is the same (various colors of lines correspond to the different values for fresh AGB in [kg/m^2]).

The average value of the module of reflection coefficient is 0.457 (see Figure 7a, gray dash-dotted line), calculated based on the optimally found parameters W_{retr} and $\sigma_{r,retr}$ in the spectrum bandwidth of impulse, and coincides with the average value of $|R_{sv}(f_0)|$ = 0.406 (see Figure 6c) at an absolute error of 5.1% (relative error 12.3%), measured based on the maximum impulse amplitudes. Figure 7a shows that model (3) in the spectrum bandwidth of the GPR impulse describes with good accuracy the measured values of the modulus of the reflection coefficient. The retrieved values for canopy biomass after each cutting-down, with a high value for the determination coefficient, coincide with the measured ones (see Figure 7b).

3.2. Experiment in GHz-Frequency Range

During the experiment on 3 September 2023, an impulse with a duration of $\Delta\tau_{GHz}$ = 0.5 ns (at a 0.5 level of the maximum envelope, see Figure 8a) with a bandwidth of 1.36 GHz (at a level of −6 dB, from 2.62 GHz to 3.98 GHz) and 2.16 GHz (at a level of −10 dB, from 2.02 GHz to 4.18 GHz), with an average frequency of 3.2 GHz (see Figure 8b) was used for the remote sensing of the wheat canopy at another test plot. The normalized time shape $s_{ref}(t)$ and envelope $\left|\dot{s}_{ref}(t)\right|$ of the GPR impulse, reflected from a metal screen (brass mesh 2 × 2 m), is shown in Figure 8a (see the solid and dashed gray curves, respectively). The timeline in Figure 8a starts from 39.0 ns for analyzing the impulses reflected from the soil surface. In accordance with the methodology, the amplitude of the impulses reflected from the vegetation–soil cover was calibrated by normalizing to the maximum envelope of the impulse, as reflected from the metal screen $\left|\dot{s}_{ref}(t)\right|_{max}$. The measured time shapes of the impulses are shown in Figure 8a (see colored curves) as the wheat cut down layer by layer from the top to the soil surface. The normalized impulse spectra, reflected from the metal screen $|S_{ref}(f)|$ and from the vegetation–soil cover $|S_{sv}(f)|$, are shown in Figure 8b.

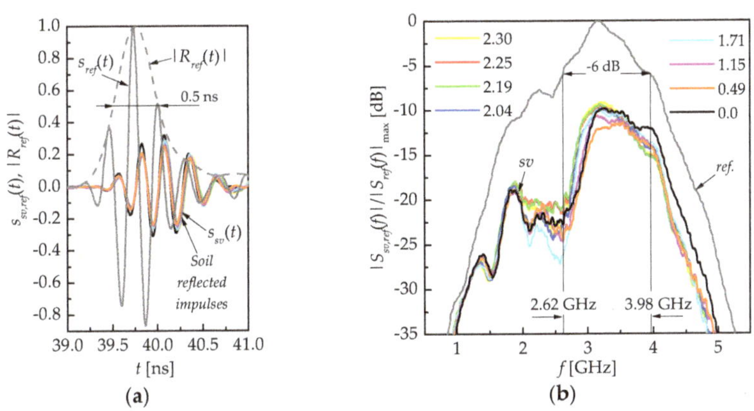

Figure 8. (**a**) Time shapes of the GPR impulses GHz-frequency range, reflected from the vegetation–soil cover $s_{sv}(t)$ (color lines) and metal reflector $s_{ref}(t)$ (gray solid line), normalized envelope of impulse, reflected from the metal screen $|R_{ref}(t)|$ (gray dashed line); (**b**) the corresponding normalized module of the impulse spectrum $|S_{sv,ref}(f)|$. Various colors of lines correspond to the different values of fresh AGB in [kg/m^2]. The color scheme is the same as in the pictures.

As the wheat is cut down and its fresh AGB value decreases from 2.30 kg/m^2 to 0.0 kg/m^2, the time delay of the impulses reflected from the soil surface decreases slightly by 0.03 ns (from 40.09 ns to 40.12 ns), and the amplitude increases by 1.3 dB (see Figure 8a). Figure 8b shows that the spectral amplitudes of impulse $|S_{sv}(f)|$, reflected from the vegetation–soil cover, in its bandwidth do not have a clear linkage with a decrease or increase in AGB. This evidence does not allow the use of impulses in the GHz-frequency range, reflected from the soil surface, for the reliable measurement of AGB.

At the same time, shown much more confidently compared to Refs. [34–36], Figure 9a,b reveals the impulses, reflected (scattered) not only by the air-canopy interface but also from internal plant elements in the canopy, located at different heights from the soil surface (time interval from ~32 ns to ~39.5 ns, the arrival time of the maximum envelope of the impulse, when reflected from the soil surface is t_0 = 39.77 ns). The normalized envelopes of the impulses reflected (scattered) by the canopy (see Figure 9c,d; time is from ~32 ns to ~39.5 ns) can be interpreted as the instantaneous value of the module of the reflection coefficient $|R_{sv}(t)|$.

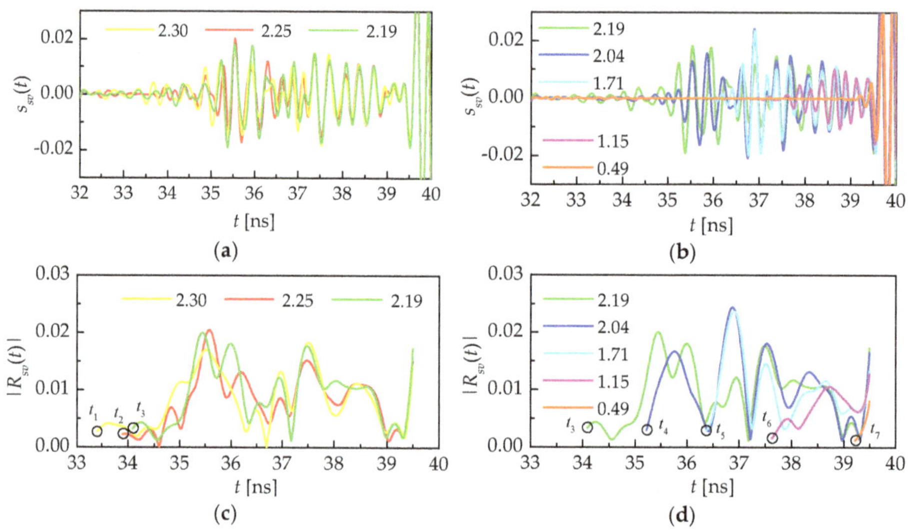

Figure 9. (**a**,**b**) Normalized time shapes of impulse $s_{sv}(t)$, reflected from the vegetation–soil cover and (**c**,**d**) their envelopes $|R_{sv}(t)| = |\dot{s}_{sv}(t)| / \left|\dot{s}_{ref}(t)\right|_{max}$ as wheat is cut down from the top to the soil surface. In the legend, the numbers indicate fresh AGB in [kg/m^2], measured in situ by the thermostat–weight method. The key for the black circles will be made clear further on.

As a result, based on Equations (8)–(10) and the data shown in Figure 9c,d, the values of $n_{can,retr}(z)$ and $\Delta v_{v,retr}(z)$ can be calculated (Figure 10).

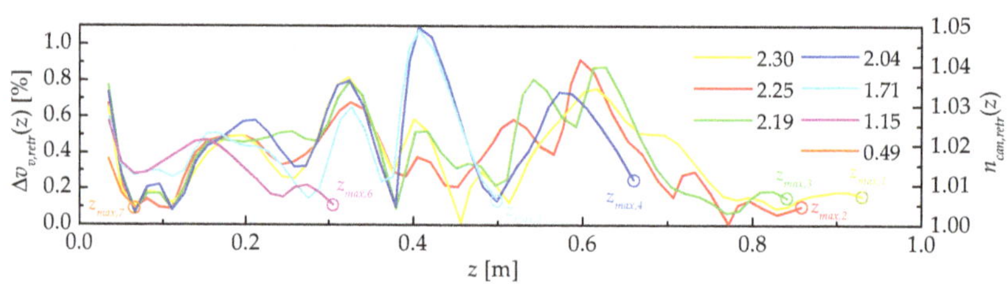

Figure 10. Retrieved local values of the volumetric contents of vegetation elements $\Delta v_{v,retr}(z)$ and the refractive index $n_{can,retr}(z)$ in the canopy. The numbers in the legend indicate the values of fresh AGB in [kg/m^2], measured by the thermostat-weight method.

Note that when calculating the dependencies (see Figure 10), the time interval (see Figure 9c,d) on the right was limited to 39.52 ns = $t_0 - \Delta\tau_{GHz}/2$. The time interval on the left was limited by the smallest value of the impulse arrival time (see Figure 9c,d, t_1, . . ., t_7), found from the criterion: $n_{can,retr}(t) > \overline{n_{can,retr}(t)} + 0.1\cdot\left(n_{can,retr}(t)|_{max} - \overline{n_{can,retr}(t)}\right)$. This criterion means a 10% excess of $n_{can,retr}(t)$ fluctuations relative to the average initial level $\overline{n_{can,retr}(t)}$ (this average value was assessed in the interval from 32 to 33 ns). As the canopy was cut down from the top to the soil surface, the position of the air-canopy interface was confidently identified, based on the criteria described above (see the black circles in Figure 9c,d, t_1,. . .,t_2, and the color circles in Figure 10, $z_{max,1}$,. . ., $z_{max,7}$). The $h_{can,retr} = z_{max,1}$,. . ., $z_{max,7}$ values found in this way are underestimated by an average of 6.7 cm relative to the wheat height measured with a ruler, and they correlate with each other, with R^2 = 0.992 and RMSE = 3.4 cm (see Figure 11). As the canopy height increases, the measured heights tend toward more underestimation, up to −11.3 cm.

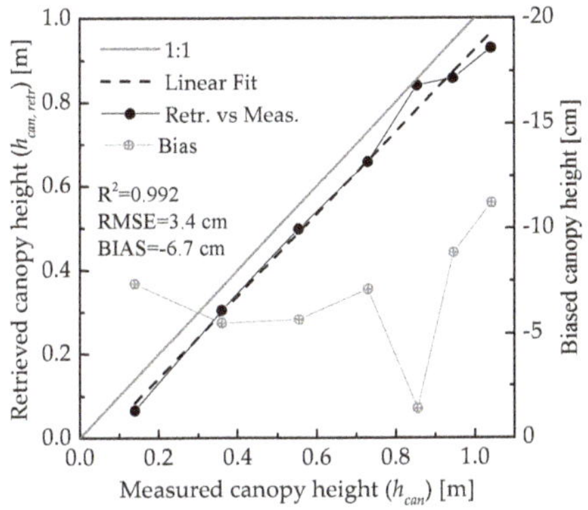

Figure 11. Dependence of the retrieved data on the measured canopy heights.

Figure 10 also shows that for six different cutting heights of vegetation, the shapes of $n_{can,retr}(z)$ and $\Delta v_{v,retr}(z)$ are not random but systematically reproduce some characteristic layered structures of local heterogeneities (reflectors/scatters) in the canopy. The retrieved profiles of the fresh AGB values, using Equation (11), are shown in Figure 12a. It can be seen that the retrieved fresh AGB values (less than ~1 kg/m^2) are underestimated, relative to the measured ones. An underestimation of B_{retr} is associated with an underestimation of $h_{can,\ retr}$ (and, therefore, $\Delta v_{v,retr}$). In addition, the relative error in $h_{can,\ retr}$ and $\Delta v_{v,retr}$ retrieval increases as the canopy height decreases. When the amount of biomass becomes significant (more than ~1 kg/m^2), apparently, the share of waves scattered by the plant elements increases, which is not taken into account in either the model of the reflection coefficient (3) or the dielectric model of the canopy (4), which leads to an overestimation of B_{retr}. In general, a high coefficient of determination $R^2 = 0.972$ and a relatively low error RMSE = 0.10 kg/m^2 of the retrieved fresh AGB values relative to the measured ones are observed (see Figure 12b).

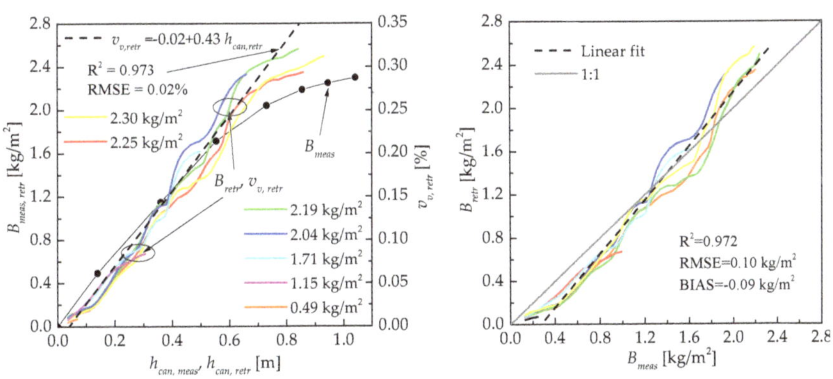

Figure 12. (**a**) The retrieved B_{retr} (color lines) and measured B_{meas} (line with black circles) for fresh AGB, depending on the retrieved $h_{can,retr}$ and measured $h_{can,meas}$ canopy heights, respectively; (**b**) correlation between the retrieved and measured fresh AGB values.

Due to the underestimation of retrieved canopy height, the retrieved fresh AGB value is also underestimated by 0.09 kg/m^2 (see Figure 12b). Figure 12a also shows the possibility of estimating the volumetric content of fresh vegetation (as can be seen from (9)), which can be described by a linear dependence on the retrieved canopy height, with $R^2 = 0.973$

and RMSE = 0.02% (see Figure 12a, dashed line). Apparently, this linear relationship is specific to each kind of plant and canopy texture.

4. Discussion

Single-day studies on the test plots when cutting down wheat made it possible to exclude the impact of soil moisture and surface roughness time-variation on the distortion of the time shape and spectrum of GPR impulses, which is a strong point for the proposed method. At the same time, the wheat was at the heading stage, which did not allow us to study the distortion of the time shapes and spectra of the GPR impulses throughout the growing period of the wheat. Future similar one-day studies are strongly recommended during the various vegetative phases to verify the proposed algorithms for measuring soil moisture, surface roughness, canopy height, and biomass. Since the OKO-3 GPR impulse (in the MHz-frequency range) weakly interacts with the canopy, this frequency band is suitable for the retrieval of soil moisture and surface roughness information. One of the significant disadvantages of the proposed method in the MHz-frequency range is its requirement of prior knowledge of the canopy height for biomass retrieval. The use of impulses in a GHz-frequency range allows us to solve this problem. To carry out measurements in the GHz-frequency range, the impulse parameters (see Section 2.2) were optimally chosen while solving the inverse problem by minimizing the norm of the difference between the measured and retrieved fresh AGB $|B_{meas}-B_{retr}|_{min}$ (see Figure 13). Figure 13 shows that when the average frequency varies from 2.0 GHz to 3.5 GHz and the spectrum half-bandwidth varies from ~1.0 GHz to 1.5 GHz of GPR impulses, there is a minimum functional of $|B_{meas}-B_{retr}|$. In accordance with the data shown in Figure 13, the spectrum half-bandwidth and center frequency for synthesizing the GPR impulse in the GHz-frequency range were chosen as Δf = 1.15 GHz and f_0 = 3 GHz, respectively (see Section 2.2).

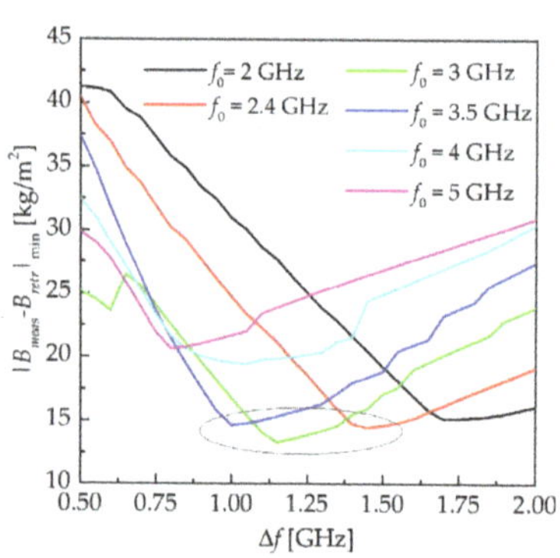

Figure 13. Relief of the norm of the difference between measured and retrieved fresh AGB values in total for all wheat-height cuts (see Figure 12a), depending on the half-bandwidth Δf and the central frequency f_0 of the Gaussian window function (see Section 2.2 and the text for Formulas (1)–(2)).

The synthesized impulse in the GHz-frequency range is apparently less susceptible to scattering by vegetation elements, compared to volumetric reflection and attenuation. As a result, the observed reflection/scattering of the GPR impulse in the GHz-frequency range, as shown, can be described by the model of the reflection coefficient of a plane wave (3) and the refractive mixing permittivity model of the canopy (4). Note that the phase-frequency method was not used for AGB retrieval in the GHz-frequency range because the impulse reflected from the soil surface should be eliminated by a time-domain window filter, which will introduce significant distortions into the reflected impulses from the bottom of the canopy. In this regard, in the GHz-frequency range, the most convenient method was the analysis of impulses reflected/scattered by the canopy in the time domain. In general, the proposed method (with combined impulses in the MHz- and GHz-frequency ranges) allowed us not only to retrieve the values for B_{retr}, W_{retr}, and $h_{r,retr}$ with significant accuracy for practical use but even the profiles of the canopy biomass and volumetric contents of vegetation elements.

It is also worth mentioning that placing radar units on a UAV will introduce special aspects to the processing and interpretation of radiated and reflected GPR impulses. Firstly, the impulse that is radiated and received by the UAV's radar will be distorted by the UAV's structural components, which are situated in the near-field region of the radar antenna. Secondly, the amplitude of the impulse reflected from the vegetation–soil layer will depend on the flight altitude of the UAV. The effect of these factors on the distortion of the time shape and the amplitude of the sensing impulses can be eliminated through the calibration of the UAV's radar, for example, as proposed in Refs. [53,55]. The findings from this study should be comparable when measured with a UAV flying at varying altitudes, with adjustments made for the corresponding in situ spatial averaging within the footprint area (requiring specific additional experimental validation).

5. Conclusions

This paper investigates the possibilities of broadband electromagnetic impulses in MHz- and GHz-frequency ranges for the remote sensing of soil moisture and the height and biomass of a wheat canopy. The broadband impulse of the MHz-frequency range (a duration of 1.2 ns) interacts negligibly with the wheat canopy (in biomass up to 1.5 kg/m^2, height up to 87 cm) and can be used for the remote sensing of soil moisture under such a canopy. In this case, variations in the impulse delay times (~0.09 ns) can also be neglected when the wheat biomass varies. It is shown that in the MHz-frequency range, a simple model of the frequency-dependent reflection coefficient (with a normal distribution of soil surface roughness) allows us to retrieve information on both soil moisture and the RMS heights of soil surface roughness under the wheat canopy. In the GHz-frequency range, the choice of an impulse with a duration of ~0.5 ns (average frequency of 3 GHz and spectrum half-bandwidth of 1.2 GHz) made it possible to confidently detect not only the time delay between impulses, reflected from the air–canopy and canopy–soil interfaces, but also the internal layered structure in the wheat canopy (fresh AGB up to 2.3 kg/m^2). It is shown that the height of wheat (up to 104 cm) can be estimated with R^2= 0.99 and a bias of −7 cm, based on measuring the time delays of GHz-frequency range impulses, as reflected from the air–canopy and canopy–soil interfaces. In this case, the vertical profile of fresh AGB with R^2 = 0.97 can be retrieved using the refractive mixing model of the canopy. The combination of the impulses of two different frequency ranges will, in the future, make it possible to create UAV-based reflectometers for the simultaneous mapping of soil moisture, height, and vegetation biomass for precision farming systems.

Author Contributions: Conceptualization, methodology, investigation, experiments, calculation, writing—original draft preparation, review and editing, project administration, and funding acquisition, K.M.; soil dielectric modeling and calculation and experiments, S.F. and A.K.; experiments, J.L.; agrofield resources and experiments, A.L. and V.R. All authors have read and agreed to the published version of the manuscript.

Funding: The investigation was supported by the Russian Science Foundation and the Krasnoyarsk Regional Science Foundation, project No. 22-17-20042.

Data Availability Statement: The original contributions presented in the study are included in the article, further inquiries can be directed to the corresponding author.

Acknowledgments: For their assistance in conducting the experiments, we thank Mikhail Mikhaylov (engineer at the Laboratory of Radiophysics of the Earth Remote Sensing Kirensky Institute of Physics Federal Research Center, KSC Siberian Branch, Russian Academy of Science).

Conflicts of Interest: The authors declare no conflicts of interest.

55. Muzalevskiy, K.; Mikhaylov, M.; Ruzicka, Z. Synthesizing of UltraWide Band Impulse by means of a Log-Periodic Dipole Antenna. Case Study for a Radar Stand Experiment. In Proceedings of the IEEE International Multi Conference on Engineering, Computer and Information Sciences (SIBIRCON), Yekaterinburg, Russia, 11–13 November 2022; pp. 1140–1143.
56. Muzalevsky, K.V. Synthesis of an Ultra-Wideband Pulse by a Log-Periodic Antenna with Continuous Excitation by Harmonic Oscillations. *Radiophys. Quantum Electron.* **2023**, *65*, 615–623. [CrossRef]
57. Mironov, L.; Bobrov, P.P.; Fomin, S.V. Dielectric model of moist soils with varying clay content in the 0.04 to 26.5 GHz frequency range. In Proceedings of the International Siberian Conference on Control and Communications (SIBCON), Tomsk, Russia, 12–13 September 2013; pp. 1–4.
58. Romanov, A.N. Dielectric Properties of Water in Saline Soil and its Solonchak Vegetation at a Frequency of 1.41 GHz. *IEEE Geosci. Remote Sens. Lett.* **2021**, *18*, 2033–2037. [CrossRef]
59. Romanov, A.N.; Kochetkova, T.D.; Suslyaev, V.I.; Shcheglova, A.S. Dielectric properties of marsh vegetation in a frequency range of 0.1–18 GHz under variation of temperature and moisture. *Russ. Phys. J.* **2017**, *60*, 803–811. [CrossRef]
60. Mironov, V.L.; Mikhaylov, M.I.; Muzalevskiy, K.V.; Sorokin, A.V.; Fomin, S.V.; Karavayskiy, A.Y. Measurement of height and moisture of an agricultural vegetation using GPS/GLONASS receiver. *Sib. Aerosp. J.* **2014**, *15*, 88–97.
61. Schmugge, T.J.; Jackson, T.J. A dielectric model of the vegetation effects on the microwave emission from soils. *IEEE Trans. Geosci. Remote Sens.* **1992**, *30*, 757–760. [CrossRef]
62. Ulaby, F.T.; El-rayes, M.A. Microwave Dielectric Spectrum of Vegetation—Part II: Dual-Dispersion Model. *IEEE Trans. Geosci. Remote Sens.* **1987**, *GE-25*, 550–557. [CrossRef]
63. Liu, S.-F.; Liou, Y.-A.; Wang, W.-J.; Wigneron, J.-P.; Lee, J.-B. Retrieval of crop biomass and soil moisture from measured 1.4 and 10.65 GHz brightness temperatures. *IEEE Trans. Geosci. Remote Sens.* **2022**, *40*, 1260–1268. [CrossRef]
64. Wigneron, J.P.; Calvet, J.C.; Chanzy, A.; Grosjean, O.; Laguerre, L. A composite discrete-continuous approach to model the microwave emission of vegetation. *IEEE Trans. Geosci. Remote Sens.* **1995**, *33*, 201–211. [CrossRef]
65. Van de Griend, A.A.; Wigneron, J.P. On the measurement of microwave vegetation properties: Some guidelines for a protocol. *IEEE Trans. Geosci. Remote Sens.* **2004**, *42*, 2277–2289. [CrossRef]
66. Van de Griend, A.A.; Wigneron, J.P. The b-factor as a function of frequency and canopy type at H-polarization. *IEEE Trans. Geosci. Remote Sens.* **2004**, *42*, 786–794. [CrossRef]
67. Chukhlantsev, A.A.; Golovachev, S.P. Attenuation of microwave radiation in vegetation [Oslablenie SVCH izlucheniya v rastitel'nom pokrove]. *J. Commun. Technol. Electron. [Radiotekhnika I Elektron.]* **1989**, *34*, 2269–2278.
68. Gill, P.E.; Murray, W. Algorithms for Nonlinear Least-Squares Problem. *SIAM J. Numer. Anal.* **1978**, *15*, 977–992. [CrossRef]

remote sensing

MDPI

Article

A Three-Dimensional Conceptual Model for Estimating the Above-Ground Biomass of Winter Wheat Using Digital and Multispectral Unmanned Aerial Vehicle Images at Various Growth Stages

Yongji Zhu [1,†], Jikai Liu [1,†], Xinyu Tao [1,†], Xiangxiang Su [1], Wenyang Li [2], Hainie Zha [3,4], Wenge Wu [1,5,*] and Xinwei Li [1,6,7,*]

1 College of Resources and Environment, Anhui Science and Technology University, Chuzhou 233100, China
2 College of Agriculture, Anhui Science and Technology University, Chuzhou 233100, China
3 School of Computer and Information, Anqing Normal University, Anqing 246133, China
4 Anhui Yigang Information Technology Co., Ltd., Anqing 246003, China
5 Rice Research Institute, Anhui Academy of Agricultural Sciences, Hefei 230001, China
6 Agricultural Waste Fertilizer Utilization and Cultivated Land Quality Improvement Engineering Research Center, Chuzhou 233100, China
7 Anhui Engineering Research Center of Smart Crop Planting and Processing Technology, Chuzhou 233100, China
* Correspondence: wuwenge@vip.sina.com (W.W.); lixw@ahstu.edu.cn (X.L.)
† These authors contributed equally to this work.

Abstract: The timely and accurate estimation of above-ground biomass (AGB) is crucial for indicating crop growth status, assisting management decisions, and predicting grain yield. Unmanned aerial vehicle (UAV) remote sensing technology is a promising approach for monitoring crop biomass. However, the determination of winter wheat AGB based on canopy reflectance is affected by spectral saturation effects. Thus, constructing a generic model for accurately estimating winter wheat AGB using UAV data is significant. In this study, a three-dimensional conceptual model (3DCM) for estimating winter wheat AGB was constructed using plant height (PH) and fractional vegetation cover (FVC). Compared with both the traditional vegetation index model and the traditional multi-feature combination model, the 3DCM yielded the best accuracy for the jointing stage (based on RGB data: coefficient of determination (R^2) = 0.82, normalized root mean square error (nRMSE) = 0.2; based on multispectral (MS) data: R^2 = 0.84, nRMSE = 0.16), but the accuracy decreased significantly when the spike organ appeared. Therefore, the spike number (SN) was added to create a new three-dimensional conceptual model (n3DCM). Under different growth stages and UAV platforms, the n3DCM (RGB: R^2 = 0.73–0.85, nRMSE = 0.17–0.23; MS: R^2 = 0.77–0.84, nRMSE = 0.17–0.23) remarkably outperformed the traditional multi-feature combination model (RGB: R^2 = 0.67–0.88, nRMSE = 0.15–0.25; MS: R^2 = 0.60–0.77, nRMSE = 0.19–0.26) for the estimation accuracy of the AGB. This study suggests that the n3DCM has great potential in resolving spectral errors and monitoring growth parameters, which could be extended to other crops and regions for AGB estimation and field-based high-throughput phenotyping.

Keywords: AGB; UAV; winter wheat; spectral features; three-dimensional conceptual model

1. Introduction

Winter wheat is one of the world's major cereal crops, accounting for 18% of the cultivated area in China [1]. Its yield is also crucial for international grain trade and global food security [2–4]. The AGB is a critical indicator in crop growth status assessment, farm management, and grain yield prediction [5,6]. Traditional measurements of AGB in the laboratory are destructive and time-consuming; the measurements are highly accurate but challenging to promote on a large scale [7,8]. Therefore, the timely, efficient, and accurate monitoring of winter wheat AGB is important for effective field management and increasing yield [9,10].

Compared with traditional measurement methods, remote sensing as a non-destructive technique has been demonstrated to have great potential in the measurement of AGB due to its simplicity and efficiency [11–13]. Various remote sensing platforms can capture crop canopy reflection spectrum signals to monitor crop biophysical/biochemical parameters [14,15]. These platforms that have been used to monitor crop AGB include near-surface hyperspectral systems [16,17], unmanned aerial vehicles (UAVs) [18–20], and satellites [21–23]. Although near-surface hyperspectral systems and satellite images have high spectral resolution and a wide field of view [24,25], UAV platforms have great potential in crop phenotype monitoring due to their low cost and simple operation [26,27]. Most studies of AGB have been conducted using vegetation indices (VIs), e.g., the normalized difference vegetation index (NDVI [28]) and excess green (ExG [29]), which have achieved remarkable research results [30–33]. However, some studies have shown that the spectral saturation effect significantly impacts the estimation of crop biochemical parameters [34–37]. In particular, VIs constructed using the red and near-infrared bands can easily result in spectral saturation under conditions of high crop coverage [35,38,39]. Especially for upright-growing crops, such as winter wheat and corn, dense and compact planting modes will inevitably produce dense canopy growth. Another issue is that VIs are insensitive to AGB during the reproductive growth stage, which is because the reflection and absorption of light of different wavelengths by the chlorophyll in the canopy are saturated at this stage [38,40]. The spectral features have nonlinear relationships with physiological and biochemical parameters, and the sensitivity of these features to crop biochemical parameters is low during the reproductive growth stage [41,42]. These factors limit the ability of VIs to estimate crop physiological and biochemical parameters at different growth stages.

Several researchers have made efforts to address the saturation problem in crop estimation, such as improving or constructing vegetation indices [39,43,44] or integrating texture features [38,45], structural features [46–48], and fractional vegetation cover (FVC) [49,50] into estimation models. Generally, the combination of multi-source features can provide higher accuracy in AGB estimation and reduce the influence of the spectral saturation effect on the model [47,51,52]. However, many studies have tended to use multiple features as independent model input factors to estimate target features, leading to the accuracy of traditional multi-feature combination models being unstable under different research and experimental conditions [53]. Therefore, to ensure the stability and universality of models, a more efficient method of feature combination must be found. For example, considering that maize AGB is composed of stems and leaves before the tasseling stage, Shu et al. [54] constructed a three-dimensional conceptual model (3DCM) for predicting maize AGB by integrating the leaf area index (LAI) and plant height (PH) to improve the accuracy of using UAV data to monitor the maize AGB at the jointing stage. However, it is still unclear whether the 3DCM can be applied to estimate the AGB of winter wheat, whether it is suitable for different growth stages, and whether the 3DCM has better accuracy than the traditional multi-feature combination model. Therefore, it is necessary to explore the potential of the 3DCM for winter wheat AGB estimation.

Recent studies have reported high-dimensional data and non-linear relationships, posing new challenges to current data processing methods [55]. Compared with traditional regression techniques, machine learning (ML) algorithms are typically better at handling high-dimensional data and non-linear relationships between the predictor variable and target variable [56–58]. Currently, ML regression algorithms such as the support vector machine (SVM) [59,60], artificial neural network (ANN) [61,62], and random forest (RF) [63,64] have been widely used to integrate multi-source input variables, including integrating VIs and plant height [48], integrating VIs and thermal characteristics [65], and integrating texture, color, and VIs [66]. However, the winter wheat AGB prediction improvement through traditional multi-source feature combinations is limited. Therefore, it is necessary to consider the contributions of characteristic variables to the estimation of AGB and accurately estimate winter wheat AGB by effectively combining the characteristic variables.

Therefore, this research aimed to establish a 3DCM for the accurate estimation of winter wheat AGB across multiple stages. The specific objectives of this study were as follows: (1) to construct a new three-dimensional conceptual model (n3DCM), (2) to evaluate the potential of the n3DCM in AGB estimation, and (3) to compare the advantages of different UAVs in AGB estimation.

2. Materials and Methods

2.1. Experimental Design

The winter wheat field experiment was conducted in the 2021 growing season. The winter wheat experiment site was located at Xiaogang Village, Fengyang County, Chuzhou City, Anhui Province in China (117°42′E, 32°16′N) (Figure 1).

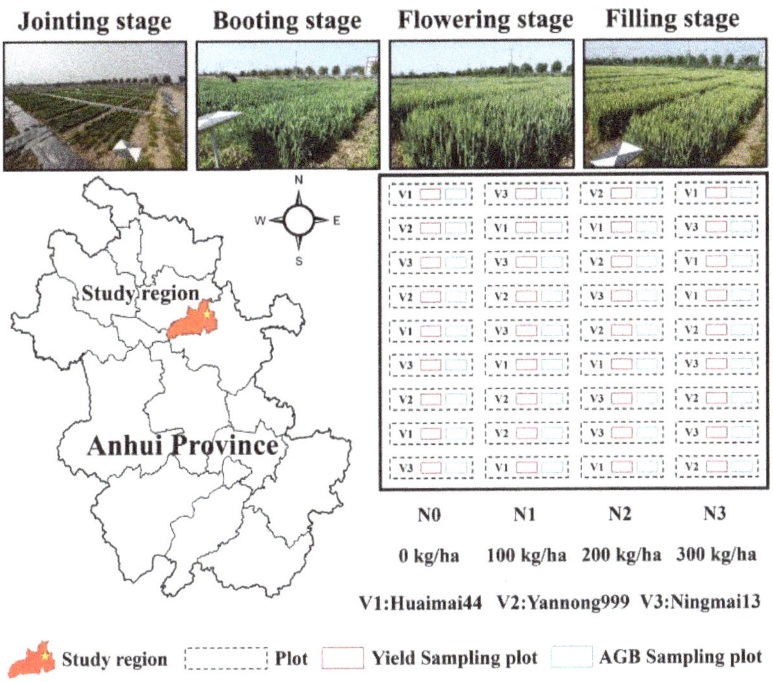

Figure 1. Location of the experimental site and the experimental design of the winter wheat field plots in 2021.

Different winter wheat cultivars and nitrogen (N) fertilizer treatments were set up in the experiment. The plot number was 36 and the plot size was 2 m × 8 m. The three winter wheat cultivars were Huaimai 44 (V1, high-gluten wheat), Yannong 999 (V2, high-gluten wheat), and Ningmai 13 (V3, low-gluten wheat), with three replicates of each. The four nitrogen fertilizer treatments were N0 (0 kg/ha), N1 (100 kg/ha), N2 (200 kg/ha), and N3 (300 kg/ha). The N fertilizer was applied in the form of urea, with 60% applied before planting and 40% applied during the jointing stage. Other management practices were consistent with local recommendations.

2.2. Field Data Collection

In 2021, 36 plots were sampled to measure the PH and winter wheat AGB at four critical growth stages. Three winter wheat plants from a sample plot were randomly selected, and their distances from the highest point to the ground were measured using a ruler. The average value was then taken as the true plant height in the sample plot.

The winter wheat AGB was measured via manually destructive sampling from two rows. Each sample was 0.5 m long. These winter wheat samples were quickly transported to the lab for leaf, stem, and spike separation. All fresh organs were oven-dried at 105 °C for 30 min and then at 75 °C for at least 24 h to achieve a constant weight. The dry weight of the winter wheat was then obtained using a balance (accuracy: 0.01 g) and the AGB was then converted to kg/ha.

At the mature stage of winter wheat, 1 m^2 of wheat with consistent growth was randomly selected from each plot in the study area. The yield and SN of winter wheat samples were obtained after threshing, drying to constant weight, and weighing.

2.3. Data Acquisition

2.3.1. Acquisition of the UAV Images

This study employed a DJI Mavic 2 (DJI Technology Co., Shenzhen, China) with an RGB digital camera to acquire high spatial-resolution image and a DJI Phantom 4 multispectral (DJI Technology Co., Shenzhen, China) to capture the multispectral image. The UAV images of winter wheat were acquired before sowing and at critical growth stages (jointing, booting, flowering, and filling). The DJI GS pro software package (https://www.dji.com/cn/downloads/djiapp/dji-gs-pro, accessed on 13 May 2023) was used to design the same flight plans for all campaigns. The flight altitude was set to 30 m (pixel size: 0.7 cm for RGB data, 1.5 cm for multispectral (MS) data) with a flight speed of 2 m/s. The forward overlap of images was higher than 90% and the side overlap was higher than 85%. Four standard reflector panels were placed on the ground for radiometric calibration, and five ground control points were evenly distributed in the field. All UAV flights were conducted from 10 a.m. to 2 p.m. on sunny and cloudless days. The UAV camera specifications and data acquisition dates are shown in Table 1.

Table 1. Camera specifications and summary of field campaigns for the wheat experiments.

Camera	Spectral Band (nm)	Date of UAV Flight	Growth Stage
RGB	Red Green Blue	14 March 2021 8 April 2021 29 April 2021 9 May 2021	Jointing Booting Flowering Filling
MS	Blue (450 ± 16 nm) Green (560 ± 16 nm) Red (650 ± 16 nm) Red edge (730 ± 16 nm) Near-infrared (840 ± 26 nm)		

2.3.2. Preprocessing of the UAV Images

The RGB and MS image mosaicking was conducted with the PIX4Dmapper software (4.4.12 version, Pix4D SA, Prilly, Switzerland) to generate ortho-mosaics from four critical growth stages. The main operations of this procedure mainly include aligning the images, adding ground control points, generating dense point clouds and texture meshes, reconstructing 3D images based on structure from a motion (SfM) algorithm [67], and, finally, obtaining the digital orthophoto model (DOM), digital surface model (DSM), and digital terrain model (DTM) images of the study area. The images of reflector panels on the ground were collected for radiometric calibration. ArcGIS (10.2 version, Environmental Systems Research Institute, Inc., Redlands, CA, USA) was used to create all plots' vector boundaries. To minimize the impact of marginal effects, the edge of each plot was omitted while creating the .shp file. The average of all the extracted pixel values of each plot was used as the corresponding feature.

2.4. Methods

The PH and FVC values extracted from the UAV data were used to construct a 3DCM for estimating the AGB of winter wheat. The critical process is shown in Figure 2. First, the canopy height model (CHM) was used to obtain the PH of winter wheat. Second, the VI was extracted from UAV images, and the FVC of each plot was extracted using the "excess green (ExG)—excess red (ExR)" method. Third, different models were trained and verified. Fourth, the accuracy of different models was compared and the AGB was visualized.

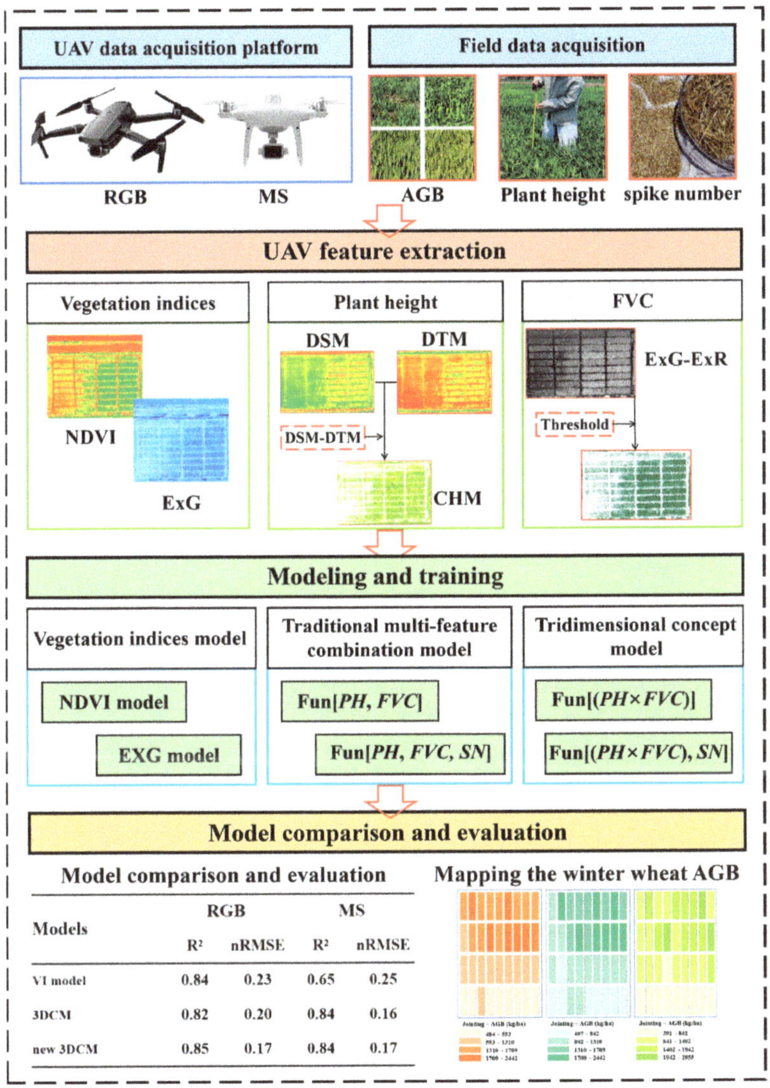

Figure 2. Research flow map.

2.4.1. PH Extraction

Before planting the winter wheat, we used UAVs to obtain the terrain model of the fields. Then, we used the UAVs to acquire the winter wheat's DSM at different growth stages and subtracted the DTM from the DSM at each growth stage to extract the plant height of the winter wheat. The calculation method is shown as Equation (1):

$$CHM = DSM_i - DTM_0, \tag{1}$$

where DSM_i represents the DSM generated in the ith stage and DTM_0 represents the terrain DTM obtained before planting. As shown in Figure 3, the measured and extracted PHs exhibited good consistency (RGB: $R^2 = 0.76$; MS: $R^2 = 0.88$). Overall, the extracted PH was slightly lower compared to the measured PH.

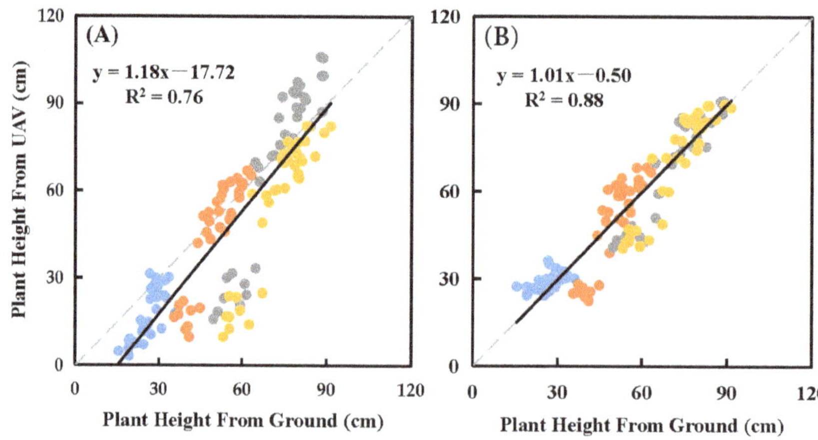

Figure 3. Comparison between the measured plant height and the plant height derived from unmanned aerial vehicle (UAV) images ((**A**): RGB; (**B**): MS).

2.4.2. FVC Calculation

FVC is usually defined as the percentage of the vertical projection area of vegetation (including branches, stems, and leaves) in a unit area [68]. In this study, the "ExG–ExR" method was used to segment soil background pixels from original images, which is effective for different soil backgrounds and has excellent performance in processing natural color digital images [69]. The FVC of each plot was calculated using Equation (2):

$$FVC = \frac{N_{\text{green}}}{N_{\text{all}}}, \tag{2}$$

where N_{all} represents the full number of pixels in one plot and N_{green} represents the number of pixels after removing the background.

2.4.3. Machine Learning Algorithm

RF, which was proposed by Breiman [70], is commonly used in the estimation of the AGB of winter wheat [71,72]. The RF model combines a large number of trees to improve accuracy [73]. RF regression not only handles a large number of input variables but also uses small subsets of variables to obtain a reasonable prediction accuracy. In addition, RF regression can help overcome the overfitting issue of simple decision trees [31,74]. There are three parameters, including the number of trees (ntree), the number of variables used as predictors for each tree (mtry), and the minimum size for each terminal mode (node size) [75]. This paper set ntree to 1000 and mtry to 1 to 2.

2.4.4. Three-Dimensional Conceptual Model

Many studies have shown a good correlation between PH and AGB [7,30,33,76]. Most studies combine the PH value with spectral and texture characteristics to estimate winter wheat biomass, but the accuracy of this method varies across different studies. Therefore, to estimate winter wheat AGB accurately and stably, this study established a 3DCM for estimating the AGB based on the work of Shu et al. [54] (Figure 4B). Before the heading stage, the winter wheat AGB was composed of stems and leaves. Different winter wheat varieties have different stem heights. The stem height is associated with stem weight [77]. The number and area of leaves determine the weight of the leaves. FVC refers to the percentage of the vertical projection area of the canopy to the total area and is highly correlated with the leaf biomass. Although the VI was the same, the biomass varied with stem height. Therefore, it was necessary to consider differences in PH to improve the accuracy of the AGB estimates. A winter wheat population can be regarded as a cube. The FVC is the base area of the winter wheat cube. The larger the FVC value, the larger the bottom area of the cube. The height of the cube is represented in the PH value. The higher the PH, the higher the height of the winter wheat cube. The volume of the cube is calculated by multiplying the area of its base by its height. Therefore, before the heading stage of winter wheat, AGB could be estimated using Equation (3).

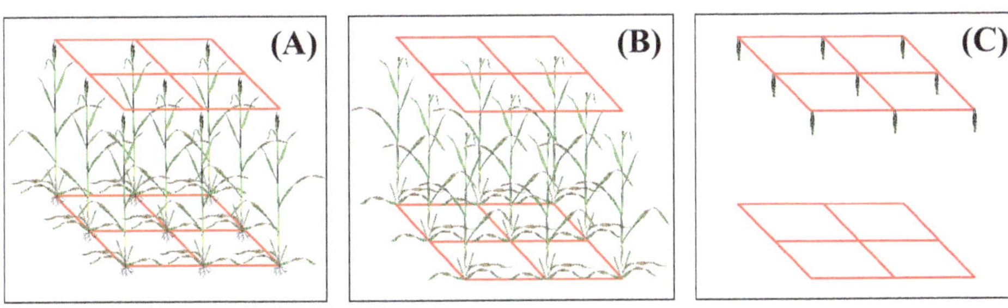

Figure 4. Conceptual map of the prediction model for above-ground biomass of winter wheat based on plant height, spike number, and fractional vegetation cover ((**A**) winter wheat population after the jointing stage; (**B**) winter wheat population at the jointing stage; (**C**) spike organs of winter wheat population).

However, Shu et al. [54] only focused on the jointing stage (no spike organ appeared). Therefore, to enhance the stability and universality of the model during the entire growth cycle, attention needed to be paid to the influence of spike organ emergence. Therefore, the present study used the SN to quantify the contribution of spike organs to the AGB (Figure 4A,C). A larger SN value indicated that there were more spike organs and that the AGB of spike organs was larger in the winter wheat population. The influence of spike organs on the AGB of winter wheat was represented by the SN, and the n3DCM was proposed to improve the accuracy of AGB estimation (Equation (4)):

$$\text{M1}: AGB = \text{Fun}[(PH \times FVC)] \tag{3}$$

$$\text{M2}: AGB = Fun[(PH \times FVC), SN] \tag{4}$$

where *PH* is the plant height, *SN* is the number of spikes, and *FVC* represents the fractional vegetation cover. Fun represents the RF algorithm.

2.5. Accuracy Evaluation

The study dataset was divided into two portions, with 70% of the samples used for calibration and 30% used for validation. This resulted in 25 calibration samples and 11 validation samples. Two metrics of the coefficient of determination (R^2) and normalized root mean square error (nRMSE) were used to evaluate the accuracy of the calibration and validation models as follows:

$$R^2 = 1 - \frac{\sum_{i=1}^{n} (y_i - x_i)^2}{\sum_{i=1}^{n} (x_i - \overline{x})^2} \quad (5)$$

$$nRMSE = \frac{\sqrt{\frac{1}{n}\sum_{i=1}^{n} (y_i - x_i)^2}}{\overline{x}} \quad (6)$$

where x_i and y_i represent the measured and predicted winter wheat AGB for sample i, respectively; $\overline{x}$ is the average measured winter wheat AGB and n is the number of samples.

3. Results

3.1. Comparison of the Ability to Estimate the AGB of Winter Wheat between the Three-Dimensional Conceptual Model (3DCM) and the Traditional VI Model of Different Growth Stages

The R^2 and nRMSE for the AGB simulated using the VI model and the 3DCM are displayed in Figure 5. In general, the two models exhibited greater estimation accuracy values in the jointing stage than in other growth stages. In addition, the RGB or MS accuracy values for the 3DCM (jointing: RGB: R^2 = 0.82, nRMSE = 0.20; MS: R^2 = 0.84, nRMSE = 0.16) were higher than those for the VI model. Among them, compared with the 3DCM, the R^2 was slightly higher for the VI model RGB-based ExG at the jointing stage, but the nRMSE of AGB estimated using the VI model was larger. The results demonstrated that the 3DCM could yield satisfactory accuracy in the jointing stage, which is similar to the finding of Shu et al. [54].

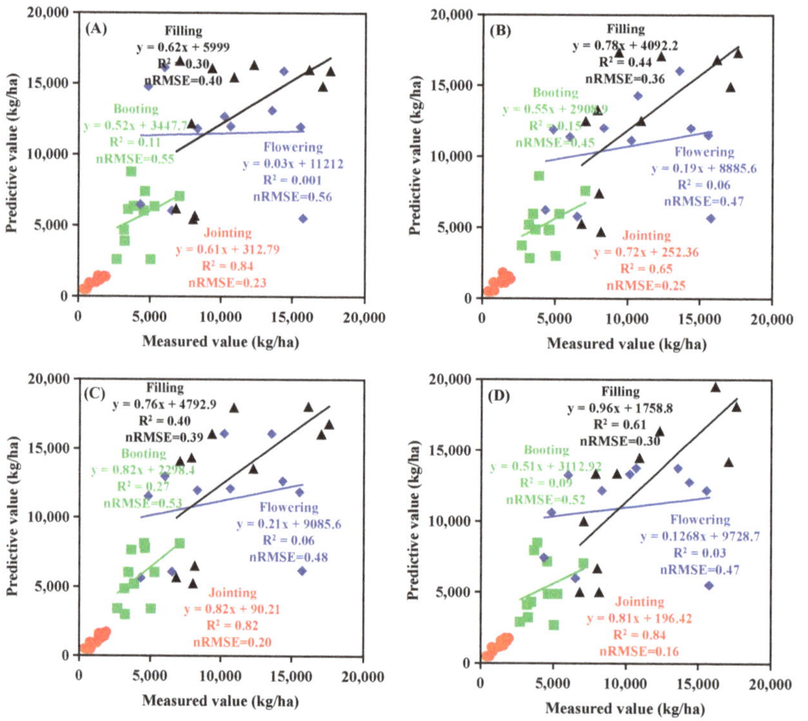

Figure 5. Relationship between measured and predicted above-ground biomass (AGB) based on the traditional vegetation model. ((**A**,**B**) Traditional vegetation model; (**C**,**D**) 3DCM; (**A**,**C**) RGB; (**B**,**D**) multispectral). Coefficient of determination, R^2; normalized root mean square error, nRMSE.

3.2. Differences between the Three-Dimensional Conceptual Model (3DCM) and the Traditional Multi-Feature Combination Model in Estimating Winter Wheat AGB

Figure 6 shows a comparison of the 3DCM and traditional multi-feature combination model for the estimation of AGB across the critical growth stages. Compared with the 3DCM, the performance of the traditional multi-feature combination model was lower than that of the 3DCM in the jointing stage. In addition, the traditional multi-feature combination model also showed a similar decrease in accuracy after the jointing stage. In the jointing stage, the traditional multi-feature combination model achieved the best accuracy (RGB: R^2 = 0.76, nRMSE = 0.21; MS: R^2 = 0.70, nRMSE = 0.21) among the four growth stages. At the stages of the emergence of spike organs, the accuracy of the traditional multi-feature combination model was higher than that of the 3DCM, indicating that the 3DCM had high consistency with the winter wheat AGB at the jointing stage without the appearance of the spike organ. However, after the formation of the spike organ, the 3DCM needed more description of spike characteristics, which resulted in the poor performance of estimating the winter wheat AGB.

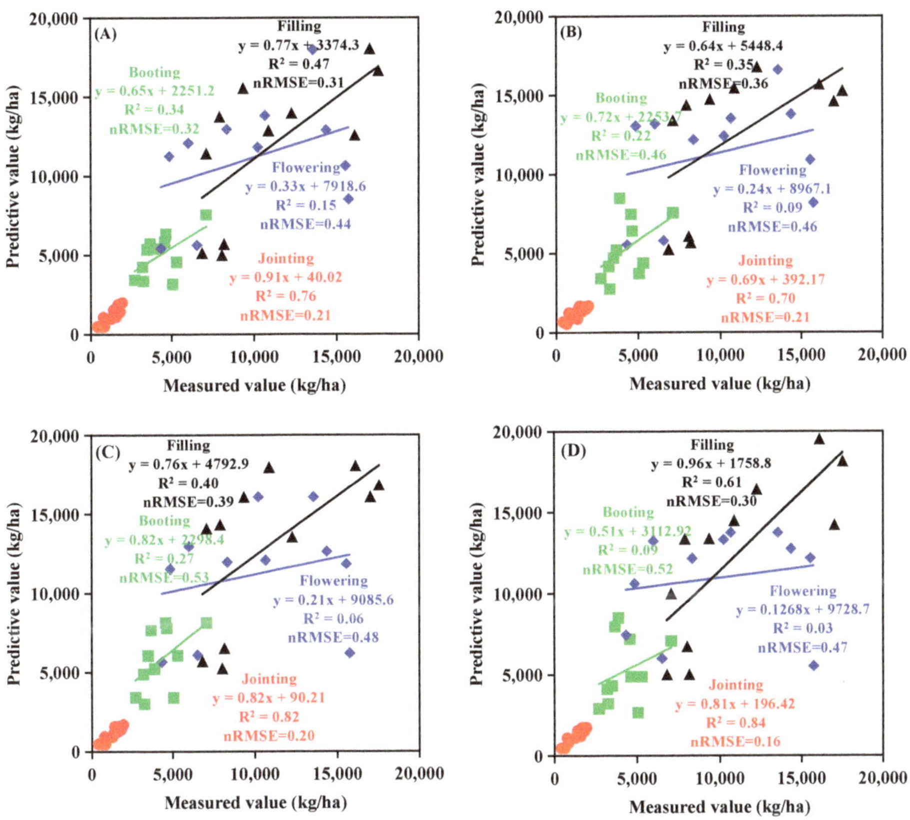

Figure 6. Traditional multi-feature combination model and 3DCM was used to estimate winter wheat above-ground biomass (AGB) at different growth stages based on RGB and multispectral (MS) UAV. ((**A**,**B**) Traditional multi-feature combination model; (**C**,**D**) 3DCM; (**A**,**C**) RGB; (**B**,**D**) MS). Coefficient of determination, R^2; normalized root mean square error, nRMSE.

3.3. The Three-Dimensional Conceptual Model (3DCM) with Spike Organ Consideration

To improve the accuracy of the 3DCM in estimating winter wheat AGB and broaden the usability of the model at different growth stages, this study introduced a feature highly correlated with spike weight: the SN. The SN and PH×FVC were used as input factors to construct an n3DCM. To explore the performance of the n3DCM in estimating the winter wheat AGB under different UAVs and growth stages, this study compared its performance with that of the n3DCM and the traditional multi-feature combination model (PH, FVC, and SN). The results are shown in Figure 7.

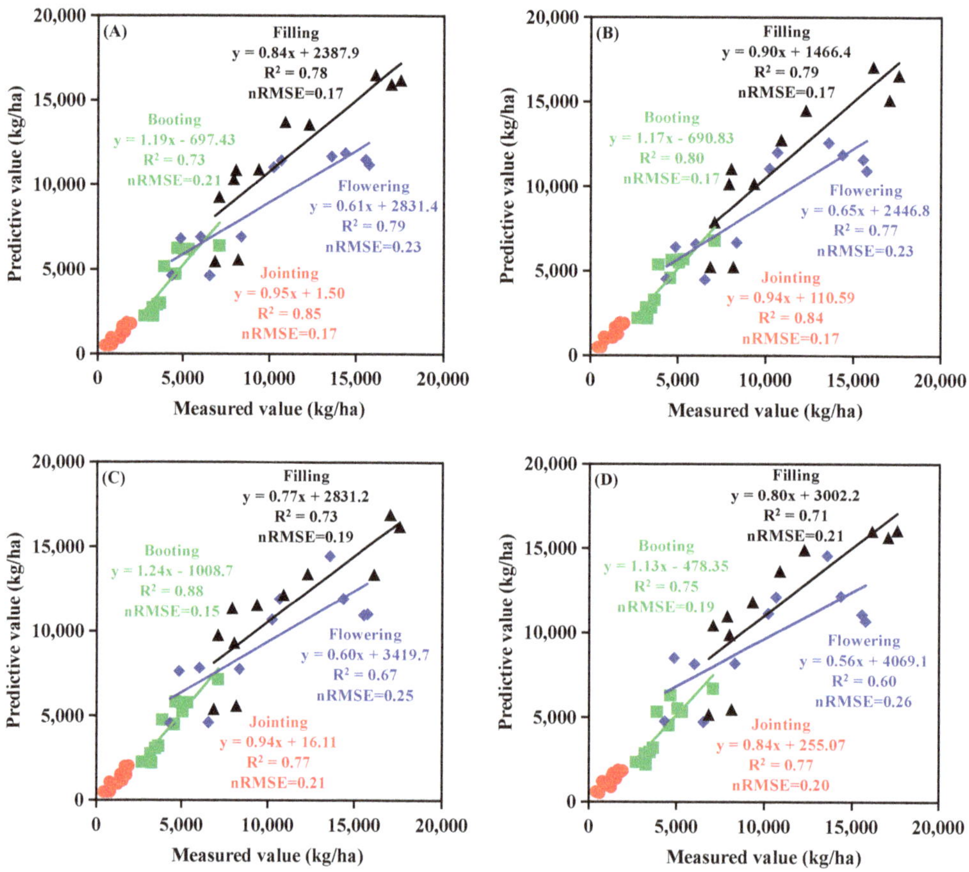

Figure 7. Traditional multi-feature combination model and n3DCM was used to estimate winter wheat above-ground biomass (AGB) at different growth stages based on RGB and multispectral (MS) UAV. ((**A**,**B**) n3DCM; (**C**,**D**) traditional multi-feature combination model; (**A**,**C**) RGB; (**B**,**D**) MS). Coefficient of determination, R^2; normalized root mean square error, nRMSE.

The results of winter wheat AGB estimation using the n3DCM are shown in Figure 7A,B). The accuracy of the n3DCM was significantly better than that of the 3DCM (Figure 6C,D). The R^2 and nRMSE of winter wheat AGB were estimated to be above 0.73 and below 0.21, respectively, using the n3DCM based on different UAV and growth stages. Compared with the 3DCM, the accuracy of the n3DCM was not significantly improved at the jointing stage, but it was significantly improved after the jointing stage. Compared with the 3DCM (Figure 6C,D), the accuracy of the n3DCM improved most significantly in estimating the AGB of winter wheat during the flowering stage; the R^2 increased from 0.06 to 0.79 and the nRMSE decreased from 0.48 to 0.23 for the RGB UAV. Under the MS UAV, the R^2 increased from 0.03 to 0.77 and the nRMSE decreased from 0.47 to 0.23. Furthermore, the n3DCM exhibits high and consistent accuracy in estimating winter wheat AGB across different UAVs and growth stages.

Based on the traditional multi-feature combination model, the FVC, PH, and SN were used as input features of the model to estimate the winter wheat AGB. The results are shown in Figure 7C,D. Overall, the accuracy of the n3DCM was higher than that of the traditional multi-feature combination model. However, the accuracy of the traditional multi-feature combination model was better than that of the n3DCM when predicting the winter wheat AGB based on RGB UAV data at the booting stage, and the R^2 and nRMSE were 0.88 and 0.15 for the traditional multi-feature combination model, respectively, and 0.73 and 0.21 for the n3DCM, respectively. The changing pattern of the traditional multi-feature combination model based on the FVC, PH, and SN was similar to that of the traditional multi-feature combination model based on the FVC and PH. Adding the SN feature significantly improved the accuracy of AGB estimation at the booting, flowering, and filling stages. However, there was no apparent improvement at the jointing stage. The 3DCM also showed the same difference. These results indicate that the SN feature has great potential in estimating the AGB during spike organ emergence. In general, the n3DCM with the SN feature had the best performance in AGB estimation, and the model had stable performance in different growth stages and with different UAVs. These results indicate that n3DCM is better than the traditional multi-feature combination model and 3DCM.

3.4. The Performance of Multi-Sensor Fusion in AGB Estimation

The PH and FVC features extracted from RGB and MS images were fused for estimating the winter wheat AGB. The results are shown in Figure 8. The accuracy of the n3DCM combining the PH and FVC extracted from different UAVs was lower than that based on a single UAV. The n3DCM that combined PH values based on MS and the FVC value based on RGB had the lowest accuracy for the jointing stage (R^2 = 0.58, nRMSE = 0.26). Overall, these results indicated that mixed multi-source UAV features did not necessarily improve the AGB estimation accuracy.

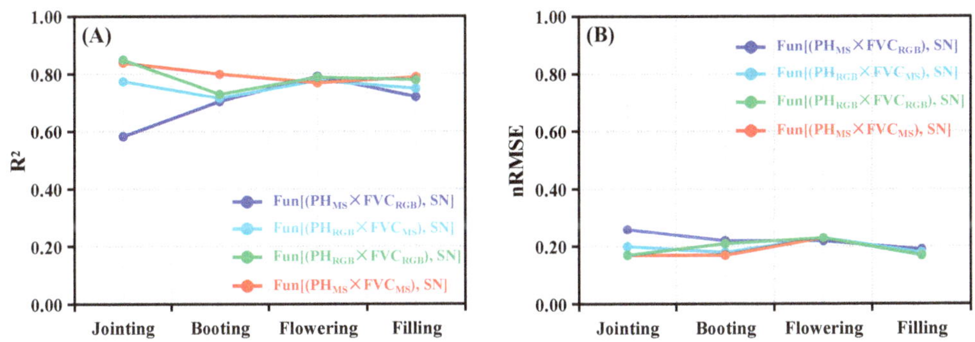

Figure 8. Results of winter wheat above-ground biomass (AGB) estimation using a new three-dimensional conceptual model integrating multi-source unmanned aerial vehicle (UAV) features. ((**A**) The determination coefficients of winter wheat AGB monitoring with UAV features and single UAV features; (**B**) nRMSE for monitoring winter wheat AGB with UAV feature fusion and single UAV features). Coefficient of determination, R^2; normalized root mean square error, nRMSE.

3.5. AGB Mapping Using the New Three-Dimensional Conceptual Model (n3DCM)

We mapped the winter wheat AGB using n3DCM and two types of UAV data (Figure 9). The n3DCM based on MS had higher accuracy in estimating AGB. The n3DCM based on RGB showed clear underestimation in the N0 region during the jointing stage. In booting images, there was an overestimation in the N0 region and an underestimation in the N3 region.

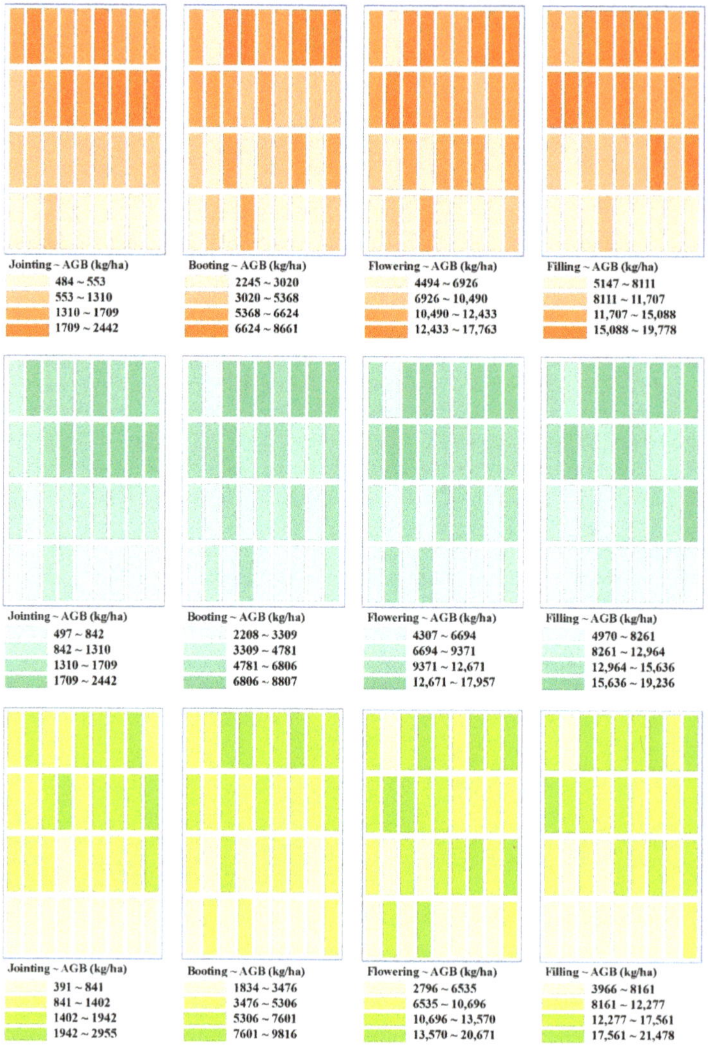

Figure 9. The map of estimated winter wheat AGB using the new three-dimensional conceptual model (first row: RGB; middle row: MS; bottom row: measured value).

4. Discussion

4.1. Limitations of Spectral Information for Monitoring Crops

Remote sensing technology allows for efficient and convenient estimates of crop biophysical/biochemical parameters using canopy spectral reflectance, but the spectral saturation phenomenon can significantly affect the accuracy of the model. Our study also showed that spectral features alone could not reasonably estimate the AGB of winter wheat during the whole growth stage (Figure 5A,B). The variation pattern of NDVI and AGB in Figure 10 shows that with increases in AGB in winter wheat, the VI produced a relatively saturated effect, resulting significant decrease in the ability of VI to estimate AGB.

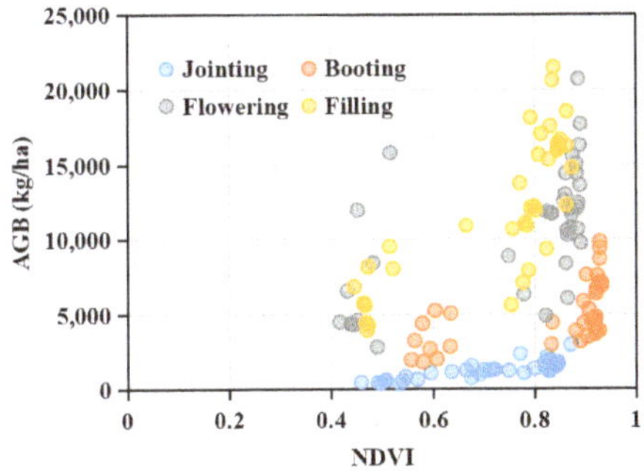

Figure 10. Changes in normalized difference vegetation index (NDVI) and above-ground biomass (AGB).

Over the past few decades, various schemes have been proposed to overcome the effect of spectral saturation on crop AGB estimates. Although the problem of saturation in spectral features has been partially overcome, spectral signals are susceptible to various factors in real situations. In the field scene, soil background, moisture, spectral acquisition time, spatial image resolution, and other factors will affect the spectral signals [16,31,78,79]. As shown in Figure 11, taking jointing stage as an example, the difference in green pixel reflectance and all pixel reflectance was determined under various N fertilizer treatments. With both UAVs, the reflectance increased when the background was removed. The vegetation coverage under the N0 treatment was relatively low, and GreenPix and AllPix differed significantly in red, red-edge, and near-infrared bands. With the increase in coverage, the gap between GreenPix and AllPix in red, red-edge, and near-infrared bands became smaller and gradually tended to be the same, only being slightly different in near-infrared bands. This shows that background has a strong influence on spectral characteristics.

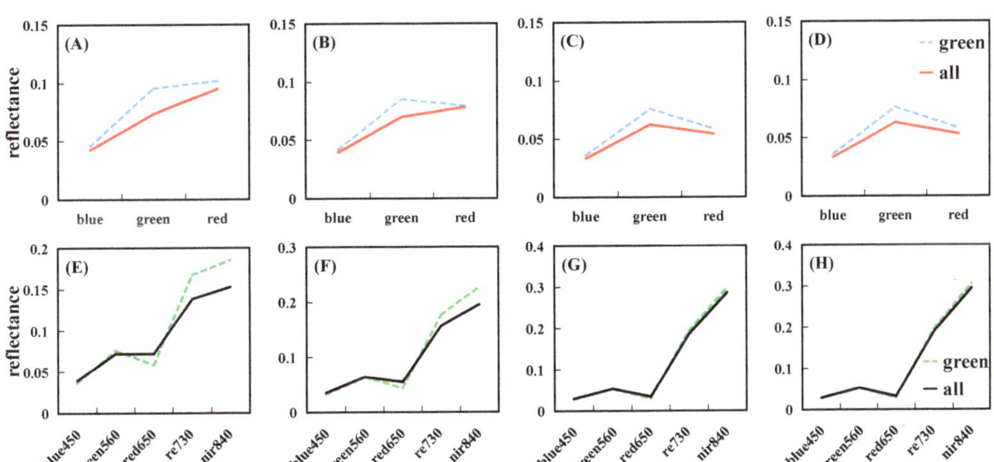

Figure 11. Comparison of the average reflectance of all pixels (all) and wheat pixels (green) under different nitrogen fertilizer treatments ((**A–D**) RGB; (**E–H**) (multispectral) MS; (**A**,**E**) nitrogen rate: 0 kg/ha; (**B**,**F**) nitrogen rate: 100 kg/ha; (**C**,**G**) nitrogen rate: 200 kg/ha; (**D**,**H**) nitrogen rate: 300 kg/ha). The solid line represents all pixels, while the dashed line represents green pixels.

The spectral signal collected by UAV are generally of the leaf canopy, which correlate well with the biochemical parameters of leaves. However, winter wheat AGB is composed of multiple organs; thus, it is not appropriate to estimate the sum of leaf, stem, and spike organs using only the spectral signal of the canopy [62]. Because the zenith angle makes it challenging to obtain spectral signals of crop stems or below the canopy, in order to collect more spectral information reflected by crop organs and reduce the contribution of the soil background to the spectral reflectance of the canopy, some studies have obtained multi-angle image data by adjusting the shooting angle of the UAV [80,81]. In addition, several studies have collected spectral reflectance at different times to obtain more spectral signals of the physiological and biochemical parameters of crops by using the changes in the solar altitude angle [19,82]. However, the dense planting pattern of winter wheat prevents the sensor from acquiring spectral signals reflected by all crop organs. Therefore, in a relatively complex field environment, it is necessary to consider using characteristic information that is not affected by natural conditions to estimate the AGB of winter wheat.

4.2. Estimating the AGB Potential of Three-Dimensional Information in Winter Wheat

The canopy reflectance of crops can be affected by the complex interaction between sunlight, vegetation, and soil, and this effect is difficult to eliminate in existing field trials [83]. Because the AGB of winter wheat contains the weight of leaves, stems, and spikes, the dense canopy structure hinders the spectral signal acquisition of stems in the middle and late growing season, and the spectral reflectance cannot reflect the weight of winter wheat stems well.

The PH is an important indicator for characterizing the AGB of the vertical growing crops. Previous studies have shown a moderate correlation between the PH and the crop AGB [46,77,84]. The present study also found a moderate correlation between the PH and the crop AGB (Table 2). Moreover, the CHM-derived PH was slightly lower than the field measurements (Figure 3). Bendig et al. [48] found that there is a degree of underestimation when UAVs are used to estimate plant height. The cause of this underestimation may be that in the field environment, the wind can blow the leaves of winter wheat, resulting in positional changes and differences in the same leaf in the overlapping images captured by the UAV. This leads to the stitched image being unable to accurately reflect the height of the winter wheat. In addition, the maximum spatial resolution of the UAV used in our study was 0.7 cm, which made it difficult to capture the height of the top of the winter wheat canopy for very narrow winter wheat plants. This also leads to the underestimation of plant height.

Table 2. Correlation between the AGB with the FVC, PH, and spike number at different growth stages.

Growth Stage	Fractional Vegetation Cover		Plant Height		Spike Number
	RGB	MS	RGB	MS	
Jointing stage	0.81	0.81	0.75	0.77	0.41
Booting stage	0.28	0.54	0.62	0.63	0.82
Flowering stage	0.37	0.51	0.61	0.67	0.91
Filling stage	0.39	0.71	0.78	0.79	0.82

The FVC is a vital feature in characterizing a canopy and is closely related to the canopy organ and the leaf area index (LAI) [85]. Compared with the LAI, acquiring the FVC is more straightforward and does not require field measurement data. As shown in Table 2, the correlation between the FVC obtained using the two UAVs and the AGB of winter wheat showed the maximum value at the jointing stage, indicating that the FVC at the jointing stage was highly correlated with the AGB of winter wheat. As shown in Figure 12, the AGB at the jointing stage was mainly composed of the leaf organ, which did not show stratification or overlap, and the FVC could well represent the leaf organ. Yue et al. [62] also showed that the leaf organ made up a large proportion in the jointing stage, and leaf features such as the FVC could effectively improve estimation accuracy.

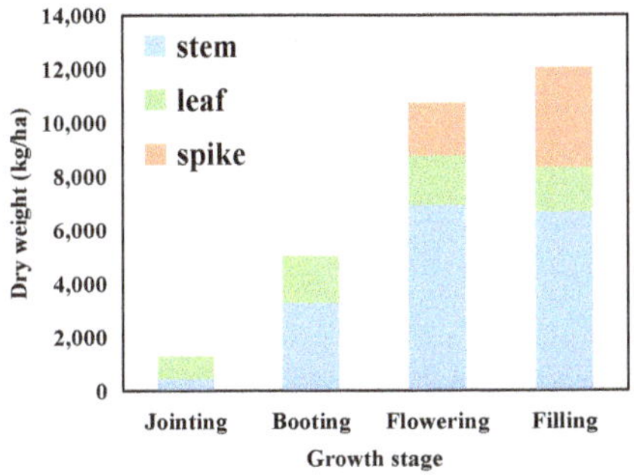

Figure 12. Proportion of different organs (stem, leaf, and spike) in the above-ground biomass at different growth stages.

The PH and FVC used in this study were derived from the CHM and orthophoto images, respectively, which were generated from overlapping images acquired by RGB and MS UAVs. The combination of the PH and FVC as input data for regression techniques is equivalent to using two types of features, namely, vertical and canopy features. The results show that the 3DCM using a combination of PH and FVC information estimated AGB with higher accuracy than models using the VI (Figures 5A,B and 6A,B). However, the accuracy of PH combined with FVC was higher only in the jointing stage, and the model's accuracy in other growth stages could not satisfy the application requirements, indicating that the influence of the spike organ on the model should be considered.

As shown in Figure 12, spike organs appeared after the booting stage, and the weight of spike organs gradually increased with the winter wheat grows, making it necessary to consider the contribution of spike organs to the AGB when estimating the AGB in winter wheat. However, most current studies estimate the AGB using information on spectral, textural, thermal characteristics, PH, and canopy features [10,38,47,54], but the relationship between these characteristics and spike organs is not significant, making it difficult to quantify the weight of spike organs in winter wheat AGB. As shown in Table 2, in the analysis of the correlation between the SN and winter wheat, the SN was better correlated with the winter wheat AGB when spike organs were appearance. Therefore, this study used SN to quantify the contributions of spike characteristics to the winter wheat AGB to enhance the ability of the model to estimate the winter wheat AGB at different growth stages. The PH, FVC, and SN were used as input characteristics to estimate the winter wheat AGB (Figure 7C,D). Adding spike characteristics significantly improved the PH and FVC models after the jointing stage. This indicates that the SN has great potential in estimating winter wheat AGB.

Three-dimensional information has great potential for estimating the AGB in winter wheat, but a simple data feature input may not improve model accuracy [86]. Therefore, the form of the feature combination must be considered to improve the estimation ability of the model.

4.3. Potential Estimation of Winter Wheat AGB Using a New Three-Dimensional Conceptual Model (n3DCM) and the Performance of Multi-Source Data Fusion

Previous studies have found that the effect of treating the maize population volume without spike organs as the AGB is more accurate than the traditional VI model [54]. However, previous studies did not compare different combinations of three-dimensional features and only performed comparisons with a single VI model. Therefore, this study explored whether this 3DCM could be applied to winter wheat and compared its performance with traditional VI model and traditional multi-feature combination model.

Compared with the traditional VI model, the 3DCM performed better in estimating the AGB of winter wheat during the jointing stage (Figure 5), which was similar to the results of Shu et al. [54]. However, the study of Shu et al. [54] did not compare the accuracy of the 3DCM with that of the traditional multi-feature combination model. Therefore, this study compared the accuracy of the 3DCM with the traditional multi-feature combination model (Figure 6). The results showed that the accuracy of the 3DCM was higher than that of the traditional multi-feature combination model at the jointing stage. However, the accuracy for the other growth stages was similar to that of the traditional multi-feature combination model. This indicates that although the volume-based 3DCM has some potential for estimating the AGB of winter wheat, it has some limitations in estimating the AGB of winter wheat during the whole reproductive stage. This may be due to the emergence of a spike organ. Many studies have shown that photosynthetic products are usually transferred to the reproductive organs of the crop (e.g., wheat spikes) at late stages of growth [62,87,88]. Therefore, considering only stem and leaf organs may lead to an underestimation of the winter wheat AGB at the reproductive growth stage.

Therefore, this study proposed the n3DCM to improve the model's universality in multiple growth stages. The n3DCM mainly considered the impact of spike organ (the SN) on AGB estimation. This study compared the n3DCM (Figure 7A,B) with the 3DCM (Figure 6C,D). The accuracy of the n3DCM was significantly improved after the jointing stage, indicating that adding the SN could effectively improve the model accuracy to estimate the winter wheat AGB during the whole growth stage. This study also compared the n3DCM with the traditional multi-feature combination model of PH, FVC, and SN (Figure 7), and the results showed that the effect of the n3DCM was better than that of the traditional multi-feature combination model. These results indicate that the 3DCM of fused SN can effectively consider the influence of the spike organ on the AGB estimation of winter wheat.

In order to further explore the performance of the n3DCM, the PH and FVC extracted from the two UAVs were combined to estimate the winter wheat AGB (Figure 8). The overall estimated accuracy was above 0.7, but the R^2 of the Fun [($PH_{MS} \times FVC_{RGB}$), SN] model at the jointing stage was 0.58, which was lower than the overall level. In addition, the n3DCM based on multi-source data fusion did not significantly improve accuracy in estimating the winter wheat AGB. RGB and MS UAVs are equipped with optical sensors, with differences only in band and resolution. Because the flight height in the current study was 30 m, the extracted PH and FVC features were less affected by spectral bands and spatial resolution. Therefore, in this study, the feature combination of multi-source UAVs did not significantly impact the n3DCM.

4.4. Limitations and Prospects

Although the n3DCM was more effective than the traditional method in estimating the AGB of winter wheat, it has some limitations. For example, the measured number of spikes was used to represent the weight of spike organ. Crop spike detection using image recognition techniques is already available [89,90], and these techniques can be used for spike counting. This study selected the "ExG–ExR" threshold method to extract the vegetation elements of winter wheat due to the convenience of operation. However, the "ExG–ExR" method, which is an effective indicator to distinguish green vegetation pixels from the original image, is strictly limited to green objects and is not sensitive to non-green objects [91]. Previous studies have shown that supervised classification methods (e.g., SVM and RF) can provide higher classification accuracy and lower uncertainty [92,93]. Therefore, supervised classification methods can be considered instead of the "ExG–ExR" threshold method in future work.

Although the n3DCM obtained good performance in estimating winter wheat AGB, the results of this study were based on four growth stages in one year and a single location consisting of a combination of varieties and N rates. Therefore, further exploration of the potential of n3DCM must be carried out by utilizing additional locations, winter wheat varieties, nitrogen rates, and growth stages to verify the portability of the model. In addition, investigating how to apply the n3DCM to satellite scales for global applications is also worthy of continued research [23]. This study evaluated the performance of the winter wheat population volume in estimating the winter wheat AGB but neglected the effect of planting density on estimating the winter wheat AGB [94]. Future work should also consider the effect of crop planting density on the estimation of the winter wheat AGB using the n3DCM.

5. Conclusions

This study investigated the potential of the 3DCM for estimating the winter wheat AGB based on UAV data. The performances of three models on the winter wheat AGB were compared at different growth stages and under different UAVs. Compared with the traditional VI model, the 3DCM performed better in the jointing stage, but its accuracy decreased significantly after the jointing stage. Compared with the traditional multi-feature combination model, the 3DCM only performed better in the jointing stage. In order to enhance the stability of the 3DCM in estimating the winter wheat AGB at different growth stages, an n3DCM was proposed. Compared with the previous three models, the accuracy of the n3DCM was significantly improved after the jointing stage. The R^2 and nRMSE values of the n3DCM were all higher than 0.73 and less than 0.23, respectively, at different growth stages of winter wheat. These results indicate that the n3DCM has great potential in estimating the AGB of winter wheat. The n3DCM provides a new way to estimate the AGB of winter wheat and has excellent potential in the accurate estimation of growth parameters for other crops.

Author Contributions: X.L., W.W., J.L. and Y.Z. were responsible for the conception and design of this research study. Y.Z. analyzed the results of the research and wrote the manuscript. J.L. debugged the algorithm code. X.L., W.W., W.L., J.L., X.T., H.Z. and X.S. repeatedly revised the manuscript. Y.Z., X.T. and X.S. were responsible for data collection and processing in this research. All authors have read and agreed to the published version of the manuscript.

Funding: This project was supported by the National Key Research and Development Program of China (no. 2022YFD2300221), National Key Field Innovation Team Program of China (no. 2021-11), scientific research projects in higher education institutions of Anhui Province (nos. 2022AH051623, 2022AH051029, KJ2021A0891, and KJ2021A0860), Science and Technology Project Program of Fengyang Country, Anhui Province, China (no. NY2022-01), and College Students' Innovation and Entrepreneurship Training Project (no. 202210879043).

Data Availability Statement: Data will be made available upon request.

Acknowledgments: We are very grateful to Xiaofang Chen, Jun Li, Xueqing Zhu, Qingyang Liu, and Weiqiang Wang for their assistance in data collection.

Conflicts of Interest: The authors declare no conflict of interest.

References

1. Fan, L.; Yang, J.; Sun, X.; Zhao, F.; Liang, S.; Duan, D.; Chen, H.; Xia, L.; Sun, J.; Yang, P. The effects of Landsat image acquisition date on winter wheat classification in the North China Plain. *ISPRS-J. Photogramm. Remote Sens.* **2022**, *187*, 1–13. [CrossRef]
2. Shiferaw, B.; Smale, M.; Braun, H.; Duveiller, E.; Reynolds, M.; Muricho, G. Crops that feed the world 10. Past successes and future challenges to the role played by wheat in global food security. *Food Secur.* **2013**, *5*, 291–317. [CrossRef]
3. Fischer, R.A.; Byerlee, D.; Edmeades, G. *Crop Yields and Global Food Security*; Aciar: Canberra, ACT, Australia, 2014; pp. 8–11.
4. Curtis, T.; Halford, N.G. Food security: The challenge of increasing wheat yield and the importance of not compromising food safety. *Ann. Appl. Biol.* **2014**, *164*, 354–372. [CrossRef] [PubMed]
5. Liu, J.; Pattey, E.; Miller, J.R.; McNairn, H.; Smith, A.; Hu, B. Estimating crop stresses, aboveground dry biomass and yield of corn using multi-temporal optical data combined with a radiation use efficiency model. *Remote Sens. Environ.* **2010**, *114*, 1167–1177. [CrossRef]
6. Ritchie, J.T.; Singh, U.; Godwin, D.C.; Bowen, W.T. Cereal growth, development and yield. In *Understanding Options for Agricultural Production*; Springer: Dordrecht, The Netherlands, 1998; pp. 79–98.
7. Lu, N.; Zhou, J.; Han, Z.; Li, D.; Cao, Q.; Yao, X.; Tian, Y.; Zhu, Y.; Cao, W.; Cheng, T. Improved estimation of aboveground biomass in wheat from RGB imagery and point cloud data acquired with a low-cost unmanned aerial vehicle system. *Plant Methods* **2019**, *15*, 17. [CrossRef]
8. Feng, H.; Tao, H.; Fan, Y.; Liu, Y.; Li, Z.; Yang, G.; Zhao, C. Comparison of winter wheat yield estimation based on near-surface hyperspectral and UAV hyperspectral remote sensing data. *Remote Sens.* **2022**, *14*, 4158. [CrossRef]

9. Huang, H.; Huang, J.; Li, X.; Zhuo, W.; Wu, Y.; Niu, Q.; Su, W.; Yuan, W. A dataset of winter wheat aboveground biomass in China during 2007–2015 based on data assimilation. *Sci. Data* **2022**, *9*, 200. [CrossRef]
10. Fu, Y.; Yang, G.; Song, X.; Li, Z.; Xu, X.; Feng, H.; Zhao, C. Improved estimation of winter wheat aboveground biomass using multiscale textures extracted from UAV-based digital images and hyperspectral feature analysis. *Remote Sens.* **2021**, *13*, 581. [CrossRef]
11. Navarro, J.A.; Algeet, N.; Fernández-Landa, A.; Esteban, J.; Rodríguez-Noriega, P.; Guillén-Climent, M.L. Integration of UAV, Sentinel-1, and Sentinel-2 data for mangrove plantation aboveground biomass monitoring in Senegal. *Remote Sens.* **2019**, *11*, 77. [CrossRef]
12. Poley, L.G.; McDermid, J.G. A systematic review of the factors influencing the estimation of vegetation aboveground biomass using unmanned aerial systems. *Remote Sens.* **2020**, *12*, 1052. [CrossRef]
13. Jin, X.; Kumar, L.; Li, Z.; Feng, H.; Xu, X.; Yang, G.; Wang, J. A review of data assimilation of remote sensing and crop models. *Eur. J. Agron.* **2018**, *92*, 141–152. [CrossRef]
14. Cavender-Bares, J.; Gamon, J.A.; Townsend, P.A. The use of remote sensing to enhance biodiversity monitoring and detection: A critical challenge for the twenty-first century. In *Remote Sensing of Plant Biodiversity*; Springer: Berlin/Heidelberg, Germany, 2020; pp. 1–12.
15. Knipling, E.B. Physical and physiological basis for the reflectance of visible and near-infrared radiation from vegetation. *Remote Sens. Environ.* **1970**, *1*, 155–159. [CrossRef]
16. Zhou, K.; Cheng, T.; Zhu, Y.; Cao, W.; Ustin, S.L.; Zheng, H.; Yao, X.; Tian, Y. Assessing the impact of spatial resolution on the estimation of leaf nitrogen concentration over the full season of paddy rice using near-surface imaging spectroscopy data. *Front. Plant Sci.* **2018**, *9*, 964. [CrossRef]
17. Yue, J.; Feng, H.; Yang, G.; Li, Z. A comparison of regression techniques for estimation of above-ground winter wheat biomass using near-surface spectroscopy. *Remote Sens.* **2018**, *10*, 66. [CrossRef]
18. Liu, J.; Zhu, Y.; Tao, X.; Chen, X.; Li, X. Rapid prediction of winter wheat yield and nitrogen use efficiency using consumer-grade unmanned aerial vehicles multispectral imagery. *Front. Plant Sci.* **2022**, *13*, 1032170. [CrossRef]
19. Wang, W.; Zheng, H.; Wu, Y.; Yao, X.; Zhu, Y.; Cao, W.; Cheng, T. An assessment of background removal approaches for improved estimation of rice leaf nitrogen concentration with unmanned aerial vehicle multispectral imagery at various observation times. *Field Crops Res.* **2022**, *283*, 108543. [CrossRef]
20. Zheng, J.; Fu, H.; Li, W.; Wu, W.; Yu, L.; Yuan, S.; Tao, W.Y.W.; Pang, T.K.; Kanniah, K.D. Growing status observation for oil palm trees using Unmanned Aerial Vehicle (UAV) images. *ISPRS-J. Photogramm. Remote Sens.* **2021**, *173*, 95–121. [CrossRef]
21. Zhou, W.; Liu, Y.; Ata-Ul-Karim, S.T.; Ge, Q.; Li, X.; Xiao, J. Integrating climate and satellite remote sensing data for predicting county-level wheat yield in China using machine learning methods. *Int. J. Appl. Earth Obs. Geoinf.* **2022**, *111*, 102861. [CrossRef]
22. Cai, Y.; Guan, K.; Lobell, D.; Potgieter, A.B.; Wang, S.; Peng, J.; Xu, T.; Asseng, S.; Zhang, Y.; You, L. Integrating satellite and climate data to predict wheat yield in Australia using machine learning approaches. *Agric. For. Meteorol.* **2019**, *274*, 144–159. [CrossRef]
23. Zheng, J.; Yuan, S.; Wu, W.; Li, W.; Yu, L.; Fu, H.; Coomes, D. Surveying coconut trees using high-resolution satellite imagery in remote atolls of the Pacific Ocean. *Remote Sens. Environ.* **2023**, *287*, 113485. [CrossRef]
24. Tian, Y.; Gu, K.; Chu, X.; Yao, X.; Cao, W.; Zhu, Y. Comparison of different hyperspectral vegetation indices for canopy leaf nitrogen concentration estimation in rice. *Plant Soil* **2014**, *376*, 193–209. [CrossRef]
25. Omer, G.; Mutanga, O.; Abdel-Rahman, E.M.; Peerbhay, K.; Adam, E. Mapping leaf nitrogen and carbon concentrations of intact and fragmented indigenous forest ecosystems using empirical modeling techniques and WorldView-2 data. *ISPRS-J. Photogramm. Remote Sens.* **2017**, *131*, 26–39. [CrossRef]
26. Xie, C.; Yang, C. A review on plant high-throughput phenotyping traits using UAV-based sensors. *Comput. Electron. Agric.* **2020**, *178*, 105731. [CrossRef]
27. Sankaran, S.; Khot, L.R.; Espinoza, C.Z.; Jarolmasjed, S.; Sathuvalli, V.R.; Vandemark, G.J.; Miklas, P.N.; Carter, A.H.; Pumphrey, M.O.; Knowles, N.R. Low-altitude, high-resolution aerial imaging systems for row and field crop phenotyping: A review. *Eur. J. Agron.* **2015**, *70*, 112–123. [CrossRef]
28. Rouse, J.W.; Haas, R.H.; Schell, J.A.; Deering, D.W. Monitoring vegetation systems in the Great Plains with ERTS. *Nasa Spec. Publ.* **1974**, *351*, 309.
29. Mao, W.; Wang, Y.; Wang, Y. Real-time detection of between-row weeds using machine vision. In Proceedings of the 2003 ASAE Annual Meeting:American Society of Agricultural and Biological Engineers, Las Vegas, NV, USA, 27–30 July 2003; p. 1.
30. Niu, Y.; Zhang, L.; Zhang, H.; Han, W.; Peng, X. Estimating above-ground biomass of maize using features derived from UAV-based RGB imagery. *Remote Sens.* **2019**, *11*, 1261. [CrossRef]
31. Wang, F.; Yang, M.; Ma, L.; Zhang, T.; Qin, W.; Li, W.; Zhang, Y.; Sun, Z.; Wang, Z.; Li, F. Estimation of above-ground biomass of winter wheat based on consumer-grade multi-spectral UAV. *Remote Sens.* **2022**, *14*, 1251. [CrossRef]
32. Wan, L.; Cen, H.; Zhu, J.; Zhang, J.; Zhu, Y.; Sun, D.; Du, X.; Zhai, L.; Weng, H.; Li, Y. Grain yield prediction of rice using multi-temporal UAV-based RGB and multispectral images and model transfer—A case study of small farmlands in the South of China. *Agric. For. Meteorol.* **2020**, *291*, 108096. [CrossRef]
33. Han, L.; Yang, G.; Dai, H.; Xu, B.; Yang, H.; Feng, H.; Li, Z.; Yang, X. Modeling maize above-ground biomass based on machine learning approaches using UAV remote-sensing data. *Plant Methods* **2019**, *15*, 10. [CrossRef]

34. Swoish, M.; Leme Filho, J.F.D.C.; Reiter, M.S.; Campbell, J.B.; Thomason, W.E. Comparing satellites and vegetation indices for cover crop biomass estimation. *Comput. Electron. Agric.* **2022**, *196*, 106900. [CrossRef]
35. Mutanga, O.; Masenyama, A.; Sibanda, M. Spectral saturation in the remote sensing of high-density vegetation traits: A systematic review of progress, challenges, and prospects. *ISPRS-J. Photogramm. Remote Sens.* **2023**, *198*, 297–309. [CrossRef]
36. Li, Z.; Taylor, J.; Yang, H.; Casa, R.; Jin, X.; Li, Z.; Song, X.; Yang, G. A hierarchical interannual wheat yield and grain protein prediction model using spectral vegetative indices and meteorological data. *Field Crops Res.* **2020**, *248*, 107711. [CrossRef]
37. Jiang, Z.; Huete, A.R.; Didan, K.; Miura, T. Development of a two-band enhanced vegetation index without a blue band. *Remote Sens. Environ.* **2008**, *112*, 3833–3845. [CrossRef]
38. Yue, J.; Yang, G.; Tian, Q.; Feng, H.; Xu, K.; Zhou, C. Estimate of winter-wheat above-ground biomass based on UAV ultrahigh-ground-resolution image textures and vegetation indices. *ISPRS-J. Photogramm. Remote Sens.* **2019**, *150*, 226–244. [CrossRef]
39. Mutanga, O.; Skidmore, A.K. Narrow band vegetation indices overcome the saturation problem in biomass estimation. *Int. J. Remote Sens.* **2004**, *25*, 3999–4014. [CrossRef]
40. Zaman-Allah, M.; Vergara, O.; Araus, J.L.; Tarekegne, A.; Magorokosho, C.; Zarco-Tejada, P.J.; Hornero, A.; Albà, A.H.; Das, B.; Craufurd, P. Unmanned aerial platform-based multi-spectral imaging for field phenotyping of maize. *Plant Methods* **2015**, *11*, 35. [CrossRef]
41. Haboudane, D.; Tremblay, N.; Miller, J.R.; Vigneault, P. Remote estimation of crop chlorophyll content using spectral indices derived from hyperspectral data. *IEEE Trans. Geosci. Remote Sens.* **2008**, *46*, 423–437. [CrossRef]
42. Cui, B.; Zhao, Q.; Huang, W.; Song, X.; Ye, H.; Zhou, X. A new integrated vegetation index for the estimation of winter wheat leaf chlorophyll content. *Remote Sens.* **2019**, *11*, 974. [CrossRef]
43. Li, F.; Miao, Y.; Feng, G.; Yuan, F.; Yue, S.; Gao, X.; Liu, Y.; Liu, B.; Ustin, S.L.; Chen, X. Improving estimation of summer maize nitrogen status with red edge-based spectral vegetation indices. *Field Crops Res.* **2014**, *157*, 111–123. [CrossRef]
44. Gnyp, M.L.; Bareth, G.; Li, F.; Lenz-Wiedemann, V.I.; Koppe, W.; Miao, Y.; Hennig, S.D.; Jia, L.; Laudien, R.; Chen, X. Development and implementation of a multiscale biomass model using hyperspectral vegetation indices for winter wheat in the North China Plain. *Int. J. Appl. Earth Obs. Geoinf.* **2014**, *33*, 232–242. [CrossRef]
45. Liu, Y.; Liu, S.; Li, J.; Guo, X.; Wang, S.; Lu, J. Estimating biomass of winter oilseed rape using vegetation indices and texture metrics derived from UAV multispectral images. *Comput. Electron. Agric.* **2019**, *166*, 105026. [CrossRef]
46. Tilly, N.; Aasen, H.; Bareth, G. Fusion of plant height and vegetation indices for the estimation of barley biomass. *Remote Sens.* **2015**, *7*, 11449–11480. [CrossRef]
47. Yue, J.; Yang, G.; Li, C.; Li, Z.; Wang, Y.; Feng, H.; Xu, B. Estimation of winter wheat above-ground biomass using unmanned aerial vehicle-based snapshot hyperspectral sensor and crop height improved models. *Remote Sens.* **2017**, *9*, 708. [CrossRef]
48. Bendig, J.; Bolten, A.; Bennertz, S.; Broscheit, J.; Eichfuss, S.; Bareth, G. Estimating biomass of barley using crop surface models (CSMs) derived from UAV-based RGB imaging. *Remote Sens.* **2014**, *6*, 10395–10412. [CrossRef]
49. Martínez-Guanter, J.; Egea, G.; Pérez-Ruiz, M.; Apolo-Apolo, O.E. Estimation of the leaf area index in maize based on UAV imagery using deep learning techniques. In *Precision Agriculture'19*; Wageningen Academic Publishers: Wageningen, The Netherlands, 2019; p. 1304.
50. Luo, S.; Jiang, X.; He, Y.; Li, J.; Jiao, W.; Zhang, S.; Xu, F.; Han, Z.; Sun, J.; Yang, J. Multi-dimensional variables and feature parameter selection for aboveground biomass estimation of potato based on UAV multispectral imagery. *Front. Plant Sci.* **2022**, *13*, 2673. [CrossRef]
51. Sadeghi, Y.; St-Onge, B.; Leblon, B.; Prieur, J.; Simard, M. Mapping boreal forest biomass from a SRTM and TanDEM-X based on canopy height model and Landsat spectral indices. *Int. J. Appl. Earth Obs. Geoinf.* **2018**, *68*, 202–213. [CrossRef]
52. Fei, S.; Hassan, M.A.; Xiao, Y.; Su, X.; Chen, Z.; Cheng, Q.; Duan, F.; Chen, R.; Ma, Y. UAV-based multi-sensor data fusion and machine learning algorithm for yield prediction in wheat. *Precis. Agric.* **2023**, *24*, 187–212. [CrossRef]
53. Bendig, J.; Yu, K.; Aasen, H.; Bolten, A.; Bennertz, S.; Broscheit, J.; Gnyp, M.L.; Bareth, G. Combining UAV-based plant height from crop surface models, visible, and near infrared vegetation indices for biomass monitoring in barley. *Int. J. Appl. Earth Obs. Geoinf.* **2015**, *39*, 79–87. [CrossRef]
54. Meiyan, S.; Mengyuan, S.; Qizhou, D.; Xiaohong, Y.; Baoguo, L.; Yuntao, M. Estimating the maize above-ground biomass by constructing the tridimensional concept model based on UAV-based digital and multi-spectral images. *Field Crops Res.* **2022**, *282*, 108491. [CrossRef]
55. Yuan, Q.; Shen, H.; Li, T.; Li, Z.; Li, S.; Jiang, Y.; Xu, H.; Tan, W.; Yang, Q.; Wang, J. Deep learning in environmental remote sensing: Achievements and challenges. *Remote Sens. Environ.* **2020**, *241*, 111716. [CrossRef]
56. Weiss, M.; Jacob, F.; Duveiller, G. Remote sensing for agricultural applications: A meta-review. *Remote Sens. Environ.* **2020**, *236*, 111402. [CrossRef]
57. Liakos, K.G.; Busato, P.; Moshou, D.; Pearson, S.; Bochtis, D. Machine learning in agriculture: A review. *Sensors* **2018**, *18*, 2674. [CrossRef]
58. Lu, D. The potential and challenge of remote sensing-based biomass estimation. *Int. J. Remote Sens.* **2006**, *27*, 1297–1328. [CrossRef]
59. Li, B.; Xu, X.; Zhang, L.; Han, J.; Bian, C.; Li, G.; Liu, J.; Jin, L. Above-ground biomass estimation and yield prediction in potato by using UAV-based RGB and hyperspectral imaging. *ISPRS-J. Photogramm. Remote Sens.* **2020**, *162*, 161–172. [CrossRef]
60. Zhu, W.; Sun, Z.; Yang, T.; Li, J.; Peng, J.; Zhu, K.; Li, S.; Gong, H.; Lyu, Y.; Li, B. Estimating leaf chlorophyll content of crops via optimal unmanned aerial vehicle hyperspectral data at multi-scales. *Comput. Electron. Agric.* **2020**, *178*, 105786. [CrossRef]

61. Li, Q.; Jin, S.; Zang, J.; Wang, X.; Sun, Z.; Li, Z.; Xu, S.; Ma, Q.; Su, Y.; Guo, Q. Deciphering the contributions of spectral and structural data to wheat yield estimation from proximal sensing. *Crop J.* **2022**, *10*, 1334–1345. [CrossRef]
62. Yue, J.; Yang, H.; Yang, G.; Fu, Y.; Wang, H.; Zhou, C. Estimating vertically growing crop above-ground biomass based on UAV remote sensing. *Comput. Electron. Agric.* **2023**, *205*, 107627. [CrossRef]
63. Wang, Q.; Che, Y.; Shao, K.; Zhu, J.; Wang, R.; Sui, Y.; Guo, Y.; Li, B.; Meng, L.; Ma, Y. Estimation of sugar content in sugar beet root based on UAV multi-sensor data. *Comput. Electron. Agric.* **2022**, *203*, 107433. [CrossRef]
64. Fu, Z.; Jiang, J.; Gao, Y.; Krienke, B.; Wang, M.; Zhong, K.; Cao, Q.; Tian, Y.; Zhu, Y.; Cao, W. Wheat growth monitoring and yield estimation based on multi-rotor unmanned aerial vehicle. *Remote Sens.* **2020**, *12*, 508. [CrossRef]
65. Berni, J.; Zarco-Tejada, P.J.; Suarez, L.; González-Dugo, V.; Fereres, E. Remote sensing of vegetation from UAV platforms using lightweight multispectral and thermal imaging sensors. *Int. Arch. Photogramm. Remote Sens. Spatial Inform. Sci.* **2009**, *38*, 6.
66. Zhang, J.; Qiu, X.; Wu, Y.; Zhu, Y.; Cao, Q.; Liu, X.; Cao, W. Combining texture, color, and vegetation indices from fixed-wing UAS imagery to estimate wheat growth parameters using multivariate regression methods. *Comput. Electron. Agric.* **2021**, *185*, 106138. [CrossRef]
67. Lowe, D.G. Distinctive image features from scale-invariant keypoints. *Int. J. Comput. Vis.* **2004**, *60*, 91–110. [CrossRef]
68. Li, L.; Mu, X.; Jiang, H.; Chianucci, F.; Hu, R.; Song, W.; Qi, J.; Liu, S.; Zhou, J.; Chen, L.; et al. Review of ground and aerial methods for vegetation cover fraction (fCover) and related quantities estimation: Definitions, advances, challenges, and future perspectives. *ISPRS-J. Photogramm. Remote Sens.* **2023**, *199*, 133–156. [CrossRef]
69. Meyer, G.E.; Neto, J.C. Verification of color vegetation indices for automated crop imaging applications. *Comput. Electron. Agric.* **2008**, *63*, 282–293. [CrossRef]
70. Breiman, L. Random forests. *Mach. Learn.* **2001**, *45*, 5–32. [CrossRef]
71. Belgiu, M.; Drăguţ, L. Random forest in remote sensing: A review of applications and future directions. *ISPRS-J. Photogramm. Remote Sens.* **2016**, *114*, 24–31. [CrossRef]
72. Zhou, X.; Zhu, X.; Dong, Z.; Guo, W. Estimation of biomass in wheat using random forest regression algorithm and remote sensing data. *Crop J.* **2016**, *4*, 212–219.
73. Hastie, T.; Tibshirani, R.; Friedman, J.; Hastie, T.; Tibshirani, R.; Friedman, J. Unsupervised learning. In *The Elements of Statistical Learning: Data Mining, Inference, and Prediction*; Springer: Berlin/Heidelberg, Germany, 2009; pp. 485–585.
74. Hutengs, C.; Vohland, M. Downscaling land surface temperatures at regional scales with random forest regression. *Remote Sens. Environ.* **2016**, *178*, 127–141. [CrossRef]
75. Zhang, Y.; Xia, C.; Zhang, X.; Cheng, X.; Feng, G.; Wang, Y.; Gao, Q. Estimating the maize biomass by crop height and narrowband vegetation indices derived from UAV-based hyperspectral images. *Ecol. Indic.* **2021**, *129*, 107985. [CrossRef]
76. Madec, S.; Baret, F.; de Solan, B.; Thomas, S.; Dutartre, D.; Jezequel, S.; Hemmerlé, M.; Colombeau, G.; Comar, A. High-Throughput Phenotyping of Plant Height: Comparing Unmanned Aerial Vehicles and Ground LiDAR Estimates. *Front. Plant Sci.* **2017**, *8*, 2002. [CrossRef]
77. Li, W.; Niu, Z.; Chen, H.; Li, D.; Wu, M.; Zhao, W. Remote estimation of canopy height and aboveground biomass of maize using high-resolution stereo images from a low-cost unmanned aerial vehicle system. *Ecol. Indic.* **2016**, *67*, 637–648. [CrossRef]
78. Huete, A.R.; Jackson, R.D.; Post, D.F. Spectral response of a plant canopy with different soil backgrounds. *Remote Sens. Environ.* **1985**, *17*, 37–53. [CrossRef]
79. Klemas, V.; Smart, R. The influence of soil salinity, growth form, and leaf moisture on-the spectral radiance of. *Photogramm. Eng. Remote Sens.* **1983**, *49*, 77–83.
80. Zhou, X.; Yang, M.; Chen, X.; Ma, L.; Yin, C.; Qin, S.; Wang, L.; Lv, X.; Zhang, Z. Estimation of Cotton Nitrogen Content Based on Multi-Angle Hyperspectral Data and Machine Learning Models. *Remote Sens.* **2023**, *15*, 955. [CrossRef]
81. He, L.; Liu, M.; Guo, Y.; Wei, Y.; Zhang, H.; Song, X.; Feng, W.; Guo, T. Angular effect of algorithms for monitoring leaf nitrogen concentration of wheat using multi-angle remote sensing data. *Comput. Electron. Agric.* **2022**, *195*, 106815. [CrossRef]
82. Li, D.; Chen, J.M.; Zhang, X.; Yan, Y.; Zhu, J.; Zheng, H.; Zhou, K.; Yao, X.; Tian, Y.; Zhu, Y. Improved estimation of leaf chlorophyll content of row crops from canopy reflectance spectra through minimizing canopy structural effects and optimizing off-noon observation time. *Remote Sens. Environ.* **2020**, *248*, 111985. [CrossRef]
83. Thomas, S.; Kuska, M.T.; Bohnenkamp, D.; Brugger, A.; Alisaac, E.; Wahabzada, M.; Behmann, J.; Mahlein, A. Benefits of hyperspectral imaging for plant disease detection and plant protection: A technical perspective. *J. Plant Dis. Prot.* **2018**, *125*, 5–20. [CrossRef]
84. Ehlert, D.; Horn, H.; Adamek, R. Measuring crop biomass density by laser triangulation. *Comput. Electron. Agric.* **2008**, *61*, 117–125. [CrossRef]
85. Wan, L.; Zhu, J.; Du, X.; Zhang, J.; Han, X.; Zhou, W.; Li, X.; Liu, J.; Liang, F.; He, Y. A model for phenotyping crop fractional vegetation cover using imagery from unmanned aerial vehicles. *J. Exp. Bot.* **2021**, *72*, 4691–4707. [CrossRef]
86. Li, Z.; Zhao, Y.; Taylor, J.; Gaulton, R.; Jin, X.; Song, X.; Li, Z.; Meng, Y.; Chen, P.; Feng, H. Comparison and transferability of thermal, temporal and phenological-based in-season predictions of above-ground biomass in wheat crops from proximal crop reflectance data. *Remote Sens. Environ.* **2022**, *273*, 112967. [CrossRef]
87. Makanza, R.; Zaman-Allah, M.; Cairns, J.E.; Magorokosho, C.; Tarekegne, A.; Olsen, M.; Prasanna, B.M. High-throughput phenotyping of canopy cover and senescence in maize field trials using aerial digital canopy imaging. *Remote Sens.* **2018**, *10*, 330. [CrossRef] [PubMed]

88. Wang, Y.; Zhang, K.; Tang, C.; Cao, Q.; Tian, Y.; Zhu, Y.; Cao, W.; Liu, X. Estimation of rice growth parameters based on linear mixed-effect model using multispectral images from fixed-wing unmanned aerial vehicles. *Remote Sens.* **2019**, *11*, 1371. [CrossRef]
89. Sun, J.; Yang, K.; Chen, C.; Shen, J.; Yang, Y.; Wu, X.; Norton, T. Wheat head counting in the wild by an augmented feature pyramid networks-based convolutional neural network. *Comput. Electron. Agric.* **2022**, *193*, 106705. [CrossRef]
90. Zaji, A.; Liu, Z.; Xiao, G.; Bhowmik, P.; Sangha, J.S.; Ruan, Y. AutoOLA: Automatic object level augmentation for wheat spikes counting. *Comput. Electron. Agric.* **2023**, *205*, 107623. [CrossRef]
91. Tian, K.; Li, J.; Zeng, J.; Evans, A.; Zhang, L. Segmentation of tomato leaf images based on adaptive clustering number of K-means algorithm. *Comput. Electron. Agric.* **2019**, *165*, 104962. [CrossRef]
92. Buciu, I.; Kotropoulos, C.; Pitas, I. Demonstrating the stability of support vector machines for classification. *Signal Process.* **2006**, *86*, 2364–2380. [CrossRef]
93. Rodriguez-Galiano, V.F.; Chica-Olmo, M.; Abarca-Hernandez, F.; Atkinson, P.M.; Jeganathan, C. Random Forest classification of Mediterranean land cover using multi-seasonal imagery and multi-seasonal texture. *Remote Sens. Environ.* **2012**, *121*, 93–107. [CrossRef]
94. Bates, J.S.; Montzka, C.; Schmidt, M.; Jonard, F. Estimating Canopy Density Parameters Time-Series for Winter Wheat Using UAS Mounted LiDAR. *Remote Sens.* **2021**, *13*, 710. [CrossRef]

remote sensing

MDPI

Article

Estimation of Biochemical Compounds in Tradescantia Leaves Using VIS-NIR-SWIR Hyperspectral and Chlorophyll a Fluorescence Sensors

Renan Falcioni [1,*], Roney Berti de Oliveira [1], Marcelo Luiz Chicati [1], Werner Camargos Antunes [1], José Alexandre M. Demattê [2] and Marcos Rafael Nanni [1]

[1] Department of Agronomy, State University of Maringá, Av. Colombo, 5790, Maringá 87020-900, Paraná, Brazil; rboliveira@uem.br (R.B.d.O.); mlchicati@uem.br (M.L.C.); wcantunes@uem.br (W.C.A.); mrnanni@uem.br (M.R.N.)

[2] Department of Soil Science, Luiz de Queiroz College of Agriculture, University of São Paulo, Av. Pádua Dias, 11, Piracicaba 13418-260, São Paulo, Brazil; jamdemat@usp.br

* Correspondence: renanfalcioni@gmail.com or rfalcioni2@uem.br; Tel.: +55-4430118940

Abstract: An integrated approach that utilises hyperspectral and chlorophyll a fluorescence sensors to predict biochemical and biophysical parameters represents a new generation of remote-sensing research. The main objective of this study was to obtain a detailed spectral profile that correlates with plant physiology, thereby enhancing our understanding and management of plant health, pigment profiles, and compound fingerprints. Leveraging datasets using non-imaging or passive hyperspectral and chlorophyll fluorescence sensors to collect data in Tradescantia species demonstrated significant differences in leaf characteristics with pigment concentrations and structural components. The main goal was to use principal component analysis (PCA) and partial least squares regression (PLS) methods to analyse the variations in their spectra. Our findings demonstrate a strong correlation between hyperspectral data and chlorophyll fluorescence, which is further supported by the development of hyperspectral vegetation indices (HVIs) that can accurately evaluate fingerprints and predict many compounds in variegated leaves. The higher the integrated analytical approach and its potential application in HVIs and fingerprints, the better the selection of wavelengths and sensor positions for rapid and accurate analysis of many different compounds in leaves. Nonetheless, limitations arose from the specificity of the data for the Tradescantia species, warranting further research across diverse plant types and compounds in the leaves. Overall, this study paves the way for more sustainable and informed agricultural practices through breakthroughs in the application of sensors to remote-sensing technologies.

Keywords: biochemical compounds; HVI; hyperspectral sensors; partial least squares regression; principal component analysis; purple leaves

1. Introduction

The integration of hyperspectral sensors with chlorophyll fluorescence techniques represents a significant advancement in leaf signature analysis [1]. These cutting-edge methodologies provide a detailed understanding of the physiological and biochemical states of vegetation, enabling us to understand plant responses to various environmental conditions [2,3]. These tools not only improve the accuracy of traditional assessments but also open up new possible innovative approaches for monitoring plant health and managing agriculture [4–6].

Chlorophyll fluorescence (ChlF) curves are an essential tool for assessing plant health because they allow for the accurate mapping of pigment concentrations and biochemical components based on 1 s curves [7,8]. By measuring the fluorescence emitted by chlorophyll a, these curves provide valuable insights into the photosynthetic efficiency and stress response of plants. The data obtained from the ChlF curves can reveal variations in chlorophyll content, as well as changes in other pigments and biochemical markers, which are crucial for understanding the physiological state of the plant [9–11]. This technique is particularly useful for detecting early signs of stress before visible symptoms appear, enabling proactive management and mitigation strategies for crop cultivation and environmental monitoring or pigment profiling in leaves [12,13].

Hyperspectral curves derived from both imaging and non-imaging sensors provide a comprehensive spectral profile of plant leaves and capture detailed information over a wide range of wavelengths [14–17]. Non-imaging hyperspectral sensors offer distinct advantages. These sensors facilitate rapid data acquisition without the need for spatial context, making them highly efficient for large-scale or remote assessments. The flexibility and precision of non-imaging hyperspectral sensors enable the detection of subtle physiological changes, enhancing the capacity to monitor plant stress responses with exceptional accuracy [11,18–21]. Consequently, these tools are invaluable for advancing our understanding of plant dynamics and improving agricultural practices.

With the intricate cellular and foliar architecture of plants, an array of chloroplastic pigments, such as chlorophylls and carotenoids, and non-chloroplastic compounds, including anthocyanins, flavonoids, and phenolic compounds, have been identified [22–24]. Moreover, structural components such as lignin and cellulose play critical roles in the biomechanical integrity of plant tissues. The concentrations of these biochemical constituents can vary significantly and are influenced by factors such as the expansion of leaf area, leaf thickness, and the number and structural alterations of cells [21,23,25]. These variations are pivotal because they reflect the biophysical and biochemical dynamics within the plant and offer insights into its adaptive responses to environmental conditions.

Principal component analysis (PCA) is an advanced statistical method that is widely applied to address the complexity and high dimensionality of hyperspectral and fluorescence data [22,26–28]. This method effectively separates and recognises patterns by reducing data dimensionality while maintaining most of the variance, thus revealing the underlying variability among the samples. One of the main benefits of PCA is its ability to select the optimal number of principal components (PCs) required to capture significant data features [27,29,30]. This choice is vital because it balances the maximisation of information retention with minimising noise. The β-loadings obtained from PCA provide a clear illustration of the spectral peaks, offering "fingerprints" of the chemical and physical properties within the dataset [22,23]. Furthermore, PCA can be combined with regression coefficients obtained from various spectral curves, such as OJIP, which represent the fluorescence kinetics over the first few seconds of illumination, and hyperspectral reflectance, transmittance, and absorbance curves. This combination allows for more comprehensive analysis by combining biochemical and biophysical insights [31]. Such a multifaceted approach enhances the understanding of plant responses and interactions with their environment, aiding in more accurate and predictive modelling of plant physiology and agronomy by remote-sensing techniques [4–6,32].

Hyperspectral vegetation indices (HVIs) are useful for analysing large datasets from both chlorophyll fluorescence and hyperspectral measurements [15,33–35]. By simplifying complex spectral data into understandable indices, HVIs enable the effective large-scale surveillance and mapping of more relevant parameters. These indices can be used to systematically identify areas of specific interest wavelengths by locating regions of interest in which key biochemical and biophysical components or fingerprint indicators show significant changes [22,23]. For example, specific HVIs can be designed to detect changes in chlorophyll content, water stress, and nutrient levels [25,29,36–38]. The combination of these indices with chlorophyll fluorescence data improves the ability to spatially differentiate areas with different photosynthetic efficiencies or stress reactions, whereas hyperspectral data can be used to map the distribution of various biochemical markers across a landscape. Ultimately, the application of HVIs provides a powerful tool for precision agriculture and environmental monitoring. By converting complex spectral data into actionable information, these indices enable the development of targeted intervention strategies, maximisation of resource use, and improvement of crop management practices.

Partial least squares regression (PLSR) is a general method for analysing hyperspectral data for predictive modelling because it can effectively handle highly collinear and multivariate data [22,26,27,39,40]. This method is particularly useful when there are more predictor variables than observations, which is often the case in spectral analysis. PLSR works by finding the most relevant information from the predictors (in this case, spectral bands) by projecting them onto a new subspace defined by the latent variables. These latent variables are selected not only for their ability to account for the variance in the predictors but also for their correlation with the response variable, which is essential for making accurate predictions [27,40,41]. One of the main benefits of PLSR is its ability to handle multicollinearity among spectral bands well, where traditional regression methods may not work or yield unreliable coefficients. PLSR reduces the predictors to a smaller set of uncorrelated components while maintaining the ability to capture key patterns related to the response variable.

PLSR is useful not only for prediction but also for exploratory data analysis as it can uncover hidden patterns and associations in the data. It can be very effective when combined with other techniques, such as cross-validation, to increase model stability and assess predictive performance [27,42]. PLSR stands out for its flexibility and efficiency in dealing with complex and large datasets that are common in hyperspectral imaging, making it a preferred method for both academic research and practical applications in fields such as remote sensing, chemometrics, and precision agriculture [27,40,41]. For those who want to know more about this method, detailed applications and comparisons with other techniques are often found in the scientific literature related to spectroscopy and data analysis [22,26,27,39,40].

This study aimed to improve the prediction of chlorophyll a fluorescence parameters together using hyperspectral sensors. The main objective of this study was to identify specific spectral bands by HVI using hyperspectral data that are strongly correlated with chlorophyll a fluorescence to aid in the estimation of seventeen biochemical and biophysical parameters in Tradescantia plants. This concerns considering the shape of leaf structures, which is relevant to plant physiology. The hypothesis of this study is that by combining and enhancing the use of advanced hyperspectral sensors for reflectance, transmittance, and absorbance data, along with powerful multivariate statistical methods such as PCA and PLSR, it is possible to increase the prediction of these data parameters (Figure 1).

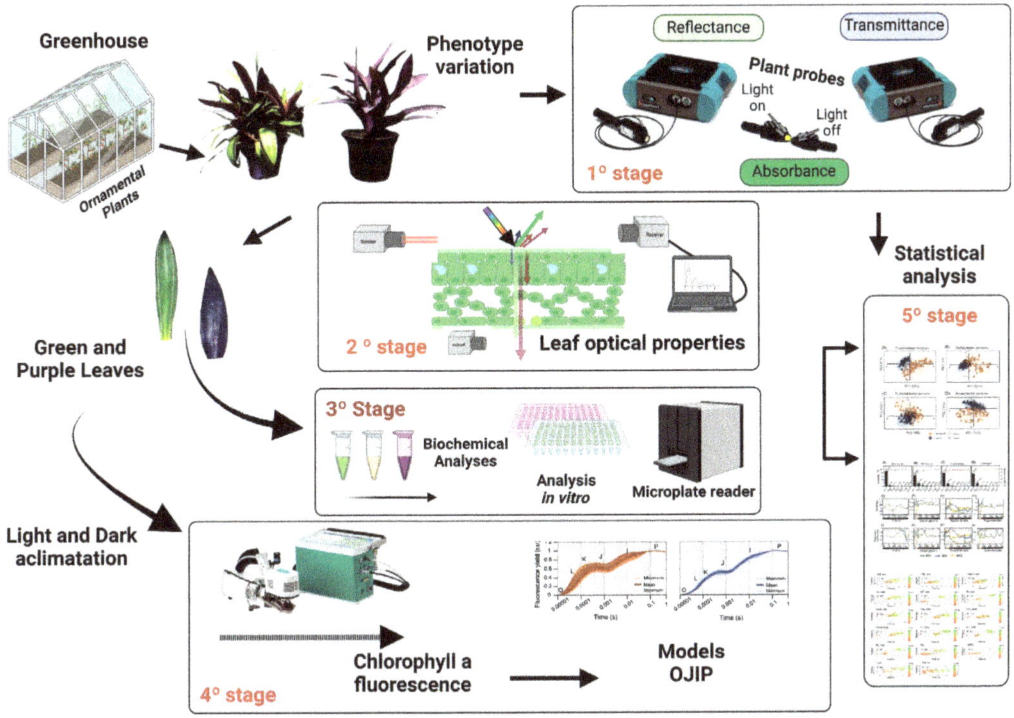

Figure 1. A flowchart showing how to predict the biochemical compounds in *Tradescantia spathacea* (L.) Olof Swartz and *Tradescantia pallida* (Rose) D.R. Hunt. plants, using two hyperspectral and chlorophyll sensors. Stage 1 involved growing plants in a greenhouse and using two hyperspectral sensors to measure the reflectance, transmittance, and absorbance spectra of their leaves. Stage 2 involves examining leaves to detect changes in their optical properties. In Stage 3, the levels of biochemical compounds in the leaves were measured using a microplate reader. In Stage 4, the leaves were exposed to dark conditions to measure chlorophyll a fluorescence and evaluate the prediction models. Stage 5 involves analysing the data using PLS and other multivariate statistical methods for the classification and prediction of biochemical and biophysical parameters. Created with BioRender.com.

2. Materials and Methods

2.1. Plant Materials and Experimental Design

The model plants *Tradescantia spathacea* (L.) Olof Swartz and *Tradescantia pallida* (Rose) D.R. Hunt., plants that exhibit variations in pigment concentration and leaf thickness, were cultivated in 2 L pots at the Botanical Garden of the State University of Maringá, Brazil. These plants were grown under greenhouse conditions, benefiting from natural light, and maintained within a temperature range of 22 °C to 26 °C under a 16-h photoperiod. Regular watering was conducted twice daily, at 8 a.m. and 6 p.m., to ensure consistent hydration. Leaves of various ages and positions (apex, middle, and base) were sampled from different sections of the plants. The investigation involved hyperspectral reflectance analysis and leaf biochemical profiling of a total of 200 samples. All measurements were meticulously performed between 11 a.m. and 1 p.m. to maintain consistency in the data collection. A summary of the analytical procedure is shown in Figure 1.

2.2. OJIP Chlorophyll a Fluorescence Transient

The leaves were analysed using an infrared gas exchange analyser (IRGA) with a Multiphase Flash^{TM} Fluorometer (LI-6800-01; LI-COR Inc., Lincoln, NE, USA) equipped with a constant concentration of 400 µmol mol^{-1} in the chamber sample (CO_2_sample) and a relative humidity of 60% in the sample chamber (%RH_sample). A flow rate of 700 µmol s^{-1}, a fan speed of 10,000 rpm, and a sample heat exchanger temperature of 25 °C were maintained within a 6 cm^2 sample chamber. The sensor operates at >720 nm, specifically for chlorophyll a fluorescence [23].

To elicit chlorophyll a fluorescence transients, the leaves were subjected to dark acclimation for 12 h in the dark. Thereafter, a clipping chamber was used, and a saturating light pulse of 15,000 µmol m^{-2} s^{-1} was applied for 1 s in induction mode, ensuring the closure of all reaction centres [13].

2.3. Hyperspectral Optical Leaf Properties

A FieldSpec® 3 spectroradiometer with an ASD Contact PlantProbe® (ASD Inc., Boulder, CO, USA) with a diameter of 10 mm was used to measure the reflectance (R) and transmittance (T) of the leaves. The equipment consisted of a VNIR detector with a 512-element silicon array for wavelengths ranging from 350 to 1000 nm (3 nm spectral resolution), an SWIR 1 detector with a Graded Index InGaAs Photodiode, a Two-Stage TE Cooled for wavelengths from 1001 to 1800 nm (10 nm spectral resolution), an SWIR 2 detector with a Graded Index InGaAs Photodiode, and a Two-Stage TE Cooled for wavelengths from 1801 to 2500 nm (10 nm spectral resolution), with interpolation in 1 nm by spectroradiometer equipment. This spectroradiometer is based on non-imaging passive sensors. A PlantProbe® leaf clip was used to minimise atmospheric effects. ViewSpec Pro software version 6.2 (ASD Inc., Boulder, CO, USA) was used to preprocess the data and change the sensor at 1000 and 1800 nm. Standard white reference plates were used to calibrate and optimise the equipment. A high-intensity light beam (1500 µmol m^{-2} s^{-1}) was measured at 1 cm from the light source with an irradiance sensor measured by LI-180 (LI-COR Inc., Lincoln, NE, USA), and from one plant probe was directed to the upper (adaxial) surface of the leaf, whereas another probe, without its light beam, assessed the lower (abaxial) surface of the leaf. The reflectance and transmittance for each wavelength were recorded simultaneously, and the absorbance was calculated using the formula [$A = 1 - (R + T)$].

2.4. Evaluation of Biochemical and Biophysical Leaf Tissue Composition

2.4.1. Measurement of Chlorophyll and Carotenoid Contents

We used a modified version of the method by Gitelson and Solovchenko (2018) [43] to determine the concentrations of chlorophyll *a*, chlorophyll *b*, total chlorophyll (*a*+*b*), and carotenoids, including carotenes and xanthophylls. The absorbance of the methanol extract from the apolar phase of chloroform:methanol (2:1) extraction was measured at 470, 652, and 665 nm [44]. We calculated the concentrations of these pigments using these formulas and expressed the final concentrations in mg cm^{-2} and mg g^{-1} [44].

2.4.2. Measurement of Anthocyanins and Flavonoids

To measure anthocyanins, we acidified the water-methanol phase with hydrochloric acid and measured its absorbance at λ530 nm using the molar absorption coefficient of Gitelson and Solovchenko (2018) [43]. To measure flavonoids, we examined the polar fraction of the methanol extract at a wavelength of 358 nm. We also used molar absorption coefficients according to the method described by Gitelson and Solovchenko (2018) [43].

2.4.3. Evaluation of Antioxidant Capacity

To measure the total antioxidant capacity of the samples, we followed a modified version of the DPPH assay, based on the method described by Llorach et al. (2008) [45]. In this assay, we incubated the methanolic extract with 1 mM DPPH solution and recorded the absorbance of the mixture for colour changes.

2.4.4. Measurement of Phenolic Compounds in Leaves

We used a modified version of the method described by Ragaee (2006) [46] to measure the soluble phenolic compounds. The methanolic extract was mixed with Folin–Ciocalteu reagent, sodium carbonate (Na_2CO_3), and deionised water. The mixture was incubated in the dark and centrifuged to separate the phases. The absorbance of the supernatant was measured at a wavelength of 725 nm.

2.5. Hyperspectral Vegetation Indices Using Optimal Wavelengths for JIP-Test and Hyperspectral Parameters

The hyperspectral bands and chlorophyll a fluorescence were calculated using the normalised difference vegetation index formula (Equation (1)), as outlined by Crusiol et al. (2023) [27]. This procedure yielded unique hyperspectral vegetation indices (HVIs). Each HVI was then correlated with relevant cross-sections pertaining to chlorophyll a kinetic parameters. These correlations were quantified using the Pearson correlation coefficient and the coefficient of determination (R^2) using a custom IDL code. The data were collected using a ground-based sensor, which captured spectra across a range of 350–2500 nm, and the results are presented in a contour map.

$$HVI = \frac{Wavelength\ 1 - Wavelength\ 2}{Wavelength\ 1 + Wavelength\ 2} \quad (1)$$

2.6. Partial Least Squares Regression (PLSR) by Analysis of Spectroscopy Data

The hyperspectral data were centred on the mean and subjected to PLSR to create prediction models for JIP test parameters. To achieve this, the spectral data of the various parameters of the 200 samples were divided into two groups: 75% (150) of the samples were allocated to the training group, whereas the remaining 25% (50) were designated as the prediction group. This allocation was chosen to ensure that the resulting estimates were valid and accurate. Validity was ensured by preventing an overestimation of the accuracy, which was maximised by minimising the overestimation of the approximation error. This approach was based on the analysis described in [22,23].

Calibration (Cal) and cross-validation (Cva) were employed to predict quality attributes based on the JIP test. Furthermore, the predictive capabilities of the calibration model were assessed by calculating metrics, such as the coefficient of determination. (R^2; $1 - \frac{SS_{res}}{SS_{tot}}$), offset, root mean square error (RMSE; $\sqrt{\sum_{i=1}^{n} \frac{(\hat{Y}i - Yi)^2}{n}}$), the ratio of performance to deviation (RPD; $\frac{1}{\sqrt{1-R_x^2}}$), and bias were used to assess the quality, precision, and accuracy of the model, as described in [23].

2.7. Statistical Analyses

2.7.1. Descriptive, Univariate, and Multivariate Statistical Analyses

Descriptive statistics were used to describe the biochemical parameters. For each parameter, assessments included the count (n), mean, median, minimum, maximum, and coefficient of variation (CV, %). The CV was categorised according to the criteria proposed by Zar (2010) [47]. Pearson's correlation methodology was employed to determine the interrelationships between biochemical and biophysical attributes. For these analytical tasks, we utilised Statistica 10® (StatSoft Inc., Tulsa, OK, USA) and the R-Studio software version 2023.12.1 (Posit Software, PBC, Boston, MA, USA) framework. Graphical representations were generated using a range of applications: SigmaPlot 10.0® (Systat Inc., Santa Clara, Silicon Valley, CA, USA), R-Studio software, Excel 365 version 2404 (Microsoft Inc., Silicon Valley, CA, USA), and CorelDraw 2024® version 25 (Corel Corp., Ottawa, ON, Canada).

2.7.2. Principal Component Analysis (PCA)

Unscrambler X software, version 10.4 (CAMO Software, Oslo, Norway), was used for principal component analysis (PCA) of the growth parameter data. This was achieved with a predetermined statistical significance level of $p < 0.01$. To ensure that the analysis was not subject to underfitting or overfitting, the optimal number of principal components was determined based on the first maximum value of overall accuracy, as outlined in [22,23].

3. Results

3.1. Statistical Description of the Biochemical Compounds

Table 1 provides a comprehensive statistical analysis of various biochemical compounds measured in the leaves of *Tradescantia spathacea* (L.) Olof Swartz and *Tradescantia pallida* (Rose) D.R. Hunt., species based on 200 samples per parameter. The data included the mean, median, minimum, maximum, and coefficient of variation for each compound (Table 1).

Table 1. The descriptive statistics of biochemical compound parameters measured in the leaves of *Tradescantia spathacea* (L.) Olof Swartz and *Tradescantia pallida* (Rose) D.R. Hunt. species. For each parameter, data were collected for 200 samples, including the mean, median, minimum, and maximum values and the coefficient of variation (CV%). (n = 200).

Parameter	Count (n)	Mean	Median	Minimum	Maximum	CV (%)
Chl*a* (mg m^{-2})	200	765.25	760.47	480.20	996.52	10.92
Chl*b* (mg m^{-2})	200	487.48	469.65	262.06	875.10	18.99
Chl*a+b* (mg m^{-2})	200	1252.73	1231.39	742.26	1871.61	13.89
Car (mg m^{-2})	200	263.54	264.23	185.89	362.00	9.24
AnC (nmol cm^{-2})	200	23.78	23.59	18.36	27.48	6.52
Flv (nmol cm^{-2})	200	34.02	32.94	17.97	51.74	18.21
Chl*a*/*b* ratio	200	1.59	1.61	1.14	1.94	7.63
Chl*a* (mg g^{-1})	200	10.53	10.30	0.96	17.50	28.99
Chl*b* (mg g^{-1})	200	6.64	6.85	0.64	11.77	29.01
Chl*a+b* (mg g^{-1})	200	17.16	17.46	1.60	27.88	28.68
Car (mg g^{-1})	200	3.64	3.57	0.33	6.40	29.58
AnC (µmol g^{-1})	200	3.37	2.92	0.24	5.75	37.07
Flv (µmol g^{-1})	200	4.94	3.75	0.33	11.32	46.51
Phe (mL L^{-1})	200	57.91	57.59	29.02	111.31	29.66
DPPH	200	91.73	91.68	88.58	99.30	1.35
Lignin (mg g^{-1})	200	307.67	303.22	178.09	422.13	19.68
Cellulose (nmol mg^{-1})	200	725.52	671.16	322.95	1386.90	37.39

Chlorophyll *a* (Chl*a*, mg m^{-2}) had a mean of 765.25, a median of 760.47, a minimum of 480.20, and a maximum of 996.52, with a coefficient of variation of 10.92%. Chlorophyll *b* (Chl*b*, mg m^{-2}) had a mean of 487.48, a median of 469.65, a minimum of 262.06, and a maximum of 875.10, with a high variation coefficient of 18.99%. Total chlorophyll *a+b* (Chl*a+b*, mg m^{-2}) had a mean of 1252.73, a median of 1231.39, a minimum of 742.26, and a maximum of 1871.61, with a variation coefficient of 13.89%. Carotenoids (Car, mg m^{-2}) had a mean of 263.54, a median of 264.23, a minimum of 185.89, and a maximum of 362.00, showing a lower variability of 9.24%. The mean chlorophyll *a*/*b* ratio was 1.59, the median was 1.61, the minimum was 1.14, and the maximum was 1.94, with a variation coefficient of 7.63% (Table 1).

The anthocyanin contents (AnC, nmol cm^{-2}) were 23.78, 23.59, 18.36, and 27.48, respectively, with a variation coefficient of 6.52%. The mean flavonoid content (Flv, nmol cm^{-2}) was 34.02, the median was 32.94, the minimum was 17.97, and the maximum was 51.74, with a coefficient of variation of 18.21%.

On a mass basis, chlorophyll *a* (mg g^{-1}) had a mean of 10.53, a median of 10.30, a minimum of 0.96, and a maximum of 17.50, showing high variability with a coefficient of 28.99%. Similarly, chlorophyll b (mg g^{-1}) exhibited high variability, with a mean of 6.64, a median of 6.85, a minimum of 0.64, and a maximum of 11.77, with a coefficient of variation of 29.01%. The mean total chlorophyll *a+b* concentration (Chl*a+b*, mg g^{-1}) was 17.16, the median was 17.46, the minimum was 1.60, and the maximum was 27.88, with a variation of 28.68%. On a mass basis (Car, mg g^{-1}), the mean carotenoid content was 3.64, the median was 3.57, the minimum was 0.33, and the maximum was 6.40, with a high coefficient of variation of 29.58%.

The mean anthocyanin content (AnC, μmol g^{-1}) was 3.37, with a median of 2.92, a minimum of 0.24, and a maximum of 5.75, with a variability of 37.07%. The mean flavonoid content (Flv, μmol g^{-1}) was 4.94, with a median of 3.75, a minimum of 0.33, and a maximum of 11.32, with the highest coefficient of variation at 46.51%. The mean phenolic compound content (Phe, mL L^{-1}) was 57.91, the median was 57.59, the minimum was 29.02, and the maximum was 111.31, with a coefficient of variation of 29.66%.

The mean DPPH radical scavenging activity was 91.73, with a median of 91.68, a minimum of 88.58, and a maximum of 99.30, indicating minimal variability with a coefficient of variation of 1.35%. Lignin (mg g^{-1}) had a mean of 307.67%, a median of 303.22%, a minimum of 178.09%, and a maximum of 422.13%, with a coefficient of variation of 19.68%. Finally, cellulose (nmol mg^{-1}) displayed a mean of 725.52, a median of 671.16, a minimum of 322.95, and a maximum of 1386.90, showing significant variability with a coefficient of variation of 37.39% (Table 1).

3.2. Chlorophyll a Fluorescence Kinetics

The two Tradescantia species displayed different chlorophyll a fluorescence kinetics in their leaves (Figure 2). The OJIP curves follow the names of the distinct phases O (origin), L, K, J, I, and P (peak), which are essential for calculating the JIP test parameters based on a logarithmic scale.

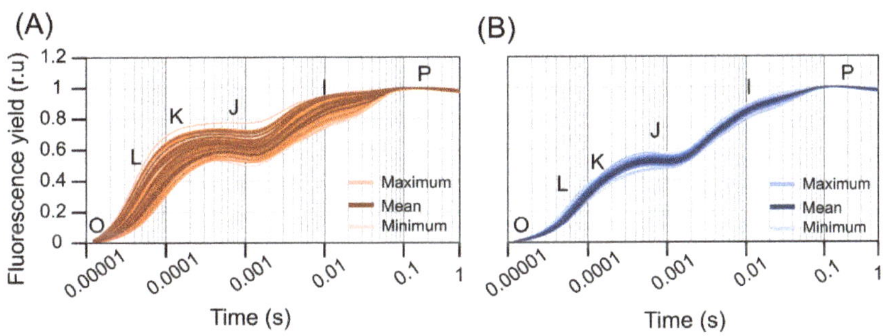

Figure 2. Spectral chlorophyll a fluorescence kinetics in leaves. (**A**) *Tradescantia spathacea* (L.) Olof Swartz. (**B**) *Tradescantia pallida* (Rose) DR. Hunt., species. The O, L, K, J, I, and P phases are based on a logarithmic scale (Time, s). (n = 100).

The OJIP curves indicated significant differences in pigments between the two species ($p < 0.01$), as measured by the photosynthetic performance. Significant reductions in variable fluorescence were observed at key points of 20 μs (ΔL), 300 μs (ΔK), 2 ms (ΔJ), 10 ms (ΔI), and 40 ms (ΔP). The curves illustrate different patterns of chlorophyll a fluorescence kinetics between *Tradescantia spathacea* and *Tradescantia pallida* plants (Figure 2A,B).

Further analysis revealed that points O and P had almost the same chlorophyll a fluorescence intensity, based on fluorescence yield for both species. However, *Tradescantia pallida* consistently showed greater fluorescence at points L, K, J, and I than *T. spathacea*, indicating possible differences in photosynthetic apparatus efficiency.

3.3. Hyperspectral Reflectance, Transmittance, and Absorbance Curves

There were noticeable differences in the reflectance between *Tradescantia spathacea* and *Tradescantia pallida* at specific wavelengths within each spectral range (Figure 3A,B). In the VIS spectrum (400–700 nm), a significant difference was observed at 544 nm. The largest difference in the NIR range (700–1300 nm) was observed at 700 nm. For the SWIR1 spectrum (1300–1800 nm), the most evident contrast was observed at 1441 nm, and in the SWIR2 range (1800–2500 nm), the most marked change was observed at 2488 nm. The consistently low p-values ($p < 0.01$) highlight the statistical importance of these results, implying that these wavelengths are essential for separating the two *Tradescantia* species based on their reflectance.

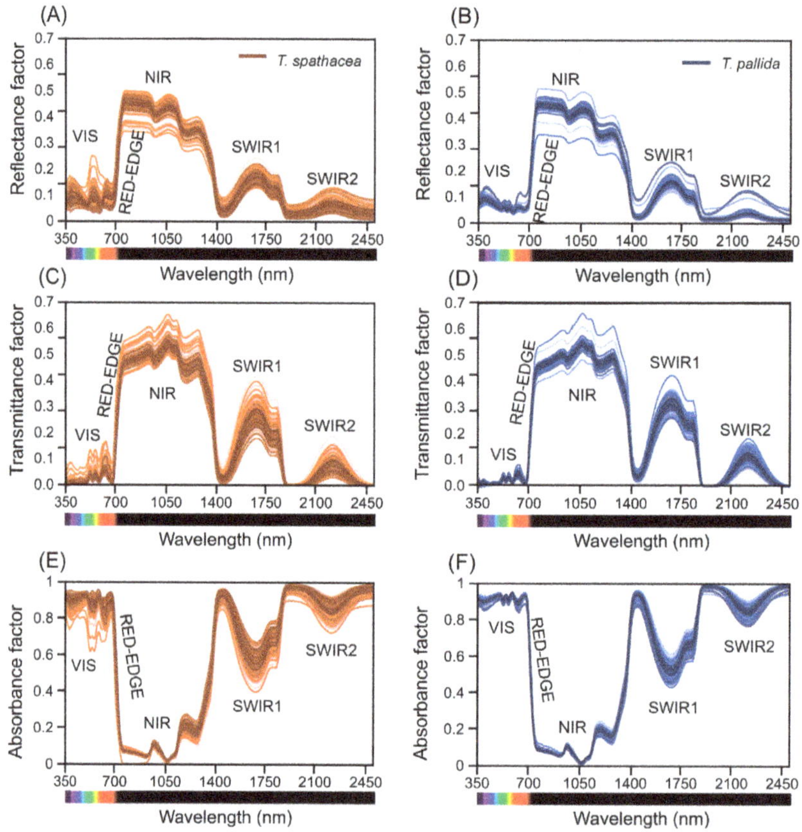

Figure 3. Spectral leaf reflectance, transmittance, and absorbance curves from 350 to 2500 nm for *Tradescantia spathacea* (L.) Olof Swartz and *Tradescantia pallida* (Rose) D.R. Hunt., species. (**A**,**B**) Reflectance curves. (**C**,**D**) Transmittance curves. (**E**,**F**) Absorbance curves. For clarity, *Tradescantia spathacea* is represented by orange lines, while *Tradescantia pallida* is indicated by blue lines ($n = 100$).

The transmittance values also showed substantial differences between the species at certain wavelengths within each spectral band (Figure 3C,D). In the VIS spectrum, the largest difference was observed at 400 nm. The peak difference within the NIR spectrum was at 1125 nm, whereas in the SWIR1 spectrum, it was at 1607 nm, and the SWIR2 spectrum peaked at 2175 nm. These significantly low *p*-values indicate that transmittance at these selected wavelengths can be used to distinguish *Tradescantia spathacea* from *Tradescantia pallida* species.

In the absorbance analysis, significant differences were detected at specific wavelengths across spectral bands (Figure 3E,F). The most notable changes were observed at 495 nm within VIS-Blue, 498 nm in VIS-Blue-Green, 733 nm in VIS-Red-Far-Red, 800 nm in NIR-Far-Red, 1117 nm in the NIR, 1575 nm in SWIR1, and 2175 nm in SWIR2. The extremely low p-values associated with these wavelengths verify their statistical significance and suggest that absorbance at these wavelengths is crucial for distinguishing *Tradescantia spathacea* from *Tradescantia pallida* species (Figure 3).

3.4. Principal Component Analysis for Fluorescence, Reflectance, Transmittance, and Absorbance Sensors

Figure 4 shows a principal component analysis (PCA) that reveals the spectral differences in the leaves of *Tradescantia spathacea* and *Tradescantia pallida* using various sensors for fluorescence, reflectance, transmittance, and absorbance (Figure 4A–D).

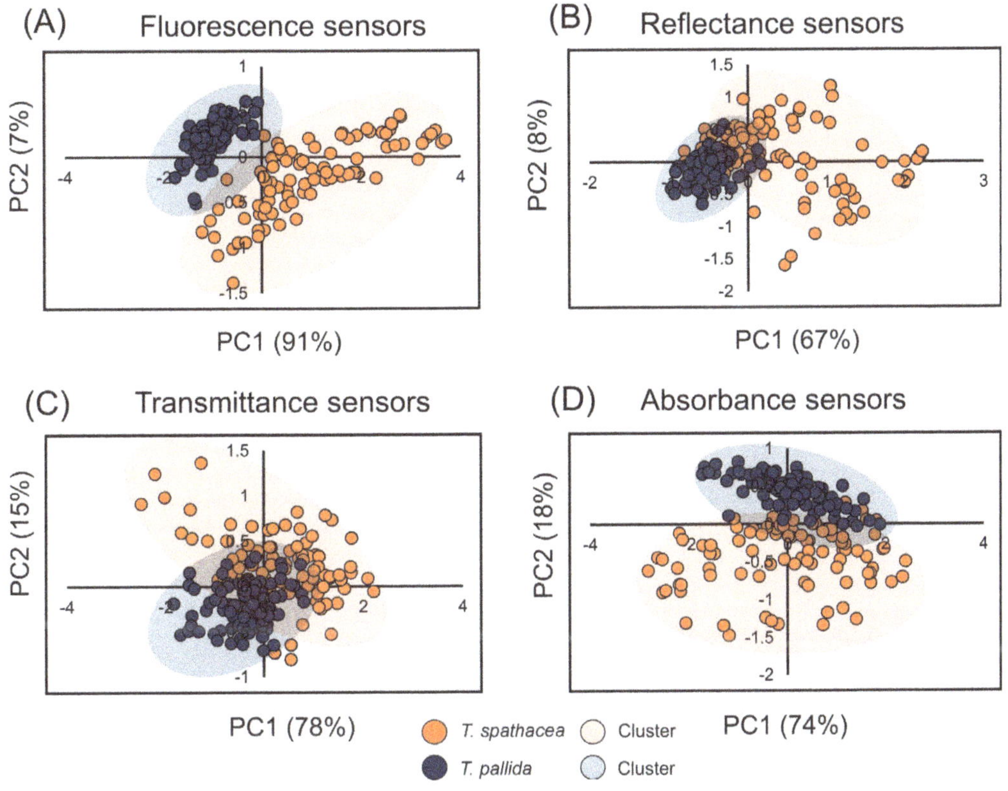

Figure 4. Principal component (PC) from 350 to 2500 nm in the leaves of *Tradescantia spathacea* (L.) Olof Swartz and *Tradescantia pallida* (Rose) D.R. Hunt., plants. (**A**) Fluorescence sensors. (**B**) Hyperspectral reflectance sensors. (**C**) Hyperspectral transmittance sensors. (**D**) Hyperspectral absorbance sensors. Clustering-coloured leaves are displayed as orange (*T. spathacea*) and blue (*T. pallida*) circles (n = 100).

Figure 4A shows the PCA for the fluorescence sensors, where *Tradescantia spathacea* is in orange and *Tradescantia pallida* is shown in blue. There was a clear separation along Principal Component 1 (PC1), which accounted for 91% of the variance, highlighting distinct fluorescence patterns for each species.

Figure 4B shows the PCA of the reflectance sensors. Here, a moderate difference was observed in PC1, which accounted for 67% of the total variance, indicating different reflectance features between the two species.

Figure 4C shows the PCA for transmittance sensors, showing a noticeable distinction between *Tradescantia spathacea* and *Tradescantia pallida* along both PC1 and PC2, explaining 78% and 15% of the variance, respectively. This implies that there were significant species-specific transmittance signatures.

Figure 4D shows the PCA for the absorbance sensors, with PC1 explaining 74% of the variance and PC2 accounting for 18%. This separation suggests strong differences in absorbance between the species.

The shaded regions within each shape show clusters of data points, reflecting the diversity within each species and the level of resemblance between them. The PCA results demonstrated the value of these spectral measurements for distinguishing between the two species of Tradescantia.

By analysing Figure 5A–L, each of which shows the variability and loadings across different spectral measurements, one can delineate the principal component contributions to spectral data interpretation for fluorescence, reflectance, transmittance, and absorbance (Figure 5).

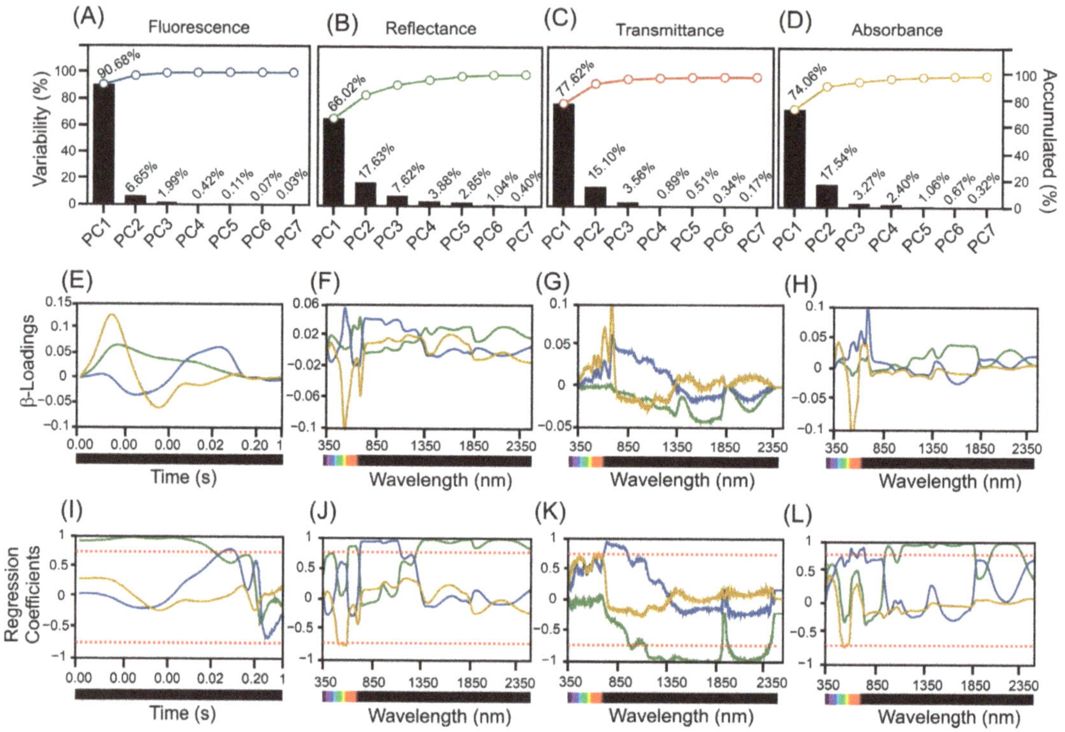

Figure 5. Displays scores, β-loadings, and regression coefficients obtained from fluorescence sensor, reflectance, transmittance, and absorbance hyperspectral analyses of *Tradescantia spathacea* (L.) Olof Swartz and *Tradescantia pallida* (Rose) D.R. Hunt. plants. **(A–D)** Variability and accumulation (%) based on three principal components. **(E–H)** β-Loading, corresponding to the sensors. **(I–L)** Regression coefficients for PC1-3 from 350 to 2500 nm. The green line represents PC1. The blue line represents PC2. The orange line represents PC3. The dashed red line delimits −0.75 to +0.75.

Figure 5A shows the variance captured by the principal components in the fluorescence data, with PC1 accounting for the majority of the variance (90.68%), followed by significantly smaller contributions from subsequent components. The reflectance data in Figure 5B show that PC1 was the dominant factor explaining 60.02% of the variability. The other components progressively contributed less, with PC2 and beyond explaining less than 20% of the variance. Figure 5C shows the transmittance data, with PC1 being pivotal and capturing 77.82% of the variance. PC2 also plays a more substantial role than the reflectance data, accounting for 15.10% of the variability. The absorbance variability in Figure 5D was primarily determined by PC1, which explained 74.06% of the total variance, followed by smaller yet significant contributions from PC2 and PC3.

Figure 5E–H presents the β-loadings across the time or wavelength range for each principal component, reflecting their weight in each spectral band. Figure 5I–L correlates these findings with the regression coefficients to indicate the influence of each wavelength on the respective spectral measurements. Figure 5F shows the leading wavelengths for PC1 located in the blue, green, red, NIR, SWIR1, and SWIR2 bands. The reflectance datasets for PC2 and PC3 also highlighted similar influential wavelengths, confirming their significance across the spectrum. Figure 5G shows the crucial wavelengths for the transmittance of PC1 in the blue and SWIR2 bands. The subsequent principal components, depicted in Figure 5J,K, corroborate the importance of these wavelengths, suggesting consistency in the influential spectral bands across different components.

The absorbance measurements in Figure 5H for PC1 show the selection of key wavelengths from the blue to the SWIR2 range. This is in line with the absorbance results for PC2 and PC3, as shown in Figure 5K,L, which further confirms the relevance of the wavelengths.

A comprehensive examination of these findings, in conjunction with the regression coefficients depicted in Figure 5I–L, provides a profound understanding of the most influential wavelengths across the reflectance, transmittance, and absorbance spectra. The variance explained by the principal components underscores the significant spectral regions that differentiate the studied variables (Figure 5A–L).

3.5. Hyperspectral Vegetation Index for Chlorophyll a Fluorescence, Reflectance, Transmittance, and Absorbance

Figure 6 shows a contour plot that maps the coefficient of determination (R^2) values from linear regression analyses, which evaluates the relationship between the levels of various biochemical compounds and chlorophyll fluorescence (ChlF) over a time logarithmic scale of 0.00001 to 1 s (Figure 6A–Q).

Figure 6A,B shows the R^2 values for chlorophyll *a* and chlorophyll *b*, respectively, measured in mg m^{-2}, over the time scale. Areas that changed from dark to light red indicate higher R^2 values, indicating stronger relationships at certain time points. In Figure 6C, the total chlorophyll (Chl*a*+*b*) content is plotted, showing the R^2 values over time, indicating the time points at which the fluorescence data best predicted the total chlorophyll content. Figure 6D–F show the contour maps for carotenoids, anthocyanins, and flavonoids, measured in mg m^{-2} and nmol cm^{-2}, respectively. These plots show the temporal patterns of the correlation between chlorophyll fluorescence and the levels of these compounds.

Figure 6G–I focus on the chlorophyll *a*/*b* ratio, chlorophyll *a*, and chlorophyll *b* on a mass basis (mg g^{-1}). The plots show different correlations, with some timeframes showing higher R^2 values. Figure 6J,K,L shows the total chlorophyll (Chl*a*+*b*), carotenoids, and anthocyanins per mass, highlighting the times when fluorescence is most indicative of the presence of these compounds. In Figure 6M,N, the maps for flavonoids and phenolic compounds, measured in μmol g^{-1} and mL L^{-1}, respectively, show areas of stronger and weaker correlations over the fluorescence time scale. Figure 6O shows the R^2 values for the DPPH assay, which is a measure of antioxidant activity, showing less variation over time.

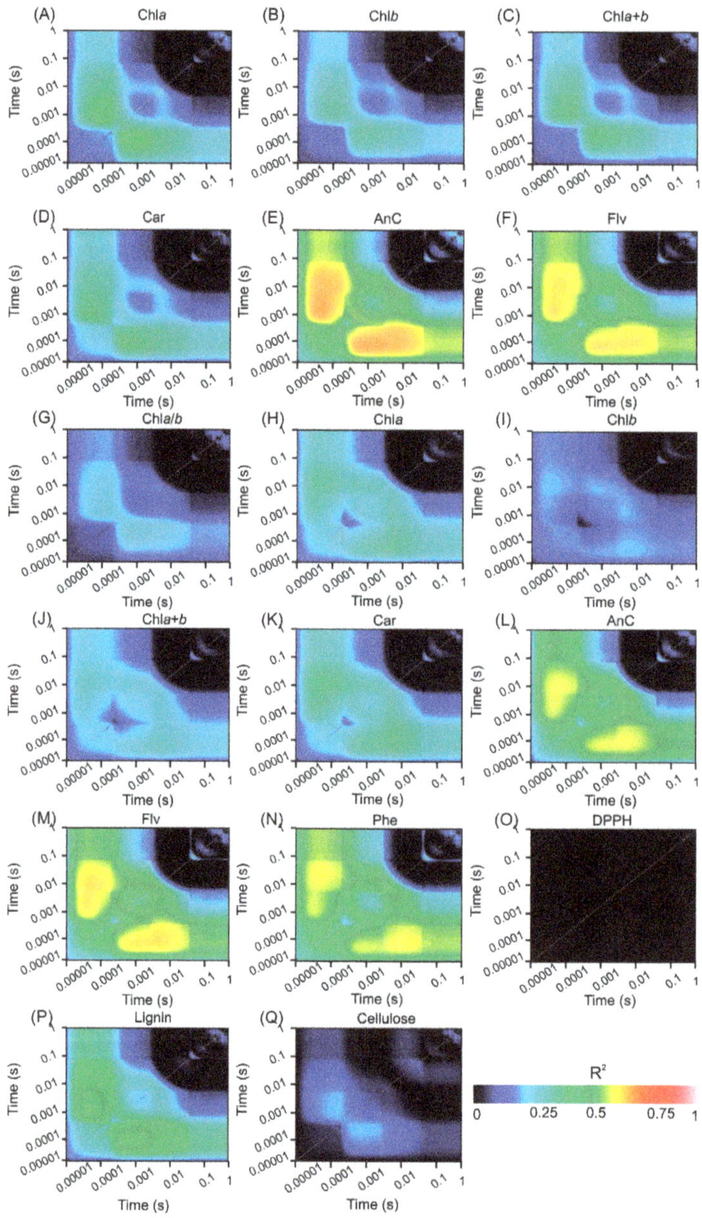

Figure 6. Count plot map of the coefficient of correlation (R^2) from the linear regression between the concentration of compounds and wavelength1 vs. wavelength2 from ChlF from 0.00001 to 1 s. (**A**) Chlorophyll *a* (mg m^{-2}). (**B**) Chlorophyll *b* (mg m^{-2}). (**C**) Total chlorophyll (*a*+*b*) (mg m^{-2}). (**D**) Carotenoids (mg m^{-2}). (**E**) Anthocyanins (nmol cm^{-2}). (**F**) Flavonoids (nmol cm^{-2}). (**G**) Chl *a*/*b* ratio. (**H**) Chlorophyll *a* (mg g^{-1}). (**I**) Chlorophyll *b* (mg g^{-1}). (**J**) Total chlorophyll (*a*+*b*) (mg g^{-1}). (**K**) carotenoids (mg g^{-1}). (**L**) Anthocyanins (μmol g^{-1}). (**M**) Flavonoids (μmol g^{-1}). (**N**) Phenolic compounds (mL L^{-1}). (**O**) DPPH. (**P**) Lignin (mg g^{-1}). (**Q**) Cellulose (nmol mg^{-1}). Dark blue to light red indicate increased associations. (n = 200).

Figure 6P,Q shows the lignin and cellulose contents, measured in mg g^{-1} and nmol mg^{-1}, respectively. This figure shows specific time intervals with strong relationships between fluorescence and compound levels.

Overall, these contour maps provide a visual representation of the temporal and quantitative relationships between chlorophyll fluorescence dynamics and the levels of various biochemical compounds in plant leaves. The gradation from dark to light red areas shows where the relationship is strongest, offering valuable insights into the moments when ChlF is the most informative of the compound levels.

Figure S1 shows a series of contour plots that illustrate the strength of the correlation, as indicated by the coefficient of determination (R^2), across two wavelengths (wavelength1 and wavelength2) for various biochemical compounds using hyperspectral reflectance data (Figure S1A–Q).

Figure S1A–C displays the relationships for chlorophyll *a*, chlorophyll *b*, and total chlorophyll (Chl*a*+*b*), respectively, measured in mg m^{-2}. Areas with higher R^2 values, which changed from dark blue to red, showed stronger correlations, especially for specific wavelength pairings. In Figure S1D, the R^2 values for the carotenoids (mg m^{-2}) are plotted, showing regions where the correlation between the reflectance at certain wavelengths and the carotenoid concentration is more evident. Figure S1E,F, which represents anthocyanins (nmol cm^{-2}) and flavonoids (nmol cm^{-2}), respectively, reveals the spectral zones in which the reflectance data have greater explanatory power for the concentrations of these compounds. The chlorophyll *a*/*b* ratio is shown in Figure S1G, with regions of stronger association indicating wavelengths that are more closely related to this particular ratio.

For chlorophyll *a*+*b*, on a mass basis (mg g^{-1}), Figure S1H,I illustrates how some wavelength combinations correlated more strongly with their concentrations. Figure S1J–L presents the R^2 values for total chlorophyll (Chl*a*+*b*), carotenoids, and anthocyanins per mass of plant material, showing key wavelengths where reflectance data correlated strongly with compound concentrations. For flavonoids (µmol g^{-1}) and phenolic compounds (mL L^{-1}), Figure S1M,N reveals significant spectral areas where the correlations between reflectance and concentration are strongest. Figure S1O, which shows DPPH, an antioxidant activity marker, showed a nearly uniform correlation across all wavelength pairs, indicating a less clear relationship in the reflectance data. Finally, Figure S1P,Q shows the correlation between lignin (mg g^{-1}) and cellulose (nmol mg^{-1}). Here, the selected wavelength pairings were shown to have a stronger association with the concentrations of these structural compounds.

Together, these contour plots reveal the complex relationships between reflectance at various wavelengths and the concentrations of different biochemical compounds, highlighting the possibility of using hyperspectral reflectance data to estimate compound concentrations in plant leaves. The change in colour from dark blue to red in the plots indicates the range of correlation strengths, with warmer colours indicating areas of greater predictive accuracy (Figure S1A–Q).

Figure S2 shows the correlations between different wavelengths of light passing through the plant tissues and their biochemical compounds. The R^2 values in the figure show which wavelengths of light are most related to the compound levels in plants.

Chlorophyll *a* and *b*, as shown in Figure S2A,B, had strong correlations with some visible and NIR wavelengths, especially when they interacted with specific NIR bands. Figure S2C shows that the transition from red to NIR light is highly predictive of the total chlorophyll (Chl*a*+*b*) content. As shown in Figure S2D, there were strong correlations between the levels of carotenoids at the edge of the visible and NIR light, indicating that these wavelengths affect carotenoid levels. The anthocyanin and flavonoid concentrations in Figure S2E,F exhibited sharp peaks and many correlations across different wavelengths, indicating that their spectral reflectance varied between species.

Figure S2G shows that some wavelengths were strongly related to the Chl *a*/*b* ratio, as indicated by the high R^2 values. Likewise, the chlorophyll *a* and *b* per mass in Figure S2H,I and the total chlorophyll (Chl*a*+*b*) per gram in Figure S2J had areas of high R^2 values, showing the wavelengths that tell us a lot about these chlorophyll levels.

The carotenoid and anthocyanin contents per mass, as shown in Figure S2K,L, exhibit a mixed pattern with strong hotspots, revealing the wavelengths that strongly reflect these compounds. Figure S2M,N, which shows flavonoids and phenolic compounds per gram, respectively, has high correlations in some spectral areas, revealing the regions that are most predictive of these compounds.

In contrast, the DPPH assay results in Figure S2O show no strong linear relationship between the wavelength and antioxidant activity, as seen in the even plot (Figure S2, see scale). Figure S2P,Q shows that lignin and cellulose have relatively high correlation values. These regions have wavelengths that are good indicators of the levels of these structural compounds.

Together, these findings demonstrate the complex links between spectral transmittance and biochemical compounds, providing a spectral signature that can be used to analyse plant constituents without destroying them. The colours in each plot show the strength of these links, with warmer colours showing regions of higher accuracy in the hyperspectral transmittance data (Figure S2A–Q).

Figure S3 shows how the absorbance data reveal how wavelengths and plant biochemical compounds interact according to their concentrations. Peaks with high correlations appear clearly in some spectral zones, showing that the absorbance at one wavelength is most useful for predicting the compound concentration when combined with another wavelength.

The chlorophyll *a* and *b* concentrations were highly correlated in the near-infrared region at approximately 700 nm. This trend is also true for the total chlorophyll content (Chl*a*+*b*), where wavelengths near 700 nm and shortwave infrared regions are strongly related to the chlorophyll content. The chlorophyll *a*/*b* ratio showed a similar correlation pattern, especially within the near-infrared range (Figure S3).

Carotenoid levels have noticeable correlations, especially within the overlap of the visible light range and the lower part of the near-infrared spectrum. Anthocyanin concentrations show a different pattern, with the highest correlations occurring over a wider range of wavelengths, indicating that multiple factors are involved in predicting anthocyanin levels through absorbance.

Flavonoid concentrations, shown in their contour plot, also had areas of high correlation, particularly in the interactions that occurred from the visible light range to the near-infrared spectrum. This finding implies a consistent effect of these wavelengths on the prediction of the flavonoid content (Figure S3).

The plots of structural compounds, such as lignin and cellulose, revealed that the concentrations of some wavelength combinations, especially those that cross from the near-infrared region to the shortwave infrared region, are somewhat related to their concentrations. In these contour plots, a range of correlations was observed, with the colour intensity representing the minor of the relationship. The gradients in these plots helped us identify the wavelength interactions that were most predictive of the concentrations of these important plant compounds (Figure S3A–Q).

3.6. Parameters Predicted by Biochemical Compounds

3.6.1. Calibration and Validation Models

Table S1 shows the statistical metrics from the PLSR models for different modalities in the comprehensive evaluation of spectrometric methods for estimating biochemical pigment parameters. The aim of this PLSR model was to compare the calibration and cross-validation results of chlorophyll and carotenoid predictions using fluorescence, reflectance, transmittance, and absorbance measurements in *Tradescantia* species (Table S1).

The fluorescence sensor calibration for chlorophyll a had an R^2 of 0.56, with a small decrease to 0.55 in cross-validation and corresponding RPDs of 1.21 and 1.19, indicating moderate model strength. Carotenoid predictions under fluorescence showed higher calibration accuracy, with an R^2 of 0.64 and an RPD of 1.31, which slightly decreased to an R^2 of 0.61 and an RPD of 1.26 in cross-validation, suggesting a more reliable model.

The reflectance measurements displayed similar trends, with chlorophyll a having an R^2 of 0.58 in calibration and 0.53 in cross-validation and carotenoids having R^2 values of 0.61 and 0.56, respectively, implying consistent performance but with some room for improvement in cross-validation. Transmittance was highly effective, especially for carotenoids, which showed an impressive calibration R^2 of 0.84. However, the cross-validation phase indicated a reduction in the predictive accuracy, with an R^2 of 0.59. The absorbance data for chlorophyll a showed a strong calibration R^2 value of 0.61, with a slight decrease to 0.56 in cross-validation. The carotenoids measured via absorbance had high calibration and cross-validation R^2 values of 0.64 and 0.59, confirming the effectiveness of this modality in evaluating pigment concentration (Table S1).

Statistical parameters such as slope, offset, RMSE, RPD, and bias present across these sensors provide a detailed understanding of each model's predictive power and potential limitations. Notably, anthocyanin concentration predictions stand out with an R^2 reaching up to 0.92 in calibration and maintained in cross-validation for the fluorescence sensor, highlighting the high quality of this modality for this specific pigment.

Overall, the data presented offer a thorough quantitative analysis of spectrometric techniques for the non-destructive estimation of biochemical compounds (Table S1).

3.6.2. Predicted

Table S2 shows the predictive performance of PLSR across different spectroscopic methods for estimating biochemical compound concentrations in the Tradescantia species. The table benchmarks performance metrics comprising the correlation coefficient (r), R-square for model fit (R^2), slope, offset, SEP, RMSEP, RPD, and bias, offering a precision selection for each sensor.

Fluorescence-based predictions revealed moderate predictability for chlorophyll *a*, with an R^2 value of 0.20. Carotenoids had limited accuracy, as indicated by an R^2 value of 0.13. Conversely, anthocyanins demonstrated a higher model fit, with an R^2 value of 0.42, suggesting enhanced predictability with this sensor.

Reflectance-based assessments delivered slightly superior R^2 values for chlorophyll *a* (Chl*a*) and carotenoids of 0.26 and 0.16, respectively, indicating moderate precision. Anthocyanins outperformed the other tested compounds, with an R^2 value of 0.52, indicating increased reliability. Transmittance measurements yielded analogous R^2 values for chlorophyll *a* and carotenoids of 0.23 and 0.10, respectively, highlighting the predictive limitations of this technique for these compounds. However, anthocyanins exhibited robust predictability with an R^2 of 0.52, mirroring the reflectance findings.

The absorbance modality improved the R^2 values for chlorophyll *a* and carotenoids to 0.24 and 0.12, respectively. The R^2 of 0.53 for anthocyanins confirmed the sensor's ability to predict these biochemical compounds. The RMSEP and RPD values across all sensors demonstrated variable precision and reliability, with higher RPD values indicating superior predictive capabilities, particularly for anthocyanins in most spectroscopic modalities. Bias values pinpointed the deviations from an ideal zero, accentuating opportunities for model refinement.

Further detailed examination of the specific compounds using the maximum factors in PLS revealed varying degrees of predictability. For example, phenolics (Phe) exhibited an R^2 of 0.53 with a PLS factor of 7, denoting a moderately strong fit, whereas lignin with the same factor showed a weak fit with an R^2 of 0.02. The anthocyanin content, as predicted by PLS with a factor of 5, showed a strong R^2 of 0.42 and an RPD of 1.31, indicating the reliability of the model.

A comparison of the predicted and observed values in four different scatter plots showed that absorbance was the most consistent method, with better correlations for some parameters than for chlorophyll fluorescence, reflectance, transmittance, and absorbance data. As shown in Figure 7, for chlorophyll a fluorescence, the R^2 values for chlorophyll *a* (Chl*a*)area and mass were moderate, indicating some correlation but with variability. The carotenoid area had a weak prediction, as shown by the low R^2 value, and this pattern continued for the Chl*a*/*b* ratio. However, flavonoid and anthocyanin mass measurements had higher predictability with relatively high R^2 values.

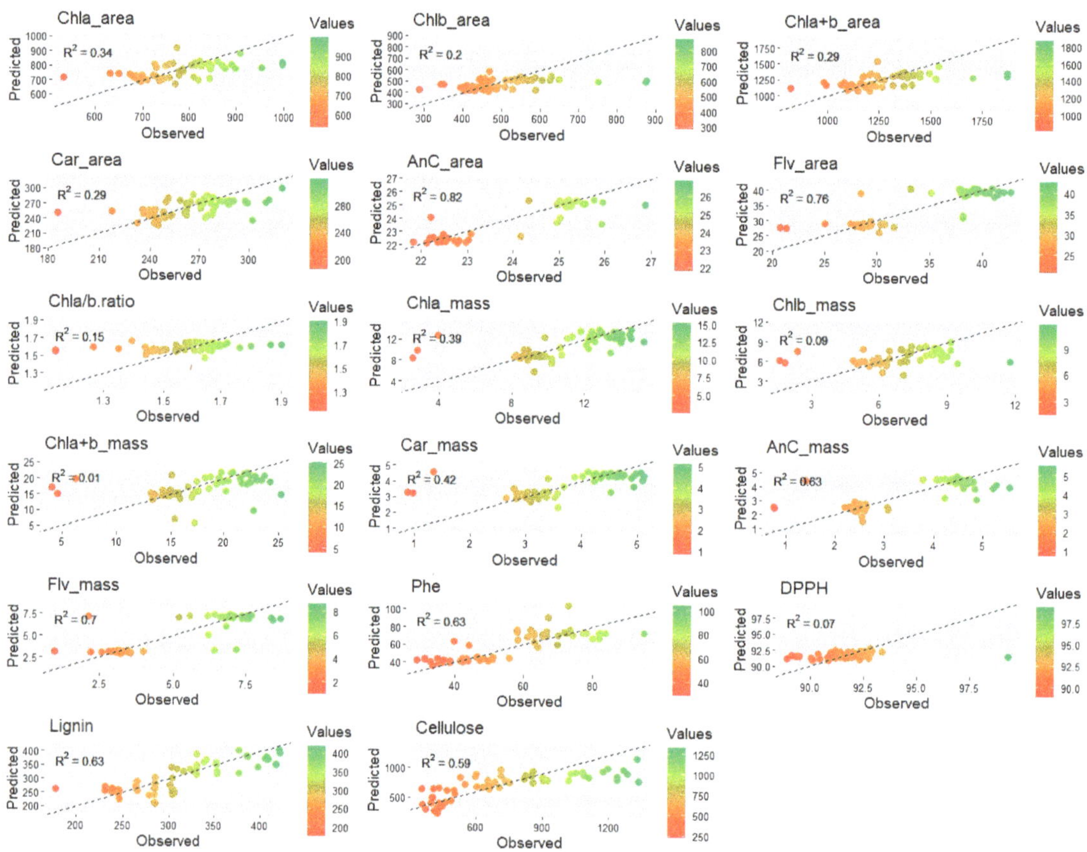

Figure 7. Observed vs. predicted data estimated by partial least squares regression (PLSR) with hyperspectral ChlF data. The R^2 value was adjusted using a linear equation. The red to green dots represent increased values, and the black dashed lines represent regression and 1:1 ratios, respectively. (n = 50).

As shown in Figure S4, the reflectance data were fairly consistent for the chlorophyll *a* area, with moderate R^2 values. Carotenoid area and anthocyanin mass also had reasonable predictive abilities. The reflectance was especially strong in predicting the flavonoid area and phenolic content, as shown by the higher R^2 values. However, the Chl*a*/*b* ratio and cellulose content were less reliably predicted by the reflectance, with lower R^2 values (Figure S4).

As shown in Figure S5, the overall transmittance data exhibited weaker correlations. However, anthocyanin mass predictions were much more accurate, unlike the Chl*a*/*b* ratio, which remained poorly predicted across all the sensors. The flavonoid mass maintained a strong relationship with the observed transmittance, similar to its effect on the reflectance. The lignin content had moderate predictability with respect to the transmittance (Figure S5).

Finally, the absorbance data in Figure S6 correlated moderately with the observed values for the chlorophyll *a* (Chl*a*)-based area, with slight improvements in the ability of the other methods to predict the carotenoid content. The anthocyanin mass predictions remained strong, and the trend of weak predictability for the Chl*a*/*b* ratio continued. The flavonoid mass showed a good correlation, although it was slightly lower than that of the transmittance data. The predictions for lignin and cellulose content by absorbance were moderate but improved compared to those for reflectance and transmittance (Figure S6).

The plots had greater green colour intensity, especially in the absorbance data, showing stronger correlations for specific parameters, suggesting that absorbance could be a more reliable predictor of biochemical content (Figures S4–S6).

4. Discussion

The combination of hyperspectral sensors in our study has proven to be highly effective in advancing the predictive capabilities of remote sensing and aligns with plant physiological research (Figures 1–7 and S1–S6). These sensors not only capture a wide spectrum of data but also facilitate a deeper understanding of biochemical and biophysical compound predictions that align physiological processes, revealing more than what meets the eye at the superficial level. By integrating hyperspectral vegetation indices (HVIs) with other analytical tools, we have deepened our analysis and demonstrated significant improvements in monitoring and predicting plant health and better understanding fingerprints that use different sensors for analyses.

This enhanced approach allowed us to construct a detailed spectrum of plant responses to pigments and structural compounds, which was corroborated by our findings that showed a positive impact on the accuracy of chlorophyll a fluorescence predictions following [22,48,49]. The integration of various sensor technologies in our research established a robust framework for conducting nuanced and comprehensive plant analyses, effectively extending the capabilities of traditional methods and providing new insights into remote sensing for environmental and agricultural analyses [2,26,50].

Our results underscore the benefits of sensor integration, validating the approach as a transformative step in the field of precision agriculture and improving environmental monitoring. This is a promising direction for future research, potentially leading to more refined strategies with SFI or non-imaging for crop management and ecological assessments [27,51–53].

The application of hyperspectral sensors in predicting chlorophyll a fluorescence parameters has recently gained considerable attention in remote-sensing research [22,26,27,39,40]. The interactions between light and plant tissues, including absorption, reflection, and transmission, provide valuable insights beyond the more accurate prediction of compounds in relation to integrated sphering or methods for analysing single sensors. They reveal crucial physiological processes and adaptive mechanisms.

Hyperspectral vegetation indices (HVIs) are powerful tools in precision agriculture because of their ability to measure a wide range of physiological, biochemical, and structural parameters in leaves of different thicknesses [18,22,54,55]. These indices enable the discrimination and monitoring of different environmental stresses, such as water and nitrogen deficiency, by analysing the spectral reflectance patterns of crops or studies on different plants [6,14,36,56,57].

For instance, certain narrow-band HVIs are particularly sensitive to changes in water and nitrogen levels, allowing for a nuanced assessment of crop responses under varying conditions of irrigation and fertilisation. The DATT index and HVI, which focus on near-infrared and red-edge wavelengths, have shown efficacy in correlating with chlorophyll content, whereas indices such as the double difference index (DD) are highly correlated with leaf gas exchange, highlighting their potential for identifying and differentiating between water and nitrogen stress levels in crops [20,25,38,58,59].

Moreover, HVIs can integrate data from chlorophyll fluorescence and hyperspectral measurements, providing a comprehensive map that identifies regions with specific biochemical and biophysical attributes. This integration is crucial for generating accurate maps that guide agricultural interventions, optimise resource use, and improve crop management strategies.

4.1. Hyperspectral and Principal Component Analysis by Reflectance, Transmittance, and Absorbance

Hyperspectral sensors provide detailed, in-depth spectral data, enabling the comprehensive analysis of plant biochemical and biophysical characteristics [23,60]. Reflectance data offer insights into the surface and internal structures of leaves, indicating variations in chlorophyll concentrations and potential cellular modifications. This finding aligns with previous research that demonstrated how changes in reflectance can signify physiological changes within plant tissues [7,27]. Similarly, transmittance data are critical for understanding how light diffuses within a leaf, thereby providing additional data points that enhance our understanding of leaf structure and function [61,62].

However, hyperspectral datasets require sophisticated data-reduction techniques, such as principal component analysis (PCA). In this study, PCA was effectively utilised to identify critical spectral regions that correlate with variations in chlorophyll a fluorescence, which is crucial for developing robust remote-sensing applications [59,63]. This precise identification significantly enhances the accuracy of the remote-sensing tools. Additionally, the predictive capabilities of these hyperspectral measurements were rigorously evaluated, focusing on the coefficients of variation and range of values obtained to ensure data reliability across a broad electromagnetic spectrum [15,64]. Our findings demonstrate that when these advanced passive sensor techniques are applied correctly, they provide detailed insights into plant health and photosynthetic performance, which are crucial for accurate plant phenotyping and health monitoring, as well as available fingerprints in leaves with different pigments and depths.

Finally, the integration of different sensor types, both hyperspectral and chlorophyll fluorescence, was explored to enhance the predictive modelling capabilities. This synergy allows broader application of the data, enhancing the ability to effectively predict and monitor various plant health parameters. This comprehensive approach underscores the potential of hyperspectral non-imaging to revolutionise plant physiological research and agricultural practices by providing a deeper understanding of plant dynamics at the molecular level with fast and accurate methods.

4.2. Predictive Modelling-Based Reflectance, Transmittance, and Absorbance

The fusion of hyperspectral data and partial least squares (PLS) modelling has emerged as a revolutionary approach in plant science, significantly enhancing our ability to predict and understand complex physiological traits [23,58,65,66]. The integration of reflectance, transmittance, and absorbance measurements with advanced multivariate algorithms, such as PLS, not only substantiates the vital role of these parameters as indicators of photosynthetic performance and the functionality of the electron transport chain but also boosts the precision of our predictive models.

Variable importance in projection (VIP) scores and hyperspectral vegetation indices (HVIs) are tools for isolating the most informative wavelengths from hyperspectral datasets, refining the predictive accuracy of models, and enabling a more detailed understanding of plant characteristics [22,23,67]. Such methodologies underscore the utility of identifying spectral regions that are rich in information and are directly related to the physiological state of plants [27,64,68,69].

The use of principal component analysis (PCA) to handle a substantial amount of large-scale hyperspectral data simplifies the complexity by identifying primary spectral regions indicative of changes in chlorophyll a fluorescence parameters. These spectral signatures are essential for crafting remote-sensing tools that can noninvasively assess plant properties, such as chlorophyll and potassium and nitrogen content [38,50].

The predictive models developed from this integrated approach support real-time with high-speed fluorescence lifetime imaging for analysis with a microscope and non-imaging spectroradiometer methods reinforce the power of remote sensing in broad-scale monitoring, conforming to contemporary perspectives that acknowledge the transformative potential of these technologies for global monitoring and productivity management. Real-time monitoring is pivotal for informed decision-making in agriculture, forestry, and other remote-sensing-dependent sectors, leading to enhanced productivity and sustainability [28,29]. In future applications, compressed FLIM has a striking advantage in acquiring a widefield lifetime image within a single camera snapshot. This eliminates motion artifacts and enables fast recording of biological events. There is also the possibility of associating other sensors for remote sensing [70].

However, it is essential to recognise that while our study has made significant strides in the application of hyperspectral and PLS models, further research is needed to extend these techniques to various plant species and environmental conditions.

Whole-spectrum models, such as PLSR, LDA, and SVR, have shown exceptional efficacy in classifying and predicting leaf properties, offering invaluable insights for interpreting chlorophyll a fluorescence data that are critical for JIP-test evaluations [30,58,71,72]. By leveraging the full spectrum of available data, these models ensure a comprehensive analysis of intricate leaf attributes, including the interactions between leaf optical properties and the complex chemistry of molecules in variegated leaves.

The combination of hyperspectral sensors and chlorophyll a fluorescence has proven to be highly effective in predicting biochemical compounds in Tradescantia leaves. Our findings, which align with other studies and perspectives, demonstrate the consistent effects of spectral resolution (SR) and sensor altitude on the accuracy of solar-induced fluorescence (SIF) quantification. In contrast to sub-nanometre sensors, which are precise but costly and difficult to operate, narrow-band sensors are more accessible and can be installed on drones and lightweight aircraft. We suggest that future studies utilise a combination of sensors, particularly when analysing plants and leaves with multiple overlapping pigments, to evaluate the efficiency of narrow-band sensors in producing SIF760 estimates. Furthermore, the incorporation of machine learning, deep learning, and other hyperspectral vegetation indices could significantly enhance these analyses.

5. Conclusions

This study has shown the comprehensive ability of hyperspectral remote sensing to estimate biochemical and structural compounds in Tradescantia species by utilising the intricate synergy between chlorophyll fluorescence, reflectance, transmittance, and absorbance measurements. The accuracy of the multivariate statistical models validates the effectiveness of these methods in remote-sensing applications, and the identified spectral regions, spanning from blue to shortwave infrared, were confirmed to be critical for the non-destructive evaluation of plant physiological status.

The strategic application of hyperspectral vegetation indices (HVIs) in selecting informative wavelengths has notably refined the results of partial least squares (PLS) regression models. The precision of these models attests to the significant role of hyperspectral sensors in the remote assessment of plant photosynthesis and health.

For broader remote sensing, the findings of this study can serve as a benchmark for the potential of also applying other passive sensors and hyperspectral imaging in diverse plant studies. Future research should extend these approaches to a larger variety of species and incorporate them into different field conditions. Such expansions could enhance the accuracy and generalisability of the models, as well as other methods that align with hyperspectral sensors, as tools in the fields of plant remote sensing and agricultural monitoring of variegatum leaves.

Supplementary Materials: The following supporting information can be downloaded at: https://www.mdpi.com/article/10.3390/rs16111910/s1, Table S1. Statistical metrics from the PLSR model in the calibration and cross-validation phases. R-square for model goodness-of-fit (R^2), slope, offset, root mean squared error (RMSE), ratio of performance to deviation (RPD), and bias to base models (a prediction using an independent sample coupled to calibrated models), biochemical compound from ChlF (single sensor), reflectance (single sensor), transmittance (single sensor), and absorbance (two sensors) hyperspectral data of *Tradescantia spathacea* (L.) Olof Swartz and *Tradescantia pallida* (Rose) D.R. Hunt. plants. (n = 150); Table S2. Statistical metrics of the PLSR model in the predicted phases. R-square for model goodness-of-fit (R^2), slope, offset, root mean squared error (RMSE), ratio of performance to deviation (RPD), and bias to base models (a prediction using an independent sample coupled to calibrated models), biochemical compound from ChlF (single sensor), reflectance (single sensor), transmittance (single sensor), and absorbance (two sensors) hyperspectral data of *Tradescantia spathacea* (L.) Olof Swartz and *Tradescantia pallida* (Rose) D.R. Hunt. plants. (n = 50); Figure S1. Count plot map of the coefficient of correlation (R^2) from the linear regression between the concentration compounds and wavelength1 vs. wavelength2 from hyperspectral reflectance from 350 to 2500 nm. (A) Chlorophyll *a* (mg m^{-2}). (B) Chlorophyll *b* (mg m^{-2}). (C) Total chlorophyll (*a*+*b*) (mg m^{-2}). (D) Carotenoids (mg m^{-2}). (E) Anthocyanins (nmol cm^{-2}). (F) Flavonoids (nmol cm^{-2}). (G) Chl *a*/*b* ratio. (H) Chlorophyll *a* (mg g^{-1}). (I) Chlorophyll *b* (mg g^{-1}). (J) Total chlorophyll (*a*+*b*) (mg g^{-1}). (K) Carotenoids (mg g^{-1}). (L) Anthocyanins (μmol g^{-1}). (M) Flavonoids (μmol g^{-1}). (N) Phenolic compounds (mL L^{-1}). (O) DPPH. (P) Lignin (mg g^{-1}). (Q) Cellulose (nmol mg^{-1}). Dark blue to light red indicate increased associations. (n = 200); Figure S2. Count plot map of the coefficient of correlation (R^2) from the linear regression between the concentration compounds and wavelength1 vs. wavelength2 from hyperspectral transmittance from 350 to 2500 nm. (A) Chlorophyll *a* (mg m^{-2}). (B) Chlorophyll *b* (mg m^{-2}). (C) Total chlorophyll (*a*+*b*) (mg m^{-2}). (D) Carotenoids (mg m^{-2}). (E) Anthocyanins (nmol cm^{-2}). (F) Flavonoids (nmol cm^{-2}). (G) Chl *a*/*b* ratio. (H) Chlorophyll *a* (mg g^{-1}). (I) Chlorophyll *b* (mg g^{-1}). (J) Total chlorophyll (*a*+*b*) (mg g^{-1}). (K) and carotenoids (mg g^{-1}). (L) Anthocyanins (μmol g^{-1}). (M) Flavonoids (μmol g^{-1}). (N) Phenolic compounds (mL L^{-1}). (O) DPPH. (P) Lignin (mg g^{-1}). (Q) Cellulose (nmol mg^{-1}). Dark blue to light red indicate increased associations. (n = 200); Figure S3. Count plot map of the coefficient of correlation (R^2) from the linear regression between the concentration of compounds and wavelength1 vs. wavelength2 from the hyperspectral absorbance from 350 to 2500 nm. (A) Chlorophyll *a* (mg m^{-2}). (B) Chlorophyll *b* (mg m^{-2}). (C) Total chlorophyll (*a*+*b*) (mg m^{-2}). (D) Carotenoids (mg m^{-2}). (E) Anthocyanins (nmol cm^{-2}). (F) Flavonoids (nmol cm^{-2}). (G) Chl *a*/*b* ratio. (H) Chlorophyll *a* (mg g^{-1}). (I) Chlorophyll *b* (mg g^{-1}). (J) Total chlorophyll (*a*+*b*) (mg g^{-1}). (K) Carotenoids (mg g^{-1}). (L) Anthocyanins (μmol g^{-1}). (M) Flavonoids (μmol g^{-1}). (N) Phenolic compounds (mL L^{-1}). (O) DPPH. (P) Lignin (mg g^{-1}). (Q) Cellulose (nmol mg^{-1}). Dark blue to light red indicate increased associations. (n = 200); Figure S4. The observed vs. predicted data were estimated using partial least squares regression (PLSR) with hyperspectral reflectance data. The R^2 value was adjusted using a linear equation. Dotted (red) lines represent regression and 1:1, respectively. (n = 50); Figure S5. Observed vs. predicted data estimated by partial least squares regression (PLSR) with hyperspectral transmittance data. The R^2 value was adjusted using a linear equation. The dotted (red) lines represent regression and 1:1, respectively. (n = 50); Figure S6. Observed vs. predicted data estimated by partial least squares regression (PLSR) of hyperspectral absorbance data. The R^2 value was adjusted using a linear equation. The dotted (red) lines represent regression and 1:1, respectively. (n = 50).

Author Contributions: Conceptualisation, R.F.; data curation, R.F. and J.A.M.D.; formal analysis, R.F., W.C.A., J.A.M.D. and M.R.N.; funding acquisition, R.F., R.B.d.O., M.L.C., J.A.M.D. and M.R.N.; investigation, R.F., W.C.A. and M.R.N.; methodology, R.F., R.B.d.O., M.L.C., W.C.A., J.A.M.D. and M.R.N.; project administration, R.F. and M.R.N.; resources, R.F.; software, R.F., R.B.d.O., M.L.C., J.A.M.D. and M.R.N.; supervision, R.F. and M.R.N.; validation, R.F., R.B.d.O., M.L.C., W.C.A. and M.R.N.; visualisation, R.F.; writing—original draft, R.F., R.B.d.O., M.L.C., W.C.A., J.A.M.D. and M.R.N.; writing—review and editing, R.F., R.B.d.O., M.L.C., W.C.A., J.A.M.D. and M.R.N. All authors have read and agreed to the published version of the manuscript.

Funding: National Council for Scientific and Technological Development: Programa de Apoio à Fixação de Jovens Doutores no Brasil 168180/2022−7; Fundação Araucária: CP 19/2022—Jovens Doutores; Coordenação de Aperfeiçoamento de Pessoal de Nível Superior: 001; Fundação de Amparo à Pesquisa do Estado de São Paulo, FAPESP pn 2021/05129−8 for sensor financial support. CEAGRE—Centro de Excelência em Agricultura Exponencial for financial support.

Data Availability Statement: Data are contained within the article and Supplementary Materials.

Acknowledgments: We thank Programa de Pós-Graduação em Agronomia (PGA-UEM) at the State University of Maringá and FAPESP for their support.

Conflicts of Interest: The authors declare no conflicts of interest. The funders had no role in the study design, collection, analyses, interpretation of the data, writing of the manuscript, or decision to publish the results.

References

1. Cotrozzi, L.; Lorenzini, G.; Nali, C.; Pellegrini, E.; Saponaro, V.; Hoshika, Y.; Arab, L.; Rennenberg, H.; Paoletti, E. Hyperspectral Reflectance of Light-Adapted Leaves Can Predict Both Dark- and Light-Adapted Chl Fluorescence Parameters, and the Effects of Chronic Ozone Exposure on Date Palm (*Phoenix dactylifera*). *Int. J. Mol. Sci.* **2020**, *21*, 6441. [CrossRef] [PubMed]
2. Kycko, M.; Zagajewski, B.; Lavender, S.; Dabija, A. In Situ Hyperspectral Remote Sensing for Monitoring of Alpine Trampled and Recultivated Species. *Remote Sens.* **2019**, *11*, 1296. [CrossRef]
3. Vilfan, N.; van der Tol, C.; Muller, O.; Rascher, U.; Verhoef, W. Fluspect-B: A Model for Leaf Fluorescence, Reflectance and Transmittance Spectra. *Remote Sens. Environ.* **2016**, *186*, 596–615. [CrossRef]
4. Ahmed, H.F.A.; Elnaggar, S.; Abdel-Wahed, G.A.; Taha, R.S.; Ahmad, A.; Al-Selwey, W.A.; Ahmed, H.M.H.; Khan, N.; Seleiman, M.F. Induction of Systemic Resistance in *Hibiscus sabdariffa* Linn. to Control Root Rot and Wilt Diseases Using Biotic and Abiotic Inducers. *Biology* **2023**, *12*, 789. [CrossRef] [PubMed]
5. Prabhakara, K.; Dean Hively, W.; McCarty, G.W. Evaluating the Relationship between Biomass, Percent Groundcover and Remote Sensing Indices across Six Winter Cover Crop Fields in Maryland, United States. *Int. J. Appl. Earth Obs. Geoinf.* **2015**, *39*, 88–102. [CrossRef]
6. de Oliveira, M.R.R.; Ribeiro, S.G.; Mas, J.F.; dos Santos Teixeira, A. Advances in Hyperspectral Sensing in Agriculture: A Review. *Rev. Cienc. Agron.* **2020**, *51*, e20207739. [CrossRef]
7. Kior, A.; Sukhov, V.; Sukhova, E. Application of Reflectance Indices for Remote Sensing of Plants and Revealing Actions of Stressors. *Photonics* **2021**, *8*, 582. [CrossRef]
8. Shi, M.; Gu, J.; Wu, H.; Rauf, A.; Emran, T.B.; Khan, Z.; Mitra, S.; Aljohani, A.S.M.; Alhumaydhi, F.A.; Al-Awthan, Y.S.; et al. Phytochemicals, Nutrition, Metabolism, Bioavailability, and Health Benefits in Lettuce: A Comprehensive Review. *Antioxidants* **2022**, *11*, 1158. [CrossRef] [PubMed]
9. Kaňa, R.; Špundová, M.; Ilík, P.; Lazár, D.; Klem, K.; Tomek, P.; Nauš, J.; Prášil, O. Effect of Herbicide Clomazone on Photosynthetic Processes in Primary Barley (*Hordeum vulgare* L.) Leaves. *Pestic. Biochem. Physiol.* **2004**, *78*, 161–170. [CrossRef]
10. Andreeva, A.; Stoitchkova, K.; Busheva, M.; Apostolova, E. Changes in the Energy Distribution between Chlorophyll-Protein Complexes of Thylakoid Membranes from Pea Mutants with Modified Pigment Content. I. Changes Due to the Modified Pigment Content. *J. Photochem. Photobiol. B Biol.* **2003**, *70*, 153–162. [CrossRef] [PubMed]
11. Falcioni, R.; Antunes, W.C.; Demattê, J.A.M.; Nanni, M.R. Biophysical, Biochemical, and Photochemical Analyses Using Reflectance Hyperspectroscopy and Chlorophyll a Fluorescence Kinetics in Variegated Leaves. *Biology* **2023**, *12*, 704. [CrossRef] [PubMed]
12. Cheng, T.; Song, R.; Li, D.; Zhou, K.; Zheng, H.; Yao, X.; Tian, Y.; Cao, W.; Zhu, Y. Spectroscopic Estimation of Biomass in Canopy Components of Paddy Rice Using Dry Matter and Chlorophyll Indices. *Remote Sens.* **2017**, *9*, 319. [CrossRef]
13. Li, K.-Y.; de Lima, R.; Burnside, N.G.; Vahtmäe, E.; Kutser, T.; Sepp, K.; Cabral Pinheiro, V.H.; Yang, M.-D.; Vain, A.; Sepp, K. Toward Automated Machine Learning-Based Hyperspectral Image Analysis in Crop Yield and Biomass Estimation. *Remote Sens.* **2022**, *14*, 1114. [CrossRef]
14. Aneece, I.; Thenkabail, P.S. Classifying Crop Types Using Two Generations of Hyperspectral Sensors (Hyperion and DESIS) with Machine Learning on the Cloud. *Remote Sens.* **2021**, *13*, 4704. [CrossRef]
15. da Silva Junior, C.A.; Nanni, M.R.; Shakir, M.; Teodoro, P.E.; de Oliveira-Júnior, J.F.; Cezar, E.; de Gois, G.; Lima, M.; Wojciechowski, J.C.; Shiratsuchi, L.S. Soybean Varieties Discrimination Using Non-Imaging Hyperspectral Sensor. *Infrared Phys. Technol.* **2018**, *89*, 338–350. [CrossRef]
16. Baio, F.H.R.; Santana, D.C.; Teodoro, L.P.R.; de Oliveira, I.C.; Gava, R.; de Oliveira, J.L.G.; da Silva Junior, C.A.; Teodoro, P.E.; Shiratsuchi, L.S. Maize Yield Prediction with Machine Learning, Spectral Variables and Irrigation Management. *Remote Sens.* **2023**, *15*, 79. [CrossRef]
17. Belwalkar, A.; Poblete, T.; Longmire, A.; Hornero, A.; Hernandez-Clemente, R.; Zarco-Tejada, P.J. Evaluation of SIF Retrievals from Narrow-Band and Sub-Nanometer Airborne Hyperspectral Imagers Flown in Tandem: Modelling and Validation in the Context of Plant Phenotyping. *Remote Sens. Environ.* **2022**, *273*, 112986. [CrossRef]

18. Fernandes, A.M.; Fortini, E.A.; Müller, L.A.d.C.; Batista, D.S.; Vieira, L.M.; Silva, P.O.; do Amaral, C.H.; Poethig, R.S.; Otoni, W.C. Leaf Development Stages and Ontogenetic Changes in Passionfruit (*Passiflora edulis* Sims.) Are Detected by Narrowband Spectral Signal. *J. Photochem. Photobiol. B Biol.* **2020**, *209*, 111931. [CrossRef]
19. Shurygin, B.; Chivkunova, O.; Solovchenko, O.; Solovchenko, A.; Dorokhov, A.; Smirnov, I.; Astashev, M.E.; Khort, D. Comparison of the Non-Invasive Monitoring of Fresh-Cut Lettuce Condition with Imaging Reflectance Hyperspectrometer and Imaging PAM-Fluorimeter. *Photonics* **2021**, *8*, 425. [CrossRef]
20. Jia, M.; Li, D.; Colombo, R.; Wang, Y.; Wang, X.; Cheng, T.; Zhu, Y.; Yao, X.; Xu, C.; Ouer, G.; et al. Quantifying Chlorophyll Fluorescence Parameters from Hyperspectral Reflectance at the Leaf Scale under Various Nitrogen Treatment Regimes in Winter Wheat. *Remote Sens.* **2019**, *11*, 2838. [CrossRef]
21. Sobejano-Paz, V.; Mikkelsen, T.N.; Baum, A.; Mo, X.; Liu, S.; Köppl, C.J.; Johnson, M.S.; Gulyas, L.; García, M. Hyperspectral and Thermal Sensing of Stomatal Conductance, Transpiration, and Photosynthesis for Soybean and Maize under Drought. *Remote Sens.* **2020**, *12*, 3182. [CrossRef]
22. Falcioni, R.; Antunes, W.C.; de Oliveira, R.B.; Chicati, M.L.; Demattê, J.A.M.; Nanni, M.R. Assessment of Combined Reflectance, Transmittance, and Absorbance Hyperspectral Sensors for Prediction of Chlorophyll a Fluorescence Parameters. *Remote Sens.* **2023**, *15*, 5067. [CrossRef]
23. Falcioni, R.; Gonçalves, J.V.F.; de Oliveira, K.M.; de Oliveira, C.A.; Reis, A.S.; Crusiol, L.G.T.; Furlanetto, R.H.; Antunes, W.C.; Cezar, E.; de Oliveira, R.B.; et al. Chemometric Analysis for the Prediction of Biochemical Compounds in Leaves Using UV-VIS-NIR-SWIR Hyperspectroscopy. *Plants* **2023**, *12*, 3424. [CrossRef]
24. Falcioni, R.; dos Santos, G.L.A.A.; Crusiol, L.G.T.; Antunes, W.C.; Chicati, M.L.; de Oliveira, R.B.; Demattê, J.A.M.; Nanni, M.R. Non-Invasive Assessment, Classification, and Prediction of Biophysical Parameters Using Reflectance Hyperspectroscopy. *Plants* **2023**, *12*, 2526. [CrossRef]
25. Asner, G.P.; Jones, M.O.; Martin, R.E.; Knapp, D.E.; Hughes, R.F. Remote Sensing of Native and Invasive Species in Hawaiian Forests. *Remote Sens. Environ.* **2008**, *112*, 1912–1926. [CrossRef]
26. Falcioni, R.; Antunes, W.C.; Demattê, J.A.M.; Nanni, M.R. Reflectance Spectroscopy for the Classification and Prediction of Pigments in Agronomic Crops. *Plants* **2023**, *12*, 2347. [CrossRef] [PubMed]
27. Crusiol, L.G.T.; Nanni, M.R.; Furlanetto, R.H.; Sibaldelli, R.N.R.; Sun, L.; Gonçalves, S.L.; Foloni, J.S.S.; Mertz-Henning, L.M.; Nepomuceno, A.L.; Neumaier, N.; et al. Assessing the Sensitive Spectral Bands for Soybean Water Status Monitoring and Soil Moisture Prediction Using Leaf-Based Hyperspectral Reflectance. *Agric. Water Manag.* **2023**, *277*, 108089. [CrossRef]
28. Boshkovski, B.; Doupis, G.; Zapolska, A.; Kalaitzidis, C.; Koubouris, G. Hyperspectral Imagery Detects Water Deficit and Salinity Effects on Photosynthesis and Antioxidant Enzyme Activity of Three Greek Olive Varieties. *Sustainability* **2022**, *14*, 1432. [CrossRef]
29. Crusiol, L.G.T.; Sun, L.; Sun, Z.; Chen, R.; Wu, Y.; Ma, J.; Song, C. In-Season Monitoring of Maize Leaf Water Content Using Ground-Based and UAV-Based Hyperspectral Data. *Sustainability* **2022**, *14*, 9039. [CrossRef]
30. Crusiol, L.G.T.; Sun, L.; Sibaldelli, R.N.R.; Junior, V.F.; Furlaneti, W.X.; Chen, R.; Sun, Z.; Wuyun, D.; Chen, Z.; Nanni, M.R.; et al. Strategies for Monitoring Within-Field Soybean Yield Using Sentinel-2 Vis-NIR-SWIR Spectral Bands and Machine Learning Regression Methods. *Precis. Agric.* **2022**, *23*, 1093–1123. [CrossRef]
31. Wójtowicz, J.; Grzyb, J.; Szach, J.; Mazur, R.; Gieczewska, K.B. Bean and Pea Plastoglobules Change in Response to Chilling Stress. *Int. J. Mol. Sci.* **2021**, *22*, 11895. [CrossRef] [PubMed]
32. Nalepa, J. Recent Advances in Multi- and Hyperspectral Image Analysis. *Sensors* **2021**, *21*, 6002. [CrossRef] [PubMed]
33. Ge, Y.; Atefi, A.; Zhang, H.; Miao, C.; Ramamurthy, R.K.; Sigmon, B.; Yang, J.; Schnable, J.C. High-Throughput Analysis of Leaf Physiological and Chemical Traits with VIS–NIR–SWIR Spectroscopy: A Case Study with a Maize Diversity Panel. *Plant Methods* **2019**, *15*, 66. [CrossRef] [PubMed]
34. Ferri, C.P.; Formaggio, A.R.; Schiavinato, M.A. Narrow Band Spectral Indexes for Chlorophyll Determination in Soybean Canopies [*Glycine max* (L.) Merril]. *Braz. J. Plant Physiol.* **2004**, *16*, 131–136. [CrossRef]
35. Ling, B.; Goodin, D.G.; Raynor, E.J.; Joern, A. Hyperspectral Analysis of Leaf Pigments and Nutritional Elements in Tallgrass Prairie Vegetation. *Front. Plant Sci.* **2019**, *10*, 142. [CrossRef] [PubMed]
36. Xu, X.; Yang, G.; Yang, X.; Li, Z.; Feng, H.; Xu, B.; Zhao, X. Monitoring Ratio of Carbon to Nitrogen (C/N) in Wheat and Barley Leaves by Using Spectral Slope Features with Branch-and-Bound Algorithm. *Sci. Rep.* **2018**, *8*, 10034. [CrossRef] [PubMed]
37. Thornley, R.H.; Verhoef, A.; Gerard, F.F.; White, K. The Feasibility of Leaf Reflectance-Based Taxonomic Inventories and Diversity Assessments of Species-Rich Grasslands: A Cross-Seasonal Evaluation Using Waveband Selection. *Remote Sens.* **2022**, *14*, 2310. [CrossRef]
38. Pandey, P.; Ge, Y.; Stoerger, V.; Schnable, J.C. High Throughput In Vivo Analysis of Plant Leaf Chemical Properties Using Hyperspectral Imaging. *Front. Plant Sci.* **2017**, *8*, 1348. [CrossRef] [PubMed]
39. Wang, L.; Chang, Q.; Li, F.; Yan, L.; Huang, Y.; Wang, Q.; Luo, L. Effects of Growth Stage Development on Paddy Rice Leaf Area Index Prediction Models. *Remote Sens.* **2019**, *11*, 361. [CrossRef]
40. Fu, Y.; Yang, G.; Song, X.; Li, Z.; Xu, X.; Feng, H.; Zhao, C. Improved Estimation of Winter Wheat Aboveground Biomass Using Multiscale Textures Extracted from UAV-Based Digital Images and Hyperspectral Feature Analysis. *Remote Sens.* **2021**, *13*, 581. [CrossRef]

41. Wang, H.; Mortensen, A.K.; Mao, P.; Boelt, B.; Gislum, R. Estimating the Nitrogen Nutrition Index in Grass Seed Crops Using a UAV-Mounted Multispectral Camera. *Int. J. Remote Sens.* **2019**, *40*, 2467–2482. [CrossRef]
42. Bendig, J.; Bolten, A.; Bennertz, S.; Broscheit, J.; Eichfuss, S.; Bareth, G. Estimating Biomass of Barley Using Crop Surface Models (CSMs) Derived from UAV-Based RGB Imaging. *Remote Sens.* **2014**, *6*, 10395–10412. [CrossRef]
43. Gitelson, A.; Solovchenko, A.; Viña, A. Foliar Absorption Coefficient Derived from Reflectance Spectra: A Gauge of the Efficiency of in Situ Light-Capture by Different Pigment Groups. *J. Plant Physiol.* **2020**, *254*, 153277. [CrossRef] [PubMed]
44. Lichtenthaler, H.K.; Wellburn, A.R. Determinations of Total Carotenoids and Chlorophylls a and b of Leaf Extracts in Different Solvents. *Biochem. Soc. Trans.* **1983**, *11*, 591–592. [CrossRef]
45. Llorach, R.; Martínez-Sánchez, A.; Tomás-Barberán, F.A.; Gil, M.I.; Ferreres, F. Characterisation of Polyphenols and Antioxidant Properties of Five Lettuce Varieties and Escarole. *Food Chem.* **2008**, *108*, 1028–1038. [CrossRef] [PubMed]
46. Ragaee, S. Antioxidant Activity and Nutrient Composition of Selected Cereals for Food Use. *Food Chem.* **2006**, *98*, 32–38. [CrossRef]
47. Zar, J.H. *Biostatistical Analysis*, 5th ed.; Pearson Education: Upper Saddle River, NJ, USA, 2010; ISBN 0-13-100846-3.
48. Pearcy, R.W.; Muraoka, H.; Valladares, F. Crown Architecture in Sun and Shade Environments: Assessing Function and Trade-Offs with a Three-Dimensional Simulation Model. *New Phytol.* **2005**, *166*, 791–800. [CrossRef] [PubMed]
49. Nielsen, S.L.; Nielsen, H.D. Pigments, Photosynthesis and Photoinhibition in Two Amphibious Plants: Consequences of Varying Carbon Availability. *New Phytol.* **2006**, *170*, 311–319. [CrossRef]
50. Yendrek, C.R.; Tomaz, T.; Montes, C.M.; Cao, Y.; Morse, A.M.; Brown, P.J.; McIntyre, L.M.; Leakey, A.D.B.; Ainsworth, E.A. High-Throughput Phenotyping of Maize Leaf Physiological and Biochemical Traits Using Hyperspectral Reflectance. *Plant Physiol.* **2017**, *173*, 614–626. [CrossRef] [PubMed]
51. Saad, A.G.; Pék, Z.; Szuvandzsiev, P.; Gehad, D.H.; Helyes, L. Determination of Carotenoids in Tomato Products Using Vis/NIR Spectroscopy. *J. Microbiol. Biotechnol. Food Sci.* **2017**, *7*, 27–31. [CrossRef]
52. Pontius, J.; Martin, M.; Plourde, L.; Hallett, R. Ash Decline Assessment in Emerald Ash Borer-Infested Regions: A Test of Tree-Level, Hyperspectral Technologies. *Remote Sens. Environ.* **2008**, *112*, 2665–2676. [CrossRef]
53. Apan, A.; Held, A.; Phinn, S.; Markley, J. Formulation and Assessment of Narrow-Band Vegetation Indices from EO-1 Hyperion Imagery for Discriminating Sugarcane Disease. In Proceedings of the 2003 Spatial Sciences Institute Biennial Conference: Spatial Knowledge Without Boundaries (SSC2003), Canberra, Australia, 22–27 September 2003; pp. 1–13.
54. Yoosefzadeh-Najafabadi, M.; Tulpan, D.; Eskandari, M. Using Hybrid Artificial Intelligence and Evolutionary Optimization Algorithms for Estimating Soybean Yield and Fresh Biomass Using Hyperspectral Vegetation Indices. *Remote Sens.* **2021**, *13*, 2555. [CrossRef]
55. Chen, J.; de Hoogh, K.; Gulliver, J.; Hoffmann, B.; Hertel, O.; Ketzel, M.; Bauwelinck, M.; van Donkelaar, A.; Hvidtfeldt, U.A.; Katsouyanni, K.; et al. A Comparison of Linear Regression, Regularization, and Machine Learning Algorithms to Develop Europe-Wide Spatial Models of Fine Particles and Nitrogen Dioxide. *Environ. Int.* **2019**, *130*, 104934. [CrossRef] [PubMed]
56. Wang, D.; Cao, W.; Zhang, F.; Li, Z.; Xu, S.; Wu, X. A Review of Deep Learning in Multiscale Agricultural Sensing. *Remote Sens.* **2022**, *14*, 559. [CrossRef]
57. Thenkabail, P.; Gumma, M.K.; Teluguntla, P.; Ahmed, M.I. Hyperspectral Remote Sensing of Vegetation and Agricultural Crops. *Photogramm. Eng. Remote Sens.* **2014**, *80*, 697–723.
58. Fan, K.; Li, F.; Chen, X.; Li, Z.; Mulla, D.J. Nitrogen Balance Index Prediction of Winter Wheat by Canopy Hyperspectral Transformation and Machine Learning. *Remote Sens.* **2022**, *14*, 3504. [CrossRef]
59. Feng, W.; Yao, X.; Tian, Y.; Cao, W.; Zhu, Y. Monitoring Leaf Pigment Status with Hyperspectral Remote Sensing in Wheat. *Aust. J. Agric. Res.* **2008**, *59*, 748–760. [CrossRef]
60. Nagler, P.L.; Inoue, Y.; Glenn, E.P.; Russ, A.L.; Daughtry, C.S.T. Cellulose Absorption Index (CAI) to Quantify Mixed Soil–Plant Litter Scenes. *Remote Sens. Environ.* **2003**, *87*, 310–325. [CrossRef]
61. Galvão, L.S.; Formaggio, A.R.; Tisot, D.A. Discrimination of Sugarcane Varieties in Southeastern Brazil with EO-1 Hyperion Data. *Remote Sens. Environ.* **2005**, *94*, 523–534. [CrossRef]
62. Prats-Mateu, B.; Felhofer, M.; de Juan, A.; Gierlinger, N. Multivariate Unmixing Approaches on Raman Images of Plant Cell Walls: New Insights or Overinterpretation of Results? *Plant Methods* **2018**, *14*, 52. [CrossRef] [PubMed]
63. Serbin, S.P.; Dillaway, D.N.; Kruger, E.L.; Townsend, P.A. Leaf Optical Properties Reflect Variation in Photosynthetic Metabolism and Its Sensitivity to Temperature. *J. Exp. Bot.* **2012**, *63*, 489–502. [CrossRef] [PubMed]
64. Chicati, M.S.; Nanni, M.R.; Chicati, M.L.; Furlanetto, R.H.; Cezar, E.; De Oliveira, R.B. Hyperspectral Remote Detection as an Alternative to Correlate Data of Soil Constituents. *Remote Sens. Appl. Soc. Environ.* **2019**, *16*, 100270. [CrossRef]
65. Zimmer, G.F.; Santos, R.O.; Teixeira, I.D.; Schneider, R. de C. de S.; Helfer, G.A.; Costa, A. Ben Rapid Quantification of Constituents in Tobacco by NIR Fiber-optic Probe. *J. Chemom.* **2020**, *34*, e3303. [CrossRef]
66. Jensen, J.S.; Egebo, M.; Meyer, A.S. Identification of Spectral Regions for the Quantification of Red Wine Tannins with Fourier Transform Mid-Infrared Spectroscopy. *J. Agric. Food Chem.* **2008**, *56*, 3493–3499. [CrossRef] [PubMed]
67. Zhou, Q.; Yu, L.; Zhang, X.; Liu, Y.; Zhan, Z.; Ren, L.; Luo, Y. Fusion of UAV Hyperspectral Imaging and LiDAR for the Early Detection of EAB Stress in Ash and a New EAB Detection Index NDVI(776,678). *Remote Sens.* **2022**, *14*, 2428. [CrossRef]
68. Iqbal, I.M.; Balzter, H.; Bareen, F.E.; Shabbir, A. Identifying the Spectral Signatures of Invasive and Native Plant Species in Two Protected Areas of Pakistan through Field Spectroscopy. *Remote Sens.* **2021**, *13*, 4009. [CrossRef]

69. Bloem, E.; Gerighausen, H.; Chen, X.; Schnug, E. The Potential of Spectral Measurements for Identifying Glyphosate Application to Agricultural Fields. *Agronomy* **2020**, *10*, 1409. [CrossRef]
70. Ma, Y.; Lee, Y.; Best-Popescu, C.; Gao, L. High-Speed Compressed-Sensing Fluorescence Lifetime Imaging Microscopy of Live Cells. *Proc. Natl. Acad. Sci. USA* **2021**, *118*, e2004176118. [CrossRef] [PubMed]
71. Chen, S.; Zhang, F.; Ning, J.; Liu, X.; Zhang, Z.; Yang, S. Predicting the Anthocyanin Content of Wine Grapes by NIR Hyperspectral Imaging. *Food Chem.* **2015**, *172*, 788–793. [CrossRef] [PubMed]
72. El-Hendawy, S.; Al-Suhaibani, N.; Mubushar, M.; Tahir, M.U.; Marey, S.; Refay, Y.; Tola, E. Combining Hyperspectral Reflectance and Multivariate Regression Models to Estimate Plant Biomass of Advanced Spring Wheat Lines in Diverse Phenological Stages under Salinity Conditions. *Appl. Sci.* **2022**, *12*, 1983. [CrossRef]

remote sensing

MDPI

Article

Estimating Plant Nitrogen by Developing an Accurate Correlation between VNIR-Only Vegetation Indexes and the Normalized Difference Nitrogen Index

Yücel Çimtay

Computer Engineering, TED University, Ankara 06420, Turkey; yucel.cimtay@tedu.edu.tr

Abstract: Nitrogen is crucial for plant physiology due to the fact that plants consume a significant amount of nitrogen during the development period. Nitrogen supports the root, leaf, stem, branch, shoot and fruit development of plants. At the same time, it also increases flowering. To monitor the vegetation nitrogen concentration, one of the best indicators developed in the literature is the Normalized Difference Nitrogen Index (NDNI), which is based on the usage of the spectral bands of 1510 and 1680 nm from the Short-Wave Infrared (SWIR) region of the electromagnetic spectrum. However, the majority of remote sensing sensors, like cameras and/or satellites, do not have an SWIR sensor due to high costs. Many vegetation indexes, like NDVI, EVI and MNLI, have also been developed in the VNIR region to monitor the greenness and health of the crops. However, these indexes are not very well correlated to the nitrogen content. Therefore, in this study, a novel method is developed which transforms the estimated VNIR band indexes to NDNI by using a regression method between a group of VNIR indexes and NDNI. Training is employed by using VNIR band indexes as the input and NDNI as the output, both of which are calculated from the same location. After training, an overall correlation of 0.93 was achieved. Therefore, by using only VNIR band sensors, it is possible to estimate the nitrogen content of the plant with high accuracy.

Keywords: agriculture; land cover; remote sensing; fertilizer; yield

1. Introduction

Numerous physiological activities in leaves, including photosynthesis, respiration, and transpiration, are primarily regulated by nitrogen [1–3]. Nitrogen is also closely related to chlorophyll concentration, light utilization efficiency, and net crop production [4–6]. In addition to frequently being a limiting factor for plant growth [7–9], nitrogen is a crucial input in the cycle of ecological processes [10,11]. Leaf nitrogen content has also been suggested as one of the crucial biodiversity variables for the monitoring of the progress towards the Aichi Biodiversity Targets by the remote sensing and ecology communities, who acknowledge the significant role of leaf nitrogen in biodiversity and ecosystem functioning [12,13].

Despite being a relatively minor element of leaves (up to 6.5–7%), nitrogen has been reliably recovered using leaf- and canopy-level hyperspectral data [14,15]. By offering contiguous, narrow spectral band data, hyperspectral data can be used to identify the nitrogen's small absorption properties. Compared to the conventional destructive sample procedures, this provides an effective and economical way to assess leaf nitrogen. The spectra from leaf powder, dry leaves, and fresh leaves were employed in previous research on the determination of nitrogen concentration in vegetation, as well as estimates at the canopy level [16–18]. The mask of the significant water absorption [17,19], the confounding effects coming from the canopy structure, illumination/viewing geometry, and background [20,21], and other obstacles make it difficult to retrieve nitrogen at the canopy level.

Based on the previous studies conducted in the literature to estimate the nitrogen content of the plant, the contributions of this study are as follows:

- Using the radiance values provided by Hyperion data directly without applying any atmospheric correction.
- Developing a proper deep model which transforms VNIR-only vegetation indexes to NDNI with a high correlation.
- Removing the necessity to have high-cost special cameras like SWIR to measure the nitrogen content of the crop.
- Enabling the farmers to follow the nitrogen content of the crop progressively and decide when to/not to fertilize.

2. Related Work

To improve the nitrogen content estimation performance, numerous methods have been employed. One method is spectral transformation, which includes employing first/second derivatives and reflectance log transformation [22,23]. There are also other studies, which include continuum removal [17,24], water removal [25,26], and wavelet analysis [27]. Numerous studies have been proposed to estimate the nitrogen content over forests [18,23,28–30], grasslands [31–33], and crop ecosystems [34–36]. A variety of artificial intelligence techniques, including support vector regression, neural networks, and Bayesian model averaging [32,36,37], as well as traditional regression techniques like stepwise multiple linear regression and partial least square regression, are used to retrieve nitrogen concentration.

Vegetation indices are one of the simplest and most popular empirical methodologies for estimating the biochemical content of leaves, including the nitrogen level. The main sources of nitrogen in leaf cells are proteins and chlorophylls [38]. Since there is a strong correlation between nitrogen and chlorophyll in a variety of species [1,2,39], nitrogen has been estimated using vegetation indices which are proposed and used for chlorophyll estimation [40]. For measuring chlorophyll, spectral wavelengths around 550 nm and 700 nm, as well as the red-edge area (680–780 nm), have been used [35,41], leading to a significant variety of indices [42–44]. In contrast to chlorophyll, there are fewer studies that offer particular indices for nitrogen estimate; the majority of these indices were established for crops [45–48], while just a small number were developed for forests [49].

Given that canopy structure is the primary cause of changes in canopy reflectance, the calculation of foliar nitrogen using canopy spectral data is complicated. According to the study in [7], the NIR reflectance (800–850 nm) and canopy foliar mass-based nitrogen concentration (%N) have a significant association that can be utilized to predict nitrogen, and in [50] the researchers pointed out the association between NIR reflectance and canopy structure. The study in [51] suggested that the biological associations between nitrogen and structural characteristics that affect NIR scattering and reflectance served as the foundation for their ideas. Additionally, in [14,52], scientists indicated that the canopy structure and leaf characteristics may co-vary among plant functional types, contradicting the study in [53], which claimed that the %N-NIR correlation is inherently false.

The purpose of the study in [54] was to assess how well 32 vegetation indicators collected from airborne hyperspectral imaging performed when used to calculate canopy foliar nitrogen in a mixed temperate forest. For comparison, the widely used partial least squares regression was carried out. These vegetation indicators can be divided into three groups, most of which are connected to the biochemical and structural characteristics of vegetation (e.g., nitrogen, chlorophyll, and leaf area index (LAI)). The nitrogen indicators are selected based on how nitrogen absorption characteristics' physical underpinnings affect canopy reflectance. The biological connections between nitrogen, chlorophyll, and canopy structure were used to justify the inclusion of the structural and chlorophyll indices in this study. Nitrogen (N) losses and the ensuing environmental issues are what define the production of vegetable crops [55–57]. The most frequent environmental issues include nitrous oxide (N_2O) emissions, ground and surface water contamination, and the eutrophication of surface waters [58,59]. These issues are frequently a result of the extensive use of N fertilizer [60], which typically exceeds the requirement of the crops [57,61,62], which is performed to ensure optimal growth and production. In order to decrease N contamination of water bodies by intensive vegetable production, it is necessary to understand crop nitrogen requirements and match crop demand with nitrogen supply [57,63,64].

There are numerous techniques available for tracking crop nitrogen status [57,65]. Leaf nutritional analysis is a common method, but it is time-consuming and labor-intensive in the lab, and it typically cannot quantify the temporal and geographical variability of nitrogen status [66,67]. These are significant drawbacks, since it is much easier to match the supply of nitrogen to crop requirements when one is aware of the temporal and spatial variability of crop nitrogen status [68].

Optical sensors are tools that quickly, accurately, and nondestructively monitor the crop's nitrogen status in the field [57,69]. They make it possible to regularly evaluate a crop and evaluate spatial variability. Canopy reflectance sensors, which are among the proximal optical sensors, have two highly advantageous characteristics in that they can monitor huge portions of a crop while they are in motion [70]. Field crops' nitrogen status can be evaluated via measures of crop reflectance [65]. These measures are based on the differential reflection of light wavelengths [57], which, depending on crop nitrogen status [69], are absorbed and reflected by the crop in varying amounts. Typically, red, green, and near-infrared light wavelengths are employed for nitrogen estimation [65]. Recently, the red edge has been suggested as a solution for nitrogen estimation of the red band's apparent saturation [71,72].

The nitrogen nutrition index (NNI) [67,73] is another commonly utilized strategy. The critical crop nitrogen content [74,75] is the lowest crop nitrogen content required for non-limiting growth, and it is used to calculate the NNI by dividing the actual crop nitrogen content by it. Any variation from 1 indicates either excess nitrogen (i.e., NNI > 1) or insufficient nitrogen (i.e., NNI1) crop status, with values of NNI equal to 1 indicating adequate nitrogen feeding [76].

Due to the high cost of SWIR band sensors, a regression-based method should be developed which maps the VNIR band indexes to SWIR band indexes. The majority of studies have been performed on cereal crops [77,78] like wheat [12,79] and rice [80–82]; very few have been carried out on vegetable crops like sweet pepper.

In [83], the crop nitrogen status of sweet pepper was estimated using eight vegetation indices that were computed from canopy reflectance data taken with two separate proximate sensors. First, crop NNI calibration regression models were fitted for each vegetation index. Second, a different dataset was used to validate these regression equations. Thirdly, sufficient values for each vegetative index for optimal nitrogen nutrition, for the main phenological stages of sweet pepper crops, were obtained utilizing the validated equations between vegetation indices and crop NNI.

The findings of the study [84] supported the use of the normalized difference vegetation index (NDVI) as a useful tool for determining the nitrogen status of cotton leaves at various growth stages. Using vegetation indices, the study in [85] calculated the nitrogen nutrition index (NNI), canopy nitrogen density (CND), and leaf nitrogen content of winter wheat over the course of the entire growth period. This study demonstrated that the correlations between each nitrogen index and the Vogelmann red-edge index (VOG), simple ratio pigment index (SRPI), modified red-edge simple ratio index, and red-edge position based on the linear interpolation method (REPliner) were not significantly influenced by growth period, and the estimation model R^2 for CND was higher than 81%. The estimation model's accuracy was higher than NNI; however, it would become saturated if CND was calculated using just one vegetation index. The red-edge chlorophyll index, CIred-edge, was demonstrated by [86] to be responsive to the canopy structure. The correlation between the nitrogen content of cotton leaves and several spectral ratio measures was examined in [87], who also conducted a cluster analysis based on prediction accuracy and overall accuracy.

The ratio of the red-edge position to the near-infrared band was shown to have a pretty high prediction accuracy and overall accuracy. The estimation of the winter wheat spectral index was investigated by [88] in a variety of environments, seasons, varieties, and growth stages. According to their findings, the growth stage had a significant impact on the performance of various vegetation indices and the choice of a sensitive wavelength for plant nitrogen concentration (PNC) estimation. The simple ratio of reflectivity at 370 nm and 400 nm (R_{370}/R_{400}) displayed the most consistent estimation accuracy in an indoor experiment ($R^2 = 0.58$) and field experiment ($R^2 = 0.51$). According to the studies, there are obvious changes in the relevant spectral index for different crops, or for various kinds and ecological zones of the same crop, when employing the spectral index to estimate crop nitrogen [89,90].

Additionally, compared to employing sensitive spectral features alone or vegetation indexes, modeling techniques like deep machine learning can produce greater prediction effects [91]. These techniques can also be used to monitor agricultural nutrients and growth indicators [92–94]. Support vector machine regression (SVR) was shown to be the most effective method for assessing crop nutrient contents in [95], which evaluated artificial neural network and SVR methods. The authors proposed that the creation of models with large sample sizes is appropriate for an artificial neural network. The hyperspectral reflectance of leaves was used in [90] to study the generalized partial least-squares regression (PLSR) model, and this approach was successful in retrieving leaf nitrogen concentration ($r = 0.85$).

The study in [96] is based on data for two types of drip-irrigated cotton at various growth stages from April 2019 to September 2020. The data include canopy nitrogen density (CND) and leaf nitrogen concentration (LNC) values. Pearson's correlation analysis was used to determine which of the thirty hyperspectral vegetation indexes and the two nitrogen indexes (LNC and CND) that were used in the three modeling techniques of simple multiple linear regression (MLR), PLSR, and support vector regression (SVR) were relatively stable. The models were employed to investigate the possibility of measuring the nitrogen nutrient status of cotton in each growth period based on a multi-vegetation index in order to give a theoretical background for the application of remote sensing technology in cotton nutrition monitoring and diagnostics.

The nitrogen attitude of paddy rice was studied in [97], including plant nitrogen content (PNC), leaf nitrogen content (LNC), plant nitrogen accumulation (PNA), and leaf nitrogen accumulation (LNA). The data used in this study were collected by using a hyperspectral camera integrated to an unmanned aerial vehicle (UAV). The results handled in this study report that the correlation between the nitrogen traits and biochemical traits, canopy chlorophyll content, leaf chlorophyll content and aboveground biomass, depend on the growth stage of the crop.

The study in [98] fused the information from different sensors and developed new spectral indices based on a coverage-adjustment and estimated the content of leaf nitrogen of maize in different stages of the growth. According to the results, CASIs perform better than the traditional vegetation indices.

According to the results of the study in [99], which developed an estimation method of potato nitrogen, combining the visible light vegetation indexes and plant morphological properties provides a better estimation of nitrogen, since by using multiple linear regression methods it achieves a 0.79 R^2 score.

Researchers developed a new method in [100] which extracts the leaf region from the color images and computes the color similarity between the extracted leaf with some predefined color information. In particular, a green color intensity was used for the reference of nitrogen content. The proposed method was tested on a Spinacia oleracea dataset and results showed that there exists a high correlation between the laboratory analysis and the analysis of the color images.

3. Materials and Methods

Image data of the Hyperion sensor were used in this study. As a push-broom hyperspectral instrument, Hyperion is housed on the EO-1 satellite, which is depicted in Figure 1.

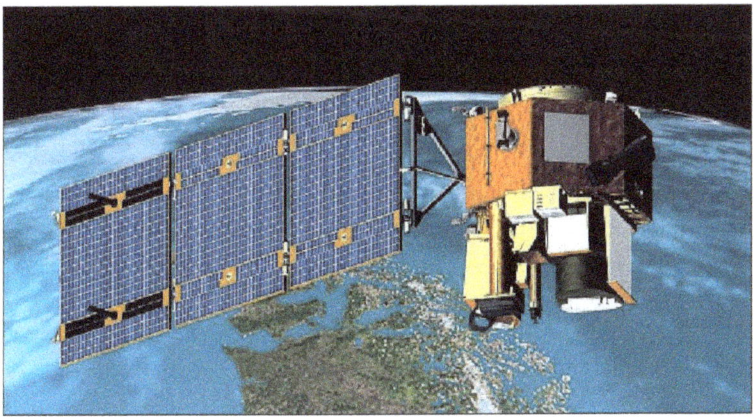

Figure 1. EO-1 Satellite View [101].

With a 10 nm bandwidth spanning from 357 nm to 2576 nm, it collects 220 different spectral channels. All bands have a spatial resolution of (30 × 30) m^2. The VNIR band, SWIR band, and VNIR-SWIR band indices can all be estimated from the same image data because Hyperion includes both the VNIR and SWIR bands. There is no need for a geometric correction because the Hyperion images have already been rectified geometrically. In addition, no atmospheric correction is applied to the data. This is due to the fact that atmospheric correction tools are not free to use, so, bring high financial costs. In addition, they cannot achieve a perfect correction, which produces incorrect reflectance values among the pixels and affects the results negatively. The properties of the Hyperion sensor are given in Table 1.

Table 1. Hyperion sensor parameters.

Parameters	Hyperion Sensor Details
Spectral range	400–2500 nm
Spatial resolution	30 m
Radiometric resolution	12 bits
Swath width	7.5 km
Spectral resolution	10 nm
Spectral coverage	Continuous
Number of rows, columns, bands	3271, 871, 220

Different test images were collected from Hyperion data on the *Harran* region based in the south-west of Turkey. Google Earth and Earth explorer views of *Harran* and the Hyperion image are shown in Figure 2.

The Harran Plain is a region that starts from the southeast of the city of Şanlıurfa and extends to the Syrian border. It is a plain with very fertile soil. It is located between the 36°43′–37°08′N parallels and 38°57′–39°55′E meridians in the Upper Mesopotamian area of Şanlıurfa province.

In the main, corn and cotton farming is carried out. In the Harran Plain, under the influence of the Mediterranean climate, the continental climate is dominant. Winters are cold and rainy, and summers are very hot and dry. Annual precipitation is 365 mm, annual evaporation is 1848 mm, and annual average temperature is 17.2 °C.

Figure 2. Google Earth view of Harran (**top**) and Earth Explorer view of Hyperion (color image) (**bottom**).

The Hyperion image downloaded from Earth Explorer covers roughly 900 km^2, which is both required and sufficient to investigate the reliability of the proposed method. The QGIS Geographic Information Software Tool was used to determine the area of the Hyperion images [102]. Figure 3 shows the image data taken from the *Harran* region, in which a large amount of corn, cotton and wheat planting is undertaken by farmers. The image acquisition time was 8 August 2016, when the crop was dense and mature. The image's latitude and longitude values and the scale of the map are given on the figure as well.

Figure 3. Hyperion data. RGB Image of *Harran* Region.

Figure 4 shows a drone camera view and a ground image of a region from Harran taken in July 2019.

Figure 4. Harran plain. Drone camera image (**top**). Ground image from a cotton field (**bottom**) [103].

In the *Harran* region, to show the vegetation density and the spreading over the area, an NDVI estimation was first applied. The Hyperion image and the resulting NDVI index map are shown in Figure 5. The Hyperion image has a spatial resolution of 3241 $\times$ 1241, totaling 4,022,081 pixels, where 2,859,262 pixels are the black regions surrounding the target region. Therefore, the vegetation index analysis is implemented on 1,162,819 pixels. Each pixel corresponds to 30 $\times$ 30 m^2 ground area. By recalling that NDVI values can be changed from -1 to 1, in Table 2 it can be seen that the number of pixels with a high NDVI value, like >0.75, was lower, relatively speaking. An important reason for this is the ground spatial resolution of the Hyperion sensor, in which one pixel covers 30 $\times$ 30 m^2. This is, relatively, a large area in which spectral mixing occurs, and therefore the spectra of soil, water and vegetation is mixed, which may reduce the NDVI indices [104]. Nonetheless, the data are powerful and exhibit a good distribution, which enables an accurate analysis of vegetation indices.

Table 2. Number of pixels falling in specific intervals of NDVI values.

NDVI < 0	0 ≤ NDVI < 0.25	0.25 ≤ NDVI < 0.5	0.5 ≤ NDVI < 0.75	0.75 ≤ NDVI < 1
447,396	193,177	214,010	269,860	49

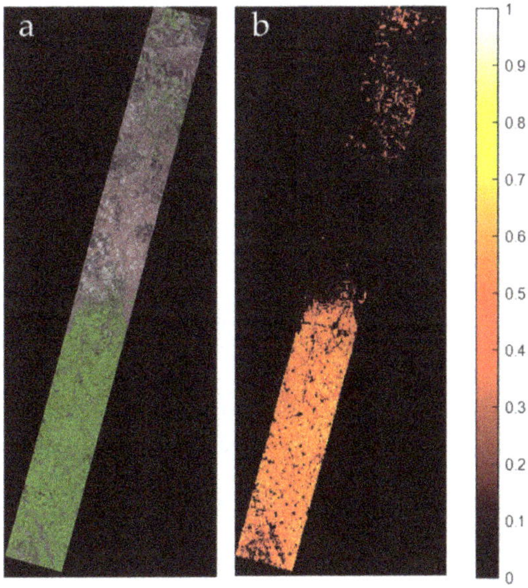

Figure 5. Hyperion image and NDVI Map for *Harran*. (**a**) Hyperion color image (**b**) NDVI Map.

To increase the accuracy, the pixels with NDVI values higher than 0.2 were taken into account. This is due to the typical vegetation pixel having an NDVI greater than 0.2.

The study in [105] states that NDNI can be used effectively for the estimation of the nitrogen content of the vegetation. Since, in this study, we develop a deep model which established a correlation between VNIR band vegetation indices and NDNI, the most important vegetation indices which hold information about the nitrogen content of the plants were estimated. These indices are NDVI [106], GNDVI [107], EVI [108], GOSAVI [109], GSAVI [109], MCARI2 [110], and VREI2 [111]. To establish the correlation, NDNI [112] was estimated as well. Table 3 shows the corresponding indices, the bands or wavelengths, and the equations which were used to estimate them.

Table 3. Vegetation indices, bands or wavelengths and equations.

Index	Bands and/or Wavelengths	Equation for Estimation
NDVI [106]	NIR, RED	$\frac{NIR - Red}{NIR + Red}$
GNDVI [107]	NIR, Green	$\frac{NIR - Green}{NIR + Green}$
EVI [108]	NIR, Green, Blue	$2.5 * \frac{NIR - Red}{NIR + 6 * Red - 7.5 * Blue + 1}$
GOSAVI [109]	NIR, Green	$\frac{NIR - Green}{NIR + Green + 0.16}$
GSAVI [109]	NIR, Green	$1.5 * \frac{NIR - Green}{NIR + Green + 0.5}$
MCARI2 [110]	$\rho_{800}, \rho_{670}, \rho_{550}$	$\frac{1.5 * [2.5(\rho_{800} - \rho_{670}) - 1.3(\rho_{800} - \rho_{670})]}{\sqrt{(2 * \rho_{800} + 1)^2 - (6 * \rho_{800} - 5 * \sqrt{\rho_{670}}) - 0.5}}$
VREI2 [111]	$\rho_{734}, \rho_{747}, \rho_{726}, \rho_{715}$	$\frac{\rho_{734} - \rho_{747}}{\rho_{715} + \rho_{726}}$
NDNI [112]	ρ_{1510}, ρ_{1680}	$\frac{\log\left(\frac{1}{\rho_{1510}}\right) - \log\left(\frac{1}{\rho_{1680}}\right)}{\log\left(\frac{1}{\rho_{1510}}\right) + \log\left(\frac{1}{\rho_{1680}}\right)}$

The black regions on the Hyperion data were excluded first. Then, each vegetation index was estimated for the pixels left. N was the number of pixels in each index map, and a vector of index values was created, as shown in Equation (1), where Map_{vi} was the index map of the corresponding vegetation index and $index_i$ was the estimated index value at pixel i.

$$Map_{vi} = [index_1, index_2 \ldots index_N] \quad (1)$$

Then, new index data were created, as shown in Equation (2), where $I_{v.i.ab}$ was the estimated index for the (b). pixel of vegetation index (a). (i.e., 3rd pixel of NDVI map).

$$data = \begin{bmatrix} I_{v.i.11} & \cdots & I_{v.i.1N} \\ \vdots & \ddots & \vdots \\ I_{v.i.M1} & \cdots & I_{v.i.MN} \end{bmatrix} \quad (2)$$

Since this study uses 7 vegetation indices from the VNIR region, a total of 7 Map_{vi} were created at the beginning. Therefore, the size of the data matrix was (7 × 1,162,819). After handling the data matrix, a further analysis was carried out.

- Due to the division by 0, some index values were calculated as infinite and/or NaN. Therefore, those kinds of pixels were found and the corresponding column was deleted.
- Another analysis was also carried out for the pixels with an abnormally large vegetation index. Therefore, the index values which had an absolute value above 5 were also deleted from the data.
- Finally, 1,113,529 pixel values were used, and to normalize the effect of the environment at the time of the capturing, each index row in the data was normalized between −1 and 1. To normalize the data, the *normalize* function of *Matlab* was used with a 'range' parameter.

Similarly, the above operations were also applied on the NDNI Map. Finally, the input data had the shape of (7 × 1113529) and the output data had (1 × 1113529).

To train a model which matches the input data to the output data, *Matlab deep learning toolbox* [113] was used. By using this tool, a deep neural network was designed with 4 dense (hidden) layers, each with 25 neurons. Figure 6 shows the designed neural network. The number of input neurons was 7 due to the shape of the input data and 1 for output, hence that was the NDNI index value.

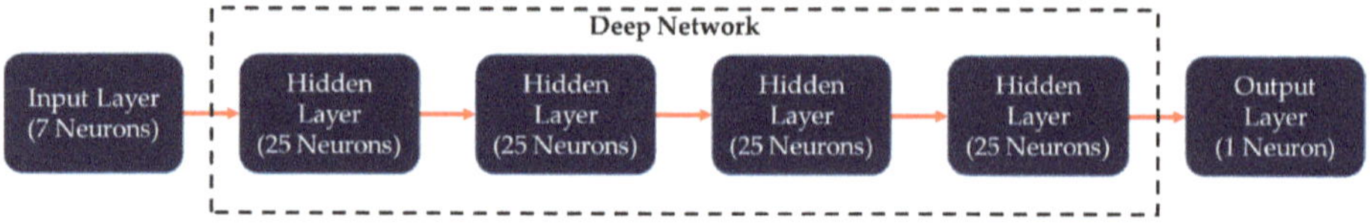

Figure 6. Feed forward deep neural network (proposed).

Data were split into train, validation, and test datasets with the default ratio of 0.7:0.15:0.15. The number of epochs was set as 1000. Training function and adaption learning functions were set as TRAINLM (Levenberg–Marquardt) and LEARNGDM. LEARNGDM is a gradient descent algorithm with momentum. The cost can be pushed farther to go around a saddle point by adding a momentum element to the gradient descent, even if the current gradient is insignificant. The performance function is MSE. Training was carried out on CPU on a Windows PC with 8 GB Ram and an 11th Gen Intel(R) Core(TM) i7-1165G7 @ 2.80 GHz processor. The reason not to use GPU was that in *Matlab*, the TRAINLM function is not supported.

The Levenberg–Marquardt [114] technique, which was developed for minimizing functions that are sums of squares of nonlinear functions, is derived from Newton's method [115]. The Levenberg–Marquardt algorithm is designed to minimize sum-of-square error functions of the form (3). In (3), err_k is the error in the kth instance and err is a vector with element at k. A Taylor series can be used to expand the error vector to first order if the difference between the old and new weight vectors is modest.

$$E = \frac{1}{2}\sum k(err_k)^2 = \frac{1}{2}||err||^2 \tag{3}$$

$$err(j+i) = err_j + \frac{\partial err_k}{\partial w_i}(w(j+1) - w(j)) \tag{4}$$

As a result, the error function can be expressed as

$$E = \frac{1}{2}\left\|err(j) + \frac{\partial err_k}{\partial w_i}(w(j+1) - w(j))\right\|^2 \tag{5}$$

After minimizing the error function with respect to the updated weight vector, (6) can be written.

$$w(j+1) = w(j) - \left(Z^T Z\right)^{-1} Z^T err(j) \tag{6}$$

where

$$Z_{ki} \equiv \frac{\partial err_k}{\partial w_i} \tag{7}$$

Since the Hessian for the sum-of-square error function is as shown in (8),

$$H_{ij} = \frac{\partial^2 E}{\partial_{w_i}\partial_{w_j}} + \sum\{(\frac{\partial err_k}{\partial w_i})\left(\frac{\partial err_k}{\partial w_i}\right) + err_k(\frac{\partial^2 err_k}{\partial w_i \partial w_i})\} \tag{8}$$

By ignoring the second term, Hessian can be written as:

$$H = Z^T Z \tag{9}$$

For nonlinear networks, updating the weights therefore entails the inverse Hessian. Since the Hessian is based on first order derivatives with respect to the network weights, which can be easily handled by back propagation, it can be calculated rather quickly. Although iterative application of the updating formula to reduce the error function is an option, this may provide a step size that is too big, invalidating the linear approximation that the method is based on.

The Levenberg–Marquardt approach minimizes the error function while maintaining a small step size to guarantee the accuracy of the linear approximation. Utilizing a form's customized error function allows for this.

$$E = \frac{1}{2}\left\|err(j) + \frac{\partial err_k}{\partial w_i}(w(j+1) - w(j))\right\|^2 + \alpha||(w(j+1) - w(j))||^2 \tag{10}$$

where α is a parameter adjusting the step size. When the modified error is minimized with respect to $w(j+1)$, (11) is handled.

$$w(j+1) = w(j) - \left(Z^T Z + \alpha I\right)^{-1} Z^T e(j) \tag{11}$$

With very large values of α, Levenberg–Marquardt approaches standard gradient descent, whereas for very small values of α it approaches the Newton method.

This study aims to investigate the relation between VNIR-only vegetation indexes and NDNI. For that purpose, linear regression was employed by using a deep neural network. Linear regression can be explained as follows:

$$Y = a + bX + \varepsilon \tag{12}$$

where

$$a = \frac{(\sum y)(\sum x^2) - (\sum x)(\sum xy)}{n(\sum x^2) - (\sum x)^2} \quad (13)$$

$$b = \frac{n(\sum xy) - (\sum x)(\sum y)}{n(\sum x^2) - (\sum x)^2} \quad (14)$$

In Equation (12), Y is the dependent (outcome) variable, a is y-intercept, b is the slope of the regression line, X is the independent variable, and ε is the error term. The calculation of linear regression includes 3 steps:

1. First, the values of formula components a and b are found by using $\sum x$, $\sum y$, $\sum xy$, and $\sum x^2$;
2. Then, the values derived in the first step are substituted into a and b;
3. Finally, a and b values are used with the formula $Y = a + bX + \varepsilon$ to establish the linear relationship between X and Y variables.

Since a deep neural network is used in this study, the calculation is performed by the neural network tool defined in *Matlab* and linear regression is employed.

4. Results

Regression and loss plots are given in Figures 7 and 8, respectively, for training, validation, test, and overall data. The R^2 values for test and validation data are above 0.91 and 0.93, respectively, which is very promising. Similarly, the MSE loss values are all below 10^{-4}. The best validation loss score is 7.01×10^{-5}, which means 70 over 1 million. As can be observed from Figure 7, although the number is low, there are some outlier values which do not fit the regression line. They are the points which are far from the regression line and whose correlation error is generally high. Therefore, the outliers affect the regression score negatively. Those points are generally the anomaly points/regions in the flat areas. The best validation score was achieved at epoch 124, and therefore the training was stopped at epoch 130.

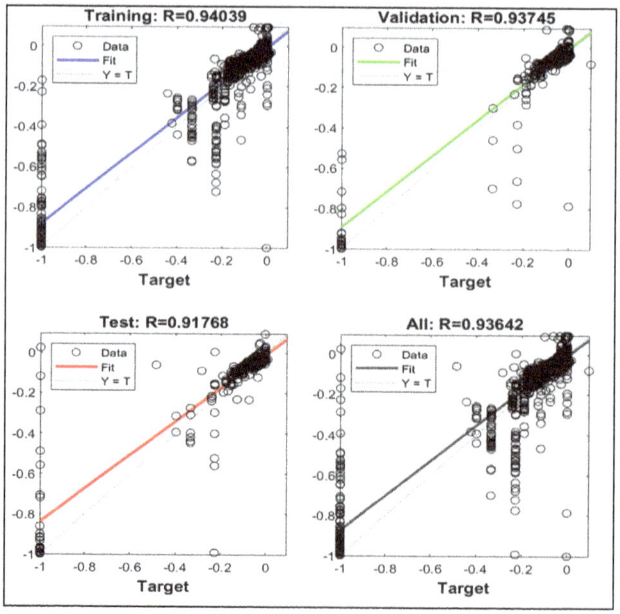

Figure 7. Regression plots for training, validation, test and all data.

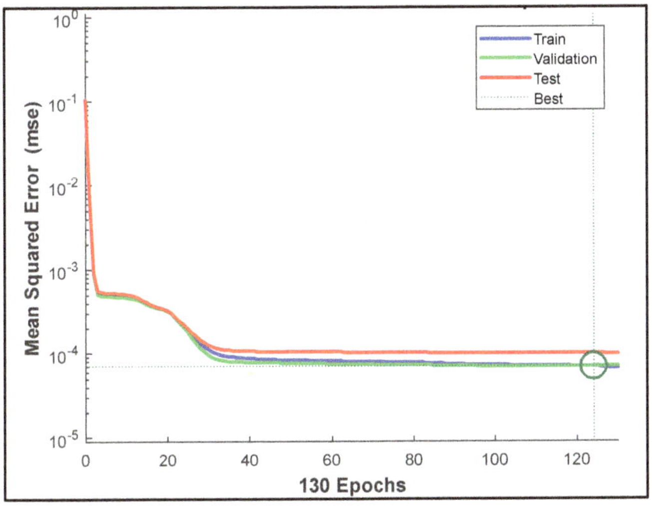

Figure 8. Loss (MSE) for training, validation, test and all data.

The regression equations between input and output handled for training, validation, test and all data are given in Table 4.

Table 4. Regression equations between output and target.

Data	Equation for Estimation
Training	$Output = 0.87 * Target + 0.0066$
Validation	$Output = 0.89 * Target + 0.0059$
Test	$Output = 0.83 * Target + 0.0089$
All	$Output = 0.87 * Target + 0.0069$

Various machine learning methods based on regression were also trained and tested. In Table 5, the best regression scores handled are given for comparison with the proposed method. It can be obviously seen from the table that the proposed method achieves the best and superior results compared to all other methods.

Table 5. Benchmark of the proposed method with various regression models.

Method	Regression Score (R^2)
Linear Regression	−0.29
SVM Regression	0.15
Gradient-boosted decision trees (GBDT)	0.37
Random Forest Regressor	0.46
Stochastic Gradient Descent (SGD)	0.35
PLSRegression	0.36
Proposed	0.91

Ablation Study

In this study, a deep neural network was employed to investigate the correlation between VNIR-Only vegetation indexes and the NDNI index. For this purpose, various combinations of different networks on normalized and/or unnormalized data were tried. Figure 9 shows the regression results when the depth of the network was reduced to two deep layers and data were normalized. Even if test score was improved a bit, validation and all data scores were not good as the proposed network.

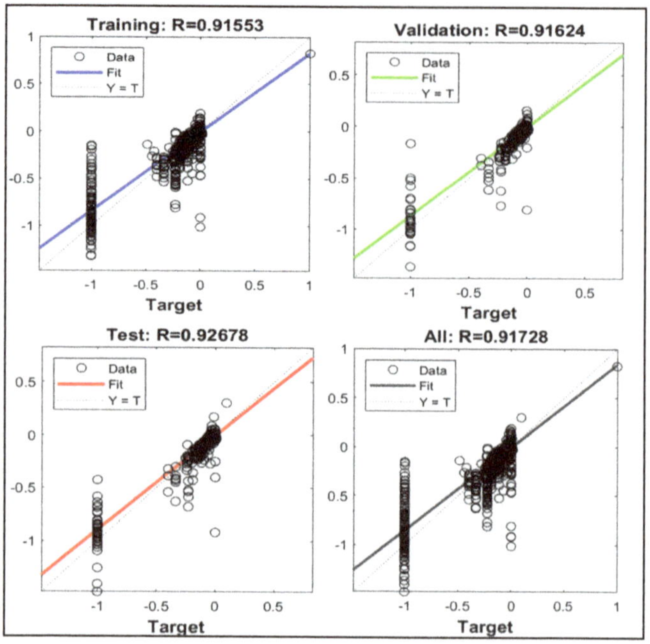

Figure 9. Two-deep layer with 25 neurons on Normalized Data.

Figure 10 shows the regression result for two deep layers on unnormalized data, which were worse and unbalanced among training, validation and test data. Therefore, when the network is not deep enough, normalization of the data is crucial.

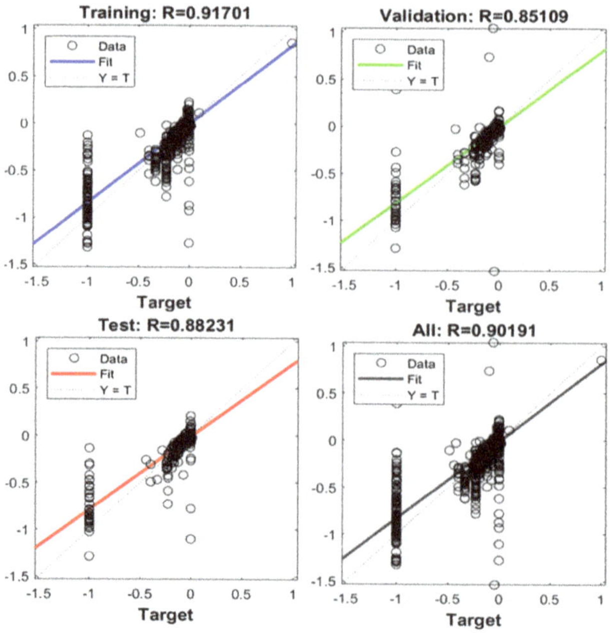

Figure 10. Two-deep layer with 25 neurons on unnormalized data.

When the depth of the network is kept and data are not normalized, similar regression results to the proposed network can be seen (Figure 11). However, the results are still a bit better when the data are normalized. In addition, when the data are normalized, the depth of the network can be reduced to two with very little and tolerable reduction in accuracy. In this way, the response time of the network to new data can be reduced, which is crucial for near real-time and/or real-time applications.

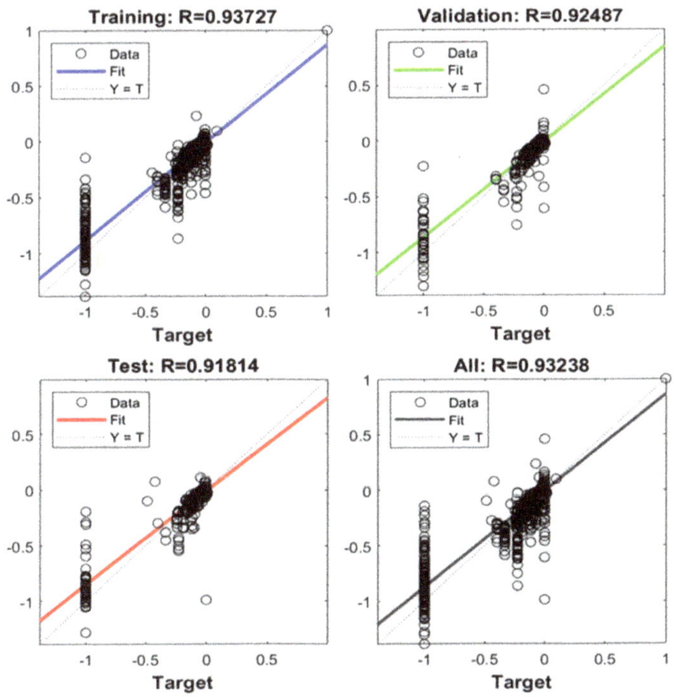

Figure 11. Four-deep layer with 25 neurons on unnormalized data.

Various neural networks with different numbers of deep layers and neurons were trained with the normalized data, and the obtained regression scores for training, validation, test, and all data are given in Table 6. The best scores are colored in red and the second-best scores are colored in blue. As (#L, #N) shows the number of deep layers and neurons at each deep layer, (4,15) includes the three best scores; however, the validation score is low. Similarly, (5,15) includes the three best scores; however, the test score is low. (3,25) and (4,25) have the three best scores, and the total score of (4,25) was above (3,25). Other different combinations had two best/second-best scores, one best/second-best score or no best/second-best scores. Therefore, in this study, the combination of (4,25) is proposed.

After training the network with (4,25), the trained model was tested on the Hyperion image. Figure 12 shows the difference image between NDNI and the estimated NDNI with the proposed neural network. It can observed from the figure that the difference between the estimated and actual NDNI is very low, especially for the regions where the vegetation density is high and farming is being carried out actively.

Table 6. Regression scores obtained by training various neural networks.

Number of Deep Layers	Number of Neurons	Regression Scores (Train-Validation-Test-All)
2	10	0.93-0.90-0.85-0.91
3	10	0.93-0.92-0.91-0.92
4	10	0.93-0.91-0.92-0.93
5	10	0.93-0.93-0.90-0.93
2	15	0.92-0.92-0.88-0.91
3	15	0.93-0.91-0.90-0.92
4	15	0.95-0.89-0.93-0.94
5	15	0.94-0.94-0.87-0.93
2	20	0.93-0.92-0.91-0.92
3	20	0.93-0.88-0.91-0.92
4	20	0.95-0.92-0.89-0.94
5	20	0.91-0.92-0.90-0.91
2	25	0.91-0.91-0.92-0.91
3	25	0.94-0.90-0.92-0.93
4	25	0.94-0.93-0.91-0.93
5	25	0.92-0.88-0.89-0.91

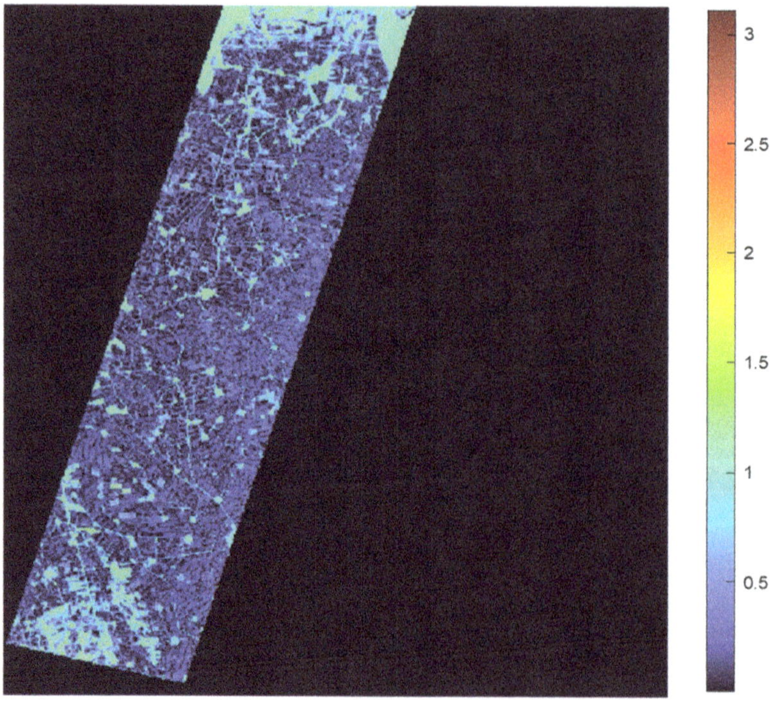

Figure 12. Difference image between actual NDNI and estimated NDNI with proposed network.

5. Discussion

In this study, the correlation between VNIR-only indexes and the NDNI index was investigated and a deep neural network was trained to establish that correlation. The results show that there exists a high correlation between them. The most important contribution of this study is proving that the VNIR-Only band vegetation indexes have a high correlation with NDNI, which is calculated by using the SWIR band region of the electromagnetic spectrum. Results show that when VNIR-only indexes are chosen and combined properly and used as the input for a deep neural network, it is possible to establish a high correlation. In this way, researchers and the farmers do not need to use an SWIR band camera, which generally means a high cost for them. By using a VNIR-Only band multispectral/hyperspectral camera and/or satellite, it is possible to estimate the nitrogen content of the plant progressively with a high accuracy. This will enable farmers to detect the regions with high and/or low amounts of nitrogen, so that they can reduce or increase the fertilization specific to different regions in a field.

To this point, the vegetation index studies in the literature have been based on either a single electromagnetic region (like VNIR) or multiple regions (VNIR-SWIR). The most important improvement of this study is in investigating and establishing the correlation between VNIR-only vegetation indexes and the NDNI index. So, without using any SWIR band cameras and/or satellites, it can be possible to estimate the nitrogen content easily and with high accuracy and very little loss. The bands used in this study from the VNIR region were Red, Green, Blue, NIR, 550 nm, 670 nm, 715 nm, 726 nm, 747 nm, 734 nm, and 800 nm of Hyperion image data. As is given in detail in the results section, the correlation (r^2) values were handled above 91% for the training, validation, and test data by using the proposed deep neural network.

6. Conclusions

In this study, an NDNI index which can be calculated by using SWIR bands from the electromagnetic spectrum was estimated by using a proper combination of VNIR band indexes. Seven different vegetation indexes were used as the input and NDNI was used as the output (target) in the training. As a result, very high accuracy was achieved since the correlation for target data was achieved above 91%. Therefore, by using the proposed network, the researchers can estimate the nitrogen content of the plant with respect to NDNI without the calculation of NDNI. SWIR band cameras are generally expensive and not easy to access. Therefore, the most important contribution of this study is in removing the necessity to have an SWIR band camera and atmospheric correction tool to estimate the nitrogen content. In addition, by using the VNIR-only vegetation indexes which are proposed in this study, a specific camera which has the capability of estimating the nitrogen content directly can be produced in the future. It can be used either standalone or by integrating on a satellite. When it is used standalone, the real-time tracking of the nitrogen content of the vegetation can be achieved. This study employs a deep neural network to achieve that purpose. In addition, the Hyperion data used in this study and the trained network are shared at https://github.com/ycimtay/VNIR_to_NDNI (accessed on 3 July 2023).

Funding: This research received no external funding.

Data Availability Statement: Publicly available datasets were analyzed in this study. This data can be found here: [https://earthexplorer.usgs.gov/].

Conflicts of Interest: The authors declare no conflict of interest.

References

1. Field, C.; Mooney, H.A. The photosynthesis-nitrogen relationship in wild plants. In *On the Economy of Plant Form and Function*; Givnish, T.J., Ed.; Cambridge University Press: Cambridge, UK, 1986; pp. 25–55.
2. Evans, J. Photosynthesis and nitrogen relationships in leaves of C3 plants. *Oecologia* **1989**, *78*, 9–19. [CrossRef]
3. Reich, P.B.; Ellsworth, D.S.; Walters, M.B. Leaf structure (specific leaf area) modulates photosynthesis–nitrogen relations: Evidence from within and across species and functional groups. *Funct. Ecol.* **1998**, *12*, 948–958. [CrossRef]
4. Smith, M.L.; Ollinger, S.V.; Martin, M.E.; Aber, J.D.; Hallett, R.A.; Goodale, C.L. Direct estimation of aboveground forest productivity through hyperspectral remote sensing of canopy nitrogen. *Ecol. Appl.* **2002**, *12*, 1286–1302. [CrossRef]
5. Green, D.S.; Erickson, J.E.; Kruger, E.L. Foliar morphology and canopy nitrogen as predictors of light-use efficiency in terrestrial vegetation. *Agric. For. Meteorol.* **2003**, *115*, 163–171. [CrossRef]
6. Ollinger, S.V.; Smith, M.L. Net primary production and canopy nitrogen in a temperate forest landscape: An analysis using imaging spectroscopy, modeling and field data. *Ecosystems* **2005**, *8*, 760–778. [CrossRef]

7. Ollinger, S.V.; Richardson, A.D.; Martin, M.E.; Hollinger, D.Y.; Frolking, S.E.; Reich, P.B.; Plourde, L.C.; Katul, G.G.; Munger, J.W.; Oren, R.; et al. Canopy nitrogen, carbon assimilation, and albedo in temperate and boreal forests: Functional relations and potential climate feedbacks. *Proc. Natl. Acad. Sci. USA* **2008**, *105*, 19336–19341. [CrossRef]
8. Sievering, H.; Fernandez, I.; Lee, J.; Hom, J.; Rustad, L. Forest canopy uptake of atmospheric nitrogen deposition at eastern US conifer sites: Carbon storage implications? *Glob. Biogeochem. Cycles* **2000**, *14*, 1153–1159. [CrossRef]
9. Lamarque, J.F.; Kiehl, J.T.; Brasseur, G.P.; Butler, T.; Cameron-Smith, P.; Collins, W.D.; Collins, W.J.; Granier, C.; Hauglustaine, D.; Hess, P.G.; et al. Assessing future nitrogen deposition and carbon cycle feedback using a multimodel approach: Analysis of nitrogen deposition. *J. Geophys. Res. Atmos.* **2005**, *110*, 1–21. [CrossRef]
10. Plummer, S.E. Perspectives on combining ecological process models and remotely sensed data. *Ecol. Model.* **2000**, *129*, 169–186. [CrossRef]
11. Zhang, C.; Li, C.; Chen, X.; Luo, G.; Li, L.; Li, X.; Yan, Y.; Shao, H. A spatial-explicit dynamic vegetation model that couples carbon, water, and nitrogen processes for arid and semiarid ecosystems. *J. Arid Land* **2013**, *5*, 102–117. [CrossRef]
12. Pereira, H.M.; Ferrier, S.; Walters, M.; Geller, G.N.; Jongman, R.H.G.; Scholes, R.J.; Bruford, M.W.; Brummitt, N.; Butchart, S.H.M.; Cardoso, A.C.; et al. Essential biodiversity variables. *Science* **2013**, *339*, 277–278. [CrossRef]
13. Skidmore, A.K.; Pettorelli, N.; Coops, N.C.; Geller, G.N.; Hansen, M.; Lucas, R.; Mücher, C.A.; O'Connor, B.; Paganini, M.; Pereira, H.M.; et al. Environmental science: Agree on biodiversity metrics to track from space. *Nature* **2015**, *523*, 403–405. [CrossRef] [PubMed]
14. Wright, I.J.; Reich, P.B.; Westoby, M.; Ackerly, D.D.; Baruch, Z.; Bongers, F.; Cavender-Bares, J.; Chapin, T.; Cornellssen, J.H.C.; Diemer, M.; et al. The worldwide leaf economics spectrum. *Nature* **2004**, *428*, 821–827. [CrossRef] [PubMed]
15. Kokaly, R.F.; Asner, G.P.; Ollinger, S.V.; Martin, M.E.; Wessman, C.A. Characterizing canopy biochemistry from imaging spectroscopy and its application to ecosystem studies. *Remote Sens. Environ.* **2009**, *113*, S78–S91. [CrossRef]
16. Curran, P.J. Remote sensing of foliar chemistry. *Remote Sens. Environ.* **1989**, *30*, 271–278. [CrossRef]
17. Kokaly, R.F.; Clark, R.N. Spectroscopic determination of leaf biochemistry using band-depth analysis of absorption features and stepwise multiple linear regression. *Remote Sens. Environ.* **1999**, *67*, 267–287. [CrossRef]
18. Martin, M.E.; Plourde, L.C.; Ollinger, S.V.; Smith, M.L.; McNeil, B.E. A generalizable method for remote sensing of canopy nitrogen across a wide range of forest ecosystems. *Remote Sens. Environ.* **2008**, *112*, 3511–3519. [CrossRef]
19. Fourty, T.; Baret, F. On spectral estimates of fresh leaf biochemistry. *Int. J. Remote Sens.* **1998**, *19*, 1283–1297. [CrossRef]
20. Asner, G.P. Biophysical and biochemical sources of variability in canopy reflectance. *Remote Sens. Environ.* **1998**, *64*, 234–253. [CrossRef]
21. Zarco-Tejada, P.J.; Miller, J.R.; Noland, T.L.; Mohammed, G.H.; Sampson, P.H. Scaling-up and model inversion methods with narrowband optical indices for chlorophyll content estimation in closed forest canopies with hyperspectral data. *IEEE Trans. Geosci. Remote Sens.* **2001**, *39*, 1491–1507. [CrossRef]
22. Yoder, B.J.; Pettigrew-Crosby, R.E. Predicting nitrogen and chlorophyll content and concentrations from reflectance spectra (400–2500 nm) at leaf and canopy scales. *Remote Sens. Environ.* **1995**, *53*, 199–211.
23. Coops, N.C.; Smith, M.L.; Martin, M.E.; Ollinger, S.V. Prediction of eucalypt foliage nitrogen content from satellite-derived hyperspectral data. *IEEE Trans. Geosci. Remote Sens.* **2003**, *41*, 1338–1346.
24. Huang, Z.; Turner, B.J.; Dury, S.J.; Wallis, I.R.; Foley, W.J. Estimating foliage nitrogen concentration from HYMAP data using continuum removal analysis. *Remote Sens. Environ.* **2004**, *93*, 18–29. [CrossRef]
25. Schlerf, M.; Atzberger, C.; Hill, J.; Buddenbaum, H.; Werner, W.; Schueler, G. Retrieval of chlorophyll and nitrogen in Norway spruce (*Picea abies* L. *Karst.*) using imaging spectroscopy. *Int. J. Appl. Earth Obs. Geoinf.* **2010**, *12*, 17–26.
26. Ramoelo, A.; Skidmore, A.K.; Schlerf, M.; Mathieu, R.; Heitkönig, I.M.A. Water-removed spectra increase the retrieval accuracy when estimating savanna grass nitrogen and phosphorus concentrations. *ISPRS J. Photogramm. Remote Sens.* **2011**, *66*, 408–417. [CrossRef]
27. Ferwerda, J.G.; Jones, S.D. Continuous wavelet transformations for hyperspectral feature detection. In *Progress in Spatial Data Handling*; Riedl, A., Kainz, W., Elmes, G.A., Eds.; Springer: Berlin/Heidelberg, Germany, 2006; pp. 167–178.
28. Asner, G.P.; Martin, R.E. Airborne spectranomics: Mapping canopy chemical and taxonomic diversity in tropical forests. *Front. Ecol. Environ.* **2008**, *7*, 269–276. [CrossRef]
29. Gökkaya, K.; Thomas, V.; Noland, T.L.; McCaughey, H.; Morrison, I.; Treitz, P. Prediction of macronutrients at the canopy level using spaceborne imaging spectroscopy and LiDAR data in a mixedwood boreal forest. *Remote Sens.* **2015**, *7*, 9045–9069. [CrossRef]
30. Singh, A.; Serbin, S.P.; McNeil, B.E.; Kingdon, C.C.; Townsend, P.A. Imaging spectroscopy algorithms for mapping canopy foliar chemical and morphological traits and their uncertainties. *Ecol. Appl.* **2015**, *25*, 2180–2197. [CrossRef] [PubMed]
31. Mutanga, O.; Skidmore, A.K.; Prins, H.H.T. Predicting in situ pasture quality in the Kruger National Park, South Africa, using continuum-removed absorption features. *Remote Sens. Environ.* **2004**, *89*, 393–408. [CrossRef]
32. Skidmore, A.K.; Ferwerda, J.G.; Mutanga, O.; Van Wieren, S.E.; Peel, M.; Grant, R.C.; Prins, H.H.T.; Balcik, F.B.; Venus, V. Forage quality of savannas—Simultaneously mapping foliar protein and polyphenols for trees and grass using hyperspectral imagery. *Remote Sens. Environ.* **2010**, *114*, 64–72. [CrossRef]
33. Pellissier, P.A.; Ollinger, S.V.; Lepine, L.C.; Palace, M.W.; McDowell, W.H. Remote sensing of foliar nitrogen in cultivated grasslands of human dominated landscapes. *Remote Sens. Environ.* **2015**, *167*, 88–97. [CrossRef]

34. Inoue, Y.; Sakaiya, E.; Zhu, Y.; Takahashi, W. Diagnostic mapping of canopy nitrogen content in rice based on hyperspectral measurements. *Remote Sens. Environ.* **2012**, *126*, 210–221. [CrossRef]
35. Li, F.; Miao, Y.; Feng, G.; Yuan, F.; Yue, S.; Gao, X.; Liu, Y.; Liu, B.; Ustin, S.L.; Chen, X. Improving estimation of summer maize nitrogen status with red edge-based spectral vegetation indices. *Field Crops Res.* **2014**, *157*, 111–123. [CrossRef]
36. Govindasamy, P.; Muthusamy, S.K.; Bagavathiannan, M.; Mowrer, J.; Jagannadham, P.T.K.; Maity, A.; Halli, H.M.; Sujayananad, G.K.; Vadivel, R.; Das, T.K.; et al. Nitrogen use efficiency—A key to enhance crop productivity under a changing climate. *Front. Plant Sci.* **2023**, *14*, 1121073. [CrossRef] [PubMed]
37. Axelsson, C.; Skidmore, A.K.; Schlerf, M.; Fauzi, A.; Verhoef, W. Hyperspectral analysis of mangrove foliar chemistry using PLSR and support vector regression. *Int. J. Remote Sens.* **2013**, *34*, 1724–1743. [CrossRef]
38. Nitrogen in Plants. Available online: https://www.cropnutrition.com/nutrient-management/nitrogen/ (accessed on 2 July 2023).
39. Homolova, L.; Maenovsky, Z.; Clevers, J.; Garcia-Santos, G.; Schaeprnan, M.E. Review of optical-based remote sensing for plant trait mapping. *Ecol. Complex.* **2013**, *15*, 1–16. [CrossRef]
40. Le Maire, G.; Francois, C.; Soudani, K.; Berveiller, D.; Pontailler, J.Y.; Breda, N.; Genet, H.; Davi, H.; Dufrene, E. Calibration and validation of hyperspectral indices for the estimation of broadleaved forest leaf chlorophyll content, leaf mass per area, leaf area index and leaf canopy biomass. *Remote Sens. Environ.* **2008**, *112*, 3846–3864. [CrossRef]
41. Wu, C.; Niu, Z.; Tang, Q.; Huang, W. Estimating chlorophyll content from hyperspectral vegetation indices: Modeling and validation. *Agric. For. Meteorol.* **2008**, *148*, 1230–1241. [CrossRef]
42. Main, R.; Cho, M.A.; Mathieu, R.; O'Kennedy, M.M.; Ramoelo, A.; Koch, S. An investigation into robust spectral indices for leaf chlorophyll estimation. *ISPRS J. Photogramm. Remote Sens.* **2011**, *66*, 751–761. [CrossRef]
43. Sims, D.A.; Gamon, J.A. Relationships between leaf pigment content and spectral reflectance across a wide range of species, leaf structures and developmental stages. *Remote Sens. Environ.* **2002**, *81*, 337–354. [CrossRef]
44. Le Maire, G.; Francois, C.; Dufrene, E. Towards universal broad leaf chlorophyll indices using PROSPECT simulated da tabase and hyperspectral reflectance measurements. *Remote Sens. Environ.* **2004**, *89*, 1–28. [CrossRef]
45. Miphokasap, P.; Honda, K.; Vaiphasa, C.; Souris, M.; Nagai, M. Estimating canopy nitrogen concentration in sugarcane using field imaging spectroscopy. *Remote Sens.* **2012**, *4*, 1651–1670. [CrossRef]
46. Tian, Y.C.; Yao, X.; Yang, J.; Cao, W.X.; Hannaway, D.B.; Zhu, Y. Assessing newly developed and published vegetation indices for estimating rice leaf nitrogen concentration with ground- and space-based hyperspectral reflectance. *Field Crops Res.* **2011**, *120*, 299–310. [CrossRef]
47. Wang, W.; Yao, X.; Yao, X.; Tian, Y.; Liu, X.; Ni, J.; Cao, W.; Zhu, Y. Estimating leaf nitrogen concentration with three-band vegetation indices in rice and wheat. *Field Crops Res.* **2012**, *129*, 90–98. [CrossRef]
48. Gitelson, A.A.; Vina, A.; Ciganda, V.; Rundquist, D.C.; Arkebauer, T.J. Remote estimation of canopy chlorophyll content in crops. *Geophys. Res. Lett.* **2005**, *32*, 1–4. [CrossRef]
49. Fahad, S.M.; Younas, F.; Farooqi, Z.U.R.; Li, Y. Soil nitrogen dynamics in natural forest ecosystem: A review. *Front. For. Glob. Chang.* **2023**, *6*, 1144930. [CrossRef]
50. Knyazikhin, Y.; Schull, M.A.; Stenberg, P.; Mottus, M.; Rautiainen, M.; Yang, Y.; Marshak, A.; Latorre Carmona, P.; Kaufmann, R.K.; Lewis, P.; et al. Hyperspectral remote sensing of foliar nitrogen content. *Proc. Natl. Acad. Sci. USA* **2013**, *110*, E185–E192. [CrossRef]
51. Ollinger, S.V.; Reich, P.B.; Frolking, S.; Lepine, L.C.; Hollinger, D.Y.; Richardson, A.D. Nitrogen cycling, forest canopy reflectance, and emergent properties of ecosystems. *Proc. Natl. Acad. Sci. USA* **2013**, *110*, E2437. [CrossRef] [PubMed]
52. Ollinger, S. Sources of variability in canopy reflectance and the convergent properties of plants. *New Phytol.* **2011**, *189*, 375–394. [CrossRef]
53. Townsend, P.A.; Serbin, S.P.; Kruger, E.L.; Gamon, J.A. Disentangling the contribution of biological and physical properties of leaves and canopies in imaging spectroscopy data. *Proc. Natl. Acad. Sci. USA* **2013**, *110*, E1074. [CrossRef]
54. Wang, Z.; Wang, T.; Darvishzadeh, R.; Skidmore, A.K.; Jones, S.; Suarez, L.; Woodgate, W.; Heiden, U.; Heurich, M.; Hearne, J. Vegetation Indices for Mapping Canopy Foliar Nitrogen in a Mixed Temperate Forest. *Remote Sens.* **2016**, *8*, 491. [CrossRef]
55. Hartz, T.K. Vegetable production best management practices to minimize nutrient loss. *Horttechnology* **2006**, *16*, 398–403. [CrossRef]
56. Thompson, R.B.; Martínez-Gaitan, C.; Gallardo, M.; Giménez, C.; Fernández, M.D. Identification of irrigation and N management practices that contribute to nitrate leaching loss from an intensive vegetable production system by use of a comprehensive survey. *Agric. Water Manag.* **2007**, *89*, 261–274. [CrossRef]
57. Thompson, R.B.; Tremblay, N.; Fink, M.; Gallardo, M.; Padilla, F.M. Tools and strategies for sustainable nitrogen fertilisation of vegetable crops. In *Advances in Research on Fertilization Management in Vegetable Crops*; Tei, F., Nicola, S., Nincasa, B.P., Eds.; Springer: Berlin/Heidelberg, Germany, 2017; pp. 11–63.
58. Congreves, K.A.; Van Eerd, L.L. Nitrogen cycling and management in intensive horticultural systems. *Nutr. Cycl. Agroecosyst.* **2015**, *102*, 299–318. [CrossRef]
59. Padilla, F.M.; Gallardo, M.; Manzano-Agugliaro, F. Global trends in nitrate leaching research in the 1960–2017 period. *Sci. Total Environ.* **2018**, *643*, 400–413. [CrossRef]

60. Zotarelli, L.; Dukes, M.D.; Scholberg, J.M.S.; Muñoz-Carpena, R.; Icerman, J. Tomato nitrogen accumulation and fertilizer use efficiency on a sandy soil, as affected by nitrogen rate and irrigation scheduling. *Agric. Water Manag.* **2009**, *96*, 1247–1258. [CrossRef]
61. Ju, X.T.; Kou, C.L.; Zhang, F.S.; Christie, P. Nitrogen balance and groundwater nitrate contamination: Comparison among three intensive cropping systems on the North China Plain. *Environ. Pollut.* **2006**, *143*, 117–125. [CrossRef] [PubMed]
62. Soto, F.; Gallardo, M.; Thompson, R.B.; Peña-Fleitas, M.T.; Padilla, F.M. Consideration of total available N supply reduces N fertilizer requirement and potential for nitrate leaching loss in tomato production. *Agric. Ecosyst. Environ.* **2015**, *200*, 62–70. [CrossRef]
63. Zhu, J.H.; Li, X.L.; Christie, P.; Li, J.L. Environmental implications of low nitrogen use efficiency in excessively fertilized hot pepper (Capsicum frutescens L.) cropping systems. *Agric. Ecosyst. Environ.* **2005**, *111*, 70–80. [CrossRef]
64. Meisinger, J.J.; Schepers, J.S.; Raun, W.R. Crop Nitrogen Requirement and Fertilization. *Nitrogen Agric. Syst.* **2008**, *49*, 563–612. [CrossRef]
65. Fox, R.H.; Walthall, C.L. Crop monitoring technologies to assess nitrogen status. In *Nitrogen in Agricultural Systems, Agronomy Monograph No. 49*; Schepers, J.S., Raun, W.R., Eds.; American Society of Agronomy, Crop Science Society of America, Soil Science Society of America: Madison, WI, USA, 2008; pp. 647–674.
66. Yao, X.; Yao, X.; Jia, W.; Tian, Y.; Ni, J.; Cao, W.; Zhu, Y. Comparison and intercalibration of vegetation indices from different sensors for monitoring above-ground plant nitrogen uptake in winter wheat. *Sensors* **2013**, *13*, 3109–3130. [CrossRef] [PubMed]
67. Mistele, B.; Schmidhalter, U. Estimating the nitrogen nutrition index using spectral canopy reflectance measurements. *Eur. J. Agron.* **2008**, *29*, 184–190. [CrossRef]
68. Hansen, P.M.; Schjoerring, J.K. Reflectance measurement of canopy biomass and nitrogen status in wheat crops using normalized difference vegetation indices and partial least squares regression. *Remote Sens. Environ.* **2003**, *86*, 542–553. [CrossRef]
69. Padilla, F.M.; Gallardo, M.; Peña-Fleitas, M.T.; de Souza, R.; Thompson, R.B. Proximal Optical Sensors for Nitrogen Management of Vegetable Crops: A Review. *Sensors* **2018**, *18*, 2083. [CrossRef] [PubMed]
70. Samborski, S.M.; Tremblay, N.; Fallon, E. Strategies to make use of plant sensors-based diagnostic information for nitrogen recommendations. *Agron. J.* **2009**, *101*, 800–816. [CrossRef]
71. Cammarano, D.; Fitzgerald, G.J.; Casa, R.; Basso, B. Assessing the robustness of vegetation indices to estimate wheat N in mediterranean environments. *Remote Sens.* **2014**, *6*, 2827–2844. [CrossRef]
72. Basso, B.; Fiorentino, C.; Cammarano, D.; Schulthess, U. Variable rate nitrogen fertilizer response in wheat using remote sensing. *Precis. Agric.* **2015**, *17*, 168–182. [CrossRef]
73. Padilla, F.M.; Peña-Fleitas, M.T.; Gallardo, M.; Thompson, R.B. Determination of sufficiency values of canopy reflectance vegetation indices for maximum growth and yield of cucumber. *Eur. J. Agron.* **2017**, *84*, 1–15. [CrossRef]
74. Greenwood, D.J.; Gastal, F.; Lemaire, G.; Draycott, A.; Millard, P.; Neeteson, J.J. Growth rate and % N of field grown crops: Theory and experiments. *Ann. Bot.* **1991**, *67*, 181–190. [CrossRef]
75. Lemaire, G.; Jeuffroy, M.H.; Gastal, F. Diagnosis tool for plant and crop N status in vegetative stage: Theory and practices for crop N management. *Eur. J. Agron.* **2008**, *28*, 614–624. [CrossRef]
76. Lemaire, G.; Gastal, F. N Uptake and Distribution in Plant Canopies. In *Diagnosis of the Nitrogen Status in Crops*; Springer: Berlin/Heidelberg, Germany, 1997; pp. 3–43, ISBN 978-3-642-64506-8.
77. Hatfield, J.L.; Gitelson, A.A.; Schepers, J.S.; Walthall, C.L. Application of spectral remote sensing for agronomic decisions. *Agron. J.* **2008**, *100*, S117–S131. [CrossRef]
78. Liu, L.; Lindsay, P.L.; Jackson, D. Next Generation Cereal Crop Yield Enhancement: From Knowledge of Inflorescence Development to Practical Engineering by Genome Editing. *Int. J. Mol. Sci.* **2021**, *22*, 5167. [CrossRef] [PubMed]
79. Fitzgerald, G.; Rodriguez, D.; O'Leary, G. Measuring and predicting canopy nitrogen nutrition in wheat using a spectral index-The canopy chlorophyll content index (CCCI). *Field Crops Res.* **2010**, *116*, 318–324. [CrossRef]
80. Yu, K.; Li, F.; Gnyp, M.L.; Miao, Y.; Bareth, G.; Chen, X. Remotely detecting canopy nitrogen concentration and uptake of paddy rice in the Northeast China Plain. *ISPRS J. Photogramm. Remote Sens.* **2013**, *78*, 102–115. [CrossRef]
81. Cao, Q.; Miao, Y.; Wang, H.; Huang, S.; Cheng, S.; Khosla, R.; Jiang, R. Non-destructive estimation of rice plant nitrogen status with Crop Circle multispectral active canopy sensor. *Field Crops Res.* **2013**, *154*, 133–144. [CrossRef]
82. Xu, S.; Xu, X.; Blacker, C.; Gaulton, R.; Zhu, Q.; Yang, M.; Yang, G.; Zhang, J.; Yang, Y.; Yang, M.; et al. Estimation of Leaf Nitrogen Content in Rice Using Vegetation Indices and Feature Variable Optimization with Information Fusion of Multiple-Sensor Images from UAV. *Remote Sens.* **2023**, *15*, 854. [CrossRef]
83. de Souza, R.; Peña-Fleitas, M.T.; Thompson, R.B.; Gallardo, M.; Padilla, F.M. Assessing Performance of Vegetation Indices to Estimate Nitrogen Nutrition Index in Pepper. *Remote Sens.* **2020**, *12*, 763. [CrossRef]
84. Muharam, F.M.; Maas, S.J.; Bronson, K.F.; Delahunty, T. Estimating Cotton Nitrogen Nutrition Status Using Leaf Greenness and Ground Cover Information. *Remote Sens.* **2015**, *7*, 7007–7028. [CrossRef]
85. Wang, R.; Song, X.; Li, Z.; Yang, G.; Guo, W.; Tan, C.; Chen, L. Estimation of winter wheat nitrogen nutrition index using hyperspectral remote sensing. *Trans. Chin. Soc. Agric. Eng.* **2014**, *30*, 191–198.
86. Ciganda, V.S.; Gitelson, A.A.; Schepers, J. How Deep Does a Remote Sensor Sense? Expression of Chlorophyll Content in a Maize Canopy. *Remote Sens. Environ.* **2012**, *126*, 240–247. [CrossRef]

87. Tarpley, L.; Reddy, K.R.; Sassenrath-Cole, G.F. Reflectance Indices with Precision and Accuracy in Predicting Cotton LeafNitrogen Concentration. *Crop Sci.* **2000**, *40*, 1814–1819. [CrossRef]
88. Li, F.; Miao, Y.; Hennig, S.D.; Gnyp, M.L.; Chen, X.; Jia, L.; Bareth, G. Evaluating Hyperspectral Vegetation Indices for Estimating Nitrogen Concentration of Winter Wheat at Different Growth Stages. *Precis. Agric.* **2010**, *11*, 335–357. [CrossRef]
89. Patel, M.K.; Ryu, D.; Western, A.W.; Suter, H.; Young, I.M. Which Multispectral Indices Robustly Measure Canopy Nitrogen across Seasons: Lessons from an Irrigated Pasture Crop. *Comput. Electron. Agric.* **2021**, *182*, 106000. [CrossRef]
90. Wang, S.; Guan, K.; Wang, Z.; Ainsworth, E.A.; Zheng, T.; Townsend, P.A.; Li, K.; Moller, C.; Wu, G.; Jiang, C. Unique Contributions of Chlorophyll and Nitrogen to Predict Crop Photosynthetic Capacity from Leaf Spectroscopy. *J. Exp. Bot.* **2021**, *72*, 341–354. [CrossRef] [PubMed]
91. Ayhan, B.; Kwan, C.; Budavari, B.; Kwan, L.; Lu, Y.; Perez, D.; Li, J.; Skarlatos, D.; Vlachos, M. Vegetation Detection Using Deep Learning and Conventional Methods. *Remote Sens.* **2020**, *12*, 2502. [CrossRef]
92. Sun, Y.; Lao, D.; Ruan, Y.; Huang, C.; Xin, Q. A Deep Learning-Based Approach to Predict Large-Scale Dynamics of Normalized Difference Vegetation Index for the Monitoring of Vegetation Activities and Stresses Using Meteorological Data. *Sustainability* **2023**, *15*, 6632. [CrossRef]
93. Ecarnot, M.; Compan, F.; Roumet, P. Assessing Leaf Nitrogen Content and Leaf Mass per Unit Area of Wheat in the Field throughout Plant Cycle with a Portable Spectrometer. *Field Crops Res.* **2013**, *140*, 44–50. [CrossRef]
94. Li, Z.; Jin, X.; Wang, J.; Yang, G.; Nie, C.; Xu, X.; Feng, H. Estimating Winter Wheat (Triticum aestivum) LAI and Leaf Chlorophyll Content from Canopy Reflectance Data by Integrating Agronomic Prior Knowledge with the PROSAIL Model. *Int. J. Remote Sens.* **2015**, *36*, 2634–2653. [CrossRef]
95. Yao, X.; Huang, Y.; Shang, G.; Zhou, C.; Cheng, T.; Tian, Y.; Cao, W.; Zhu, Y. Evaluation of Six Algorithms to Monitor Wheat Leaf Nitrogen Concentration. *Remote Sens.* **2015**, *7*, 14939–14966. [CrossRef]
96. Ma, L.; Chen, X.; Zhang, Q.; Lin, J.; Yin, C.; Ma, Y.; Yao, Q.; Feng, L.; Zhang, Z.; Lv, X. Estimation of Nitrogen Content Based on the Hyperspectral Vegetation Indexes of Interannual and Multi-Temporal in Cotton. *Agronomy* **2022**, *12*, 1319. [CrossRef]
97. Wang, L.; Chen, S.; Li, D.; Wang, C.; Jiang, H.; Zheng, Q.; Peng, Z. Estimation of Paddy Rice Nitrogen Content and Accumulation Both at Leaf and Plant Levels from UAV Hyperspectral Imagery. *Remote Sens.* **2021**, *13*, 2956. [CrossRef]
98. Xu, X.; Fan, L.; Li, Z.; Meng, Y.; Feng, H.; Yang, H.; Xu, B. Estimating leaf nitrogen content in corn based on information fusion of multiple-sensor imagery from UAV. *Remote Sens.* **2021**, *13*, 340. [CrossRef]
99. Fan, Y.; Feng, H.; Jin, X.; Yue, J.; Liu, Y.; Li, Z.; Feng, Z.; Song, X.; Yang, G. Estimation of the nitrogen content of potato plants based on morphological parameters and visible light vegetation indices. *Front. Plant Sci.* **2022**, *13*, 1012070. [CrossRef] [PubMed]
100. Haider, T.; Farid, M.S.; Mahmood, R.; Ilyas, A.; Khan, M.H.; Haider, S.T.-A.; Chaudhry, M.H.; Gul, M. A Computer-Vision-Based Approach for Nitrogen Content Estimation in Plant Leaves. *Agriculture* **2021**, *11*, 766. [CrossRef]
101. EO-1 (Earth Observing-1). Available online: https://www.eoportal.org/satellite-missions/eo-1#eo-1-earth-observing-1 (accessed on 22 June 2023).
102. QGIS Software. Available online: https://qgis.org/en/site/ (accessed on 24 June 2023).
103. Urfa Haber. Available online: https://www.medyaurfa.com/gundem/harran-ovasi-gap-ile-ihya-oldu-h81516.html (accessed on 26 June 2023).
104. Çimtay, Y.; İlk, H.G. A novel bilinear unmixing approach for reconsideration of subpixel classification of land cover. *Comput. Electron. Agric.* **2018**, *152*, 126–140. [CrossRef]
105. Wang, L.; Wei, Y. Revised normalized difference nitrogen index (NDNI) for estimating canopy nitrogen concentration in wetlands. *Optik* **2016**, *127*, 7676–7688. [CrossRef]
106. Rouse, J.W.; Haas, R.H.; Schell, J.A.; Deering, D.W. *Monitoring Vegetation Systems in the Great Plains with ERTS*; Third ERTS Symposium; NASA: Washington, DC, USA, 1973; pp. 309–317.
107. Gitelson, A.A.; Merzlyak, M.N. Remote Sensing of Chlorophyll Concentration in Higher Plant Leaves. *Adv. Space Res.* **1998**, *22*, 689–692. [CrossRef]
108. Huete, A.; Didan, K.; Miura, T.; Rodriguez, E.P.; Gao, X.; Ferreira, L.G. Overview of the Radiometric and Biophysical Performance of the MODIS Vegetation Indices. *Remote Sens. Environ.* **2002**, *83*, 195–213. [CrossRef]
109. Sripada, R.P. Determining In-Season Nitrogen Requirements for Corn Using Aerial Color-Infrared Photography. Ph.D. Dissertation, North Carolina State University, Raleigh, NC, USA, 2005.
110. Haboudane, D.; Miller, J.R.; Pattey, E.; Zarco-Tejada, P.J.; Strachan, I.B. Hyperspectral Vegetation Indices and Novel Algorithms for Predicting Green LAI of Crop Canopies: Modeling and Validation in the Context of Precision Agriculture. *Remote Sens. Environ.* **2004**, *90*, 337–352. [CrossRef]
111. Vogelmann, J.; Rock, B.; Moss, D. Red Edge Spectral Measurements from Sugar Maple Leaves. *Int. J. Remote Sens.* **1993**, *14*, 1563–1575. [CrossRef]
112. Serrano, L.; Penuelas, J.; Ustin, S. Remote Sensing of Nitrogen and Lignin in Mediterranean Vegetation from AVIRIS Data: Decomposing Biochemical from Structural Signals. *Remote Sens. Environ.* **2002**, *81*, 355–364. [CrossRef]
113. Deep Learning Toolbox. Available online: https://www.mathworks.com/products/deep-learning.html (accessed on 28 June 2023).

114. Hagan, M.T.; Menhaj, M.B. Training feedforward networks with the Marquardt algorithm. *IEEE Trans. Neural Netw.* **1994**, *5*, 989–993. [CrossRef] [PubMed]
115. Wang, F.-Y. Control 5.0: From Newton to Merton in popper's cybersocial-physical spaces. *IEEE/CAA J. Autom. Sin.* **2016**, *3*, 233–234.

remote sensing

MDPI

Article

Cotton Seedling Detection and Counting Based on UAV Multispectral Images and Deep Learning Methods

Yingxiang Feng [1,†], Wei Chen [1], Yiru Ma [1], Ze Zhang [1], Pan Gao [2,†] and Xin Lv [1,*]

[1] Xinjiang Production and Construction Crops Oasis Eco-Agriculture Key Laboratory, College of Agriculture, Shihezi University, Shihezi 832003, China; fengyingxiang@163.com (Y.F.); m17792619205@163.com (W.C.); mayiru@stu.shzu.edu.cn (Y.M.); zhangze1227@shzu.edu.cn (Z.Z.)

[2] College of Information Science and Technology, Shihezi University, Shihezi 832003, China; gp_inf@shzu.edu.cn

* Correspondence: luxin@shzu.edu.cn

† These authors contributed equally to this work.

Abstract: Cotton is one of the most important cash crops in Xinjiang, and timely seedling inspection and replenishment at the seedling stage are essential for cotton's late production management and yield formation. The background conditions of the cotton seedling stage are complex and variable, and deep learning methods are widely used to extract target objects from the complex background. Therefore, this study takes seedling cotton as the research object and uses three deep learning algorithms, YOLOv5, YOLOv7, and CenterNet, for cotton seedling detection and counting using images at six different times of the cotton seedling period based on multispectral images collected by UAVs to develop a model applicable to the whole cotton seedling period. The results showed that when tested with data collected at different times, YOLOv7 performed better overall in detection and counting, and the T4 dataset performed better in each test set. Precision, Recall, and F1-Score values with the best test results were 96.9%, 96.6%, and 96.7%, respectively, and the R^2, RMSE, and RRMSE indexes were 0.94, 3.83, and 2.72%, respectively. In conclusion, the UAV multispectral images acquired about 23 days after cotton sowing (T4) with the YOLOv7 algorithm achieved rapid and accurate seedling detection and counting throughout the cotton seedling stage.

Keywords: cotton; seedling stage; count; detection; multispectral images; deep learning

1. Introduction

Cotton is the second largest crop after grain [1], and cotton production significantly impacts national economic development. Timely seedling inspection and replenishment during the cotton seedling stage is a prerequisite for ensuring high yield, quality, and efficiency in the later stages of cotton production [2]. Accurate estimates of the number of plants in a field crop is essential to predict yield [3,4]. Therefore, rapid and accurate detection and counting during the cotton seedling stage is essential. At present, the traditional counting method is mainly based on manual counting. Challenges such as high cost, high workload, poor timeliness, inaccurate counting, and poor data representativeness are not conducive to timely replanting. In contrast, UAV remote sensing-assisted counting can make up for the shortcomings of manual counting.

UAV remote sensing technology has recently been widely used in agriculture because of its low cost, high resolution, and fast and repeatable capture capability [5,6]. Compared with ground-based crewless vehicles and high-altitude satellite remote sensing images, UAVs are more suitable for farmland monitoring and are less affected by the atmosphere. Currently, there are more studies on monitoring seedling emergence and plant density of maize [7,8], cotton [9,10], and rice [11,12] based on UAV images. Thus, acquiring high-resolution images based on UAV remote sensing platforms is becoming an essential tool for crop emergence detection, crop growth monitoring, and yield prediction [13–15]. Most previous studies were based on RGB images acquired by UAVs for counting plants and seedlings [16–18].

However, when performing crop seedling counting, the high proportion of soil in the images and the strong influence of soil reflectance on crop color due to the small size of plants and the sensitivity of visible images to light changes pose a challenge for seedling detection and counting [19]. Furthermore, in the single-minded pursuit of high precision, the imaging requirements of RGB cameras are getting higher and higher; however, this pursuit also means an increase in cost. In contrast, the near-infrared (NIR) channel has a high reflectance and generally absorbs 10% or less of the radiation [20]. Compared with RGB images under low-illumination conditions, NIR images have a clear structure and no noise impairment [21,22]. Therefore, multispectral images with near-infrared (NIR) bands can be used more effectively for crop segmentation and counting.

The existing Phantom 4 Multispectral UAV imaging system, which does not require additional integration for image geotagging, has a low payload weight, is less burdensome to operate for acquisition [23], can also work under different lighting conditions, and is suitable for crop phenotyping studies [24]. Nevertheless, multispectral imaging systems are less used for plant seedling counting. The resolution of images acquired by RGB sensors at the same image size is lower than that of spectral sensors [25]. In contrast, hyperspectral images have a large amount of data and redundant information compared to multispectral images, which are more suitable for information extraction. Osco et al. [26] evaluated the performance of individual bands and their combinations using multispectral images in four bands (red, green, red-edge, and NIR) and the results showed that the combination of three bands, red, green, and NIR, had better performance. Multispectral imaging allows the calculation of multiple vegetation indexes, which can be used for plant phenotyping studies and the development of multivariate regression models [27]. In this multivariate approach, spectral, morphological, or textural information can be used individually or in combination with each other [28]. For example, random forests (RF) and support vector machines (SVM) are used to rapidly classify images [29]. Traditional machine learning algorithms such as random forest (RF) and support vector machine (SVM) can quickly classify images. Support vector machine models can be used to classify spectral and textural features and estimate seedling number and density [30]. For supervised classification methods, manually selecting a sufficient number of representative samples from many images is tedious and time-consuming, and the manual selection also reduces classification accuracy [31]. Therefore, more innovative algorithms are being created, tested, and improved; for example, based on deep learning models are used to build the model to identify methods with better generalizability.

Deep learning techniques can accurately extract target objects from complex backgrounds [32]. Compared to traditional methods, deep learning can automatically learn different features from images or datasets to identify and locate individual objects of interest [33]. Fan et al. [34] combined whole convolutional networks (FCNs) based on RGB images from drones to count beets, corn, and strawberries with an error of less than 4.6%. Barreto et al. [35] proposed a convolutional neural network (CNN)-based deep learning method that performs planting row identification and plant counting with high accuracy for maize and citrus. Experiments using deep learning algorithms to perform counting tasks have been conducted in various industries, but many challenges remain. For example, image resolution, weeds, plant size, plant density, and overlap directly affect detection and counting accuracies [36]. To improve detection accuracy, many researchers have developed and improved target detection algorithms according to their needs. YOLOv5, YOLOv7, and CenterNet are algorithms that have been applied to target detection tasks. YOLOv5 and YOLOv7 are anchor point-based target detection algorithms. These algorithms mainly generate candidate frames based on predefined anchor points, identify different sizes and aspect ratios of anchor points, compare them with genuine target frames, and consider them as target objects if they exceed a certain threshold; otherwise, they are considered as background or other objects. YOLOv5 has been applied to pest identification [37], tomato virus disease identification [38], and apple real-time target detection [39]. YOLOv7 has been applied to the estimation of the sparrow duck population [40], real-time detection of kiwi [41], and localization of road cracks [42]. CenterNet is an improved version of CornerNet, a key point-based target detection algorithm. After the previous key point target detection algorithm, an additional essential point matching process, the NMS post-processing process is needed. In contrast, this algorithm only predicts the location of the center point of the bounding box. It uses the center point as the key point, eliminating the post-processing process and improving the detection speed. CenterNet has been applied to construction vehicle detection [43], cotton seedling counting [44], and wheat broadleaf weed seedling detection [45]. All three algorithms have great potential for plant detection and counting.

Therefore, the multispectral images acquired by the UAV at different times were used to construct seedling detection and counting models by (1) selecting the optimal algorithm using the performance of YOLOv5, YOLOv7, and CenterNet in the six time points of collected UAV multispectral images; (2) selecting the optimal cotton seedling detection and counting time based on the selected optimal algorithm; and (3) final selection of the cotton seedling detection and counting model applicable to the whole seedling stage. Altogether, the aim of this study was to identify a method to provide a fast, highly time-efficient decision and basis for later agricultural production management.

2. Materials and Methods

2.1. Experimental Sites

As shown in Figure 1, the experiment was conducted in April–May 2022 at the Second Company of Shihezi University Agricultural Experimental Farm (44°19′N, 85°59′E; 443 m above sea level). The varieties planted in the trial area were "Xinlu Early 53" and "Xinlu Early 84", and the planting pattern was "one film, three tubes, and six rows" with a comprehensive and narrow row design. The sowing date was 15 April 2022, and the seedling emergence rate was about 85% on April 25. The trial was conducted at the cotton's 2–4-leaf stage (including cotyledons). The specific sampling dates were: 25 April 2022 (T1, 10 days after sowing), 1 May 2022 (T2, 17 days after sowing), 5 May 2022 (T3, 21 days after sowing), 7 May 2022 (T4, 23 days after sowing), 9 May 2022 (T5, 25 days after sowing), and 12 May 2022 (T6, 28 days after sowing).

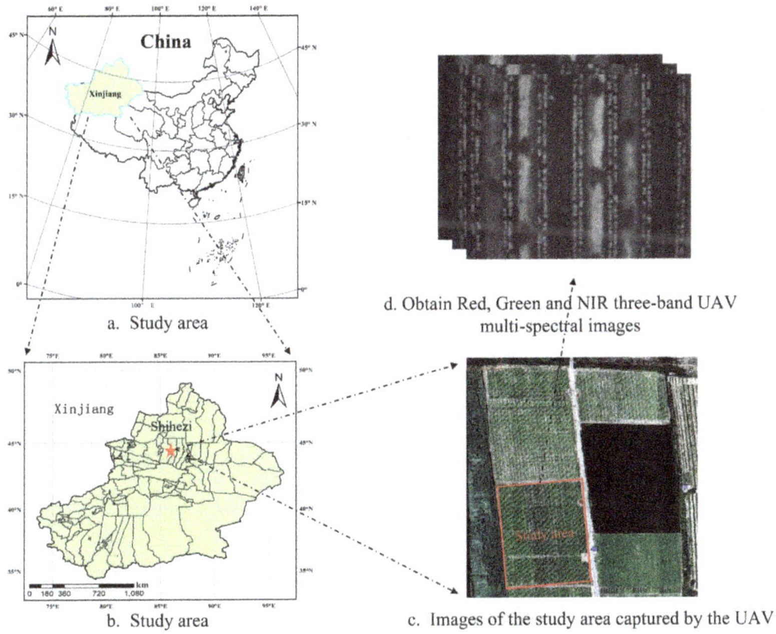

Figure 1. Study area overview: (**a**) is the map of Xinjiang, (**b**) is the map of Shihezi, (**c**) is the test site, and (**d**) is the multispectral images collected by the UAV.

2.2. Data Collection

2.2.1. Ground Data Acquisition

Company 2 of the Agricultural Experimental Farm of Shihezi University was the experimental site. The varieties planted in the experimental area were "Xinlu Early 53" and "Xinlu Early 84" from April to May 2022.

2.2.2. UAV Image Acquisition

The drone data acquisition was performed on the same day as the ground data acquisition. The lens was positioned vertically downward during image acquisition, and the interval was 2 s. The flight height was 10 m, the course overlap degree was 60%, and the side overlap degree was 60%. The parameters of the UAV are shown in Table 1. The camera parameters were as follows: FOV was 62.7°, the focal length was 5.74 mm, the aperture was f/2.2, and the monochrome sensors were 2 megapixels. The image resolution was 1600 × 1300 pixels, and the format was TIFF (multispectral imaging). Images of the red, green, and near-infrared bands were acquired, and the acquired images were stitched into orthophoto images using DJI Wisdom (China, DJI) software. The orthophoto images after stitching were stored in TIFF format.

Table 1. Phantom 4 Multispectral parameters.

Parameter	Value
UAV weight	1487 g
Max flight time	27 min
Image max resolution	1600 × 1300 (4:3.25)

2.3. Image Processing

As shown in Figure 2, in the first step, the acquired UAV images were stitched into ortho images using DJI Smart Image (DJI, China) software, and the stitched orthoimages were stored in TIFF format. In the second step, the acquired multispectral images in the red, green, and near-infrared bands were band synthesized using ENVI5.3. In the third step, a cropping operation was performed on the pre-processed images using Python 3.8. This cropping operation removed the edge data with more distortion and anomalies during the stitching process, reducing the impact of related algorithm design and model construction.

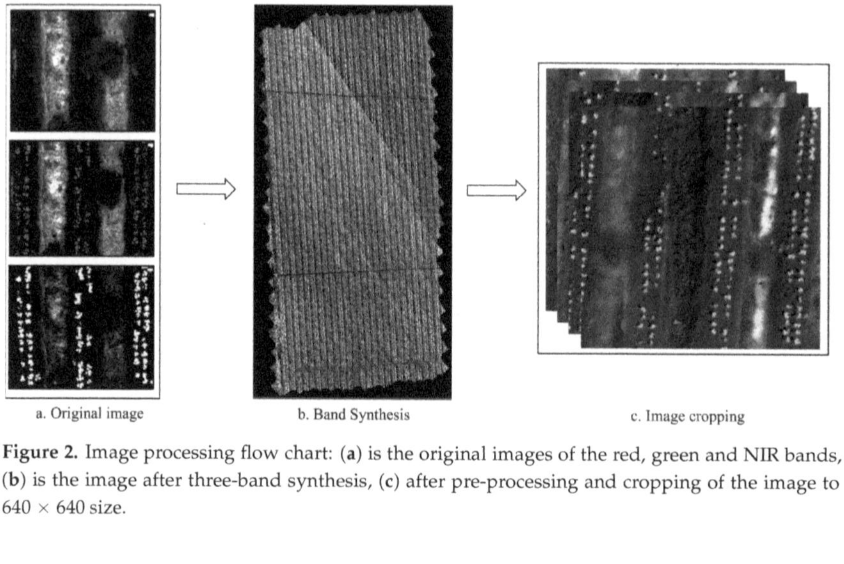

Figure 2. Image processing flow chart: (**a**) is the original images of the red, green and NIR bands, (**b**) is the image after three-band synthesis, (**c**) after pre-processing and cropping of the image to 640 × 640 size.

2.4. Dataset Creation

The segmented images were opened for labeling using the labelimg tool; 40 images were labeled each time, 240 images were labeled 6 times, and 37,840 cotton seedlings were labeled. After the labelling was completed, the six datasets were randomly divided according to the ratio of the training set/validation set = 3:1. We applied the validation sets from other time points as the test dataset at a particular time when performing the test. However, we tested the models individually each time instead of testing the models by combining the validation sets from several other times together, as shown in Table 2. For example, the test results for T1 were from testing the detection and counting models constructed for the T1 dataset against the validation sets for the T2, T3, T4, T5, and T6 datasets, individually.

Table 2. The number of cotton seedling marks in training, verification, and testing images at different time points.

Time	Train Set	Val (Test) Set	Total
T1	3234	1143	4377
T2	3715	1235	4950
T3	6284	2108	8392
T4	4192	1305	5497
T5	4160	1408	5568
T6	6770	2286	9056
Total	28,355	9485	37,840

T1–T6 were 10 days after seeding, 17 days after seeding, 21 days after seeding, 23 days after seeding, 25 days after seeding, and 28 days after seeding, respectively. Train, Val, Test, and Total represent the number of markers of cotton shoots in the training set, verification set, test set, and in total, respectively.

2.5. Deep Learning Models

2.5.1. YOLOv5

As the basic version of the YOLO series, YOOv1 is a one-stage object detection algorithm that directly generates a location and category from pictures without a region proposal process. Compared with YOLOv1, YOLOv2 improves the detection performance. A common training method is proposed to train the target detector on detection and classification data. The network structure of YOLOv3 is divided into four parts [46]: Input Terminal, Backbone, Neck, and Prediction. Yolov4 has many innovations based on YOLOv3. For example, mosaic data are used for input; CSPDarknet53, Mish activation function, and Dropblock are used for the Backbone; SPP and FPN+PAN are used for Neck; and CIOU_Loss and DIOU_nms operations are used for the output. Compared with YOLOv4 [47], the input side of YOLOv5 is still mosaic data enhancement, while adding an adaptive anchor frame calculation, adaptive picture scaling, and other operations. The Backbone adopts a Focus structure and CSP structure. The Neck is still an FPN+PAN structure [48]. The Prediction part is also the GIOU_Loss operation. The network structure diagram is shown in Figure 3. The image input size is 640 × 640, the initial training weight file was yolov5s, the optimizer selected is SGD, the batch size is 16, and the epoch is 300.

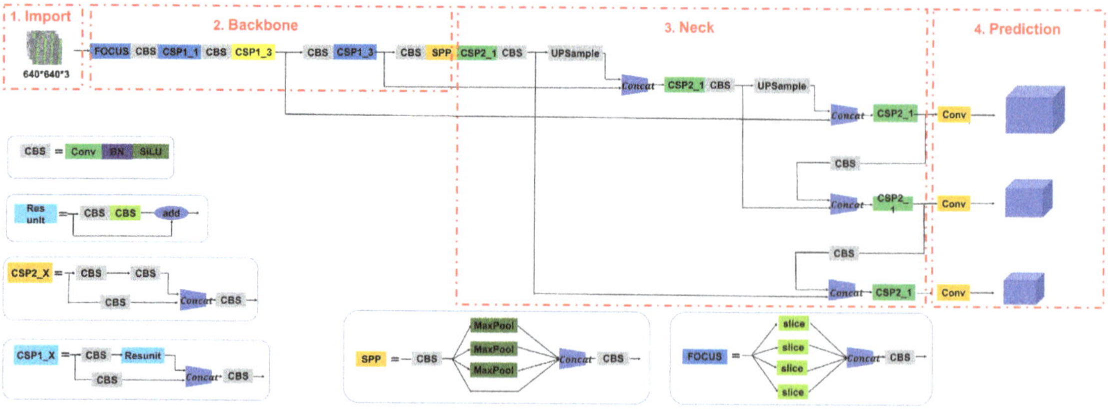

Figure 3. YOLOv5 network structure.

2.5.2. YOLOv7

YOLOv7 is inherited mainly from YOLOv5, including the overall network architecture, configuration file setup, training, reasoning, and verification processes. In addition, YOLOv7 also inherits a lot from YOLOR, including the design of different networks, the setting of hyperparameters, and the inclusion of implicit knowledge learning. It also imitates YOLOX's SimOTA strategy when matching positive samples. In addition to these structures in the existing YOLO version, YOLOv7 includes the latest tricks in recent years: efficient aggregation networks, reparameterized convolution, auxiliary training modules, model scaling, and more. In the efficient aggregation network the main factors to consider are the number of parameters, computation, and computation density. By controlling the shortest and longest gradient paths, deeper networks can learn efficiently and converge better. The role of reparameterization is to accelerate the network under the condition of ensuring the performance of the model. It mainly fuses the convolution +BN layer and different convolutions into a convolution module. The auxiliary training module uses deep supervision which is commonly used to train deep networks. The central concept is to add additional auxiliary heads in the middle layer of the network and shallow network weights guided by auxiliary losses. The role of model scaling is to scale the baseline up or down to make it applicable to different computing devices [49]. Model scaling methods usually include different scaling factors such as input size, depth, width, and stage, thus achieving a good trade-off in terms of the number of parameters, computation, reasoning speed, and network precision. The network structure diagram is shown in Figure 4. The image input size was 640 × 640, the initial training weights file was yolov7, the optimizer was adam, the batch size was 8, and the epoch was 1000.

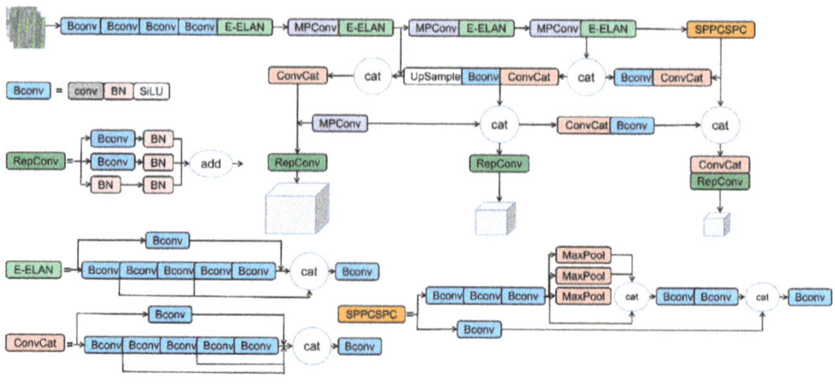

Figure 4. YOLOv7 network structure.

2.5.3. CenterNet

CenterNet is an anchorless target detection algorithm that is an improvement of the CornerNet algorithm. The algorithm removes inefficient and complex anchors, performs filtering operations directly on the heat map, removes time-consuming NMS post-processing operations, transforms the target detection problem into a critical point detection problem, and further improves the performance of the detection algorithm. In contrast to CenterNet, most target detection and recognition algorithms usually frame the target in a rectangular box. The horizontal and vertical axes of the rectangular box are parallel to the horizontal and vertical axes of the image. These detectors identify potential target locations and then classify them, which wastes time and requires additional post-processing. CenterNet, on the other hand, does not require manual thresholding of foreground or background by assigning anchors based on location rather than dense coverage on the feature map. Each object in it has only one positive sample of anchor, so there is no need for non-maximal value suppression processing, i.e., no post-processing methods are required, and only local peaks in the critical point heatmap need to be extracted. A larger output resolution is used, which eliminates the need for multiple anchors [50]. The primary process of building the target detection and recognition model is as follows: the image is fed into a fully convolutional network used to generate the heatmap, the peak position of the heatmap is the center of the target, and the image features at each peak position are used to predict the width and height of the target bounding box. Its network structure diagram is shown in Figure 5. The image input size was 640 × 640, the initial training weights file was centernet_resnet50_voc, the optimizer was chosen as adam, the batch size was 4, and the epoch was 900.

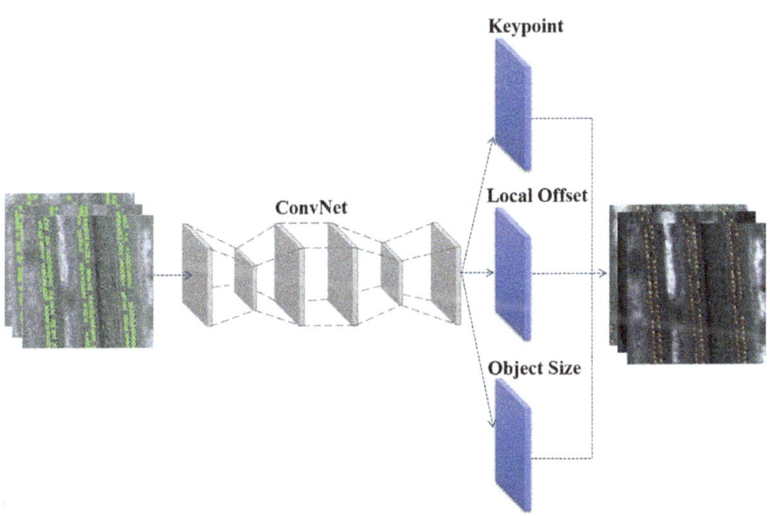

Figure 5. CenterNet network structure.

2.6. Precision Validation

In this study, *Precision*, *Recall*, and *F1* Score were used to determine the cotton detection and counting results. The calculation formula is as follows:

$$Precision = \frac{TP}{TP + FP}$$

$$Recall = \frac{TP}{TP + FN}$$

$$F1 = 2 \times \frac{Precision \times Recall}{Precision + recall}$$

TP is the true positives where the predicted result is cotton, the actual category is cotton, and the prediction is correct. TN is the true negatives where the prediction result is not cotton, a correct category is not cotton, and the prediction is correct. FP is the false positives where the proper category is not cotton, the prediction result is cotton, and the prediction is incorrect. FN is the false negatives where the correct category is cotton, the prediction result is not cotton, and the prediction is incorrect.

The coefficient of determination (R^2), root mean square error ($RMSE$), and relative root mean square error ($RRMSE$) were used as evaluation indexes to evaluate the performance of cotton seedling counting results.

$$R^2 = 1 - \frac{\sum_1^n (m_i - c_i)^2}{\sum_1^n \left(m_i - \bar{m_i}\right)^2}$$

$$RMSE = \sqrt{\frac{\sum_1^n (m_i - c_i)^2}{n}}$$

$$RRMSE = \sqrt{\frac{\sum_{i=1}^{n} (m_i - c_i)^2}{n}} \times \frac{1}{c_i}$$

where m_i, $\bar{m_i}$ and c_i are, respectively, the number of artificially labeled cotton seedlings in the image i, the average number of artificially labeled cotton seedlings in the image i, and the predicted number of cotton seedlings. n is the number of images tested.

3. Results

3.1. Model Validation

3.1.1. Model Training and Verification Test Results

As shown in Table 3, when deep learning cotton seedling detection was conducted based on YOLOv5, the performance at each time point was in the order of T3 > T6 > T4 > T2 > T5 > T1, with the best detection results at T3 and the worst at T1. When deep learning cotton seedling detection was conducted based on YOLOv7, the performance at each time point was in the order of T3 > T6 > T4 > T5 > T2 > T1. The detection results were the best at T3 and the worst at T1. When deep learning cotton seedling detection was conducted based on CenterNet, the performance at each time point was in the order of T6 > T3 > T5 > T4 > T2 > T1; the best results were detected at T6, and the worst results were detected at T1. In summary, when the Precision, Recall, and F1-Score were comprehensively evaluated, the performance of the three algorithms was in the order of YOLOv7 > YOLOv5 > CenterNet.

Table 3. Model training and validation test results.

Model	Time	Training Set			Validation Set		
		Precision (%)	Recall (%)	F1-Score (%)	Precision (%)	Recall (%)	F1-Score (%)
YOLOv5	T1	93.1	93.6	93.3	93.8	88.7	91.2
	T2	95.9	95.2	95.5	96.6	96.0	96.3
	T3	97.4	96.4	96.9	98.4	98.0	98.2
	T4	96.1	95.7	95.9	96.5	95.4	95.9
	T5	96.1	96.1	96.1	96.1	94.5	95.3
	T6	97.7	95.7	96.7	97.2	94.6	95.9
YOLOv7	T1	92.3	94.4	93.3	94.3	92.0	93.2
	T2	96.0	96.5	96.2	95.9	96.6	96.2
	T3	97.3	98.2	97.7	98.1	98.6	98.3
	T4	96.8	96.2	96.5	96.9	96.6	96.7
	T5	95.8	96.4	96.1	97.3	96.5	96.9
	T6	98.5	97.9	98.2	97.3	96.0	96.7
CenterNet	T1	89.2	79.3	83.9	85.7	79.5	82.5
	T2	93.3	82.8	87.7	92.9	82.6	87.4
	T3	96.4	87.6	91.8	96.8	88.2	92.3
	T4	95.1	83.1	88.7	94.8	83.8	89.0
	T5	95.1	84.3	89.4	96.6	85.5	90.7
	T6	98.2	93.2	95.6	97.9	93.4	95.6

3.1.2. Model Training and Verification of Counting Results

As shown in Table 4, based on the performance evaluation of YOLOv5 in cotton counting, the performance at each time point was in order of T2 > T4 > T3 > T5 > T1 > T6. The training and verification results at T2 were the best, while the training and verification results at T6 were the worst. Based on the performance evaluation of YOLOv7 in cotton counting, the performance of each time point was in the order of T2 > T3 > T5 > T4 > T1 > T6. The training and verification counting results were the best at T2 and the worst at T6. Based on the performance evaluation of CenterNet in cotton counting, the performance of CenterNet at each time was in the order of T2 > T3 > T4 > T5 > T6 > T1, with the best training and verification counting results at T2 and the worst at T1.

Table 4. Model training and verification counting results.

Model	Time	Training Set			Validation Set		
		R^2	RMSE	RRMSE (%)	R^2	RMSE	RRMSE (%)
YOLOv5	T1	0.85	9.36	8.40	0.64	12.48	11.46
	T2	0.97	5.97	4.82	0.90	6.50	5.27
	T3	0.91	9.53	4.55	0.93	9.97	4.73
	T4	0.94	5.79	4.14	0.90	4.63	3.54
	T5	0.94	7.89	5.69	0.87	5.41	3.84
	T6	0.74	17.24	7.64	0.29	22.98	10.05
YOLOv7	T1	0.88	7.25	6.50	0.65	11.10	10.20
	T2	0.97	11.48	9.27	0.91	5.21	4.22
	T3	0.92	8.32	3.97	0.94	8.03	3.81
	T4	0.92	5.82	4.16	0.90	4.32	3.31
	T5	0.92	8.36	6.03	0.92	5.39	3.83
	T6	0.78	9.17	4.06	0.57	11.61	5.08
CenterNet	T1	0.88	10.55	9.46	0.68	12.75	11.71
	T2	0.97	6.80	5.49	0.93	5.77	4.67
	T3	0.95	6.66	3.18	0.94	8.55	4.06
	T4	0.94	5.47	3.92	0.91	3.95	3.03
	T5	0.92	6.87	4.96	0.97	3.36	2.39
	T6	0.95	3.95	1.75	0.69	6.55	2.87

Figure 8 shows an example of cotton seedling detection and counting at T4. The three algorithms all overestimated the number of cotton seedlings, and visually interpreted one hundred and thirty-seven cotton seedlings. The YOLOv5 algorithm detected one hundred and forty-one cotton seedlings, and four were false positives. The YOLOv7 algorithm detected one hundred and forty cotton plants with three false positives. CenterNet algorithm detected one hundred and forty-four seedlings, with seven false positives.

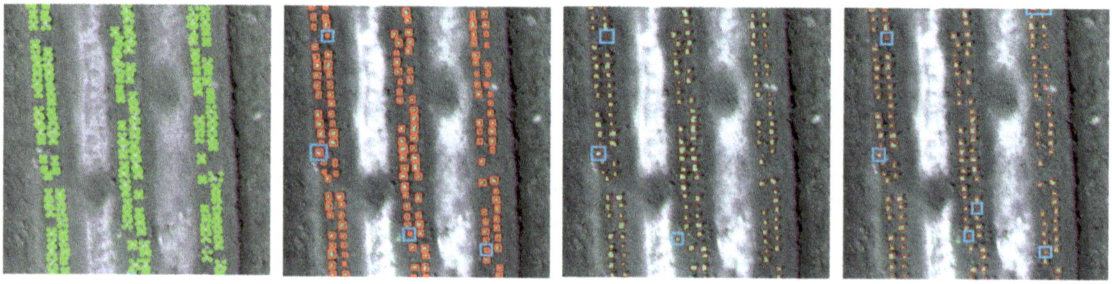

(a) (b) (c) (d)

Figure 8. An example of the results from the three algorithms for counting cotton seedlings in the T4 dataset: (**a**) is the manually labeled cotton seedling image, (**b–d**) represent the counting results using the YOLOv5, YOLOv7 and CenterNet algorithms, respectively; yellow boxes indicate missed detections, blue boxes indicate false positives.

Figure 9 shows the test results at different time points compared to T4 based on the YOLOv7 algorithm. A total of one hundred and fourteen cotton seedlings were detected in one image at T1. There were one hundred and fourteen cotton seedlings in an image at T2. The algorithm overestimated the number of seedlings and detected one hundred and eighteen cotton seedlings, with six false positives and two false negatives. A total of two hundred and one cotton seedlings were detected in an image during the T3 period. The algorithm overestimated the number of seedlings and detected two hundred and five cotton seedlings, with five false positives and one false negatives. There were one hundred and thirty-nine cotton seedlings in an image during the T5 period. The algorithm overestimated the number of seedlings and detected one hundred and forty-two cotton seedlings, with five false positives and two false negatives. There were two hundred and twenty-five cotton seedlings in an image during the T6 period. The algorithm overestimated the number of seedlings and detected 235 cotton seedlings, with 11 false positives and 1 false negative. The number of specific cotton seedlings detected and the number of false positives in the training and validation set of the T4 dataset are shown in Table 5.

Table 5. Number of specific cotton seedlings and false positives detected in the training and validation sets of the T4 dataset.

Model	Training Set				Validation Set			
	True Value	Predicted Value	False Positive	False Negative	True Value	Predicted Value	False Positive	False Negative
YOLOv5	4192	4334	150	8	1305	1339	37	3
YOLOv7	4192	4324	135	3	1305	1334	31	2
CenterNet	4192	4326	140	6	1305	1333	31	3

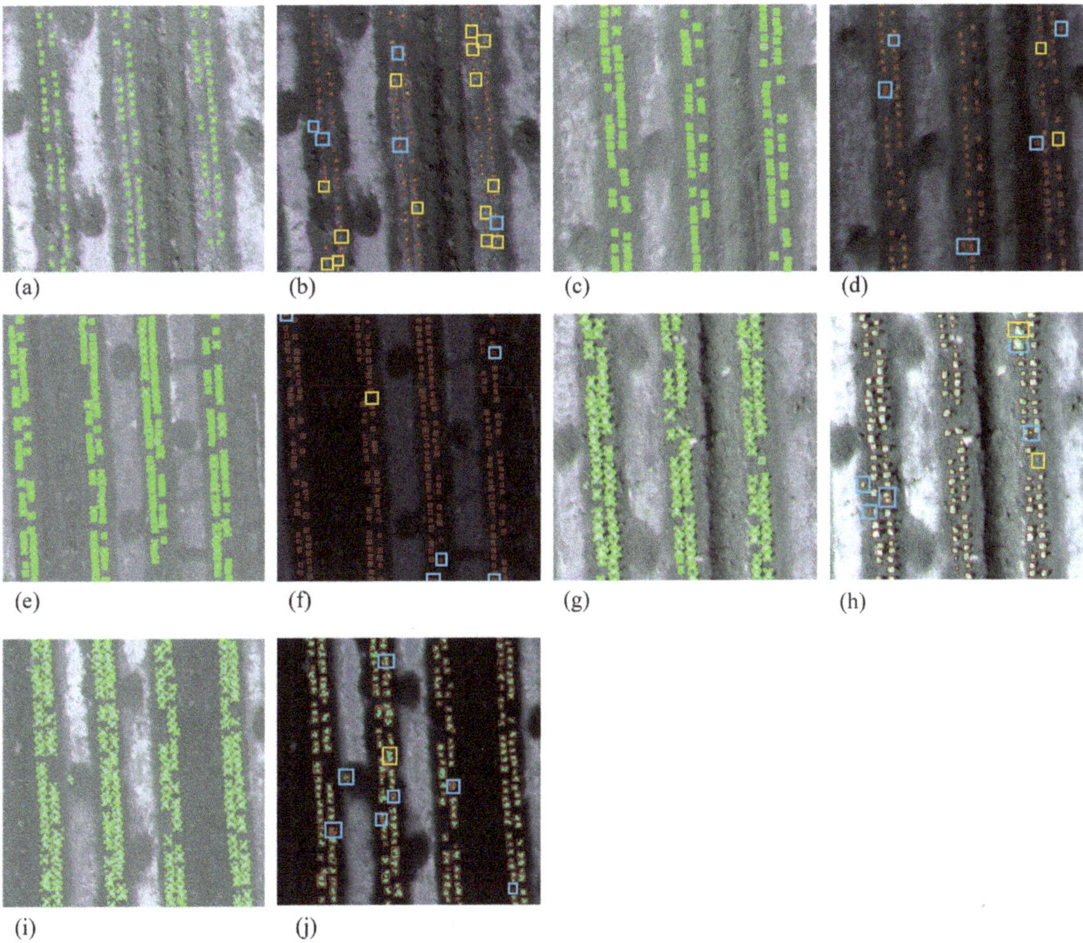

Figure 9. The T4 dataset was tested using YOLOv7, as well as the counts of the model in the other five datasets: (a,c,e,g,i) indicate manually labeled images in the T1, T2, T3, T5, and T6 datasets, respectively. (b,d,f,h,j) correspond to the count results of YOLOv7. The yellow box in the figure indicates a missed detection, and the blue box indicates a false detection. (f,j) indicate T3 and T6, which were cloudy at the time of image acquisition.

4. Discussion

As cotton seedlings gradually grew from small to large, the number of cotton leaves gradually increased. There were significant differences between the detection and counting models at different time points. Therefore, the image acquisition time point is particularly critical in cotton detection and counting, which determines cotton size. If the images are acquired too early, the seedlings are too small to be detected and counted, e.g., seedling detection and counting at T1 in this study. If the images are acquired too late, the cotton seedlings reach the four-leaf stage, and the leaves have spread out, with crossing and overlap occurring between leaves, resulting in underestimation of the cotton population, e.g., seedling detection and counting at T6 in this study, which are also the two significant challenges encountered so far [51]. Due to the short window of cotton seedlings, if the best time to replenish them is missed, it will affect the cotton yield at the later harvest. To overcome these challenges, we should mainly improve the algorithms, such as YOLOv5 and YOLOv7, which are more effective in small target detection, and CenterNet, which is more effective in detecting seedlings when they are larger, in order to combine the advantages of each algorithm to improve and solve the significant challenges caused by smaller seedlings and overlapping leaves. Because the growth rate of cotton seedlings depends on different environmental factors, such as soil type, temperature, water, and fertilizer, and weather conditions, in this study, the image collection time was from ten days after seeding to twenty-seven days after seeding, with a total of six time points for collection, which is the reference value for determining the optimal detection and counting time.

The resolution of multispectral images is mainly determined by the UAV's camera or sensor and the UAV's flying altitude. Better cameras and sensors represent a high cost. The standard minimum flying altitude is ten meters, and it is recommended to fly at most ten meters. This study used a multispectral camera to obtain multispectral images of the red, green, and near-infrared bands with sound detection and counting accuracy [52]. A multispectral sensor collected images for cotton plant detection and counting, and good results were also obtained. Compared with RGB cameras, we obtained more information about the cotton, and the presence of cotton in the image was more prominent [53,54].

The vast majority of cotton grown in Xinjiang province is sprayed with herbicide before sowing, a process that minimizes the impact of weeds. Then, machines are used to lay drip irrigation belts, planters, and plastic film. Placing the plastic film keeps weeds from growing between the cotton seedlings, ensuring that weeds do not interfere with target detection and competition for cotton nutrients. In order to prevent the plastic film from blowing away in strong winds, the plastic film is covered with a layer of soil at a specific interval. However, although this layer of soil solves the risk of the film blowing away, it also increases the difficulty of the growth of cotton seedlings [55]. About ten days after sowing, seedlings should be released. In order to prevent seedlings from being burned to death at high temperatures, seedlings should be able to grow normally from between the plastic film. Due to the small size of the cotton seedlings, some of them were not taller than the plastic film, such as the T1 period in this study, so the counting accuracy was complicated.

In this paper, cotton leaves included two–four leaves from ten days to twenty-seven days after sowing, and the morphological diversity of cotton was relatively affluent. According to the analysis of the detection and counting effects from training verification and test results, model training speed, and weight file size, the overall performance of the YOLOv7 algorithm is promising. YOLOv7 extends the E-ELAN network based on YOLOv5, and extends, disorders, and combines Cardinality [56], which can improve the network's learning ability without destroying the original gradient path. In E-ELAN's network architecture, the transition layer architecture was not changed, only the architecture in the fast computing group. The scaling method of this model is a compound model scaling method. When scaling a depth factor with fast calculation, the change of the output channel of the block should also be calculated, and the width factor scaling of the transition layer should be carried out with the exact change amount. The convolution reparameterization is introduced and improved, and the auxiliary training module is introduced to generate the level of labels from coarse to fine. The detection time of each image was 16.71 ms, and when the training step is 1000, the weight file size was 71.3 MB. YOLOv5 took 131.7 ms to detect each image, and the weight file size was 13.7 MB when the training step size was 300. The YOLOv5 algorithm is a single-stage target detection algorithm. Images at the input end are spliced using random scaling, clipping, and arrangement. This data enhancement method combines several images into one, which can not only enrich the dataset but also improves the training speed and, most importantly, reduces the memory requirements of the model. A method of adaptive anchor frame calculation and adaptive picture scaling was proposed. In terms of the benchmark network, YOLOv5 uses the CSPDarknet53 structure and the

Focus structure as the benchmark network. This module can extract some common feature representations. Although the training speed and detection accuracy could be better than YOLOv7, the small model is suitable for embedding in the mobile end [57], which provides the possibility for cotton field detection and counting. The main idea of the CenterNet algorithm is to treat the target as a critical point when creating the model, i.e., the center point of the target boundary frame [58]. The algorithm finds the central point by evaluating the critical point of the target and makes regression predictions on other attributes of the target. This algorithm had a better detection and counting effect on slightly overlapping cotton seedlings than the other two algorithms.

Weather conditions have a significant influence on field image acquisition by UAVs. In this study, the time of image collection was from noon to 5 PM. Under the background of long sunshine in Xinjiang, the light intensity in this period was the highest. Among them, the weather was cloudy when the images were collected at T3 and T6, and the soil background and cotton seedlings were dark in the images. However, the detection and counting of cotton seedlings using the three algorithms had better results. In this study, multispectral images on cloudy days were collected as a reference, and the results of cotton seedling detection and counting were good, similar to previous studies [9,10,52,55]. The results showed that in this study, six time periods between ten days and twenty-seven days after the sowing of cotton were collected for plant detection and counting, and the best period for detection and counting was determined. After determining the optimal detection time, a generalized model with high generalization ability was constructed at the cotton seedling stage. The growth rate of cotton at the seedling stage was very uneven, which changed considerably within two–three days. Therefore, the time division could be more detailed based on this study. In future studies, the application of different crops with large planting areas in Xinjiang, such as maize, wheat, and sugar beet, and different imaging techniques should be considered to validate the robustness of the model. In addition, CenterNet can be improved by integrating other detection algorithms that have a better counting effect for cotton with an overlapping phenomenon to improve the overall detection and counting effect.

With the continuous development of deep learning, AI algorithm-driven software products such as target detection-type applications are increasingly affecting our lives. The technology is developing in a longitudinal direction, such as the continuous iteration of autonomous driving. Applying formal methods for analyzing and validating AI software in future research should focus on data reliability issues: (1) whether the data set is evenly distributed; (2) the size of the dataset used to train the model; and (3) whether the samples are appropriately labelled. It is hoped that formal methods will be applied to solve the problems related to security and validation in this area of AI [59,60].

5. Conclusions

In this study, cotton images of three bands were collected by a Sprite 4 multispectral version UAV, and the acquired multispectral images were processed. Deep learning was conducted based on YOLOv5, YOLOv7, and CenterNet target-detection algorithms to obtain cotton seedling detection and counting results. For cotton seedling detection, the algorithm performance in the process of model construction was in the order of YOLOv7 > YOLOv5 > CenterNet, and the algorithm performance at each time point was in the order of T3 > T6 > T4 > T5 > T2 > T1. During the counting of cotton seedlings, the algorithm performance in the process of model construction was in the order of CenterNet > YOLOv7 > YOLOv5, and in the order of T2 > T3 > T4 > T5 > T6 > T1. When the data collected at different times were tested, the all-around performance of YOLOv7 in detecting and counting cotton seedlings in the T4 period was better. In summary, (1) six images at different time points were used for model verification, and YOLOv7 was the optimal algorithm; and (2) based on these three target detection algorithms, T4 was the most suitable time point for seedling detection and counting in the cotton seedling stage. Therefore, the multispectral images of UAV obtained at the T4 time point of the cotton seedling stage and the YOLOv7 algorithm were used to realize rapid and accurate detection and counting of cotton seedlings in the whole seedling stage. This approach can provide technical support for checking seedling and repairing seedlings in time and provide the foundation for cotton production with high efficiency, high quality, and high yield.

YOLOv5, YOLOv7, and CenterNet algorithms can accurately detect and count cotton seedlings, and the combination of target detection algorithms and UAV remote sensing for counting has a broad application prospect. However, there are significant challenges for counting under the conditions of small seedling size and considerable overlap. In future research, we need to further investigate the effects of light conditions, image resolution, and complex backgrounds on cotton seedling detection accuracy. Evaluating the optimal flight height and image resolution is another worthwhile direction.

Author Contributions: Conceptualization, P.G., X.L. and Y.F.; methodology, Y.F. and W.C.; software, Y.F., W.C. and Y.M.; validation, Y.F. and W.C.; formal analysis, Y.F.; investigation, Y.F., W.C. and Y.M.; resources, P.G., X.L. and Z.Z.; data curation, Y.F.; writing—original draft preparation, Y.F.; writing—review and editing, P.G. and X.L.; visualization, Y.F.; supervision, P.G. and X.L.; project administration, P.G. and X.L.; funding acquisition, P.G. and X.L. All authors have read and agreed to the published version of the manuscript.

Funding: This study was supported by the National Natural Science Foundation of China (Grant No. 62265015).

Data Availability Statement: Not applicable.

Conflicts of Interest: The authors declare that the research was conducted in the absence of any commercial or financial relationships that could be construed as a potential conflict of interest.

References

1. Mavridou, E.; Vrochidou, E.; Papakostas, G.A.; Pachidis, T.; Kaburlasos, V.G. Machine Vision Systems in Precision Agriculture for Crop Farming. *J. Imaging* **2019**, *5*, 89. [CrossRef]
2. Sun, S.; Li, C.; Paterson, A.H.; Chee, P.W.; Robertson, J.S. Image Processing Algorithms for Infield Single Cotton Boll Counting and Yield Prediction. *Comput. Electron. Agric.* **2019**, *166*, 104976. [CrossRef]
3. Kitano, B.T.; Mendes, C.C.T.; Geus, A.R.; Oliveira, H.C.; Souza, J.R. Corn Plant Counting Using Deep Learning and UAV Images. *IEEE Geosci. Remote Sens. Lett.* **2019**, 1–5. [CrossRef]
4. Oliveira, H.; Guizilini, V.; Nunes, I.; Souza, J. Failure Detection in Row Crops from UAV Images Using Morphological Operators. *IEEE Geosci. Remote Sens. Lett.* **2018**, *15*, 991–995. [CrossRef]
5. Verger, A.; Vigneau, N.; Chéron, C.; Gilliot, J.-M.; Comar, A.; Baret, F. Green Area Index from an Unmanned Aerial System over Wheat and Rapeseed Crops. *Remote Sens. Environ.* **2014**, *152*, 654–664. [CrossRef]
6. Shakhatreh, H.; Sawalmeh, A.H.; Al-Fuqaha, A.; Dou, Z.; Almaita, E.; Khalil, I.; Othman, N.S.; Khreishah, A.; Guizani, M. Unmanned Aerial Vehicles (UAVs): A Survey on Civil Applications and Key Research Challenges. *IEEE Access* **2019**, *7*, 48572–48634. [CrossRef]
7. Shirzadifar, A.; Maharlooei, M.; Bajwa, S.G.; Oduor, P.G.; Nowatzki, J.F. Mapping Crop Stand Count and Planting Uniformity Using High Resolution Imagery in a Maize Crop. *Biosyst. Eng.* **2020**, *200*, 377–390. [CrossRef]
8. Vong, C.N.; Conway, L.S.; Zhou, J.; Kitchen, N.R.; Sudduth, K.A. Early Corn Stand Count of Different Cropping Systems Using UAV-Imagery and Deep Learning. *Comput. Electron. Agric.* **2021**, *186*, 106214. [CrossRef]
9. Lin, Z.; Guo, W. Cotton Stand Counting from Unmanned Aerial System Imagery Using MobileNet and CenterNet Deep Learning Models. *Remote Sens.* **2021**, *13*, 2822. [CrossRef]
10. Yang, H.; Chang, F.; Huang, Y.; Xu, M.; Zhao, Y.; Ma, L.; Su, H. Multi-Object Tracking Using Deep SORT and Modified CenterNet in Cotton Seedling Counting. *Comput. Electron. Agric.* **2022**, *202*, 107339. [CrossRef]
11. Wu, W.; Liu, T.; Zhou, P.; Yang, T.; Li, C.; Zhong, X.; Sun, C.; Liu, S.; Guo, W. Image Analysis-Based Recognition and Quantification of Grain Number per Panicle in Rice. *Plant Methods* **2019**, *15*, 122. [CrossRef] [PubMed]
12. Wu, J.; Yang, G.; Yang, X.; Xu, B.; Han, L.; Zhu, Y. Automatic Counting of in Situ Rice Seedlings from UAV Images Based on a Deep Fully Convolutional Neural Network. *Remote Sens.* **2019**, *11*, 691. [CrossRef]
13. Li, B.; Xu, X.; Han, J.; Zhang, L.; Bian, C.; Jin, L.; Liu, J. The Estimation of Crop Emergence in Potatoes by UAV RGB Imagery. *Plant Methods* **2019**, *15*, 15. [CrossRef] [PubMed]
14. Schirrmann, M.; Giebel, A.; Gleiniger, F.; Pflanz, M.; Lentschke, J.; Dammer, K.-H. Monitoring Agronomic Parameters of Winter Wheat Crops with Low-Cost UAV Imagery. *Remote Sens.* **2016**, *8*, 706. [CrossRef]
15. Maresma, Á.; Ariza, M.; Martínez, E.; Lloveras, J.; Martínez-Casasnovas, J.A. Analysis of Vegetation Indices to Determine Nitrogen Application and Yield Prediction in Maize (*Zea Mays* L.) from a Standard UAV Service. *Remote Sens.* **2016**, *8*, 973. [CrossRef]

16. Bai, Y.; Nie, C.; Wang, H.; Cheng, M.; Liu, S.; Yu, X.; Shao, M.; Wang, Z.; Wang, S.; Tuohuti, N.; et al. A Fast and Robust Method for Plant Count in Sunflower and Maize at Different Seedling Stages Using High-Resolution UAV RGB Imagery. *Precis. Agric.* **2022**, *23*, 1720–1742. [CrossRef]
17. Walter, A.; Liebisch, F.; Hund, A. Plant Phenotyping: From Bean Weighing to Image Analysis. *Plant Methods* **2015**, *11*, 14. [CrossRef]
18. Feng, A.; Zhou, J.; Vories, E.; Sudduth, K.A. Evaluation of Cotton Emergence Using UAV-Based Imagery and Deep Learning. *Comput. Electron. Agric.* **2020**, *177*, 105711. [CrossRef]
19. Teixeira Crusiol, L.G.; Nanni, M.R.; Furlanetto, R.H.; Cezar, E.; Silva, G.F.C. Reflectance Calibration of UAV-Based Visible and near-Infrared Digital Images Acquired under Variant Altitude and Illumination Conditions. *Remote Sens. Appl. Soc. Environ.* **2020**, *18*, 100312. [CrossRef]
20. Huete, A.R. A Soil-Adjusted Vegetation Index (SAVI). *Remote Sens. Environ.* **1988**, *25*, 295–309. [CrossRef]
21. Senecal, J.J.; Sheppard, J.W.; Shaw, J.A. Efficient Convolutional Neural Networks for Multi-Spectral Image Classification. In Proceedings of the 2019 International Joint Conference on Neural Networks (IJCNN), Budapest, Hungary, 14–19 July 2019; pp. 1–8.
22. Su, H.; Jung, C.; Yu, L. Multi-Spectral Fusion and Denoising of Color and Near-Infrared Images Using Multi-Scale Wavelet Analysis. *Sensors* **2021**, *21*, 3610. [CrossRef]
23. Lin, Z.; Guo, W. Sorghum Panicle Detection and Counting Using Unmanned Aerial System Images and Deep Learning. *Front. Plant Sci.* **2020**, *11*, 534853. [CrossRef]
24. Banerjee, B.P.; Spangenberg, G.; Kant, S. Fusion of Spectral and Structural Information from Aerial Images for Improved Biomass Estimation. *Remote Sens.* **2020**, *12*, 3164. [CrossRef]
25. Berger, K.; Machwitz, M.; Kycko, M.; Kefauver, S.C.; Van Wittenberghe, S.; Gerhards, M.; Verrelst, J.; Atzberger, C.; van der Tol, C.; Damm, A.; et al. Multi-Sensor Spectral Synergies for Crop Stress Detection and Monitoring in the Optical Domain: A Review. *Remote Sens. Environ.* **2022**, *280*, 113198. [CrossRef] [PubMed]
26. Osco, L.P.; de Arruda, M.d.S.; Marcato Junior, J.; da Silva, N.B.; Ramos, A.P.M.; Moryia, É.A.S.; Imai, N.N.; Pereira, D.R.; Creste, J.E.; Matsubara, E.T.; et al. A Convolutional Neural Network Approach for Counting and Geolocating Citrus-Trees in UAV Multispectral Imagery. *ISPRS J. Photogramm. Remote Sens.* **2020**, *160*, 97–106. [CrossRef]
27. Lee, H.; Wang, J.; Leblon, B. Using Linear Regression, Random Forests, and Support Vector Machine with Unmanned Aerial Vehicle Multispectral Images to Predict Canopy Nitrogen Weight in Corn. *Remote Sens.* **2020**, *12*, 2071. [CrossRef]
28. Linker, R.; Cohen, O.; Naor, A. Determination of the Number of Green Apples in RGB Images Recorded in Orchards. *Comput. Electron. Agric.* **2012**, *81*, 45–57. [CrossRef]
29. Ross, N.E.; Pritchard, C.J.; Rubin, D.M.; Dusé, A.G. Automated Image Processing Method for the Diagnosis and Classification of Malaria on Thin Blood Smears. *Med. Biol. Eng. Comput.* **2006**, *44*, 427–436. [CrossRef]
30. Jin, X.; Liu, S.; Baret, F.; Hemerlé, M.; Comar, A. Estimates of Plant Density of Wheat Crops at Emergence from Very Low Altitude UAV Imagery. *Remote Sens. Environ.* **2017**, *198*, 105–114. [CrossRef]
31. Zheng, H.; Zhou, X.; He, J.; Yao, X.; Cheng, T.; Zhu, Y.; Cao, W.; Tian, Y. Early Season Detection of Rice Plants Using RGB, NIR-G-B and Multispectral Images from Unmanned Aerial Vehicle (UAV). *Comput. Electron. Agric.* **2020**, *169*, 105223. [CrossRef]
32. Wu, Y.-H.; Liu, Y.; Xu, J.; Bian, J.-W.; Gu, Y.-C.; Cheng, M.-M. MobileSal: Extremely Efficient RGB-D Salient Object Detection. *IEEE Trans. Pattern Anal. Mach. Intell.* **2022**, *44*, 10261–10269. [CrossRef] [PubMed]
33. Kamilaris, A.; Prenafeta-Boldú, F.X. Deep Learning in Agriculture: A Survey. *Comput. Electron. Agric.* **2018**, *147*, 70–90. [CrossRef]
34. Fan, Z.; Lu, J.; Gong, M.; Xie, H.; Goodman, E.D. Automatic Tobacco Plant Detection in UAV Images via Deep Neural Networks. *IEEE J. Sel. Top. Appl. Earth Obs. Remote Sens.* **2018**, *11*, 876–887. [CrossRef]
35. Barreto, A.; Lottes, P.; Ispizua Yamati, F.R.; Baumgarten, S.; Wolf, N.A.; Stachniss, C.; Mahlein, A.-K.; Paulus, S. Automatic UAV-Based Counting of Seedlings in Sugar-Beet Field and Extension to Maize and Strawberry. *Comput. Electron. Agric.* **2021**, *191*, 106493. [CrossRef]
36. Vong, C.N.; Conway, L.S.; Feng, A.; Zhou, J.; Kitchen, N.R.; Sudduth, K.A. Corn Emergence Uniformity Estimation and Mapping Using UAV Imagery and Deep Learning. *Comput. Electron. Agric.* **2022**, *198*, 107008. [CrossRef]
37. Ahmad, I.; Yang, Y.; Yue, Y.; Ye, C.; Hassan, M.; Cheng, X.; Wu, Y.; Zhang, Y. Deep Learning Based Detector YOLOv5 for Identifying Insect Pests. *Appl. Sci.* **2022**, *12*, 10167. [CrossRef]
38. Qi, J.; Liu, X.; Liu, K.; Xu, F.; Guo, H.; Tian, X.; Li, M.; Bao, Z.; Li, Y. An Improved YOLOv5 Model Based on Visual Attention Mechanism: Application to Recognition of Tomato Virus Disease. *Comput. Electron. Agric.* **2022**, *194*, 106780. [CrossRef]
39. Yan, B.; Fan, P.; Lei, X.; Liu, Z.; Yang, F. A Real-Time Apple Targets Detection Method for Picking Robot Based on Improved YOLOv5. *Remote Sens.* **2021**, *13*, 1619. [CrossRef]
40. Jiang, K.; Xie, T.; Yan, R.; Wen, X.; Li, D.; Jiang, H.; Jiang, N.; Feng, L.; Duan, X.; Wang, J. An Attention Mechanism-Improved YOLOv7 Object Detection Algorithm for Hemp Duck Count Estimation. *Agriculture* **2022**, *12*, 1659. [CrossRef]
41. Xia, Y.; Nguyen, M.; Yan, W.Q. A Real-Time Kiwifruit Detection Based on Improved YOLOv7. In *Revised Selected Papers, Proceedings of the Image and Vision Computing: 37th International Conference, IVCNZ 2022, Auckland, New Zealand, 24–25 November 2022*; Springer Nature: Cham, Switzerland, 2022; pp. 48–61.
42. Yang, Z.; Ni, C.; Li, L.; Luo, W.; Qin, Y. Three-Stage Pavement Crack Localization and Segmentation Algorithm Based on Digital Image Processing and Deep Learning Techniques. *Sensors* **2022**, 22, 8459. [CrossRef]

43. Mandal, V.; Adu-Gyamfi, Y. Object Detection and Tracking Algorithms for Vehicle Counting: A Comparative Analysis. *J. Big Data Anal. Transp.* **2020**, *2*, 251–261. [CrossRef]
44. Liu, H.; Yuan, G.; Yang, L.; Liu, K.; Zhou, H. An Appearance Defect Detection Method for Cigarettes Based on C-CenterNet. *Electronics* **2022**, *11*, 2182. [CrossRef]
45. Zhuang, J.; Li, X.; Bagavathiannan, M.; Jin, X.; Yang, J.; Meng, W.; Li, T.; Li, L.; Wang, Y.; Chen, Y.; et al. Evaluation of Different Deep Convolutional Neural Networks for Detection of Broadleaf Weed Seedlings in Wheat. *Pest Manag. Sci.* **2022**, *78*, 521–529. [CrossRef]
46. Zhao, L.; Li, S. Object Detection Algorithm Based on Improved YOLOv3. *Electronics* **2020**, *9*, 537. [CrossRef]
47. Zakria, Z.; Deng, J.; Kumar, R.; Khokhar, M.S.; Cai, J.; Kumar, J. Multiscale and Direction Target Detecting in Remote Sensing Images via Modified YOLO-V4. *IEEE J. Sel. Top. Appl. Earth Obs. Remote Sens.* **2022**, *15*, 1039–1048. [CrossRef]
48. Wu, W.; Liu, H.; Li, L.; Long, Y.; Wang, X.; Wang, Z.; Li, J.; Chang, Y. Application of Local Fully Convolutional Neural Network Combined with YOLO v5 Algorithm in Small Target Detection of Remote Sensing Image. *PLoS ONE* **2021**, *16*, e0259283. [CrossRef]
49. Gallo, I.; Rehman, A.U.; Dehkordi, R.H.; Landro, N.; La Grassa, R.; Boschetti, M. Deep Object Detection of Crop Weeds: Performance of YOLOv7 on a Real Case Dataset from UAV Images. *Remote Sens.* **2023**, *15*, 539. [CrossRef]
50. Zhang, C.; Liu, P.; Wang, H.; Jin, Y. Saliency-Based Centernet for Ship Detection in SAR Images. In Proceedings of the IGARSS 2022–2022 IEEE International Geoscience and Remote Sensing Symposium, Kuala Lumpur, Malaysia, 17–22 July 2022; pp. 1552–1555.
51. Khaki, S.; Pham, H.; Khalilzadeh, Z.; Masoud, A.; Safaei, N.; Han, Y.; Kent, W.; Wang, L. High-Throughput Image-Based Plant Stand Count Estimation Using Convolutional Neural Networks. *PLoS ONE* **2022**, *17*, e0268762. [CrossRef]
52. Feng, A.; Zhou, J.; Vories, E.; Sudduth, K.A. Evaluation of Cotton Emergence Using UAV-Based Narrow-Band Spectral Imagery with Customized Image Alignment and Stitching Algorithms. *Remote Sens.* **2020**, *12*, 1764. [CrossRef]
53. He, J.; Zhang, N.; Su, X.; Lu, J.; Yao, X.; Cheng, T.; Zhu, Y.; Cao, W.; Tian, Y. Estimating Leaf Area Index with a New Vegetation Index Considering the Influence of Rice Panicles. *Remote Sens.* **2019**, *11*, 1809. [CrossRef]
54. Suo, C.; McGovern, E.; Gilmer, A. Coastal Dune Vegetation Mapping Using a Multispectral Sensor Mounted on an UAS. *Remote Sens.* **2019**, *11*, 1814. [CrossRef]
55. Xia, L.; Zhang, R.; Chen, L.; Huang, Y.; Xu, G.; Wen, Y.; Yi, T. Monitor Cotton Budding Using SVM and UAV Images. *Appl. Sci.* **2019**, *9*, 4312. [CrossRef]
56. Zhang, Y.; Guo, Z.; Wu, J.; Tian, Y.; Tang, H.; Guo, X. Real-Time Vehicle Detection Based on Improved YOLO V5. *Sustainability* **2022**, *14*, 12274. [CrossRef]
57. Zhou, Y.; Tang, Y.; Zou, X.; Wu, M.; Tang, W.; Meng, F.; Zhang, Y.; Kang, H. Adaptive Active Positioning of Camellia Oleifera Fruit Picking Points: Classical Image Processing and YOLOv7 Fusion Algorithm. *Appl. Sci.* **2022**, *12*, 12959. [CrossRef]
58. An, K.; Chen, Y.; Wang, S.; Xiao, Z. RCBi-CenterNet: An Absolute Pose Policy for 3D Object Detection in Autonomous Driving. *Appl. Sci.* **2021**, *11*, 5621. [CrossRef]
59. Krichen, M.; Mihoub, A.; Alzahrani, M.Y.; Adoni, W.Y.H.; Nahhal, T. Are Formal Methods Applicable To Machine Learning And Artificial Intelligence? In Proceedings of the 2022 2nd International Conference of Smart Systems and Emerging Technologies (SMARTTECH), Riyadh, Saudi Arabia, 9–11 May 2022; IEEE: Piscataway, NJ, USA, 2022; pp. 48–53.
60. Seshia, S.A.; Sadigh, D.; Sastry, S.S. Toward Verified Artificial Intelligence. *Commun. ACM* **2022**, *65*, 46–55. [CrossRef]

remote sensing

MDPI

Article

Testing the Performance of LSTM and ARIMA Models for In-Season Forecasting of Canopy Cover (CC) in Cotton Crops

Sambandh Bhusan Dhal [1], Stavros Kalafatis [1], Ulisses Braga-Neto [1], Krishna Chaitanya Gadepally [1], Jose Luis Landivar-Scott [2], Lei Zhao [2,3], Kevin Nowka [1], Juan Landivar [2], Pankaj Pal [2] and Mahendra Bhandari [2,*]

[1] Department of Electrical and Computer Engineering, Texas A&M University, College Station, TX 77843, USA; sambandh@tamu.edu (S.B.D.); skalafatis-tamu@tamu.edu (S.K.); ulisses@tamu.edu (U.B.-N.); kcgadepally@tamu.edu (K.C.G.); kjnowka@tamu.edu (K.N.)

[2] Texas A&M AgriLife Research and Extension Center, Corpus Christi, TX 77406, USA; jose.landivarscott@ag.tamu.edu (J.L.L.-S.); lei.zhao@ag.tamu.edu (L.Z.); jalandivar@ag.tamu.edu (J.L.); pankaj.pal@ag.tamu.edu (P.P.)

[3] Department of Computer Science, Texas A&M University, Corpus Christi, TX 78412, USA

* Correspondence: mahendra.bhandari@ag.tamu.edu

Abstract: Cotton (*Gossypium* spp.), a crucial cash crop in the United States, requires the constant monitoring of growth parameters for informed decision-making. Recently, forecasting models have gained prominence for predicting canopy indicators, aiding in-season planning and management decisions to optimize cotton production. This study employed unmanned aerial system (UAS) technology to collect canopy cover (CC) data from a 40-hectare cotton field in Driscoll, Texas, in 2020 and 2021. Long short-term memory (LSTM) models, trained using 2020 data, were subsequently applied to forecast the CC values for 2021. These models were compared with real-time auto-regressive integrated moving average (ARIMA) models to assess their effectiveness in predicting the CC values up to 14 days in advance, starting from the 28th day after crop emergence. The results showed that multiple-input multi-step output LSTM models achieved higher accuracy in predicting the in-season CC values during the early growth stages (up to the 56th day), with an average testing RMSE of 3.86, significantly lower than other single-input LSTM models. Conversely, when sufficient testing data are available, single-input stacked-LSTM models demonstrated precision in CC predictions for later stages, achieving an average RMSE of 3.06. These findings highlight the potential of LSTM models for in-season CC forecasting, facilitating effective management strategies in cotton production.

Keywords: canopy cover; unmanned aerial system (UAS); long short-term memory (LSTM); ARIMA; multiple-input multi-step output LSTM; stacked LSTM

1. Introduction

Artificial intelligence (AI) has emerged as a transformative tool in addressing both food security and environmental sustainability concerns [1–12]. Researchers have leveraged AI techniques, such as machine learning (ML) and deep learning (DL), to optimize agricultural practices and mitigate environmental risks. For instance, in aquaponic systems, AI-based IoT monitoring systems enable real-time data collection and analysis, facilitating precise nutrient management for optimal plant growth while minimizing resource usage. Moreover, AI algorithms have been deployed to predict growth stages in crops cultivated in hydroponic setups, enhancing yield and efficiency. In addition to improving agricultural productivity, studies have demonstrated the efficacy of AI-driven approaches in reducing heavy metal toxicity in food products like soybeans and milk, thereby ensuring food safety. Furthermore, AI-powered processing techniques in the dairy sector not only enhance food quality but also contribute to environmental sustainability by reducing the need for chemical preservatives and minimizing waste. This integration of AI into food production and processing systems holds promise for promoting food security while safeguarding the environment.

One of the critical aspects of ensuring food security is effectively monitoring crop growth parameters with the goal of maximizing yield during the cultivation period. Crop growth and development are multifaceted processes influenced by genetics, the environment, management practices, and their interactions. These growth dynamics are quantified through phenotypic measures such as canopy cover (CC), canopy height (CH), and leaf area index (LAI). Traditionally, crop growth forecasts rely on process-based simulation models like the decision support system for agrotechnology (DSSAT) [13] or the Agricultural Production Systems sIMulator (APSIM) [14], despite the need for comprehensive calibration. However, there's a growing interest in exploring alternative approaches, such as machine learning (ML), particularly utilizing deep learning neural network models like long short-term memory (LSTM) networks [15] and ARIMA-based models. These ML techniques offer potentially viable options for forecasting temporal phenotypic parameters like CC, CH, and LAI, providing a complementary or alternative framework to traditional simulation models.

LSTM networks belong to the category of recurrent neural networks (RNNs) and have the ability to identify and capture long-term dependencies. These networks possess a remarkable ability to effectively acquire new knowledge, to the point that the retention of this information seems to happen effortlessly and lasts for an extended period. Some of the commonly used LSTM models for multi-temporal projections are stacked LSTM [16], vanilla LSTM, bidirectional LSTM [17], and CNN-LSTM [18,19]. The stacked LSTM design is characterized by its use of many linked LSTM layers. In contrast, the bidirectional LSTM model is designed to train two input sequences simultaneously, whereby the first and second sequences are exact replicas of each other. The architecture of this paradigm enables the facilitation of fast learning. It is a kind of neural network that exhibits the capability to capture sequential information in both forward and backward directions, allowing for the retrieval of sequences from either the future to the past or vice versa. This model is characterized by its capacity to handle input sequences in both forward and backward directions, setting it apart from the traditional LSTM models, which are limited to unidirectional input propagation. These models have traditionally been used extensively in forecasting crop outputs [20–22], commodity prices [23], and pest and disease incidence [24,25]. In these studies, five LSTM models were used to anticipate the agricultural prices using time-series data from five crops: vanilla LSTM, bidirectional LSTM, stacked LSTM, CNN-LSTM, and convolutional LSTM. The findings revealed the possibility of more accurate price forecasting one month in advance. Similarly, the efficacy of bidirectional LSTMs using multivariate time-series input to anticipate insect damage in rice crops was compared to vanilla and stacked LSTMs.

The acronym ARIMA refers to autoregressive integrated moving average models. The time-series forecasting model discussed is a commonly employed approach that integrates autoregressive (AR) and moving average (MA) components, together with differencing techniques, to achieve stationarity in the time series. ARIMA models have demonstrated efficacy in forecasting future values by using past data sources. Several studies have explored the use of ARIMA-based models to forecast crop growth. In one study [26], historical data on sugarcane productivity from Tamil Nadu was utilized to create ARIMA models for capturing time-series patterns and forecasting. The forecasts' accuracy was determined by comparing them to actual yield data. The outputs and performance indicators of the models were investigated, providing insights into the usefulness and reliability of the ARIMA approach for sugarcane crop growth forecasting. Elsamie et al. [27] employed an ARIMA dynamic time-series model to capture the temporal changes in Egyptian cotton and predicted key crop parameters.Similarly, the Box–Jenkins ARIMA [28] model was employed to better understand the cotton output in India and discovered that the ARIMA (2, 1, 1) model was appropriate for their data. The study included diagnostic tests to ensure that the model was correct. Using the chosen ARIMA model, the researchers created projections for the years 2015–16 through 2020–21. Policymakers found these estimates beneficial because they provided insight into future grain storage and import and export requirements, allowing them to plan ahead of time.

In recent years, unmanned aerial vehicles (UAVs) equipped with various sensors, collectively referred to as UAS, have been deployed to monitor plant growth at higher spatial and temporal resolutions. Phenotypic traits, such as the CC, CH, and vegetation indices (VIs) obtained from UAS, are utilized in estimating disease severity, crop input status, and crop yield. For instance, Zhao et al. [29] employed UAS-derived vegetation indicators to predict the in-season nitrogen status, while Ballester et al. [30] utilized similar techniques to predict the lint yield on a commercial farm in Australia. These aspects necessitate integration into crop management practices, such as optimizing fertilizer and pesticide usage based on the variables affecting crop growth. Integrating models for predicting canopy attributes can facilitate decision-making in crop management, including irrigation, growth regulators, fertilizers, and harvest-aid treatments. As UAS provides canopy attribute measurements at high temporal and spatial resolutions, ML models such as the long short-term memory (LSTM) or autoregressive integrated moving average (ARIMA) can be employed for the in-season predictions of these attributes as indirect measures of crop growth. Consequently, predicted attributes can be used to make real-time informed crop management decisions [31]. In this study, the use of the LSTM and ARIMA models has been assessed for in-season forecasting of crop growth, with the CC obtained from UAS serving as one of the parameters. Moreover, multiple LSTM models have been compared to classic ARIMA strategies for in-season forecasting of CC.

The main objective of this study is to compare different forecasting models, including variations of the long short-term memory (LSTM) models and the traditional autoregressive integrated moving average (ARIMA) model, to identify the most accurate model for predicting CC values 14 days in advance. An important innovation in this research involves clustering data based on field variability using the K-means algorithm. Subsequently, pairwise cluster distances are computed using the dynamic time warping (DTW) technique, with the clusters exhibiting the smallest DTW distance being used as inputs to multiple-input multi-step output LSTM models. While this approach requires significant computational resources, it provides optimal forecasting accuracy, which is particularly beneficial for predicting cotton crop growth indices during the initial growth phase. For forecasting in later growth stages, single-input LSTM models were utilized due to ample data availability, yielding results comparable to the multiple-input multi-step output LSTM models. By utilizing predicted CC values, in-season management decisions such as irrigation scheduling, application of growth regulators, and harvest-aid chemicals can be planned and optimized, thereby maximizing resource utilization and ensuring a higher yield.

2. Materials and Methods

Before delving into the analysis, a schematic of the framework employed to forecast the CC values in this approach is presented in Figure 1. As depicted in the figure, images are gathered using a UAS for both the years 2020 and 2021. Subsequently, the CC is extracted utilizing Agisoft Metashape 1.7.2 software. Initially, the CC data for 2020 is clustered using the K-means algorithm and then utilized to train the LSTM models. Similarly, the CC data for 2021 serves as the testing dataset after clustering the plots with the K-means algorithm. The model with the lowest testing root mean squared error (RMSE) for forecasting CC values 14 days in advance was selected as the best model.

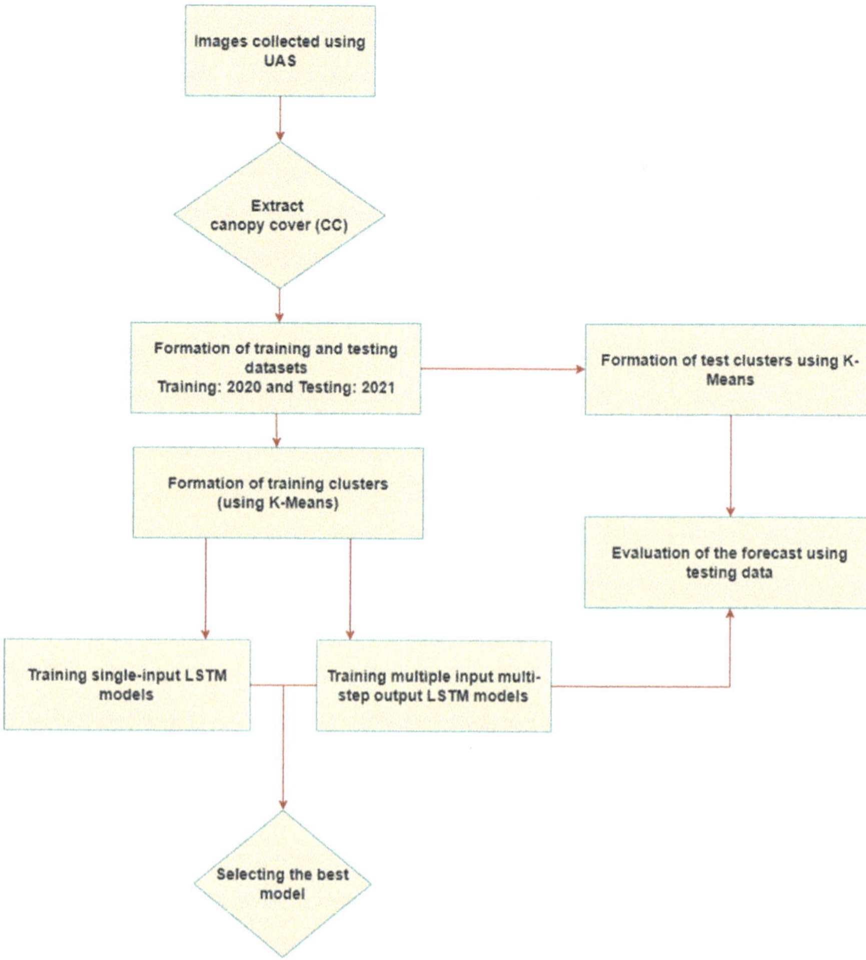

Figure 1. Flowchart of the analysis for in-season forecasting of CC obtained from unmanned aerial systems (UAS) using LSTM frameworks.

2.1. Data Collection and Feature Extraction

UAS data were collected from an 80.16 hectares commercial field located at Driscoll, Texas (27°40′06.2″N and 97°97°41′22.6″W). The field is divided into two halves and follows a cotton–sorghum rotation (Figure 2).

Data were collected in 2020 and 2021. Table 1 shows the planting date, data collection schedule, defoliation date, and harvest date for both years.

Table 1. Seeding date, defoliation date, and harvest dates of cotton in 2020 and 2021.

Year	Planting Date	Emergence Date	Defoliation Date	Harvest Date
2020	29 February 2020	12 March 2020	13 July 2020	3 August 2020
2021	27 February 2021	10 March 2021	27 July 2021	13 August 2021

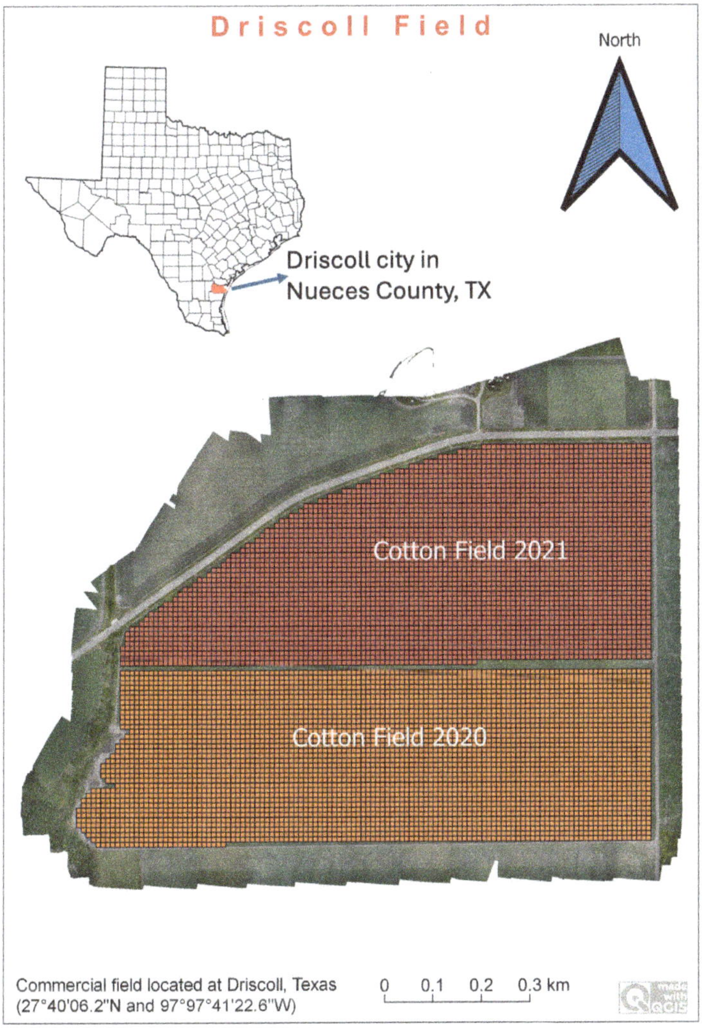

Figure 2. Data collection site of cotton field.

Phantom 4 RTK, which is equipped with a one-inch COSMOS, a red-green-blue (RGB) camera, and a Real-Time Kinematics (RTK) module, was used to collect the UAS data. The procedure for image processing and feature extraction was followed as described by Bhandari et al. [32]. The UAS flights were conducted at irregular intervals, with varying time gaps between each flight, ranging from 10 to 14 days. The collected images were processed using Agisoft Metashape PRO software version 1.8.2 (Agisoft LLC, St. Petersburg, Russia) to generate geospatial data products such as orthomosaics and surface models. The CC was obtained from the orthomosaics by employing the Canopeo algorithm [33], which classifies the image into two classes: canopy and non-canopy. A 10 m by 10 m grid was generated in QGIS software 3.36.2 and overlaid on the classified image to calculate the CC for each grid (Equation (1)). A total of 3500 grids were generated.

$$CC(\%) = \frac{\text{Number of pixels classified as canopy}}{\text{Total number of pixels in the grid}} \times 100 \quad (1)$$

Based on the duration from emergence to defoliation application and the goal to forecast two weeks in advance, it was determined to standardize the growth period to test the forecasting frameworks to 116 days. To develop a consistent data framework, irregular temporal datasets obtained during the season were interpolated using the polynomial function, and daily measurements were derived. This approach facilitated the development of equal interval time-series data across years, compensating for non-uniformity in the data collection schedule and differing planting and defoliation timings. The data obtained through the interpolation techniques, as mentioned in the Results section, was then employed as inputs for the LSTM and ARIMA models to forecast the CC values two weeks in advance, beginning from the 28th day after the cotton crop's germination.

2.2. Formation of Clusters for Analysis

Before fitting the LSTM models to the data, it was imperative to divide the plots into similar clusters for ease of training and validation of the LSTM models. Since the CC data were obtained for 3500 grids for 116 days, it was not possible to train the LSTM models, considering all the time-series sequences, as it would have resulted in millions of training sequences. Having a huge amount of training sequences would have led to a much slower computation time, and due to hardware constraints, it was decided to cluster the grids with similar CC values using the K-means algorithm. As the K-means algorithm is relatively fast and computationally efficient for high-dimensional data due to its linear time complexity, it was used because it helps us provide more control over the granularity of clustering. The continuous time-series data for all the 3500 grids for 2020 and 2021 were grouped into 14 distinct training and testing clusters, respectively, taking the data until the 116th day after emergence (DAP) into consideration. The number of plots which were grouped into each of these 14 clusters for both the years 2020 and 2021 have been shown in Table 2.

Table 2. Number of cluster-wise cultivation plots generated by K-means algorithm.

Cluster Number	Number of Cultivation Plots (2020)	Number of Cultivation Plots (2021)
1	138	73
2	136	252
3	217	168
4	179	241
5	63	157
6	238	172
7	181	197
8	297	118
9	128	149
10	158	103
11	43	269
12	99	280
13	95	133
14	91	87

2.3. Selection of Appropriate Forecasting Models

2.3.1. Using Data from Individual Cultivation Clusters as LSTM Inputs

Five different LSTM models—two stacked LSTM variants, a bidirectional LSTM, the CNN LSTM, and the encoder–decoder LSTM model—were used to predict the CC values from the 28th day after crop emergence. All these variants of LSTM models were trained on the data clusters obtained for 2020. For 2021, the average RMSE predictions over all the testing clusters were calculated separately, and the best forecasting model was chosen by a majority vote.

2.3.2. Using Data from Similar Pairwise Cultivation Clusters as LSTM Inputs

The datasets created using the information from individual clusters were used as inputs to the multiple-input multi-step output LSTM models to estimate the CC for the next 14 days. For this, the dynamic time warping (DTW) technique was used to find pairwise similar clusters to be given as inputs to the multiple-input multi-step output LSTMs. Here, DTW worked on the principle of utilizing dynamic programming to find the optimal alignment between two clusters, minimizing the total distance while allowing for local variations in the alignment.

To forecast the forthcoming CC values for each cluster, the pairwise DTW distances were computed between the cluster under consideration for the CC prediction and the remaining 13 clusters. For each early season forecast, the clusters exhibiting the minimum DTW distance were selected as inputs for the multiple-input multi-step output LSTM model. However, the training process for this type of LSTM model necessitated significant computational resources due to the pairwise training pairs, despite its potential to enhance the accuracy of the forecasting models. The major drawback of this approach is that for in-season forecasting, data needs to be available for multiple grids to be given as inputs to this type of LSTM model, making it impossible to conduct any forecasting when the CC data from only one grid was available.

2.3.3. Using ARIMA Models for a Comparative Analysis

A comparative study of the LSTM models with the traditional ARIMA-based CC forecasting has been conducted to provide a more accurate estimate.

Contrary to the LSTM models that have been described before, it was imperative to ensure the stationarity of the dataset before using an ARIMA model for analysis. A rising trend component was noted in the values of the CC. Consequently, efforts were undertaken to eliminate non-stationarity from the time-series dataset by implementing six distinct procedures, as seen in Figure 3. The stages were executed in a sequential manner, and the p-value was computed after each step until the time-series data achieved stationarity (p-value < 0.005). The stationarity of the time-series data was verified by the application of the augmented Dickey–Fuller (ADF) test.

The determination of the order of the ARIMA models was facilitated by the utilization of the partial auto-correlation (PACF) plots and the auto-correlation (ACF) plots, which provided valuable information on the major delays (p and q values) [34,35]. Hence, this methodology was employed in the prediction analysis. If the variables p and q exhibited a geometric fall when plotted together, it was inferred that the process conformed to an ARIMA model with p and q both equal to zero. If the ACF plot showed a geometric decrease and the PACF plot exhibited a complete cessation after p lags, it was inferred that the ARIMA process adhered to a (p, D, 0) distribution, where D represents the degree of differencing applied to the time-series data. In a similar vein, if the ACF plot reached zero after a certain number of lags (q), but the PACF plot exhibited a geometric decrease, it may be inferred that the ARIMA process adhered to a (0, D, q) distribution. The aforementioned methodology was employed to develop the necessary components for conducting a time-series analysis of the canopy's characteristics. As ARIMA models followed a classical statistical approach that did not require data for training the model, the data for 2021 from all the cultivation plots were averaged to gauge the efficiency of this proposed framework, and the average RMSE estimates have been shown in Table 3.

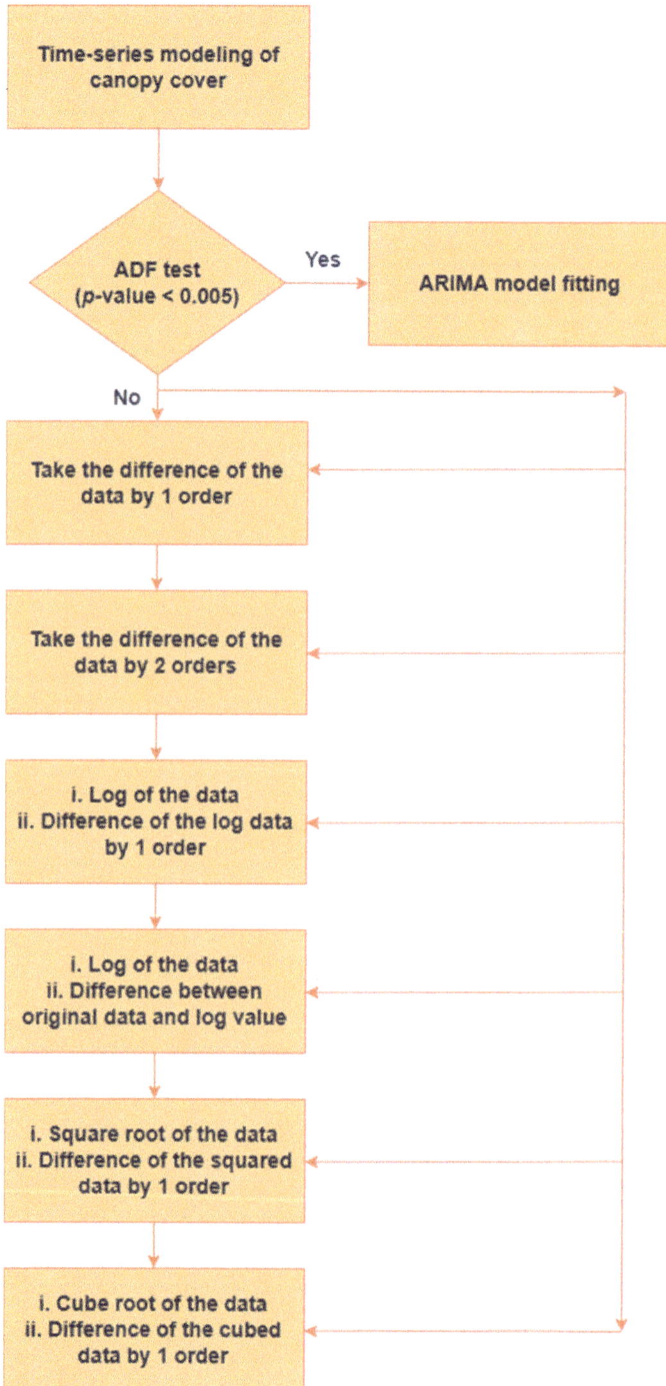

Figure 3. Pipeline to eliminate non-stationarity from CC before analyzing ARIMA models.

Table 3. Comparison of RMSE estimates for different LSTM models.

Name of the LSTM Model	Average CC RMSE Estimates over 14 Testing Clusters. (Cultivation Year 2021)										
	Number of Real Values of CC Used in the Training Set (in Days)										
	28	**35**	**42**	**49**	**56**	**63**	**70**	**77**	**84**	**91**	**98**
Stacked LSTM [a] (number of epochs = 50, batch size = 8)	6.11	5.86	5.61	5.36	5.11	4.32	3.81	3.62	3.31	3.12	2.81
Stacked LSTM [b] (number of epochs = 100, batch size = 32)	5.20	4.95	4.70	4.45	4.20	3.81	3.45	3.32	3.12	2.43	2.21
Bidirectional LSTM [c]	5.85	5.46	5.4	5.4	5.18	4.7	4.7	4.38	4.38	4.22	3.9
CNN LSTM [d]	6.11	5.86	5.61	5.36	5.11	4.86	4.61	4.36	4.11	3.86	3.61
Encoder–decoder LSTM model [e]	7.11	6.86	6.61	6.36	6.11	5.86	5.61	5.36	5.11	4.86	4.61
Multiple-input multi-step output LSTM model [f]	4.36	4.11	3.86	3.61	3.36	3.21	2.86	2.61	2.3	2.3	2.18

a = 50 input neurons in the LSTM layer, Dropout layer with 10%, 1st intermediate layer with 50 LSTM units, Dropout layer with 10%, 2nd intermediate layer with 50 LSTM units, Dropout layer with 10%, 3rd intermediate layer with 50 LSTM units, Dropout layer with 10%, Number of Dense Layers = 1, Optimizer = 'Adam'. b = Same specifications as the above-mentioned stacked LSTM with varied batch size input and number of training epochs. c = 50 input neurons in LSTM model, activation = 'relu', Number of Dense layers = 1, Optimizer = 'Adam'. d = 1D convolutional filter (number of filters = 64, kernel size = 1, activation = 'relu'), 1D Max Pooling Layer (Pool size = 2), Flatten layer, Number of neurons in LSTM model = 50, activation = 'relu', Number of Dense layers = 1, Optimizer = 'Adam', Number of epochs = 200. e = Number of LSTM units in input layer = 100, Activation layer = 'relu', RepeatVector layer with the number of timesteps to forecast as the input, Number of LSTM units in input layer = 100, Activation layer = 'relu, TimeDistributed layer with number of Dense units = 100, Activation layer = 'relu', TimeDistributed layer with number of Dense units = 1, Optimizer = 'Adam'. f = Number of LSTM units in input layer = 100, Activation layer = 'relu', Number of LSTM units in the intermediate layer = 100, Activation layer = 'relu', Number of Dense layers = 2, Optimizer = 'Adam'.

3. Results

3.1. Analysis of the Dataset

Figure 4 shows the distribution of the CC measurements obtained throughout the growing season for 2020 and 2021 for all the grids. A box plot was used to visualize the data. In general, the trend of CCs showed a slow increase early in the season, followed by a linear growth phase and steady growth. Additionally, the CC values ranged from 0 to 100% in both years, with a similar trend throughout the growing season.

In Figure 4, the box plot illustrates the CC data recorded using drone imagery. The x-axis represents "Days after emergence", while the y-axis represents "CC (%)". Each box plot, corresponding to the years 2020 and 2021, depicts the interquartile range, i.e., the difference between the first and third quartiles for each day after emergence. Additionally, the black dots signify outliers within the dataset.

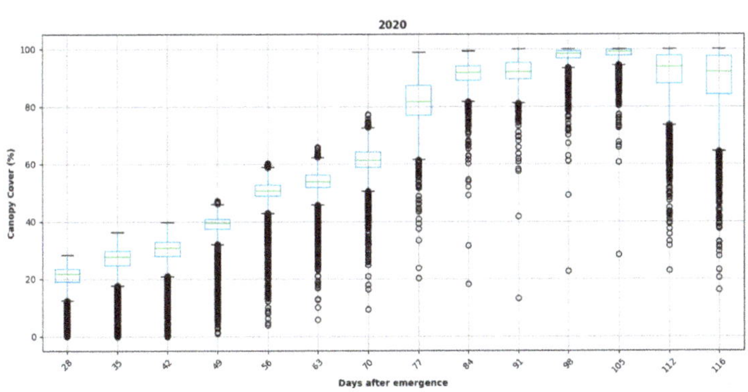

Figure 4. *Cont.*

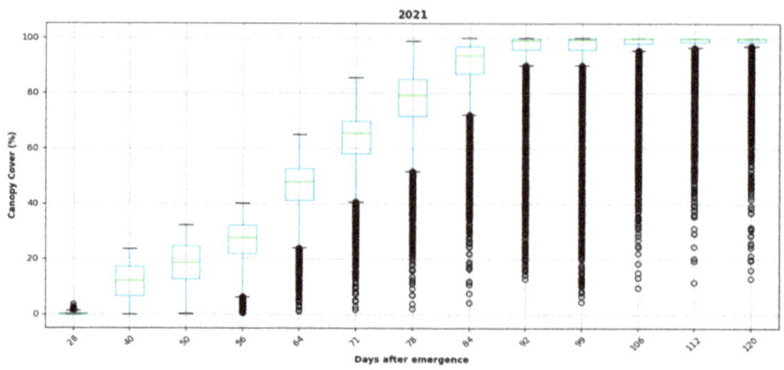

Figure 4. Box plot of CC data over 3500 distinct plots for 2020 and 2021, respectively (top to bottom).

3.2. Removal of Outliers

Upon examination of the box plot, as depicted in Figure 4, it became evident that a considerable number of outliers are present in the data collected from over 3500 cultivation grids. Consequently, it became imperative to address these outliers before proceeding with the data interpolation for the entire growth period. To accomplish this, we retained the data points falling within the range defined by quartile 1 − (1.5 × interquartile range) and quartile 3 + (1.5 × interquartile range) for analysis. Implementation of the IQR method resulted in the removal of 1101 plots and 1437 grid data points from the 2020 and 2021 cultivation years, respectively. Subsequently, data from the remaining grids were utilized for analysis, ensuring the reliability and accuracy of the subsequent interpretations and conclusions.

3.3. Interpolation of the Dataset

Given that the data were gathered over 14 days at irregular intervals, spanning from emergence to harvest, it was impractical to rely on the data from those specific days for analysis solely. Hence, considering the data's distribution, as evident from the box plots, the approach was taken to employ a five-degree polynomial interpolation [36] to interpolate the canopy data for both 2020 and 2021. This interpolation process provided enough data for all the plots throughout the 116-day growth period to design the predictive approaches. The distribution of the interpolated canopy data was visualized and is depicted in Figure 5. The interpolated canopy data from emergence to harvest has been shown in different colors to show how the distribution of the data varied over the plots.

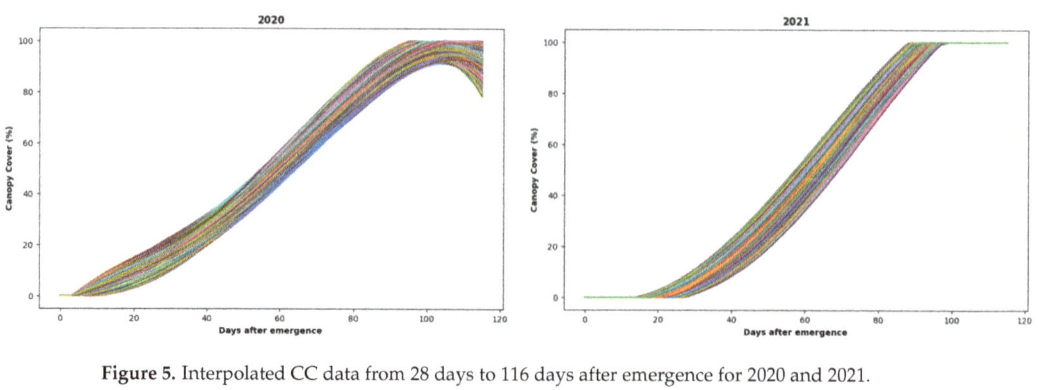

Figure 5. Interpolated CC data from 28 days to 116 days after emergence for 2020 and 2021.

The analysis of Figure 5 suggests that the CC data for both 2020 and 2021 exhibited a consistent upward trend from emergence to harvest. Consequently, given the observed improvement in the data's quality post-outlier removal, characterized by this ascending trend, the refined data were utilized as inputs to the LSTM models and the ARIMA approach, which have been elaborated in the subsequent sub-sections.

3.4. Formation of Clusters for Training LSTM Models

Before training the LSTM models, the data recorded for 2020 were clustered using K-means for ease of computation. Utilizing the elbow method, the optimal number of training clusters was determined to be 14, as the sum of squared errors (SSE) reached a plateau. Similarly, to assess the effectiveness of the trained LSTM models, the data for the year 2021 underwent clustering using the K-means algorithm. This process also resulted in choosing 14 as the optimal number of clusters. Subsequently, the selection of the best forecasting model was based on a majority vote, considering the model capable of forecasting future CC values with a minimal root mean square error (RMSE) across the majority of the testing clusters. Figure 6 illustrates the results of the elbow method employed as a metric to ascertain the optimal number of training and testing clusters.

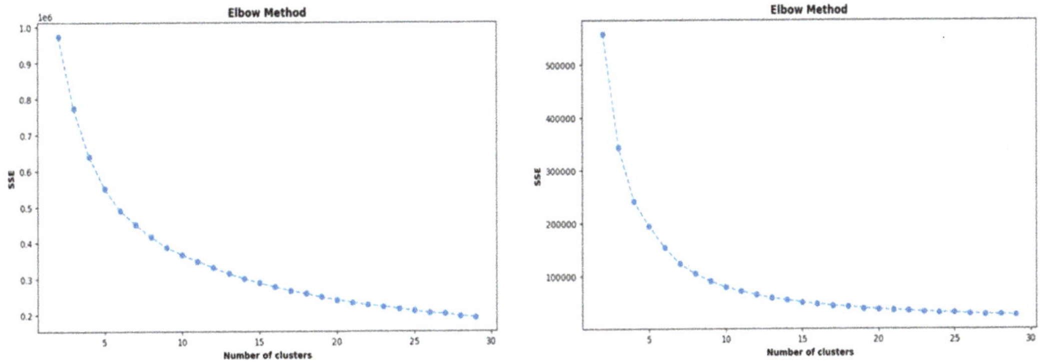

Figure 6. Number of optimal training and testing clusters obtained from the K-means algorithm for 2020 and 2021 (top to bottom).

However, before proceeding with training the LSTM models, it was imperative to visualize the average interpolated CC data for the newly formed clusters using the K-means algorithm. The average interpolated CC data have been depicted in Figure 7.

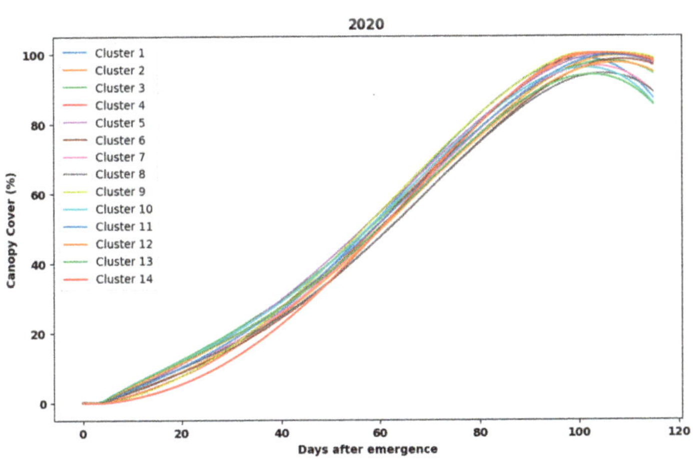

Figure 7. *Cont.*

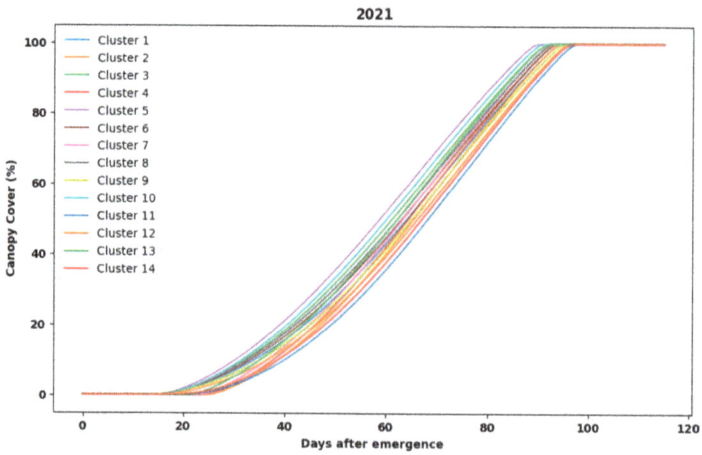

Figure 7. Average cluster-wise CC (%) data for 2020 and 2021, respectively (top to bottom).

From Figure 7, it can be inferred that the average cluster-wise CC in both 2020 and 2021 showed a steady increase in the indices, and as the line graphs are distinct, with minimal overlap between them, it ascertained the decision of the optimal number of training and testing clusters, which are chosen to be 14 in this case. The number of cultivation plots that were grouped into each distinct cluster is shown in Table 2.

3.5. *Training of Single-Input LSTM Models*

To train the single-input LSTM models, the mean cultivation data across the clusters for the year 2020 were utilized. Specifically, the training dataset comprised the canopy data for the initial 28 days as inputs, while the corresponding output sequence encompassed the canopy indices from day 29 to day 42. Thereafter, at each step, a real value of the CC was appended to the dataset, and predictions were made for the subsequent 14 days of canopy indices. This iterative process continued until the CC data for the first 98 days served as inputs, and the CC values from day 99 to day 112 were utilized as the corresponding output pair to train the single-input LSTM models. This procedure was repeated for all 14 training clusters, resulting in a total of 42,432 training sequences. Despite varying in length, each sequence maintained a consistent prediction window of 14.

These sequences were employed as inputs for various single-input LSTM models, including stacked LSTMs, the bidirectional LSTM, the CNN LSTM, and encoder–decoder LSTM models. To assess the forecasting performance of these trained LSTMs, the testing dataset for the year 2021 was partitioned into 14 clusters and identified using the K-means algorithm with the elbow method. Then, by taking the average of the testing MSEs across the 14 clusters, the LSTM model, which forecasts the values of the CC, the best has been chosen by a majority vote and has been described in detail below.

3.6. *Training of Multiple-Input Multi-Step Output LSTM Models*

However, for training the multiple-input multi-step LSTM models, for each cluster, pairwise DTW distances were calculated between the averaged CC data calculated per cluster. As the LSTM model that has been used has two inputs, the pairwise sequences that had the least DTW distances between them were given as inputs for training the LSTM model. For testing the efficiency of the trained LSTM model on the testing dataset, which in this case is the 2021 CC data, the same process of clustering is repeated, and the DTW distances are computed between the clusters. However, no training of the models is carried out. The clusters with the least DTW distances are then given as inputs to the trained model, and the results are computed.

Table 3 displays the evaluation of the LSTM models capable of processing both single-cluster and multi-cluster cultivation data. The first five models in Table 3 are trained on variable-length single-cluster data sequences and generate predictions for a 14-day period. Conversely, the final variant, termed the multiple-input multi-step output LSTM model, is trained on pairwise cluster data using time-series sequences with the shortest DTW distances between them. This training process is highly resource-intensive, demanding significant computational power to calculate the forecasted values. Hence, it is recommended to opt for the LSTMs that handle single-cluster data inputs. Nevertheless, despite its computational demands, the multiple-input multi-step output LSTM model exhibits superior performance, particularly in forecasting the early season growth indices, i.e., a prediction of the CC up to the 56th day after emergence when there is not enough data to be supplied as testing data to the trained LSTM models.

Another noteworthy observation from Table 3 is that a multiple-input multi-step output LSTM model is used as the model to predict the future values of the CC when the data from the 28th day of emergence to the 56th day after emergence are given as inputs. However, due to the resource constraints associated with training the above-stated model, it was decided that the second variant of the single-input LSTM, i.e., a stacked LSTM trained for 100 epochs with a batch size of 32, yielded comparable results at par with the multiple-input multi-step output LSTM models in forecasting the later season growth indices (starting from the 63rd day to the 98th day after emergence). The main reason for doing so is that training a stacked LSTM requires much less computational resources compared to that of a multiple-input multi-step output LSTM model.

3.7. ARIMA Model Analysis

For a more efficient performance comparison of the trained LSTM models, a classical ARIMA approach was used on the 2021 cultivation data. As the ARIMA approach did not require any model training, the cultivation data for all the 2063 plots were averaged, and the RMSE estimates were computed, which have been shown in Table 4. Based on the results from the table, it is evident that the RMSE estimates obtained for forecasting the growth parameters using initial CC data up to the 49th day of emergence were excessively high. Consequently, employing the classical ARIMA approach to forecast the CC values was deemed impractical. This comparison helped in fulfilling the objective, which was to determine the most effective estimator for forecasting future values of the CC, namely from the 28th day of emergence of the cotton crop to the conclusion of the cultivation season.

Table 4. RMSE estimates of ARIMA-based modeling on 2021 CC data.

Number of Days after Emergence in the Training Set	Methods to Standardize the Dataset	Interpretation from ACF and PACF Plots	ARIMA Model	RMSE Estimate
28 35 42 49 56	Differentiation of the original data by 2 orders	Significant spike in both ACF and PACF plots at lag 6; but none beyond that	6,2,6	27.62 21.96 20.14 10.07 8.39
63	Differentiation of the original data by 2 orders	Significant spike in both ACF and PACF plots at lag 0; but none beyond that	0,2,0	6.71
70	Cube root of the original data; differentiation of the cubed data by 2 orders	Significant spike in both ACF and PACF plots at lag 0; but none beyond that	0,2,0	5.03
77 84 91 98	Differentiation of the original data by 2 orders	Significant spike in both ACF and PACF plots at lag 0; but none beyond that	0,2,0	4.87 4.32 3.82 3.36

4. Discussion

The major goal of this study is to explore the use of ML models for in-season forecasting of crop canopy features. For this, the CC was chosen as a canopy feature as it is significantly important in measuring the canopy leaf area and subsequently for yield estimations [37–39] and irrigation scheduling [40]. Our approach is to forecast CC features two weeks in advance with accurate precision so that in-season management decisions can be made. For this, different forecasting models have been used to do a comparative analysis and to choose a model that predicted the indices with the highest accuracy at different phases of the growth cycle.

In order to simplify the analysis and ensure that the forecasting models yielded an unbiased estimate, the CC data recorded for the plots for the year 2020 were used as training data, and the CC data over the year 2021 were used to gauge the efficiency of the trained models. The recorded data for the year 2020 were clustered using the K-means algorithm for ease of training the LSTM models. Similarly, in order to compute the efficiency of the trained models, the CC data for the year 2021 were clustered, and the trained forecasting models were tested. The best forecasting model was decided by a majority vote based on the output of the models, which forecasted the values of CCs up to 14 days in advance with minimal error.

The prediction of CC values from the 28th day to the 63rd day after emergence has been achieved using a multiple-input multi-step output LSTM model. The superiority of the multiple-input multi-step output LSTM model, which utilized similar cluster cultivation data as multiple inputs to the model, over other forecasting methods, has prompted a thorough examination of the data formulation and model architecture that contributed to its enhanced prediction accuracy in predicting the early season growth indices.

Following the data preparation phase, it was crucial to examine the benefits of the resulting curated dataset when utilized as inputs to the multiple-input multi-step output and long short-term memory (LSTM) models. One significant benefit of utilizing these models lies in their ability to effectively capture relationships and dependencies among multiple interdependent input sequences. For instance, when provided with CC data for clusters with low DTW distance as inputs, these models could exploit correlations between different time-series inputs to generate more precise predictions. In this case, the DTW technique was used to measure the similarity between different clusters by stretching or compressing them along the time axis. This alignment allows similar clusters to be matched, even if they are distorted by noise. Given how the data were recorded across all plots, there is a high likelihood of the CC data being influenced by noise. Additionally, another benefit of employing DTW to evaluate the similarity between clusters is that the alignment process remains meaningful, prioritizing the alignment of genuinely similar patterns over accommodating every minor fluctuation in the data [41–43].

Similarly, the prediction of CC values, starting from the 63rd day of emergence to the end of the cultivation period, was achieved using a four-layered stacked LSTM model. These models incorporate the CC values for the year 2020 as input variables to train the model, enabling the prediction of CC indices for the year 2021. As anticipated, the root mean square error (RMSE) values for the estimation of CCs exhibited a decline with the inclusion of more actual values into the model. However, the main disadvantage of using single-input LSTM models is that they suffer from a deficiency in capturing the interactions between inputs, resulting in a decrease in predicting accuracy when there is not enough testing data to make predictions. However, it is important to exercise caution to mitigate the risk of overfitting when the input data sequences are not well aligned or curated.

Nonetheless, given the significant computational resources associated with employing a multiple-input multi-step LSTM model, it is recommended to opt for a single-input stacked LSTM architecture, as stated above, for computing growth indices starting from 63 days of cultivation. This approach ensures a more manageable computational load while still achieving a reasonably low RMSE, thus enhancing the precision of forecasting future CC indices.

Another noteworthy insight, observed in Figure 8, is the alignment between all the predicted values for the subsequent 14 days and the actual CC values. Anomalies typically occurred within the predictions around days 6 to 8 while trying to predict the early season growth indices (typically for predicting the future CC values when the real canopy values until days 28 to 35 are given as inputs to the trained LSTM models.) Hence, it suggests the potential application of more advanced time-series forecasting models like the Prophet [44], VARMAX [45], or state-space models [46,47], which can be used to address these prediction anomalies in future analyses.

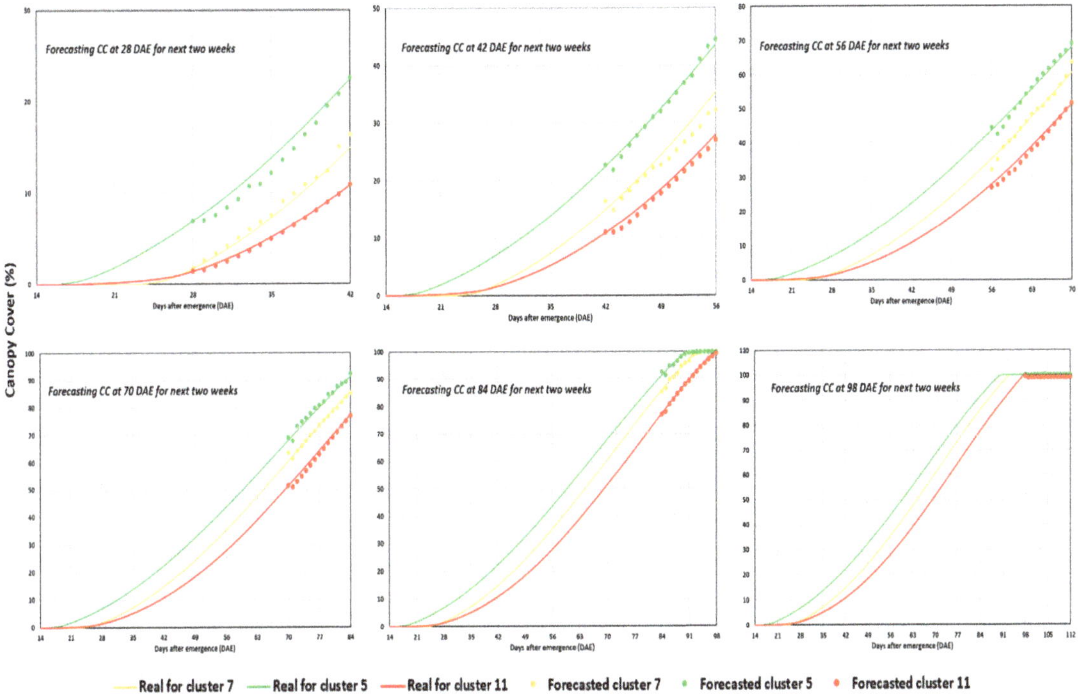

Figure 8. Bi-weekly prediction of CC from the growth period of four weeks to the end of the cultivation period (14-day prediction) for clusters 11, 5, and 7 (top to bottom).

5. Conclusions and Future Work

Utilizing cultivation data from multiple clusters with a minimal DTW distance for LSTM model training, a four-layered multiple-input multi-step output LSTM model demonstrated superior performance compared to other LSTM models and the traditional ARIMA approach. The RMSE estimates obtained from this model ranged from 4.36 to 2.18 across the entire cultivation period. However, due to computational constraints, this model was only employed for predicting growth indices up to the 56th day of emergence. Subsequently, from the 56th to the 98th day of emergence, when sufficient data became available for LSTM model testing, a stacked LSTM trained for 100 epochs with a batch size of 32 was selected over other LSTM variants due to its cost-effectiveness and relatively low average RMSE. Future research endeavors should incorporate datasets from diverse sites, soils, and climates to develop robust and versatile forecasting models that are capable of accurately predicting canopy features until the harvesting phase. Consequently, robust models are imperative for effectively predicting in-season growth, thereby optimizing management strategies and enhancing yield outcomes.

Author Contributions: Conceptualization, S.B.D., M.B. and K.C.G.; methodology, S.B.D. and U.B.-N.; software, S.B.D. and U.B.-N.; resources, S.K., J.L. and J.L.; data curation, S.B.D., J.L.L.-S., S.K., and K.C.G.; writing, S.B.D. and M.B.; writing—review and editing, M.B., K.N. and U.B.-N.; project administration, M.B., K.N., J.L., L.Z., J.L., P.P., J.L.L.-S., U.B.-N., K.N. and S.K.; funding acquisition, S.K. and M.B. All authors have read and agreed to the published version of the manuscript.

Funding: The authors would like to acknowledge Texas State Support Committee and Cotton Incorporated (project number: 19-846TX) for providing funding to collect data.

Data Availability Statement: The raw code and data may be available upon appropriate request.

Acknowledgments: The authors express their gratitude to all the members of the Digital Agriculture Research and Training Program at Texas A&M AgriLife Research and Extension Center in Corpus Christi for their invaluable assistance and collaboration during the project.

Conflicts of Interest: The authors declare no conflicts of interest.

References

1. McDonald, B.L. *Food Security*; Polity: Cambridge, UK, 2010.
2. Mahanta, S.; Habib, M.R.; Moore, J.M. Effect of high-voltage atmospheric cold plasma treatment on germination and heavy metal uptake by soybeans (*Glycine max*). *Int. J. Mol. Sci.* **2022**, *23*, 1611. [CrossRef] [PubMed]
3. Dutta, A.; Dahal, P.; Prajapati, R.; Tamang, P.; Kumar, E.S. IoT based aquaponics monitoring system. In Proceedings of the 1st KEC Conference Proceedings, Lalitpur, Nepal, 27 September 2018; Volume 1, pp. 75–80.
4. Dhal, S.B.; Jungbluth, K.; Lin, R.; Sabahi, S.P.; Bagavathiannan, M.; Braga-Neto, U.; Kalafatis, S. A machine-learning-based IoT system for optimizing nutrient supply in commercial aquaponic operations. *Sensors* **2022**, *22*, 3510. [CrossRef] [PubMed]
5. Dhal, S.B.; Bagavathiannan, M.; Braga-Neto, U.; Kalafatis, S. Nutrient optimization for plant growth in Aquaponic irrigation using machine learning for small training datasets. *Artif. Intell. Agric.* **2022**, *6*, 68–76. [CrossRef]
6. Dhal, S.B.; Bagavathiannan, M.; Braga-Neto, U.; Kalafatis, S. Can Machine Learning classifiers be used to regulate nutrients using small training datasets for aquaponic irrigation?: A comparative analysis. *PLoS ONE* **2022**, *17*, e0269401. [CrossRef] [PubMed]
7. Arvind, C.S.; Jyothi, R.; Kaushal, K.; Girish, G.; Saurav, R.; Chetankumar, G. Edge computing based smart aquaponics monitoring system using deep learning in IoT environment. In Proceedings of the 2020 IEEE Symposium Series on Computational Intelligence (SSCI), Canberra, ACT, Australia, 1–4 December 2020; pp. 1485–1491.
8. Dhal, S.B.; Mahanta, S.; Gumero, J.; O'Sullivan, N.; Soetan, M.; Louis, J.; Gadepally, K.C.; Mahanta, S.; Lusher, J.; Kalafatis, S. An IoT-based data-driven real-time monitoring system for control of heavy metals to ensure optimal lettuce growth in hydroponic set-ups. *Sensors* **2023**, *23*, 451. [CrossRef] [PubMed]
9. Habib, M.R.; Mahanta, S.; Jolly, Y.N.; Moore, J.M. Alleviating heavy metal toxicity in milk and water through a synergistic approach of absorption technique and high voltage atmospheric cold plasma and probable rheological changes. *Biomolecules* **2022**, *12*, 913. [CrossRef] [PubMed]
10. Vashisht, P.; Singh, L.; Mahanta, S.; Verma, D.; Sharma, S.; Saini, G.S.; Sharma, A.; Chowdhury, B.; Awasti, N.; Gaurav; et al. Pulsed electric field processing in the dairy sector: A review of applications, quality impact and implementation challenges. *Int. J. Food Sci. Technol.* **2024**, *59*, 2122–2135. [CrossRef]
11. Vashisht, P.; Verma, D.; Charles, A.P.R.; Saini, G.S.; Sharma, S.; Singh, L.; Mahanta, S.; Mahanta, S.; Singh, K.; Gaurav, G. Ozone processing in the dairy sector: A review of applications, quality impact and implementation challenges. *ChemRxiv* **2023**. [CrossRef]
12. Dhal, S.B.; Mahanta, S.; Gadepally, K.C.; He, S.; Hughes, M.; Moore, J.; Nowka, K.J.; Kalafatis, S. CNN-based real-time prediction of growth stage in soybeans cultivated in hydroponic set-ups. In Proceedings of the SoutheastCon 2023, Orlando, FL, USA, 1–16 April 2023; pp. 193–197.
13. Jones, J.W.; Hoogenboom, G.; Porter, C.H.; Boote, K.J.; Batchelor, W.D.; Hunt, L.A.; Wilkens, P.W.; Singh, U.; Gijsman, A.J.; Ritchie, J.T. The DSSAT cropping system model. *Eur. J. Agron.* **2003**, *18*, 235–265. [CrossRef]
14. Wang, E.; Robertson, M.J.; Hammer, G.L.; Carberry, P.S.; Holzworth, D.; Meinke, H.; Chapman, S.C.; Hargreaves, J.N.G.; Huth, N.I.; McLean, G. Development of a generic crop model template in the cropping system model APSIM. *Eur. J. Agron.* **2002**, *18*, 121–140. [CrossRef]
15. Hochreiter, S.; Schmidhuber, J. Long short-term memory. *Neural Comput.* **1997**, *9*, 1735–1780. [CrossRef] [PubMed]
16. Ullah, M.; Ullah, H.; Khan, S.D.; Cheikh, F.A. Stacked lstm network for human activity recognition using smartphone data. In Proceedings of the 2019 8th European Workshop on Visual Information Processing (EUVIP), Roma, Italy, 28–31 October 2019; pp. 175–180.
17. Graves, A.; Jaitly, N.; Mohamed, A.R. Hybrid speech recognition with deep bidirectional LSTM. In Proceedings of the 2013 IEEE Workshop on Automatic Speech Recognition and Understanding, Olomouc, Czech Republic, 8–12 December 2013; pp. 273–278.
18. LeCun, Y.; Bengio, Y.; Hinton, G. Deep learning. *Nature* **2015**, *521*, 436–444. [CrossRef] [PubMed]
19. Zhao, Y.; Xue, J.; Chen, X. Ensemble learning approaches in speech recognition. In *Speech and Audio Processing for Coding, Enhancement and Recognition*; Springer: New York, NY, USA, 2014; pp. 113–152.

20. Jiang, Z.; Liu, C.; Hendricks, N.P.; Ganapathysubramanian, B.; Hayes, D.J.; Sarkar, S. Predicting county level corn yields using deep long short term memory models. *arXiv* **2018**, arXiv:1805.12044.
21. Gavahi, K.; Abbaszadeh, P.; Moradkhani, H. DeepYield: A combined convolutional neural network with long short-term memory for crop yield forecasting. *Expert Syst. Appl.* **2021**, *184*, 115511. [CrossRef]
22. Van Klompenburg, T.; Kassahun, A.; Catal, C. Crop yield prediction using machine learning: A systematic literature review. *Comput. Electron. Agric.* **2020**, *177*, 105709. [CrossRef]
23. Yuan, C.Z.; Ling, S.K. Long short-term memory model based agriculture commodity price prediction application. In Proceedings of the 2020 2nd International Conference on Information Technology and Computer Communications, Kuala Lumpur, Malaysia, 12–14 August 2020; pp. 43–49.
24. Chen, P.; Xiao, Q.; Zhang, J.; Xie, C.; Wang, B. Occurrence prediction of cotton pests and diseases by bidirectional long short-term memory networks with climate and atmosphere circulation. *Comput. Electron. Agric.* **2020**, *176*, 105612. [CrossRef]
25. Xiao, Q.; Li, W.; Kai, Y.; Chen, P.; Zhang, J.; Wang, B. Occurrence prediction of pests and diseases in cotton on the basis of weather factors by long short term memory network. *BMC Bioinform.* **2019**, *20*, 688. [CrossRef] [PubMed]
26. Suresh, K.K.; Krishna Priya, S.R. Forecasting sugarcane yield of Tamilnadu using ARIMA models. *Sugar Tech* **2011**, *13*, 23–26. [CrossRef]
27. Elsamie, M.A.; Ali, T.; Zhou, D.Y. Using a dynamic time series model (ARIMA) for forecasting of Egyptian cotton crop variables. *J. Anim. Plant Sci.* **2021**, *31*, 810–823.
28. Poyyamozhi, S.; Mohideen, A.K. Forecasting of cotton production in India using ARIMA model. *Asia Pac. J. Res. ISSN (Print)* **2016**, *2320*, 5504.
29. Zhao, D.; Reddy, K.R.; Kakani, V.G.; Read, J.J.; Koti, S. Canopy reflectance in cotton for growth assessment and lint yield prediction. *Eur. J. Agron.* **2007**, *26*, 335–344. [CrossRef]
30. Ballester, C.; Hornbuckle, J.; Brinkhoff, J.; Smith, J.; Quayle, W. Assessment of in-season cotton nitrogen status and lint yield prediction from unmanned aerial system imagery. *Remote Sens.* **2017**, *9*, 1149. [CrossRef]
31. Pylianidis, C.; Osinga, S.; Athanasiadis, I.N. Introducing digital twins to agriculture. *Comput. Electron. Agric.* **2021**, *184*, 105942. [CrossRef]
32. Bhandari, M.; Chang, A.; Jung, J.; Ibrahim, A.M.H.; Rudd, J.C.; Baker, S.; Landivar, J.; Liu, S.; Landivar, J. Unmanned aerial system-based high-throughput phenotyping for plant breeding. *Plant Phenome J.* **2023**, *6*, e20058. [CrossRef]
33. Sullivan, D.G.; Shaw, N.L. Using smartphone technology to assess field crop stands. *Agron. J.* **2016**, *108*, 1674–1680.
34. Hyndman, R. Better acf and pacf plots, but no optimal linear prediction. *Electron. J. Stat. [E]* **2014**, *8*, 2296–2300.
35. Zakria, M.; Muhammad, F. Forecasting the population of Pakistan using ARIMA models. *Pak. J. Agric. Sci.* **2009**, *46*, 214–223.
36. Gasca, M.; Sauer, T. Polynomial interpolation in several variables. *Adv. Comput. Math.* **2000**, *12*, 377–410. [CrossRef]
37. Dhaliwal, J.K.; Panday, D.; Saha, D.; Lee, J.; Jagadamma, S.; Schaeffer, S.; Mengistu, A. Predicting and interpreting cotton yield and its determinants under long-term conservation management practices using machine learning. *Comput. Electron. Agric.* **2022**, *199*, 107107. [CrossRef]
38. Chen, C.; Chen, F. Cotton yield prediction using artificial neural networks. *Int. J. Agric. Biol. Eng.* **2014**, *7*, 144–150.
39. Zhang, C.; Kovacs, J.M.; Kafatos, M. Monitoring cotton yield and growth anomalies using AVHRR NDVI time-series data. *Int. J. Remote Sens.* **2002**, *23*, 4653–4665.
40. Risal, A.; Niu, H.; Landivar-Scott, J.L.; Maeda, M.M.; Bednarz, C.W.; Landivar-Bowles, J.; Duffield, N.; Payton, P.; Pal, P.; Lascano, R.J.; et al. Improving Irrigation Management of Cotton with Small Unmanned Aerial Vehicle (UAV) in Texas High Plains. *Water* **2024**, *16*, 1300. [CrossRef]
41. Wang, K.; Theo, G. Alignment of curves by dynamic time warping. *Ann. Stat.* **1997**, *25*, 1251–1276. [CrossRef]
42. Berndt Donald, J.; Clifford, J. Using dynamic time warping to find patterns in time series. In Proceedings of the 3rd International Conference on Knowledge Discovery and Data Mining, Seattle, WA, USA, 31 July–1 August 1994; pp. 359–370.
43. Stan, S.; Chan, P. Toward accurate dynamic time warping in linear time and space. *Intell. Data Anal.* **2007**, *11*, 561–580.
44. Gibran, K.; Bushrui, S.B. *The Prophet: A New Annotated Edition*; Simon and Schuster: New York, NY, USA, 2012.
45. Casals, J.; García-Hiernaux, A.; Jerez, M. From general state-space to VARMAX models. *Math. Comput. Simul.* **2012**, *82*, 924–936. [CrossRef]
46. Aoki, M. *State Space Modeling of Time Series*; Springer Science & Business Media: Berlin/Heidelberg, Germany, 2013.
47. Rangapuram, S.S.; Seeger, M.W.; Gasthaus, J.; Stella, L.; Wang, Y.; Januschowski, T. Deep state space models for time series forecasting. In *Advances in Neural Information Processing Systems*; Curran Associates Inc.: Red Hook, NY, USA, 2018; Volume 31.

remote sensing

MDPI

Article

Local Field-Scale Winter Wheat Yield Prediction Using VENμS Satellite Imagery and Machine Learning Techniques

Marco Spencer Chiu [1,*] and Jinfei Wang [1,2]

1 Department of Geography and Environment, The University of Western Ontario, London, ON N6G 3K7, Canada; jfwang@uwo.ca
2 The Institute for Earth and Space Exploration, The University of Western Ontario, London, ON N6A 3K7, Canada
* Correspondence: mchiu52@uwo.ca

Abstract: Reliable and accurate crop yield prediction at the field scale is critical for meeting the global demand for reliable food sources. In this study, we tested the viability of VENμS satellite data as an alternative to other popular and publicly available multispectral satellite data to predict winter wheat yield and produce a yield prediction map for a field located in southwestern Ontario, Canada, in 2020. Random forest (RF) and support vector regression (SVR) were the two machine learning techniques employed. Our results indicate that machine learning models paired with vegetation indices (VIs) derived from VENμS imagery can accurately predict winter wheat yield 1~2 months prior to harvest, with the most accurate predictions achieved during the early fruit development stage. While both machine learning approaches were viable, SVR produced the most accurate prediction with an R^2 of 0.86 and an RMSE of 0.3925 t/ha using data collected from tillering to the early fruit development stage. NDRE-1, NDRE-2, and REP from various growth stages were ranked among the top seven variables in terms of importance for the prediction. These findings provide valuable insights into using high-resolution satellites as tools for non-destructive yield potential analysis.

Keywords: precision agriculture; yield prediction; VENμS; machine learning; vegetation index; winter wheat

1. Introduction

The growing global population has heightened the need for reliable food sources and food security, underscoring the importance of advancing efficient and sustainable agricultural practices. The agriculture industry today faces substantial challenges, including rising global food demand, crop diseases, pest outbreaks, limited arable land, and the impacts of climate change. Addressing these issues is vital for ensuring a resilient and productive agricultural sector. Research by Tan and Reynolds indicates that in southwestern Ontario, water supply and demand pose the greatest challenge to the agricultural sector [1]. Interestingly, farmers in this region are less concerned about climate change compared to those in areas more frequently affected by extreme weather events [2]. The agriculture and agri-food sectors contributed approximately 7% to Canada's gross domestic product (GDP) and accounted for one in every nine jobs in 2022 [3]. While climate change may not present an immediate threat to the Canadian agricultural industry, it is wise to stay informed and proactively prepare for potential future climate variations.

Precision agriculture (PA) employs advanced technologies and data analysis techniques to optimize crop yields while minimizing resource use. This approach involves evaluating quantified spatial and in situ plant data to inform agricultural practices such as the application of water, labor, and fuel, thereby reducing costs and preventing excessive waste, including pesticide and nutrient loss. PA integrates various spatial technologies, such as geographic information systems (GIS), handheld ground-based data collection devices, and remote sensing through ground-based or aerial vehicles, to develop and implement efficient agricultural strategies [3]. Given the high demand for data collection, remote sensing techniques are employed in crop management to precisely manage, produce, and predict crop data for analysis. Accurate crop yield prediction is crucial for helping farmers address production challenges and mitigate the effects of climate variability and change on crop yield [4].

Among the various platforms of surface spectral data collection in PA, space-borne satellites are one of the most stable platforms [5–10]. A key advantage of using optical satellite images for remote sensing is the ability to obtain spectral data over large land areas in a single snapshot with high resolution. Traditionally, researchers have faced challenges with optical satellite images due to their relatively lower spatial resolution compared to ground-collected data [11]. This limitation has restricted research to regional scales rather than local, field-scale studies. For example, Landsat 8, launched in 2013 by the United States, features the Optical Land Imager (OLI) with a spatial resolution of up to 30 m [12]. Similarly, Sentinel-2, launched in 2015, features 13 multispectral bands with spatial resolutions of 10 m, 20 m, and 60 m, and a revisit time of 5 days with its constellation of twin satellites [13]. In contrast, VENµS's VSSC (Vegetation and Environment Monitoring on a New Micro-Satellite Super-Spectral Camera) captures optical images at a resolution as high as 5.3 m. Additionally, VENµS has a revisit time of 2 days, compared to Landsat 8's 16 days [12,14]. These advantages in both high spatial and temporal resolution make VENµS a superior choice for detailed crop monitoring and analyses, providing more frequent and precise data for agricultural applications.

The ease of access to satellite data offers a significant advantage over the other major remote sensing methods: ground-level and UAV-level remote sensing. Many satellite datasets, such as those from VENµS, Landsat series, Sentinel-2, MODIS, and SPOT series are publicly available. VENµS imagery can be downloaded free of charge in its predefined areas, thereby reducing both labor and monetary research costs compared to ground sampling and UAV flight operations. While crop monitoring has traditionally relied on satellite imagery, UAV-based systems often challenge their usability due to superior spatial and temporal resolution. Crop growth stages can vary week to week, making some satellite images unsuitable for timely analysis. For instance, Sentinel-2 data have yielded unsatisfactory crop yield prediction results due to cloud coverage and lower temporal resolution [15]. VENµS addresses this issue by providing higher spatial resolution data compared to most satellites, while maintaining frequent revisits of 2 days and offering a wide range of multispectral bands [14].

Furthermore, UAV operations are often constrained by weather conditions. Clear skies and low wind speeds are typically required to collect high-quality data. While UAVs offer flexible planning and scheduling, VENµS can achieve similar advantages by mitigating poor coverage with its short revisit period. Despite this, UAVs provide an edge over satellites by allowing researchers greater control over the location and timing of data collection. However, UAV flights with payloads such as multispectral cameras are often restricted under aviation regulations, and additional procedures or certifications are often required if the flight is to be conducted in a regulated aerodrome in most countries. For instance, Transport Canada mandates the registration of any remotely piloted aircrafts (RPAs) weighing between 250 g and 25 kg, which encompasses most commercially available UAVs that can carry spectral sensors as payloads [16]. Additionally, operating these RPAs categorized by Transport Canada requires the pilot to have different classes of operation licenses based on the location of flight. In contrast, satellite data can often be obtained online free of charge and without any operational requirements, making the data widely accessible. Thus, VENµS effectively combines the advantages of both satellite and UAV systems, offering high spatial resolution, frequent temporal coverage, and ease of data access.

With the spectral data collected from remote sensing imagery, vegetation index (VI) calculations become feasible. VIs are mathematical transformations of spectral bands widely used in agricultural research to determine specific plant properties, such as leaf area index (LAI), chlorophyll content, and nutrient levels [17–19]. Consequently, VIs are commonly employed for crop growth and health monitoring, including yield prediction [19,20]. For instance, vegetation indices that performed well in the study by Fu et al. were derived using the red absorption portion of the spectrum [21]. On multispectral cameras, this typically includes the red band and red-edge bands. Indices such as the normalized difference vegetation index (NDVI), normalized difference red edge (NDRE), and soil-adjusted vegetation index (SAVI) have been previously studied as effective indices in winter wheat yield monitoring [11,22]. VENµS is specifically designed for vegetation monitoring, offering more bands in the red-edge and near-infrared range than most publicly available satellite data. This enhanced spectral capability improves its ability to detect vegetation properties. Therefore, it is important to further explore VENµS's yield prediction potential using a more diverse range of vegetation indices that may be unavailable from other satellites.

Recently, machine learning regression methods, such as Random Forest (RF) and Support Vector Regression (SVR), have been extensively investigated for biomass and yield estimation [23–26]. These machine learning methods can capture complex patterns and relationships in the data that traditional methods might miss, and was proven to be viable in yield prediction [27,28]. RF, for example, can handle a large number of input variables and is less likely to overfit due to its ensemble nature. Hunt et al. successfully mapped winter wheat yield using Sentinel-2 data and RF regression models, achieving a relatively low root mean square error at 0.66 t/ha [29]. This work suggests the potential of utilizing higher spatial resolution data to capture the within-field yield variability with a common machine learning algorithm.

SVR, conversely, focuses on optimizing a margin around a hyperplane, which can result in better generalization on unseen data. While traditional regression methods are straightforward and easier to interpret, machine learning regression methods like RF and SVR offer significant advantages in terms of handling complexity, scalability, and adaptability, making them suitable for a wide range of modern data-driven applications.

Compared to most publicly available satellites, such as Sentinel-2, VENµS offers additional bands in the red-edge and near-infrared ranges, which are particularly advantageous for vegetation monitoring. It also provides relatively higher spatial and temporal resolution. Despite these benefits, VENµS has been rarely studied in yield estimation research. Therefore, to make a well-informed prediction of winter wheat yield at a local, field-scale using VENµS data, it is essential to introduce an appropriate prediction model. The objective of this study is to (i) investigate the relationships between yield and VIs at difference growth stages, (ii) to evaluate the effectiveness of RF and SVR models in predicting yield, (iii) to determine the optimal combinations of dates (growth stages) for yield prediction in a winter wheat field located in southwestern Ontario, (iv) to uncover insights in the ranked importance of VIs from different forth stages, and (v) to produce a yield prediction map.

2. Materials and Methods

2.1. Study Area and Data Collection

The study site is in Strathroy-Caradoc, Ontario, Canada, near the village of Mount Brydges, which is about 23 km southwest of the urban center of London, Ontario (Figure 1). The studied period was from May to early July of 2020, during which the average recorded temperature was 22 °C and the relative humidity averaged 73%. The climate in the area is classified as a warm-summer humid continental climate (Dfb) according to the Köppen climate classification system. The area is predominantly agricultural croplands and its major field crops include winter wheat, corn, and soybeans [30]. Winter wheat was selected as the focus of this study. A winter wheat field covering 53.7 hectares in this region was designated as the specific area for investigation.

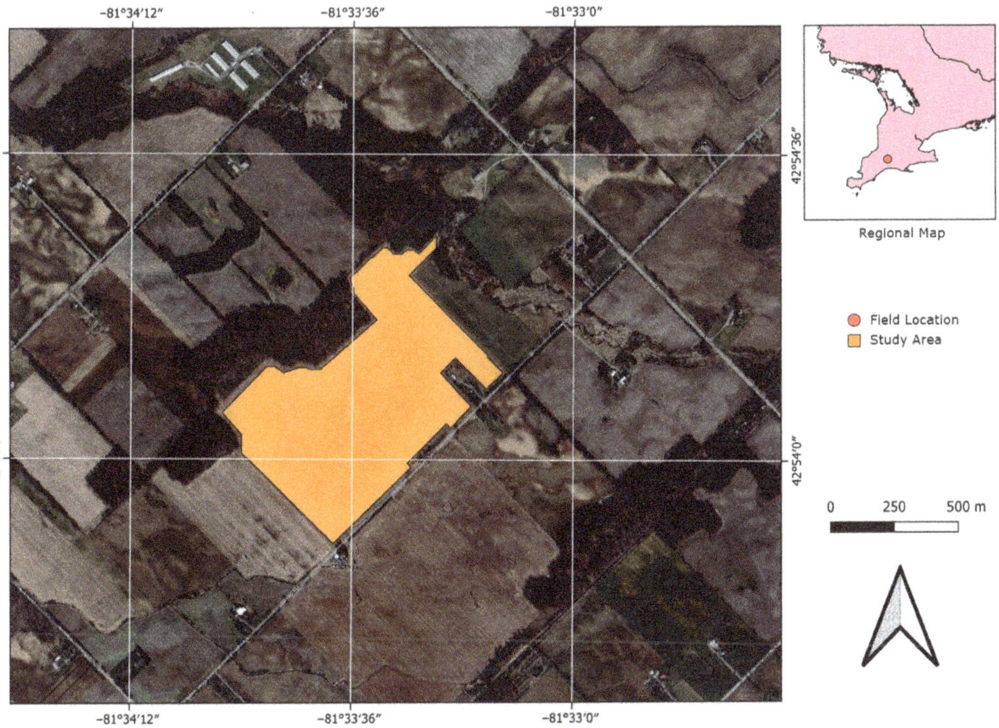

Figure 1. Location of the studied wheat field near Melbourne, ON, Canada, in an ArcGIS Pro Basemap image.

The cultivar in the studied field was soft red winter wheat, which was planted in October of 2019. In the region of Southwest Ontario, winter wheat typically lies dormant over the winter after planting, then commences shooting in late April of the following year and is harvested from early to mid-July. VENμS imagery acquisition was performed at each consequent growth stage starting at tillering, then stem elongation, booting, heading, flowering, early fruit development, and ripening. The growth stages were verified by gauging the plant's physical characteristics using the Biologische Bundesanstalt, Bundessortenamt and CHemical industry (BBCH) scale at the field, matching the satellite overpass dates (Table 1). In total, 8 cloud-free VENμS images were acquired.

Table 1. Growth stages at the study area with matching VENμS overpass dates.

Growth Stage	VENμS Overpass
Tillering-1	20200503
Tillering-2	20200513
Stem Elongation	20200521
Booting	20200525
Heading	20200606
Flowering	20200612
Early Fruit (Grain) Development	20200616
Late Fruit (Grain) Development	Cloud Cover
Ripening	20200706

2.2. VENμS Satellite Imagery and Preprocessing

The data used in this research were collected by VENμS (Vegetation and Environment Monitoring on a New MicroSatellite), which was launched in August 2017. This satellite marks the first Earth observation collaboration between France and Israel, led by the Centre National d'Etudes Spatiales (CNES) and the Israeli Space Agency (ISA). The mission aims to monitor plant growth and health status, providing valuable insights into the impacts of environmental factors, human activities, and climate change on Earth's land surface [14]. Since 2017, the VENμS VM1 mission has provided multispectral data from its 12 different bands, featuring a spatial resolution of 5.3 m, a revisiting period of 2 days, and operating at an altitude of 720 km above sea level (Table 2). As implied by its name, VENμS excels in monitoring Earth's surface vegetation, which is facilitated by its extensive red-edge and near-infrared bands.

Table 2. Spectral bands of the VENμS super-spectral camera.

Bands	Central Wavelength (nm)	Bandwidth (nm)
1	423.9	40
2	446.9	40
3	491.9	40
4	555	40
5	619.7	40
6	619.5	40
7	666.2	30
8	702	24
9	741.1	16
10	782.2	16
11	861.1	40
12	908.7	20

The imagery was categorized as level 2A (L2A) surface reflectance data, with each scene covering areas ranging from 27×27 km^2 to 27×54 km^2 at the spatial resolution of 5×5 m^2. The satellite imagery was processed and distributed by Theia MUSCATE (MUlti SATellite, multi-CApteurs, for multi-TEmporelles data), a component of the Theia Land Data Centre. This French inter-agency organization aims to provide satellite data and value-added products for scientific communities and public policy actors. MUSCATE facilitates the processing and distribution of large volumes of satellite imagery, particularly from VENμS, Sentinel-2, and Landsat satellites. This includes tasks such as atmospheric corrections and creating cloud-free surface reflectance syntheses. The processed data are used in various applications, including agriculture, forestry, urban planning, and environmental monitoring. Each of the VENμS L2A products contained two versions of surface reflectance data for the 12 bands, from B01 to B12. The first version of the surface reflectance rasters is denoted as SRE.DBL (Surface Reflectance), which is atmospherically corrected. The second version is denoted as FRE.DBL (Flat Reflectance), which is SRE.DBL files further corrected for slope effects. This correction suppresses apparent reflectance variations due to the orientation of slopes with regard to the sun, making the corrected image appear as if the land surface were flat. For this study, the FRE.DBL raster files were adopted.

The L2A surface reflectance rasters were encoded as 16-bit signed integers, necessitating preprocessing before any manipulation by dividing pixel values of each channel by 1000. This preprocessing was conducted in Python 3.9.19 using packages such as "rasterio", "gdal", and "numpy" to extract and obtain surface reflectance values from each band at the study site. Subsequently, the 12-band raster values were normalized to a range between 0 and 1 for use in later calculations.

2.3. Vegetation Indices

Vegetation indices (VIs) were used in this study as predictors of final harvested yield. The VIs were calculated as raster products using the 12 VENμS bands in Python 3.9.19, employing the same packages used in satellite image preprocessing. Additionally, several VIs that utilize spectral information in the red edge and near-infrared wavelengths, which are well represented in VENμS data, have demonstrated strong correlations with crop growth, health, and yield [17,31,32]. A total of 21 VIs were tested in this study, including 8 variations of existing VIs based on their original development formulas (Table 3). This was made possible by fitting the narrow bandwidth of VENμS bands into VI formulas initially developed with legacy sensors and satellites. For instance, NDVI was developed using the Landsat-1 Multispectral Scanner, where the NIR band 7 had a bandwidth range of 800 to 1100 nm. With the VSSC, both bands 11 and 12 fit within this NIR range, allowing for the inclusion of variations of existing VIs in the analysis.

Table 3. Vegetation indices to be tested in this study.

VI [1]	Formula [2]	Original Authors
ARVI	$\frac{NIR_{11}-[Red_7-1\times(Red_7-Blue_3)]}{NIR_{11}+[Red_7 1\times(Red_7-Blue_3)]}$	Kaufman and Tanre [33]
DVI-1	$NIR_{11}-Red_7$	Richardson and Wiegand [34]
DVI-2	$NIR_{12}-Red_7$	
EVI	$\frac{2.5\times(NIR_{11}-Red_7)}{NIR_{11}+6\times Red_7-7.5\times Blue_2+1}$	Huete et al. [35]
ISR-1	$\frac{Red_7}{NIR_{11}}$	Fernades et al. [36]
ISR-2	$\frac{Red_7}{NIR_{12}}$	
MCARI	$[(RE_8-Red_7)-0.2\times(RE_8\text{–}Green_4)]\times RE_8\div Red_7$	Daughtry et al. [37]
MSAVI-1	$\left[2\times NIR_{10}+1-\sqrt{(2\times NIR_{10}+1)^2-8\times(NIR_{10}-Red_7)}\right]\div 2$	Qi et al. [38]
MSAVI-2	$[2\times NIR_{11}+1-\sqrt{(2\times NIR_{11}+1)^2-8\times(NIR_{11}-Red_7)}]\div 2$	
NDRE-1	$\frac{(NIR_{10}-RE_8)}{(NIR_{10}+RE_8)}$	Gitelson and Merzlyak [39]
NDRE-2	$\frac{(NIR_{10}-RE_9)}{(NIR_{10}+RE_9)}$	
NDVI-1	$\frac{(NIR_{11}-Red_7)}{(NIR_{11}+Red_7)}$	Rouse et al. [40]
NDVI-2	$\frac{(NIR_{12}-Red_7)}{(NIR_{12}+Red_7)}$	
OSAVI	$[1.16\times(NIR_{11}-Red_7)]\div(NIR_{11}+Red_7+0.16)]$	Rondeaux et al. [41]
RDVI	$(NIR_{11}-Red_7)\div(\sqrt{(NIR_{11}+Red_7})$	Roujean and Breon [42]
REP	$702+40\left(\frac{\left(\frac{Red_7+NIR_{10}}{2}\right)-Red_8}{Red_9-Red_8}\right)$	Guyot and Baret [43]
RVI-1	$\frac{NIR_{11}}{Red_7}$	Jordan [44]
RVI-2	$\frac{NIR_{12}}{Red_7}$	

Table 3. *Cont.*

VI [1]	Formula [2]	Original Authors
SAVI-1	$\frac{(NIR_{10}-Red_7)}{(NIR_{10}+Red_7+0.5)}(1.5)$	Huete [45]
SAVI-2	$\frac{(NIR_{11}-Red_7)}{(NIR_{11}+Red_7+0.5)}(1.5)$	
SAVI-3	$\frac{(NIR_{12}-Red_7)}{(NIR_{12}+Red_7+0.5)}(1.5)$	

[1] ARVI, atmospherically resistant vegetation index; DVI-1 and 2, difference vegetation index; EVI, enhanced vegetation index; ISR-1 and 2, infrared simple ratio; MCARI, modified chlorophyll absorption in reflectance index; MSAVI-1 and 2, modified soil-adjusted vegetation index; NDRE-1 and 2, normalized difference red edge; NDVI-1 and 2, normalized difference vegetation index; OSAVI, optimized soil-adjusted vegetation index; RDVI, renormalized difference vegetation index; REP, red edge position; RVI-1 and 2, ratio vegetation index; SAVI-1, 2 and 3, soil-adjusted vegetation index. [2] Blue, blue reflectance; green, green reflectance; red, red reflectance; RE, red edge reflectance; NIR, near-infrared reflectance. Subscripts are the equivalent VENμS bands.

2.4. Yield Dataset

The yield data were collected at harvest on 25 July 2020, with a combine harvester equipped with a 10 m-wide and 1.5 m-long header. Yield data were generated as a point shapefile, with yield data recorded approximately every second at the center of the harvester's track. To ensure accuracy, potential outliers located at the edges of the field were removed. For this study, the shapefile was interpolated into a 5×5 m^2 spatial resolution raster using QGIS 3.22 with inverse distance weighted (IDW) interpolation, matching the VENμS imagery and the derived vegetation indices (VIs). This approach was adopted to fully utilize the high-resolution advantage of VENμS data and to produce a detailed yield prediction map.

2.5. Machine Learning Regression Modelling and Cross-Validation

In machine learning, regression models are used to predict continuous outcomes based on input variables. Two notable techniques in this domain are Random Forest (RF) regression and Support Vector Regression (SVR), both of which offer robust solutions for complex regression problems. Advantages of machine learning regression also include its ability to automatically learn from data without being explicitly programmed for each specific task. Given that the regression models in this study were based on pixel-level analysis, machine learning regression methods were ideal for our needs as they excel in handing large data sizes. In our study, we used three key metrics to evaluate the performance of our regression models: mean absolute error (MAE), R-squared (R^2), and root mean squared error (RMSE). These metrics were employed during both the cross-validation stage and the calibration and validation of the final model to ensure a comprehensive assessment of model accuracy and reliability.

RF is an ensemble learning method that constructs multiple decision trees during calibration and outputs the mean prediction of these trees. By using multiple trees, RF reduces overfitting, a common issue in single-decision tree models. Each tree is built from a random sample of the data, with a random subset of features selected at each node to decide splits. This randomness helps make the model more resilient to noise and outliers. RF can handle large, high-dimensional datasets and identify important variables in the modeled relationships. Additionally, RF provides measures of feature importance, helping to understand the impact of each variable on the prediction.

SVR, on the other hand, extends the concepts of Support Vector Machines (SVMs) from classification to regression. Like RF, SVR is also generally robust to over fitting. It is a result of its margin maximization, the use of kernel functions, the epsilon-insensitive loss function, and the reliance on support vectors. Unlike traditional methods that minimize the error between predicted and observed values, SVR attempts to fit the error within a certain threshold. It involves the creation of a hyperplane in a multidimensional space where the distance between the data points and the hyperplane is minimized, ensuring that errors do not exceed a defined threshold. This makes SVR particularly useful in cases where a margin of tolerance is specified in the predictions. SVR is highly effective in handling non-linear relationships through the use of kernel functions, making it adaptable to various types of data [46].

In this study, the data collected over 8 dates were randomly divided into a 70% calibration set and a 30% validation set. A 10-fold K-fold cross-validation approach was employed in this study to ensure the robustness and generalizability of the machine learning regression models. This method involved splitting the calibration data into multiple subsets (folds), using each subset in turn as the validation set, while the remaining data were used for training. With 10 folds, each fold used 90% of the data for training and 10% for validation. This approach ensured that each training set was large enough to effectively train the model, while each validation set was sufficient to provide a reliable evaluation without overfitting. During the cross-validation stage, MAE, R^2, and RMSE served as crucial indicators of model performance. Cross-validation involved partitioning the calibration dataset into multiple folds and iteratively training and validating the model on these folds. MAE provided the average magnitude of errors in the predictions, indicating the overall accuracy of the model without considering the direction of errors. RMSE, which penalized larger errors more significantly due to its squared component, offered insight into the model's ability to handle large deviations from observed values. R^2, representing the proportion of variance explained by the model, evaluated the goodness of fit, with values closer to 1 indicating a better fit. By averaging these metrics across all folds, we obtained a robust estimate of the model's performance and its variability, thus mitigating the risk of overfitting or underfitting to specific subsets of data. For the RF models, the RMSE dictated the optimal cross-validated RF model with an optimal number of splits at each tree node. The MAE value of that optimal RF model represents its average magnitude of the errors in the prediction. MAE served the same purpose in the SVR models, but RMSE determined the optimal SVR model with the optimal regularization parameter. The equations are as follows:

$$R^2 = 1 - \frac{\sum(y_i - \hat{y}_i)^2}{\sum(y_i - \overline{y}_i)^2} \quad (1)$$

where y_i is the observed value, $\hat{y}_i$ is the predicted value, and $\overline{y}_i$ is the mean of the observed values, and;

$$\text{RMSE} = \sqrt{\frac{\sum_{i=1}^{n}(\hat{y}_i - y_i)^2}{n}} \quad (2)$$

$$\text{MAE} = \frac{1}{n}\sum_{i=1}^{n}|\hat{y}_i - y_i| \quad (3)$$

where $\hat{y}_i$ represents the predicted yield (t/ha), y_i denotes the observed yield (t/ha), n is the total number of observations, and i serves as the summation index, incrementing by one.

After cross-validation, the final model was trained on the entire cross-validated calibration dataset and then evaluated on both the calibration and validation datasets using the same metrics. In the calibration stage, RMSE assessed the model's fit to the data it was trained on, while R^2 measures how well the model captures the underlying data patterns. High R^2 values, coupled with low RMSE, suggest a good fit. However, it is crucial to compare these metrics with those from the validation stage. The validation stage involved assessing the model on unseen data, providing an indication of its generalization ability. Consistent performance across calibration and validation sets, characterized by similar R^2, and RMSE values, indicates a robust model.

Figure 2 displays the workflow of the methodology. The modeling was written in the R programming language using RStudio by utilizing packages such as "randomForest" and "e1071" for RF and SVR, respectively. In both models, the independent variables were the VIs. Data collected over the 8 dates were ran individually, then divided into two groups of "pre-heading" and "post-heading". For each dataset, a 10-fold cross-validation was performed using packages "caret" and "kernlab". The yield prediction raster was also created using the "raster", "sp", and "rasterVis" packages in RStudio.

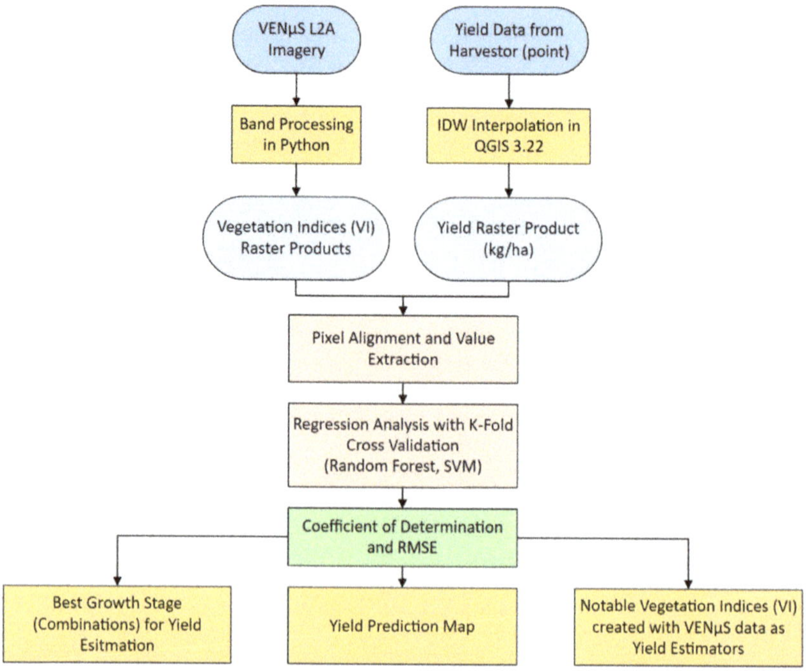

Figure 2. Methodology flowchart of this study.

3. Results

3.1. Cross-Validation of Regression Models

In our study, we performed 10-fold cross-validation on a total of 13 datasets. These datasets were divided into two categories: 8 individual growth stages and three groups of growth stages. The growth stage groups included 3 combinations of growth stages from pre-heading, 2 combinations of growth stages from post-heading, and all data. The rationale for forming grouped pre- and post-heading stage datasets is based on the fact that winter wheat undergoes a transition period marked by a slowdown in leaf growth due to shifts in developmental priorities and physiological changes. As the plant transitions to the reproductive phase, its focus shifts from vegetative to reproductive growth, including the formation and maturation of the inflorescence, causing the leaves to turn yellow. For the purpose of this study, ripening stage data were not included in the post-heading stage and all-data group because the model performance significantly dropped after the early fruit development stage.

The mean of the evaluation metrics was used to test the models' generalizability on unseen data across all 10 folds. Among the individual growth stages, the early fruit development stage performed the best, while tillering-1 performed the worst, with both machine learning models performing similarly. As seen in Figure 3, there was a trend in increasing $\overline{R^2}$, and decreasing $\overline{RMSE}$ and $\overline{MAE}$ as the growth stages progressed from tillering-1 to early fruit development. The evaluation metrics displayed a significant drop in model performance for both RF and SVR afterwards in the ripening stage. The RF model ($\overline{R^2}$ = 0.78, $\overline{RMSE}$ = 0.4832 t/ha, $\overline{MAE}$ = 0.3362 t/ha) explained the variance slightly better than the SVR model ($\overline{R^2}$ = 0.78, $\overline{RMSE}$ = 0.4834 t/ha, $\overline{MAE}$ = 0.3330 t/ha). However, the SVR model was slightly less sensitive to outliers compared to the RF model. Overall, the machine learning regression models within each growth stage were similar in terms of stability, as seen in the sizes of the whiskers in Figure 3.

Figure 3. Mean cross-validation statistics histogram: analysis by growth stage datasets and modelling approach (RF and SVR) using 21 VI variables. The whiskers display the standard deviation of the metrics.

On the other hand, models that incorporated all data and combinations from the pre- and post-heading groups showed an increase in explanatory power as more data were added to the regression models. Models using post-heading stage datasets demonstrated greater robustness, with lower mean RMSE values, compared to those using pre-heading stage datasets. However, models using all data were the least stable, as indicated by their higher $\overline{RMSE}$ standard deviation. Overall, both models demonstrated the highest generalizability on unseen data when all data were combined. The SVR ($\overline{R^2}$ = 0.86, $\overline{RMSE}$ = 0.3899 t/ha, $\overline{MAE}$ = 0.2475 t/ha) explained data variance better and had lower prediction error than the RF ($\overline{R^2}$ = 0.84, $\overline{RMSE}$ = 0.4185 t/ha, $\overline{MAE}$ = 0.2800 t/ha) model in cross-validation.

3.2. Yield Prediction Using Regression Models

Table 4 displays the calibration and validation performance of the RF and SVR models with datasets from all eight tested growth stages individually. Overall, the models best at explaining data variance could be found when the models were using early fruit development stage data. The calibration R^2 had a range of 0.54~0.96, and RMSE values had a range of 0.2039~0.7057 t/ha. The RF model had a significantly higher calibration, R^2 = 0.96, compared to the SVR model, R^2 = 0.79, indicating that the RF model fit the training data much better. This finding was consistent throughout the analysis, and is expected due to RF's ensemble nature, which excels in capturing complex patterns. In terms of validation model metrics, R^2 values had a range of 0.50~0.77, and RMSE values had a range of 0.5008~0.7421 t/ha. The validation results were also consistent with calibration that both RF and SVR had the highest R^2 when paired with data from the early fruit development stage. RF (R^2 = 0.77, RMSE = 0.5008 t/ha) slightly outperformed SVR (R^2 = 0.77, RMSE = 0.5039 t/ha), making it the best performing prediction model when using data from individual stages.

Table 4. Calibration and validation statistics: analysis by individual growth stage datasets and modelling approach (RF and SVR) using 21 VI variables [1].

Growth Stage	Model	Calibration		Validation	
		R^2	RMSE (t/ha)	R^2	RMSE (t/ha)
Tillering-1	RF	0.94	0.3017	0.50	0.7335
	SVR	0.54	0.7057	0.50	0.7421
Tillering-2	RF	0.94	0.2953	0.53	0.7116
	SVR	0.55	0.6971	0.53	0.7208
Stem Elongation	RF	0.94	0.2727	0.61	0.6510
	SVR	0.63	0.6358	0.61	0.6539
Booting	RF	0.95	0.2607	0.64	0.6264
	SVR	0.66	0.6032	0.65	0.6177
Heading	RF	0.96	0.2186	0.74	0.5283
	SVR	0.77	0.4989	0.74	0.5319
Flowering	RF	0.96	0.2181	0.75	0.5254
	SVR	0.77	0.4907	0.75	0.5183
Early Fruit Development	RF	0.96	0.2039	0.77	0.5008
	SVR	0.79	0.4696	0.77	0.5039
Ripening	RF	0.95	0.2653	0.61	0.6494
	SVR	0.61	0.6418	0.59	0.6709

[1] All models are significant at p-value < 0.001.

The analysis extended to using combinations of datasets from growth stages. Table 5 displays the calibration and validation performance of the RF and SVR models with dataset groups of pre-heading stage, post-heading stage, and all data. Collectively, models using dataset groups as variables outperformed models using individual datasets from tilling-1, tilling-2, stem elongation, and booting stage, all of which were in the pre-heading stage group. In calibration, the R^2 values had a range of 0.75~0.98, while the RMSE values had a range of 0.1640~0.5189 t/ha. Both ranges were significantly narrower compared to their counterparts in individual growth stages as we saw improved performance of SVR. Overall, the calibration R^2 was consistently higher in RF models than in SVR models. However, the validation statistics show that SVR models outperformed RF models in yield prediction as validation, with higher R^2 values and lower RMSE values in SVR models when paired with each of the three dataset groups. The R^2 values had a range of 0.72~0.86, while the RMSE values had a range of 0.3925~0.5465 t/ha in validation. The best yield prediction model was found to be the SVR model using all data from tillering-1 to the early fruit development stage (R^2 = 0.86, RMSE = 0.3925 t/ha). Although the RF model performed better in calibration, it predicted yield with slightly lower accuracy (R^2 = 0.83, RMSE = 0.4257 t/ha).

Table 5. Calibration and validation statistics: analysis by dataset groups and modelling approach (RF and SVR) using 21 VI variables [1].

Dataset Group	Growth Stage Combinations	Model	Calibration		Validation	
			R^2	RMSE (t/ha)	R^2	RMSE (t/ha)
Pre-heading Stage	Stem Elongation + Booting	RF	0.96	0.2241	0.72	0.5561
		SVR	0.75	0.5189	0.73	0.5465
	Tillering-2 + Stem Elongation + Booting	RF	0.97	0.2119	0.74	0.5353
		SVR	0.79	0.4788	0.75	0.5165
	Tillering-1, 2 + Stem Elongation + Booting	RF	0.97	0.2038	0.75	0.5210
		SVR	0.82	0.4431	0.78	0.4917
Post-heading Stage	Flowering + Early Fruit Development	RF	0.97	0.1902	0.79	0.4810
		SVR	0.81	0.4462	0.79	0.4814
	Heading + Flowering + Early Fruit Development	RF	0.97	0.1798	0.81	0.4570
		SVR	0.84	0.4116	0.81	0.4507
All Data (Ripening excluded)		RF	0.98	0.1640	0.83	0.4257
		SVR	0.89	0.3437	0.86	0.3925

[1] All models are significant at p-value < 0.001.

3.3. Ranked Importance of Vegetation Indices from Different Growth Stages

RF modeling, which utilizes numerous decision trees, was employed to generate a variable importance plot in RStudio using the "varImpPlot()" function. This plot displays increasing node purity (IncNodePurity) on the x–axis, representing the importance of each variable in predicting yield across different dates. A higher IncNodePurity value indicates that the variable is more significant as a predictor, helping to identify the key predictors in the models. The variable importance plot revealed that NDRE-1 and NDRE-2 from the heading, flowering, and early fruit development stages were among the most important predictors of yield, with the top-ranked variable being NDRE-1 from the flowering stage, as shown in Figure 4. REP from the flowering and early fruit development stages ranked 4th and 7th, respectively, on the plot. NDRE-1, NDRE-2, REP, and ARVI from the multiple growth stages constituted 17 of the top 20 ranked VI variables. Beyond the top 7 ranked VIs, the IncNodePurity values of the remaining VI variables were relatively similar and gradually decreased throughout the list of the 147 tested VI variables in total.

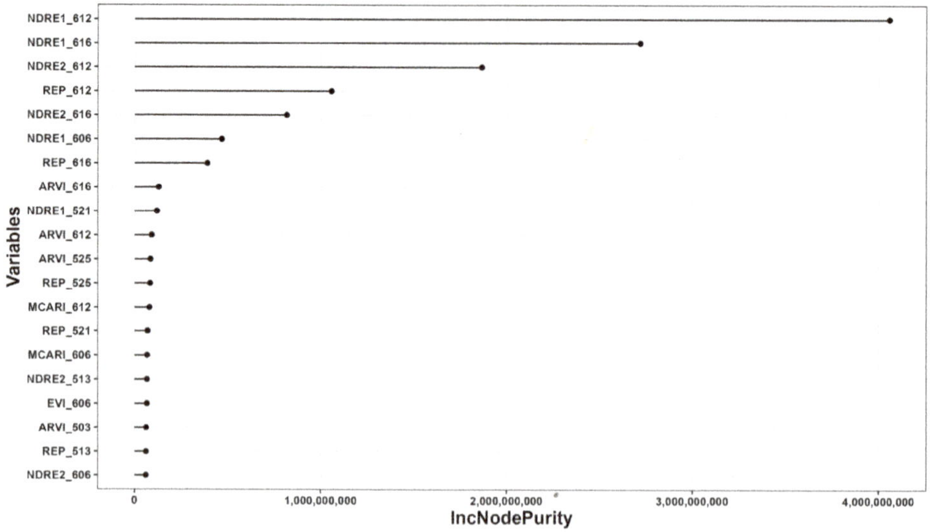

Figure 4. Variable importance plot produced with VIs with all data. Only top 20 of the 147 VI variables were displayed. Refer to Table 3 for the full names of the variables. The number denoted after the variables' abbreviation is the date of the VENμS imagery.

3.4. Visuallization of Predicted Yield

A yield prediction map helps visualize the yield variations within a field, and VENμS' higher spatial resolution enables readers to clearly identify areas of inaccuracy. Figure 5 demonstrates that the prediction generally captured the yield variations across the entire field, as reflected by both the map and the evaluation metrics. However, the prediction did not accurately capture the extreme values in the observed yield. For instance, the north side borders of the field showed extreme lows in the observed yield, but the predicted yield map did not reflect values as extreme. Similarly, in areas of extreme highs, the prediction failed to capture the highest values and sometimes incorrectly predicted the yield as a markedly different value.

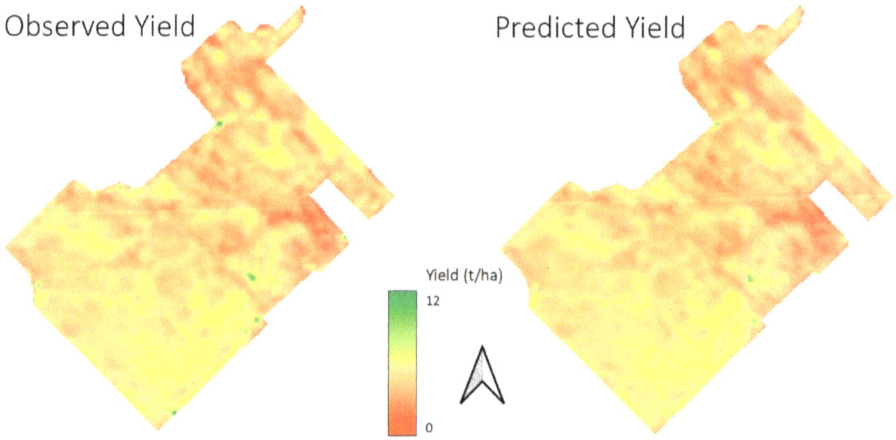

Figure 5. The map of comparison between the observed and predicted yields.

4. Discussion

Implications of Model Performance on Yield Prediction with VENμS Imagery

PA uses advanced technologies and data analysis to optimize agricultural practices and assist in management decisions, with the goal of minimizing input while maximizing output and efficiency. We proposed using VENμS imagery for yield prediction as an alternative to other publicly available satellite data with its higher spatial and temporal resolution. The differences of performance of the machine learning regression models have been discussed in detail above. Though similar in prediction performance, SVR was the overall better machine learning regression model when more data were added to the regression, while RF was more accurate when predicting yield with data from individual stages. Our findings aligned with the study conducted by Han et al., and we were able to suggest that both RF and SVR were high performance techniques in yield prediction [27,28]. However, potential overfitting was observed in the RF models, even after careful tuning. Although this overfitting decreased as more growth stage data were added, we recognize that RF models can be prone to overfitting, especially when dealing with complex data. This limitation prompted the inclusion of SVR in the study, which exhibited less overfitting and proved to be the more reliable algorithm in this context.

The regression models were able to determine that the early fruit development stage was the best growth stage to predict yield from. This finding agreed with Hassan et al.'s study, in which the yield prediction accuracy increased as the growth stages progressed [47]. Overall, our study was able to achieve a higher accuracy by incorporating all data from tillering to the early fruit development stage. Among all the test VIs, NDRE is the most important predictor of yield as tested, which is consistent with previous studies [11]. As reported, NDRE-1, NDRE-2, REP, and ARVI from multiple growth stages made up 17 of the top 20 most important variables in predicting the final yield, with NDRE-1, NDRE-2, and REP being the major contributors to the prediction. The common characteristics of the three VIs are that they all used bands 8, 9, and 10 of VENμS, which are at the central wavelengths of 702, 741.1, and 782.2 nm. These bands fall in between the red-edge and NIR regions of the spectrum, and the VIs based on this wavelength range were previously proven to be effective at predicting grain yield [30].

Our results, when compared to studies based on different satellite data, displayed a similar or even higher prediction accuracy, often accompanied by lower errors [8,10]. Given that grouped stages of data performed better in the prediction models, we conducted an additional test with Sentinel-2 data, applying the same methodology and using overpass dates as close as possible to those used with VENμS data. Table 6 presents the regression statistics of the yield prediction models using Sentinel-2 data with grouped growth stages. Of the 21 VIs tested, 20 were recreated using Sentinel-2 data. Unfortunately, data from the Tillering-2 stage could not be included in the analysis due to cloud cover. The best prediction results obtained were at R^2 = 0.79 and RMSE = 0.5147 t/ha with SVR using all data.

The accuracy of the prediction model plateaued when using post-heading stage data only, with a minor decrease in RMSE as more data were added. Additionally, compared to the best prediction model using VENμS imagery, the model prediction error with Sentinel-2 data was still significantly higher. This could have contributed to Sentinel-2's lower spatial resolution, as VENμS has four times more data than Sentinel-2. Although we were able to optimize and successfully create a robust and accurate winter wheat yield prediction model with VENμS data at a local, field-scale, it is not without its drawbacks. In contrast to most publicly available satellites which provide frequent coverage of Earth's land surface, VENμS does not cover Earth's entire land surface. Instead, it focuses on specific sites of interest and revisits these selected sites frequently. This means that the site of researchers' interests may not be covered, even though the data are publicly available. Researchers are required to apply for VENμS coverage at their location of interest.

Table 6. Calibration and validation statistics: analysis by dataset groups and modelling approach (RF and SVR) using 20 VI variables created using Sentinel-2 bands, matched to equivalent VENμS bands [1].

Dataset Group	Growth Stage Combinations	Model	Calibration		Validation	
			R^2	RMSE (t/ha)	R^2	RMSE (t/ha)
Pre-heading Stage	Stem Elongation + Booting	RF	0.96	0.2557	0.70	0.6280
		SVR	0.76	0.5452	0.72	0.5997
	Tillering-1 + Stem Elongation + Booting	RF	0.96	0.2476	0.71	0.6106
		SVR	0.78	0.5237	0.74	0.5835
Post-heading Stage	Flowering + Early Fruit Development	RF	0.97	0.2167	0.78	0.5379
		SVR	0.82	0.4728	0.79	0.5238
	Heading + Flowering + Early Fruit Development	RF	0.97	0.2121	0.78	0.5310
		SVR	0.83	0.4615	0.79	0.5190
All Data (Ripening excluded)		RF	0.97	0.2091	0.78	0.5287
		SVR	0.84	0.4434	0.79	0.5147

[1] All models are significant at p-value < 0.001.

5. Conclusions

This study evaluated the effectiveness of VENμS multispectral imagery in predicting winter wheat yield in southwestern Ontario using machine learning methods. A total of 21 VIs, including eight variations of existing VIs based on their original development formulas, were tested. The best prediction result demonstrated a high correlation between VENμS data and observed yield, with an $R^2 = 0.86$ and an RMSE = 0.3925 t/ha using an SVR model. According to our results, a reliable prediction of yield can be achieved two months prior to harvest using the combined pre-heading stage data, and the best result can be obtained 39 days prior when using all data from the pre- and post- heading stages. The findings suggest that VENμS data can offer superior yield prediction accuracy compared to other publicly available satellites, and could potentially serve as a viable alternative to UAV data for local, field-scale studies.

Though machine learning algorithms are effective at capturing complex patterns among variables, it is important to recognize the empirical nature of these models. They rely on existing datasets for validation, and can only approximate the observed yield, which is only verifiable at harvest. This intrinsic limitation highlights the potential discrepancies between predicted and actual outcomes. Such limitations underscore the necessity for ongoing calibration and testing of these models under varied agricultural conditions and across different crop cycles to ensure their reliability and accuracy.

Additionally, while k-fold cross-validation and a 70/30 train-test split were employed in this study due to their broad adoption and effective use of the data, future work could explore spatial splitting as a viable alternative. Spatial splitting, which divides the dataset based on geographic location rather than by random subsets, may provide a more realistic evaluation of the model's robustness across different parts of the field by better addressing spatial autocorrelation. Investigating this approach could enhance the model's performance in capturing spatial variability within the field.

VENμS, as mentioned above, does not provide worldwide coverage, which is a significant drawback limiting the use of its superior high-resolution multispectral data. Although this study showed that Sentinel-2 is a less effective alternative, it remains the next best option for predicting yield with publicly available satellite data using our method. Its worldwide frequent coverage can produce comparable results to VENμS at the field-scale and potentially similar results at a regional scale. This research highlights the potential of high-resolution satellite data with multispectral cameras for yield prediction. Future studies may also consider using commercial satellites such as PlanetScope and WorldView-3 as alternatives for high-resolution multispectral data. Combining these satellite data with yield estimation models could lead to advancements in low labor costs, and non-destructive yet highly accurate yield predictions, providing a more detailed understanding of crop yield potential and distribution.

Author Contributions: Conceptualization, M.S.C. and J.W.; methodology, M.S.C. and J.W.; software, M.S.C.; validation, J.W.; formal analysis, M.S.C.; investigation, M.S.C.; resources, J.W.; data curation, M.S.C.; writing—original draft preparation, M.S.C.; writing—review and editing, M.S.C. and J.W.; visualization, M.S.C.; supervision, J.W.; project administration, J.W.; funding acquisition, J.W. All authors have read and agreed to the published version of the manuscript.

Funding: This study was funded by the Natural Science and Engineering Research Council of Canada (NSERC) Discovery Grant (grant number RGPIN-2022-05051), awarded to Wang. Additional funding was from the Western Graduate Research Scholarship provided by The University of Western Ontario, granted to Chiu.

Data Availability Statement: The data collected for this paper are publicly available online through Theia's website at https://theia.cnes.fr/atdistrib/rocket/#/home (accessed on 4 June 2024) for VENµS data, and Copernicus explorer https://browser.dataspace.copernicus.eu/ (accessed on 28 June 2024) for Sentinel-2 data.

Acknowledgments: The authors would like to thank A&L Canada Laboratories Inc. and the members of Wang's GITA lab for their invaluable assistance with data collection, lab processing, and overall support. Special thanks go to Bo Shan, Robin Kwik, Naythan Samuda, Chunhua Liao, Jody Yu, and Yang Song for their dedicated help and guidance. Additionally, the authors extend their gratitude to Yu for her expertise and guidance in programming the machine learning analyses, and to James Brackett for conducting preliminary testing on the VENµS datasets. The authors would also like to thank the anonymous reviewers for their time, helpful comments, and feedback on this manuscript.

Conflicts of Interest: The authors declare no conflicts of interest.

References

1. Tan, C.S.; Reynolds, W.D. Impacts of Recent Climate Trends on Agriculture in Southwestern Ontario. *Can. Water Resour. J.* **2003**, *28*, 87–97. [CrossRef]
2. Reid, S.; Smit, B.; Caldwell, W.; Belliveau, S. Vulnerability and Adaptation to Climate Risks in Ontario Agriculture. *Mitig. Adapt. Strateg. Glob. Change* **2007**, *12*, 609–637. [CrossRef]
3. Agriculture and Agri-Food Canada. Overview of Canada's Agriculture and Agri-Food Sector. Available online: https://agriculture.canada.ca/en/sector/overview (accessed on 25 May 2024).
4. Hammer, G. Applying Seasonal Climate Forecasts in Agricultural and Natural Ecosystems—A Synthesis. In *Applications of Seasonal Climate Forecasting in Agricultural and Natural Ecosystems*; Hammer, G.L., Nicholls, N., Mitchell, C., Eds.; Springer Netherlands: Dordrecht, The Netherlands, 2000; pp. 453–462. [CrossRef]
5. Shafi, U.; Mumtaz, R.; García-Nieto, J.; Hassan, S.A.; Zaidi, S.A.R.; Iqbal, N. Precision Agriculture Techniques and Practices: From Considerations to Applications. *Sensors* **2019**, *19*, 3796. [CrossRef] [PubMed]
6. Liao, C.; Wang, J.; Shan, B.; Shang, J.; Dong, T.; He, Y. Near Real-Time Detection and Forecasting of within-Field Phenology of Winter Wheat and Corn Using Sentinel-2 Time-Series Data. *ISPRS J. Photogramm. Remote Sens.* **2023**, *196*, 105–119. [CrossRef]
7. Yu, J.; Wang, J.; Leblon, B.; Song, Y. Nitrogen Estimation for Wheat Using UAV-Based and Satellite Multispectral Imagery, Topographic Metrics, Leaf Area Index, Plant Height, Soil Moisture, and Machine Learning Methods. *Nitrogen* **2022**, *3*, 1–25. [CrossRef]
8. Skakun, S.; Franch, B.; Vermote, E.; Roger, J.-C.; Justice, C.; Masek, J.; Murphy, E. Winter Wheat Yield Assessment Using Landsat 8 and Sentinel-2 Data. In *IGARSS 2018—2018 IEEE International Geoscience and Remote Sensing Symposium*; IEEE: Valencia, Spain, 2018; pp. 5964–5967. [CrossRef]
9. Zhang, C.; Marzougui, A.; Sankaran, S. High-Resolution Satellite Imagery Applications in Crop Phenotyping: An Overview. *Comput. Electron. Agric.* **2020**, *175*, 105584. [CrossRef]
10. Zhao, Y.; Potgieter, A.B.; Zhang, M.; Wu, B.; Hammer, G.L. Predicting Wheat Yield at the Field Scale by Combining High-Resolution Sentinel-2 Satellite Imagery and Crop Modelling. *Remote Sens.* **2020**, *12*, 1024. [CrossRef]
11. Fu, Z.; Jiang, J.; Gao, Y.; Krienke, B.; Wang, M.; Zhong, K.; Cao, Q.; Tian, Y.; Zhu, Y.; Cao, W.; et al. Wheat Growth Monitoring and Yield Estimation Based on Multi-Rotor Unmanned Aerial Vehicle. *Remote Sens.* **2020**, *12*, 508. [CrossRef]
12. United States Geological Survey (USGS). *Landsat 8 (L8) Data Users Handbook*; USGS: Sioux Falls, SD, USA, 2019; pp. 1–93.
13. European Space Agency (ESA). *Sentinel-2 User Handbook*; ESA: Paris, France, 2015; pp. 1–64.
14. Centre National d'Etudes Spatiales (CNES); Israeli Space Agency (ISA). *The VENµS Mission and Products*; CNES: Paris, France; ISA: Tel Aviv, Israel, 2023; pp. 1–26.

remote sensing

MDPI

Article

Research on Cotton Field Irrigation Amount Calculation Based on Electromagnetic Induction Technology

Jianwen Han [1], Mingyue Wang [2], Nan Wang [3], Jiawen Wang [1], Jie Peng [1] and Chunhui Feng [4,*]

[1] College of Agriculture, Tarim University, Alar 843300, China; 10757212049@stumail.taru.edu.cn (J.H.)
[2] College of Life Sciences and Technology, Tarim University, Alar 843300, China; mingyue_w7@163.com
[3] Institute of Agricultural Remote Sensing and Information Technology Application, College of Environmental and Resource Sciences, Zhejiang University, Hangzhou 310058, China
[4] College of Horticulture and Forestry, Tarim University, Alar 843300, China
* Correspondence: chunhui.f@taru.edu.cn

Abstract: The rapid and efficient acquisition of field-scale farmland soil profile moisture-distribution information is very important for achieving precise irrigation and the adjustment and deployment of irrigation strategies in farmland. EM38-MK2 is a portable, non-invasive device that induces electric currents in soil to generate secondary magnetic fields for the rapid measurement of apparent electrical conductivity in the field. In this study, cotton fields were used as experimental objects to obtain soil apparent conductivity data for three periods, which were combined with soil-moisture content data collected simultaneously from soil samples and measured in the laboratory to construct an apparent soil-profile moisture regression model. A simple kriging interpolation method was used to map the distribution of the irrigation volume in the field, considering only the highest irrigation volume in the field as the maximum water-holding capacity in the field. The results showed that EM38 could accurately detect the spatial variation of soil moisture in the field. The R^2 of the linear fit between measured and predicted soil-water content ranged from 0.51 to 0.89; the RMSE ranged from 0.66 to 1.87; and the R^2 and RPD of each soil-layer water content model of the single-period model were higher than those of the full-period model. By plotting the distribution of field irrigation, it could be seen that by comparing the predicted field irrigation with the actual irrigation, at least 160 m^3 ha^{-1} of irrigation could be saved in all three periods at an irrigation depth of 40 cm, which is about 30% of the actual irrigation; at an irrigation depth of 60 cm, about 30% and 15% of irrigation could be reduced in July and August, respectively. There are three areas in the study area with high fixed-irrigation volumes located in the northwest corner, near 500 m in the northern half of the study area and 750 m east of the southern half of the study area. The results of this study proved that the use of EM38-MK2 to monitor and evaluate the soil-moisture content of the farmland at different periods can, to a certain extent, guide the irrigation amount needed to achieve efficient and precise irrigation in the field.

Keywords: soil moisture; apparent soil conductivity; fixed-rate irrigation; field scale

1. Introduction

Soil moisture is an essential and vital component of soil, which functions as a fundamental solvent for plant nutrient transport and delivery, a primary option for regulating soil temperature and reducing salinity. Accurate information on the spatial and temporal variability of soil moisture throughout the crop growing period is important for efficiently using the resources (e.g., water and nutrients) [1,2].

In addition, changes in multiple soil properties caused by changes in soil moisture can further affect the actual crop water requirements in localized areas of the field. Especially in arid regions with low salinization, untimely surveys of the spatial distribution of soil moisture can lead to slower crop growth and, more seriously, lower yields [3]. On the other hand, over-irrigated is more likely to causing the water infiltrate into groundwater and consequently pollutes groundwater quality [4,5]. Therefore, real-time and accurate acquisition of spatial information of soil moisture at field-scale is beneficial for timely adjustment of crop irrigation strategies and refinement of irrigation schemes in local areas, which is helpful for promoting crop growth and improving yields.

Usually, field-scale soil-moisture content monitoring methods not only limited by measurement points, but also take a lot of time, which makes it difficult to investigate the moisture content of soil at a certain depth effectively. In addition, traditional field-scale soil moisture monitoring methods (e.g., mass drying method) do provide accurate soil-moisture content data, but often cause damage to the original soil structure. The measuring device is radioactive (e.g., neutron source) [6], posing a potential threat to the safety of the device itself. All these reasons make it extremely difficult to monitor the soil moisture at a certain depth at a largescale. Therefore, there is an urgent need to adopt an accurate, fast and efficient soil moisture monitoring method that can be applied to larger scales. In recent years, monitoring various soil properties using electromagnetic induction has been intensively studied by a wide range of scholars [7,8], such as soil salinity [9–11], soil moisture [12,13], pH [14–16], soil capacity [17], soil texture [18], clay content [19], calcium carbonate [20], and soil organic carbon [21–23]. Electromagnetic induction techniques are commonly used to determine the weighted average of apparent conductivity of soils at a specific depth [24], and the soil apparent conductivity is a combination of several key properties [25], including soil-moisture content, soil soluble salt content, clay content, and soil temperature, making the use of electromagnetic induction techniques to obtain. Therefore, it is possible to use electromagnetic induction to obtain moisture content in the soil space [26]. Among the studies that used electromagnetic induction to obtain soil moisture, Kachanoski et al. (1988) were one of the first researchers who used electromagnetic induction instruments to obtain soil moisture [27]. Early results showed that the apparent soil conductivity data measured by electromagnetic induction could explain 77–96% of the variability in soil moisture. In addition, linear and second-order polynomial regression models could be developed on this basis. Calmita et al. used soil apparent conductivity data obtained by electromagnetic induction to predict the temporal variability of soil-moisture content with $R^2 > 0.5$ [28]. The results demonstrated that although soil pore water is spatially variable, solid particle properties and pore water conductivity remain constant in time. Hanson and Kaita investigated the accuracy of soil-water content obtained from inversion models based on apparent soil conductivity data at three different levels of salt content [29]. The results showed that the R^2 of the horizontal direction dipole inversion model was 0.81, 0.89, and 0.92, and the R^2 of the vertical direction dipole model was 0.76, 0.94, and 0.95 for the three salt content levels of low, medium and high, respectively. This study was performed by calibrating the EM38-MK2 to the soil-moisture content estimations, which was determined by the neutron method, and each neutron probe tube of 0.3 m was measured using EM38-MK2 throughout the experiment. But this method would cause errors in the apparent conductivity values from EM38-MK2. Previous studies such as Huang and Hossain provided theoretical support for the application of electromagnetic induction technique for soil moisture monitoring in agricultural fields [30–32]. However, previous studies still lacked the application in practical irrigation period. In many oasis farmlands in the arid zone of South Xinjiang, due to the combination of various factors such as local climate, the soil-moisture content in the surface layer is often very low and spatial variability is high, but the soil-moisture content in the bottom layer near the water table is high and spatial variability is low [33]. This phenomenon will not only allow farmers to misjudge the soil-moisture content at the field scale, but also easily cause over-irrigation. Therefore, it is especially important to obtain accurate soil-moisture content at the field scale, especially at a certain depth. Electromagnetic induction technology helped obtain soil apparent conductivity data non-destructively and over a large area, and showed superiority in inverting soil capacitance, field water-holding capacity and soil-water content to predict the irrigation volume of farmland, refine field-scale irrigation strategies, and provide guidance for timely monitoring and management of soil moisture conditions in local areas.

Take these all into consideration, this study takes typical cotton fields in the arid zone of South Xinjiang as the research field, and takes advantage of the electromagnetic induction technology to obtain the information of physical and chemical properties of soil profiles quickly and efficiently. The main contents of this study include:

(1) Using EM38-MK2 geodesic conductivity meter to collect apparent conductivity data of a few profile samples, combined with the laboratory measurement simultaneously. A linear regression model based on multiple linear regression method is used to construct soil moisture, soil capacity and field water-holding capacity with high accuracy.
(2) Establishing multi-period model and single-period model to explore the applicability of the instrument.
(3) Calculating predicted irrigation volume at multi-sites based on the field irrigation volume calculation method and using the simple kriging interpolation method to map the spatial distribution of predicted irrigation volume to refine the irrigation strategy and provide guidance for farmland irrigation.

2. Materials and Methods

2.1. Study Area

The study area is located in the National Agricultural Science and Technology Park in Alar, Xinjiang, China, as shown in Figure 1, with its central coordinates of 81°17′8″E and 40°31′8″N. The study area is approximately 900 m long from north to south and 200 m long from east to west, the study area is 18 ha, with a shortest linear distance from the Tarim river to the north of 110 m. The irrigation water source is drawn from the Aksu and Tarim rivers, the main cotton is Xinluzhong 78, the planting method is mulching [32]. The irrigation mode is drip irrigation during the cotton reproductive period. The spring and winter irrigation is diffuse irrigation, and the water table is buried at a depth of 1.2~1.5 m. The highest temperature in the study area in a year occurred in July (37.8 °C) and the lowest temperature was in July. The maximum and minimum temperatures were 37.8 °C and −8.6 °C in July and January (−8.6 °C), respectively, and the evapotranspiration ratio was about 40:1. The average sunshine duration between April and October was about 9.5 h. The annual temperature was above 10 °C and the annual total temperature reached 4113 °C. Cotton was irrigated six times during the reproductive period, with one winter irrigation and five drip irrigations (22 June, 9 July, 25 July, 13 August and 25 August). Among them, the first drip irrigation was carried out on 22 June at 450 m^3/ha, and the remaining four times were carried out on 9 July, 25 July, 13 August and 25 August at 600 m^3/ha, respectively, and winter irrigation was executed on November 20 at 3, 300 m^3/ha.

2.2. EM38-MK2 Measurement

The EM38-MK2 consists of a transmitting coil (Tx) and two receiving coils (Rx) with a length of 1 m and a fixed operating frequency (14.6 KHz). By passing AC current through the transmitting coil and generating a primary magnetic field in the soil that gradually weakens with increasing soil depth, the magnetic field strength changes dynamically with time, causing an induced current to form in the soil, and the current induces a secondary magnetic field. The receiving coil receives both the primary magnetic field strength and the secondary magnetic field strength, and the signal receiving end can receive both the primary and secondary magnetic field signals. In automatic mode, the instrument can collect apparent conductivity data in only one mode, i.e., horizontal mode (horizontal dipole moment) or vertical mode (vertical dipole moment). In manual mode, the instrument can collect soil apparent conductivity data for both horizontal and vertical modes. The distance between the transmitter coil and the two receiver coils is 0.5 m and 1 m, respectively, and the measurement depths are 0.375 m and 0.75 m in the horizontal mode and 0.75 m and 1.5 m in the vertical mode. The new EM38-MK2 model also adopts new technology to automatically perform temperature compensation, correct circuit faults, and eliminate data drift caused by the temperature variations. the instrument has a built-in GPS.

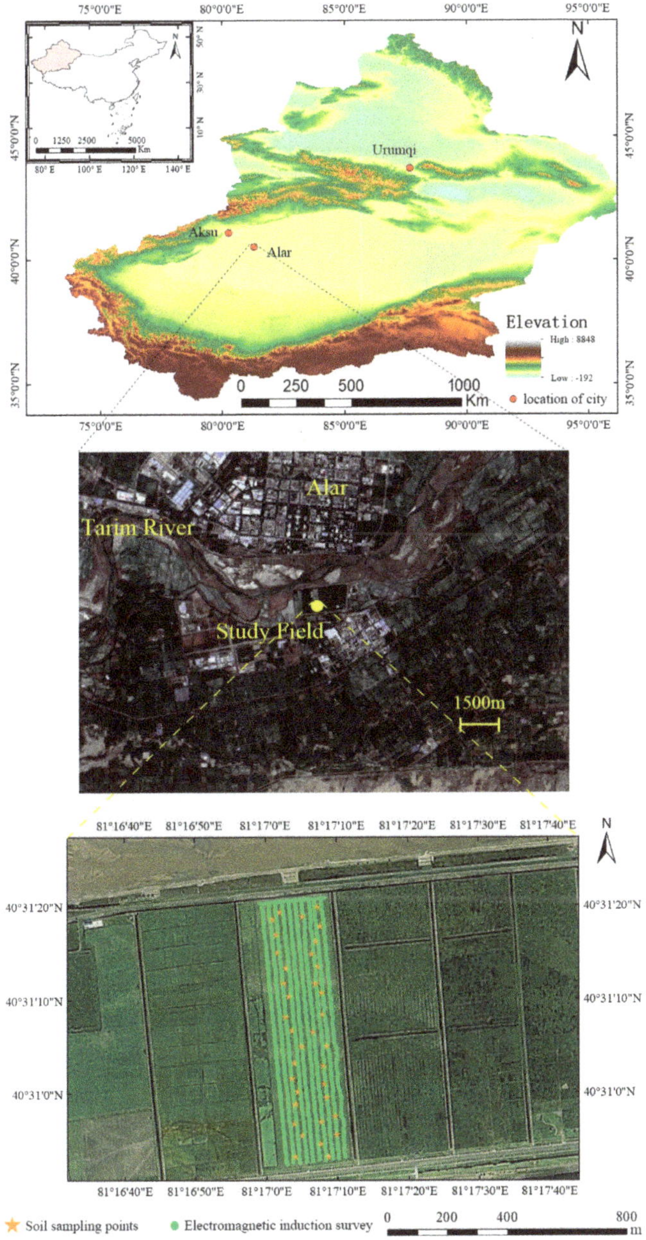

Figure 1. Location of study area, sampling points of electromagnetic induction survey. and soil sampling.

2.3. Irrigation and Rainfall Events

Soil samples and apparent conductivity data were collected three times in June, July, and August. The key reasons for choosing these three periods for the study were, first, that all three periods were times of high-water demand and high irrigation in oasis cotton fields. Second, that the actual irrigation time in the study area was mostly concentrated in June, July, and August during the cotton growth period. In addition, considering that the study area had not been irrigated once from the end of winter irrigation last year to the beginning of June, and that the first drip irrigation was carried out on 22 June, the collection time was 20 June. 450 m^3/h^2 was irrigated by drip irrigation on 22 June. In addition, the rainfall in the sample area was difficult to influence the actual irrigation amount because the planting method was mulching, and the water obtained from rainfall was difficult to penetrate into the soil.

2.4. ECa Data Collection

The experiments were conducted using a geodetic conductivity meter EM38-MK2 for apparent electrical conductivity (ECa, mS m^{-1}) measurements, which was divided into 10 measurement rows with a spacing of 20 m according to the width of the test area. Data were collected on 20 June (before the first drip irrigation), 7 July (before the second drip irrigation), and 15 August (before the third drip irrigation), 2018, and a total of three times for apparent conductivity data, using EM38-MK2 vertical and horizontal measurement modes once each, and a total of 10 measurement rows from south to north, with the instrument set to automatic recording mode and a frequency of one set of data collection per second The distribution of EM38-MK2 measurement points and soil sampling profile points is shown in Figure 1.

2.5. Soil Samples Collection

A total of three collections of apparent conductivity and soil-profile samples were conducted on 20 June, 7 July, and 15 August, 2018, and after the EM38 automatic mode collection was completed, the range of apparent conductivity in the study area was determined based on the size of the measured apparent conductivity dataset with the maximum and minimum values as the upper and lower limits, respectively, and the obtained apparent conductivity dataset was divided into 36 gradients, and in turn, according to the divided The manual mode apparent conductivity data and soil-profile samples were collected simultaneously according to the divided apparent conductivity gradient; the apparent conductivity data of the sampling points were recorded, and 36 soil-profile sample points were collected each time (Figure 1). Soil profiles were sampled in layers from 0 to 20, 20 to 40, 40 to 60, 60 to 80, and 80 to 100 cm, and the collected soil-profile samples were placed in self-sealing bags and numbered, and brought back to the laboratory for timely soil moisture determination using the mass drying method. In 2018 a total of three surveys were conducted in June, July and August, each with 36 profiles, and a total of 180 different soil-profile samples were collected in a single survey, for a total of 540 soil-profile samples throughout the year.

To calculate the irrigation volume needed to obtain soil capacity and field water-holding data, soil profile excavation and ring knife soil samples were collected on 27 October 2018, after soil auger-sampling was completed. The sample locations were selected by the EM38-MK2 automatic mode to obtain high and low values of apparent conductivity points to determine the range of modeling independent variables, and 30 of them were selected according to the apparent conductivity data close to a certain gradient, and each point was first collected for apparent conductivity data. Then, the soil profile was excavated to a depth of 70 cm, and one ring knife soil sample was taken at every 20 cm depth to collect a depth of 60 cm, for a total of 90. A total of 90 ring-knife soil samples were collected to determine soil bulk and field water-holding capacity data.

2.6. Establishing Model between Soil Water and ECa

The measured water contents of 36 sets of soil-profile samples collected in each cycle were sorted according to their numerical values, and the modeling and validation samples were drawn in a ratio of 2:1, i.e., two of every three adjacent samples were randomly selected as modeling data with the remaining one as validation data, and these were finally divided into 24 sets of modeling data and 12 sets of validation data. With the soil apparent conductivity data measured by the EM38-MK2 vertical model as the independent variable and the measured soil-moisture value as the dependent variable, the decomposition model between the soil-moisture content and soil apparent conductivity was constructed by the multiple linear regression method, and the modeling ideas were divided into two kinds of local modeling and global modeling, with local modeling as a single-period model and monthly modeling in June, July and August, respectively, and a total of three models using local modeling as a single-period model. June, July and August were modeled separately, and a total of three models were built. The global model is a multi-period mixed model, i.e., a unified model was built for all samples of the three periods. Determination coefficient (R^2), root mean square error (RMSE), relative percent deviation (RPD) and mean relative error (MRE) were used to evaluate the stability and prediction accuracy of the model. Among them, the coefficient of determination reflected the degree of fit between the predicted and measured values; the root mean square error measured the deviation between the observed and true values; the mean relative error reflected the actual error of the predicted values; and the relative analytical error was an indicator of the predictive ability of the model, which was the ratio of the sample standard deviation to the root mean square error [34].

$$R^2 = 1 - \frac{\Sigma_i(\hat{y}_i \quad y_i)^2}{\Sigma_i(y_i - \overline{y})^2} \tag{1}$$

$$\mathrm{RMSE} = \sqrt{\frac{\Sigma_i(\hat{y}_i - y_i)^2}{n}} \tag{2}$$

$$RPD = \frac{SD}{RSME} \tag{3}$$

$$\mathrm{MRE} = \frac{\Sigma_i(\hat{y}_i - y_i)^2}{ny_i} \tag{4}$$

where $\hat{y}_i$ is the predicted value, and y_i is the measured value. where $\overline{y}_i$ is the average value. n was the sample number. SD is the standard deviation.

2.7. Calculation Method of Drip Irrigation Cotton Field Soil Irrigation

The irrigation data in this study were the difference between the field water-holding capacity and the actual soil volumetric water content, where the field water-holding capacity was a stable property of the soil with little temporal variability, so it was considered as a stable value. The value was considered as the average of the measured field water-holding capacity. The actual soil volumetric water content was the product of the mass water content and the soil bulk weight, and the mass water content was obtained from the inversion of the apparent conductivity of each soil layer in each period. The mass water content was calculated from the apparent conductivity inversion model for each period. Soil capacity was also considered as a stable property of the soil, and was considered as the average of the measured soil capacity data to facilitate the irrigation volume calculation. taking into account only the maximum irrigation volume in the field as the field water-holding capacity. The formula for calculating the irrigation volume was:

$$\theta_\mathrm{i} = \mathrm{S} \times \mathrm{h} \times \rho \times \theta_\mathrm{m} \tag{5}$$

where θ_i is the irrigation volume in m^3 ha^{-1}, S is the area per hectare in m^2, h is the soil depth in m, ρ is the soil bulk weight in g cm^{-3}, and θ_m is the mass water content of the soil to be irrigated in g kg^{-1}.

The irrigation amount for different depth profiles of soil was calculated differently. The irrigation amount for 0~40 cm was the sum of 0~20 cm and 20~40 cm, the irrigation amount for 0~60 cm was the sum of 0~20 cm, 20~40 cm, and 40~60 cm, and so on.

3. Results

3.1. Statistics Assessment of Soil Moisture Data

Table 1 shows an overview of the measured water content data for each soil profile in three periods. Given the proximity of the test area to the Tarim River and the burial depth of groundwater mostly located at 1.2~1.5 m, the maximum, minimum and average values of soil-water content increased with the increase of soil depth in the same period. In terms of spatial variability of soil moisture in the test area, the coefficient of variation of soil-moisture content in Table 1 decreased as soil depth increased in the same period. The spatial variability of soil moisture in the surface layer (0–20 cm) was large, and the spatial variability of soil moisture in the bottom layer 80–100 cm was not obvious. From multiple periods in the same soil layer, the spatial variability of soil-moisture content in the surface layer 0–20 cm decreased gradually as the irrigation frequency increased. The variability coefficients of soil-water content in the bottom 60~80 cm and 80~100 cm had less variability in the three periods. After a preliminary analysis, from June to August, the environmental temperature kept rising and, theoretically, the rate of soil-water dissipation increased, but after several rounds of irrigation and the elevation of groundwater levels due to the flood season of Tarim River, the water content of the bottom layer, especially the 60~80 cm and 80~100 cm soil layers, increased and maintained a small spatial variability both in space and time.

Table 1. Statistics of measured soil moisture. Note: Max, Maximum; Min, Minimum; Mean, Arithmetic mean; CV, Coefficient of Variation.

Month	Depth (cm)	Max (%)	Min (%)	Mean (%)	CV(%)
June	0~20	17.34	8.25	12.38	23.91
	20~40	21.89	14.15	17.63	14.55
	40~60	25.82	13.91	21.16	13.43
	60~80	28.96	19.59	24.65	8.23
	80~100	30.37	20.95	26.39	8.22
July	0~20	27.19	13.27	17.32	18.06
	20~40	28.15	17.42	21.04	11.38
	40~60	27.83	15.92	23.44	15.29
	60~80	29.52	18.82	26.34	9.39
	80~100	32.43	24.36	27.95	8.40
August	0~20	21.84	11.98	15.39	14.99
	20~40	25.80	15.47	19.39	12.67
	40~60	27.32	17.30	23.78	13.32
	60~80	32.27	21.25	27.57	9.21
	80~100	32.50	23.52	28.27	6.97

3.2. Comparison of Accuracy of Soil Moisture Inversion Models

Multiple linear regression relationships between soil-moisture content and ECa at five different depths and three different times are given in Table 2. 24 profiles (modeling dataset) and were established between ECa values and validated using the remaining 18 profiles (validation dataset) at two depths measured by EM38-MK2; the R^2 obtained ranged from 0.61~0.89.

Table 2. Predicted relationships of soil-water content at different depths and periods.

Month	Depth (cm)	Models	R^2
June	20	$y = 0.009X_1 + 0.090X_2 + 7.032$	0.87
	40	$y = 0.045X_1 + 0.027X_2 + 14.529$	0.89
	60	$y = -0.027X_1 + 0.110X_2 + 16.929$	0.76
	80	$y = -0.053X_1 + 0.126X_2 + 20.500$	0.67
	100	$y = -0.037X_1 + 0.102X_2 + 22.730$	0.61
July	20	$y = -0.042X_1 + 0.082X_2 + 13.166$	0.87
	40	$y = -0.057X_1 + 0.081X_2 + 18.841$	0.62
	60	$y = 0.043X_1 - 0.080X_2 + 27.092$	0.77
	80	$y = 0.037X_1 - 0.063X_2 + 28.947$	0.75
	100	$y = -0.032X_1 + 0.007X_2 + 31.02$	0.74
August	20	$y = -0.054X_1 - 0.005X_2 + 18.27$	0.88
	40	$y = 0.033X_1 - 0.067X_2 + 22.116$	0.65
	60	$y = -0.085X_1 + 0.035X_2 + 27.41$	0.79
	80	$y = -0.017X_1 - 0.035X_2 + 30.971$	0.71
	100	$y = 0.061X_1 - 0.091X_2 + 30.154$	0.7

Note: X_1 means ECv0.75, X_2 means ECv1.5.

Table 3 shows the fit between the predicted soil-moisture content and the soil-moisture content of the reserved validation set for each soil layer in the three periods. The *p*-values obtained by F-test of all models were less than 0.01. The R^2 of the apparent conductivity inversion soil moisture model for the surface layer 0–20 cm in June, July and August were all higher than 0.80, and the RPD values were around 2.50, indicating that the predicted soil-moisture content of the surface layer (0–20 cm) in these three periods fit well with the measured values. The R^2 and RPD values of the inversion model of the apparent conductivity of 80–100 cm in June and August were the lowest among the five soil layers in the same period, indicating that the prediction error of the inversion model of the apparent conductivity of 80–100 cm in June and August was higher than that of the other soil layers. After preliminary analysis, considering the leaching effect of winter irrigation on the salts in the soil, the salts were leached to below 1 m. However, the cotton field did not have any irrigation activity after the previous year's winter irrigation until the first irrigation in 2018, and with the gradual recovery of ground temperature in spring, some of the soluble soil salts also formed a re-salt zone with the rising movement of soil moisture, which in turn affected the apparent conductivity values in the re-salt zone, leading to the stability of the model and its prediction. The stability of the model and its prediction ability decreased.

From the end of winter irrigation in the previous year to June, along with the gradual increase of ambient temperature in the study area, the apparent conductivity inversion model R^2 of the soil layer deeper than 20 cm showed a decrease trend with increasing soil depth, and so did RPD. In addition to the influence cause by soil salinity, the degree of spatial variability of soil moisture itself can further cause error variation. As shown in Table 1, the coefficient of variation of soil-moisture content in different soil layers in the same period decreased as the soil depth increased, from which it was inferred that the spatial variability of soil-moisture content in the bottom layer (80–100 cm) in June was smaller, and the degree of spatial variability of soil moisture was relatively low. The prediction error of the inverse model prediction increased, and its predictive ability was not as good as that of other soil layers in the same period.

Comparing the results in June with July, first, in terms of influence caused by crop growth metabolic activities in July, the water requirement of cotton reached its highest at the boll stage and the root system was most active. Second, in terms of soil moisture changes, after the first irrigation in the cotton field, the root layer under the film, especially the surface soil moisture, was fully replenished. Finally, in terms of changes in the apparent conductivity inversion model of the same soil layer for two periods, the R^2, RMSE and RPD values of the apparent conductivity inversion model at 0–20 cm changed less while the MRE decreased. Additionally, in July, the R^2 and RPD values at 20–40 cm were the lowest and MRE was the highest among the five soil layers, so the stability and accuracy of the inversion model of this layer were relatively low.

Table 3. Indices of cross-validation Soil Moisture Model. Note: R^2, coefficient of determination; RMSE, root mean square error; RPD, Relative percent deviation; MRE, Mean relative error.

Month	Depth (cm)	R^2	RMSE (%)	RPD	MRE (%)
June	0–20	0.87	1.80	2.44	1.26
	20–40	0.89	1.33	2.89	1.10
	40–60	0.73	1.07	1.70	2.32
	60–80	0.64	0.98	1.38	0.89
	80–100	0.58	1.39	1.19	1.08
July	0~20	0.86	0.86	2.50	0.75
	20~40	0.60	1.80	1.13	2.50
	40~60	0.75	1.87	1.75	2.30
	60~80	0.73	0.91	1.81	1.56
	80~100	0.71	1.17	1.36	1.79
August	0–20	0.88	0.66	2.69	0.57
	20–40	0.59	1.73	1.20	2.99
	40–60	0.51	1.48	1.01	2.20
	60–80	0.72	1.17	1.62	0.88
	80–100	0.66	0.79	1.38	0.69

The average monthly temperature in August was at the highest temperature of the year, and the metabolic activities of cotton slowed down compared with July, and the water demand gradually decreased. Although the cotton field was irrigated several times, the water content of the surface soil still decreased compared with that in July. The five soil apparent conductivity inversion models for the same period did not have regularity under the interactions of multiple factors dominated by temperature. Compared with the same soil layer apparent conductivity inversion model in July, both R^2 and RPD values obtained by apparent conductivity model at the 20–40 cm soil layer increased in August, so the stability and predictive ability of the model were improved.

From the evaluation indicators in Table 3, the linear inversion model soil moisture was possible in most cases. For agricultural fields in arid regions, the water–salt ratio in the soil not only directly affects the soil apparent conductivity values, but also is a crucial factor for high crop yield. In the following, the influence of two aspects on the predictive ability of the model, the degree of spatial variability in different soil layers and soil salinity, will be discussed. First, in terms of the spatial variability of soil moisture in different soil layers, as shown in Tables 1 and 3, when the degree of spatial variability of soil moisture is large (e.g., 0–20 cm soil layer in the same period), the R^2 value of the multivariate linear model was high, and the RPD value was also at a high level, indicating that the predictive ability of the model was high. In contrast, when the spatial variability of soil moisture was small (e.g., 80–100 cm depth in the same period), the predictive ability of the multivariate linear model was lower. This relationship was not sufficient to fully account for the higher spatial variability of soil moisture, because the soil texture in the study area is homogeneous and the mulching technique was used, which aimed to increase the temperature and retain moisture and to slow down the natural loss of soil moisture and soil temperature as much as possible. Therefore, whether the degree of spatial variability of soil moisture was more favorable for model fitting and prediction for farmland with heterogeneous soil texture needed further study.

Finally, in terms of soil salinity, soil salinity was bound to affect the inversion of apparent conductivity of soil moisture to some extent. In this study (Table 4), the mean value of apparent conductivity at 0.375 m in June (35.21 mS m^{-1}) was lower than the mean value of apparent conductivity at 0.75 m (54.30 mS m^{-1}), based on the positive correlation between apparent conductivity and soil-salinity content in agricultural soils, as well as previous related studies on the spatial and temporal variability of soil salinity [35], indicating that the soil-salt content located in the rhizosphere, especially in the 20–40 cm soil layer, was lower than that in the non-rhizosphere (below 60 cm) in June. the predictive ability of the 20–40 cm apparent conductivity model was better than that of the non-root layer apparent conductivity model. However, the mean values of apparent conductivity in July were 117.03 mS m^{-1} and 112.60 mS m^{-1} at 0.375 m and 0.75 m, respectively, and 78.75 mS m^{-1} at 1.5 m, indicating that the difference in soil salinity content between 0.375 m and 0.75 m during this period was not significant. While the soil salinity content at 1.5 m was very low, indicating that its soil salinity was The R^2 of the apparent conductivity model at 20–40 cm in July was 0.60, and the accuracy of the model was reduced compared with that in June. Therefore, although salinity had a certain influence on soil moisture inversion in a few soil layers, and this influence effect reduced the degree of fit between the predicted and measured values of the model, the model still had considerable predictive ability and could be applied practically.

Table 4. The statistical characteristic values of geospatial electromagnetic induction measurements of apparent electrical conductivity (ECa) at different periods.

Date	ECa	Min (mS m^{-1})	Max (mS m^{-1})	Mean (mS m^{-1})
June	$EC_{h0 \cdot 375}$	102.422	3.75	35.21
	$EC_{h0 \cdot 75}$	100	10.547	54.30
	$EC_{V0 \cdot 75}$	173.359	13.086	65.20
	$EC_{V1 \cdot 5}$	139.102	20.313	73.18
July	$EC_{h0 \cdot 375}$	145	34.004	117.03
	$EC_{h0 \cdot 75}$	163.535	23.516	112.06
	$EC_{V0 \cdot 75}$	120.891	35.898	86.95
	$EC_{V1 \cdot 5}$	160.195	18.516	78.75
August	$EC_{h0 \cdot 375}$	141.328	12.3635	65.33
	$EC_{h0 \cdot 75}$	159.1605	6.035	84.22
	$EC_{V0 \cdot 75}$	173.6525	16.641	82.29
	$EC_{V1 \cdot 5}$	165.0975	17.91	75.21

3.3. Comparison between Multi-Period and Single-Period Model

To investigate whether EM38-MK2 could be directly applied to multi-period applications, the full-period model and the single-period model were developed in this study (Table 5), and the comparison of evaluation indexes of each model is shown in Table 6. Comparing the two modeling ideas for the same soil layer, it can be seen that the R^2 and RPD values of the single-period model for each soil layer water content model were higher than the full-period model, and the MRE value was lower than the full-period model. After preliminary analysis, on the one hand, agricultural soils are non-homogeneous, and soil salinity is constantly moving up and down in the vertical direction by irrigation and evapotranspiration. On the other hand, the influence of higher ambient temperature easily triggers evapotranspiration water consumption, which can affect the variability of soil-water content in the horizontal direction. The highest RPD of the full period model was 1.38 and the lowest RPD of the single period model was 1.33, indicating that the multi-period model of apparent conductivity inversion of soil-water content has good predictive ability and high stability. The lowest coefficient of determination was found in the full-period model at 40–60 cm, which is presumed to be the result of soil water uptake by directional growth of a few main crop roots at this depth, coupled with changes in ambient temperature. Since the predictive ability of the full-period model was not as good as that of the single-period model, this suggests that the parameter of multiple-period model cannot be applied to a simple linear model at a specific period, but a separate set of linear model parameters should be used for each period.

Table 5. Predicted relationships of soil-water content at different depths for the whole period.

Method	Depth (cm)	Models	R^2
Multi-period	0~20	$Y = 0.097X_1 - 0.061X_2 + 12.052$	0.54
	20~40	$Y = 0.061X_1 - 0.033X_2 + 17.410$	0.51
	40~60	$Y = 0.070X_1 - 0.084X_2 + 23.876$	0.33
	60~80	$Y = 0.065X_1 - 0.077X_2 + 26.993$	0.60
	80~100	$Y = 0.026X_1 - 0.029X_2 + 27.734$	0.40

Table 6. Accuracy assessment of single period model and multi-period model. Note: R^2, coefficient of determination; RMSE, root mean square error; RPD, Relative percent deviation; MRE, Mean relative error.

Method	Depth (cm)	R^2	RMSE (%)	RPD	MRE (%)
Multi-period	0~20	0.52	1.29	0.96	0.89
	20~40	0.47	2.42	1.01	1.74
	40~60	0.26	2.65	0.54	2.21
	60~80	0.58	1.57	1.28	1.5
	80~100	0.35	1.34	1.38	1.58
Single period	0~20	0.89	1.21	1.79	0.68
	20~40	0.64	1.75	1.36	1.46
	40~60	0.79	1.86	1.63	1.74
	60~80	0.62	1.57	1.77	1.34
	80~100	0.77	1.47	1.33	0.84

3.4. Distribution of Irrigation Amount

Table 7 shows the statistical results of soil bulk density and field capacity of the soil samples. The results show that the coefficient variation of both at the field scale in the study area was not higher than 10%, and the degree of variation was small. Therefore, the average values of 1.48 g cm^3 and 25.44% for soil-bulk density and soil-field capacity can be used as the desired target values for both in field-scale irrigation calculations. This value can be used as soil capacity and field water-holding capacity in the calculation of irrigation volume at the field scale.

Table 7. Statistic of soil-bulk density and field capacity. Note: Max, Maximum; Min, Minimum; Mean, mean; CV, Coefficient of Variation.

Soil Properties	Max	Min	Mean	CV
Bulky density (g cm^{-3})	1.63	1.25	1.48	5%
Field Capacity (%)	34.69	20.31	25.44	10%

Kriging, also known as spatial local interpolation, is a method for te unbiased optimal estimation of regionalized variables in a finite area based on variance function theory and structural analysis and is one of the main elements of geo-statistics. In this study, the soil apparent conductivity data obtained from EM38 automatic model was brought into the soil-moisture estimation model to calculate the soil-water content in the study area, and the irrigation amount in the study area was calculated by Equation (5). The ordinary kriged land statistical in inversion interpolation method was selected for irrigation volume distribution mapping. The interpolated irrigation volume distribution map was first rasterized, and then the rasterized data were reclassified according to the legend in Figure 2 as the grading standard, and the number of rasterized cells at each level was counted. The theoretical irrigation volume was calculated by taking the median value at each level. Figure 2 shows the distribution of irrigation amount in June, July, and August, respectively.

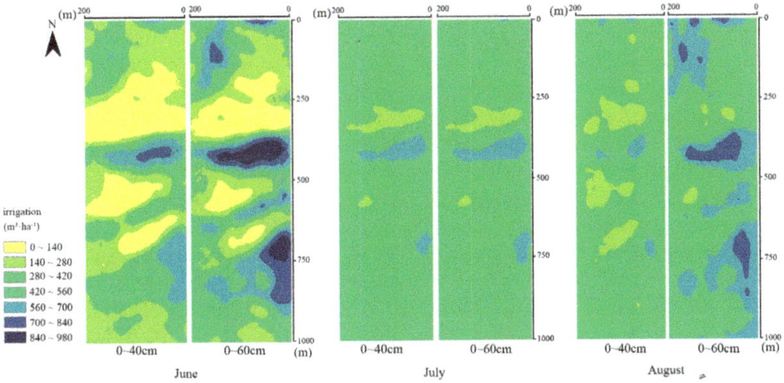

Figure 2. Distribution of irrigation in June, July and August.

First, from the overall spatial distribution, the northern part of the study area is adjacent to the Tarim River, and most of the area has less irrigation water than the southern part. The high irrigation-volume amount in the northern part of the study area is mainly located in a small part of the northeast corner of the study area, and a small part of about 500 m from north to south. The high irrigation-volume amount in the northern part of the study area is mainly due to the high apparent soil conductivity. By combining previous studies on apparent conductivity and soil salinity [35,36], it was shown that in areas with a high apparent conductivity, soil-salinity content is also high [37]. So, the soil salinity content in the high irrigation volume area is slightly higher than other areas in the study area. In addition, during the field survey, it was found that a small portion of the bare soil in the high irrigation area appeared to have a white color at the topsoil, and the cotton crop planted was short with a very low seedling emergence rate. It can be judged that the soil-salt concentration in this area exceeded the salt-tolerance threshold of the crop, and thus affected the growth of the crops. The accumulation of salt crusts caused the "whitening phenomenon" in the topsoil. A small part of the northeast corner of the study area with high irrigation is mainly affected by the flood the Tarim River in dry periods. The area of high irrigation in the southern of the study area is located in the eastern of the study area from north to south for 750 m. The field survey found that this high irrigation area is also affected by high apparent soil conductivity. Although the soil salinization is similar to the high irrigation area in the northern of the study area for 500 m, it exists only at topsoil (10 cm). Unlike the area with high irrigation in the northern for 500 m, the eastern part for 750 m rarely has seedling emergence, so it is assumed that the soil with high apparent conductivity in the topsoil (10 cm) does not threatens the growth of crops in this area. The height and emergence rate of cotton crops are consistent with the surrounding area, and the top does not appear to have the "whitening phenomenon".

Second, in terms of the temporal variation, the distribution of irrigation amount at depths of 0–40 cm and 0–60 cm in June tended to be consistent with the overall color distribution at both depths in June. The highest irrigation volume was greater than 700 m^3 ha^{-1} at the above-mentioned highly irrigated areas. The average monthly ambient temperature in July increased compared to June, and the rate of water loss from the topsoil located in the non-film covered areas increased compared to June, as can be seen in Figure 2. The yellow area with irrigation volume lower than 140 m^3 ha^{-1} disappeared in July, both the minimum irrigation volume at the depths of 0–40 cm and 0–60 cm increased compared to June. The gray area with irrigation amount of 420–560 m^3 ha^{-1} accounted for the largest percentage, indicating that the irrigation amount increased significantly in July compared to June. From July to August, although the water demand of cotton roots gradually slowed down, the average monthly temperature was still increasing, as shown by a significant decrease in the percentage of gray area with irrigation volume of 420–560 m^3 ha^{-1} but still concentrated in the northeast corner, 500 m area from north to south and 750 m east area. Comparing the locations of the high irrigation areas in June, we can see that the locations are basically the same of the above three areas in August. Therefore, in the actual irrigation process, we should specify the appropriate irrigation strategy to avoid the reduction of crop yield in cotton fields due to insufficient irrigation.

With the research on soil water management plans for agricultural fields in recent years [38], the monitoring and management of soil water dynamics has received much attention. As a typical arid farmland in South Xinjiang, the soil moisture in this study area is strongly heterogeneous in space due to the arid climate and high evapotranspiration ratio. The soil-moisture distribution is described as "dry at the top and wet at the bottom layer", which is not conducive to farmers' accurate estimation of soil-moisture content of farmland and causes excessive irrigation. On the other hand, at present, the irrigation scheme mostly adopts a same irrigation strategy to the total farmland. This irrigation method not only causes waste of soil water in the local area with low irrigation volume, but also leads to insufficient irrigation water in the local area with high irrigation volume, which leads to yield reduction.

Compared with the actual irrigation volume, the irrigation amount obtained by inversion model in this study saved 163.07, 161.32, and 208.46 m^3 ha^{-1} in June, July, and August at the depth of 0–40 cm, respectively; saved 58.43, 156.24, and 91.79 m3 ha^{-1} in June, July, and August at the depth of 0–60 cm, respectively. The 0–60 cm saved 58.43, 156.24 and 91.79 m^3 ha^{-1} of irrigation in June, July, and August, respectively. Thus, only considering soil moisture, the method used in this study can reduce irrigation amount by at least 160 m^3 ha^{-1} for crops with shallow root depths and reduce about 30% and 15% in July and August for crops or fruit trees at deep root depths, but less in June. By contrast to the results of previous studies, this study aimed to reduce the waste of soil moisture by using a fine-grained regional irrigation amount. The field-scale inversion of soil moisture is more effective in keeping an eye on soil-moisture conditions in highly irrigated areas, while facilitating rapid information on soil-moisture distribution at the farm scale. However, only the soil-moisture condition was considered in this study, and the content of soil moisture requiring salt leaching in highly irrigated areas was missing. Therefore, future studies will subsequently concentrate on the assessment of the effect of soil-salt concentrations on the uptake of soil moisture by crops in multiple water-demand periods, so that the irrigation amount can effectively alleviate the physiological drought of crops, and be applied to the leaching of soil salts to meet the requirements for more demand under-membrane drip irrigation systems in arid areas of Xinjiang.

4. Conclusions

In this study, an inversion of field-scale soil-moisture data was performed using the apparent soil conductivity of cotton fields obtained by EM38-MK2. The results from the inversion model showed that the linear-inversion approach of soil moisture using soil apparent conductivity data was feasible. Moreover, the ability of the inversion model to be directly applied to multiple periods was also investigated, and the results showed that the predictive ability of the full-period model was not as good as that of the single-period model, indicating that the inversion model of soil-moisture content for multiple periods cannot be directly applied to a simple model for a specific period, and a separate set of models should be used for each period separately, which can improve the accuracy of prediction of soil moisture. In this study, soil-irrigation volume distribution was also mapped by simple kriging interpolation method combined with soil-moisture capacity and field water-holding capacity data, taking into account only soil-moisture conditions. By comparing these with the actual irrigation volume, the predicted field-irrigation volume for all three periods was less than the actual irrigation volume, refining the regional irrigation volume and reducing the waste of soil moisture. Therefore, the geodetic conductivity meter used in this study can achieve the purpose of guiding irrigation amounts to a certain extent by the inversion of soil moisture, soil-moisture capacity and field water-holding capacity data under the premise of considering soil moisture only.

Author Contributions: All authors contributed in a substantial way to the manuscript. J.H.: conceived and designed the research themes analyzed the data. C.F.: contribution to data analysis. N.W.: contributed to the revision and translation. M.W.: contributed to revision and translation. J.W.: contributed to the revision. J.P.: conceived and designed the research themes analyzed the data. All authors have read and agreed to the published version of the manuscript.

Funding: This research was supported by grants from the Tarim University President's Fund (Grant Nos. TDZKCX202205, TDZKSS202227, TDZKSS202350), the Bingtuan Science and Technology Program (Grant No. 2020CB032), the National Key Research and Development Program of China (Grant No. 2018YFE0107000).

Data Availability Statement: Not applicable.

Conflicts of Interest: The authors declare no conflict of interest.

References

1. Fereres, E.; Soriano, M.A. Deficit Irrigation for Reducing Agricultural Water Use. *J. Exp. Bot.* **2007**, *58*, 147–159. [CrossRef]
2. Misra, R.K.; Padhi, J. Assessing Field-Scale Soil Water Distribution with Electromagnetic Induction Method. *J. Hydrol.* **2014**, *516*, 200–209. [CrossRef]
3. Wijewardana, Y.G.N.S.; Galagedara, L.W. Estimation of Spatio-Temporal Variability of Soil Water Content in Agricultural Fields with Ground Penetrating Radar. *J. Hydrol.* **2010**, *391*, 24–33. [CrossRef]
4. Li, P.; He, S.; He, X.; Health, R.T.-E. *Seasonal Hydrochemical Characterization and Groundwater Quality Delineation Based on Matter Element Extension Analysis in a Paper Wastewater Irrigation Area*; Springer: Berlin/Heidelberg, Germany, 2018; Volume 10, pp. 241–258. [CrossRef]
5. Foster, S.; Chilton, J.; Nijsten, G.J.; Richts, A. Groundwater-a Global Focus on the "Local Resource". *Curr. Opin. Environ. Sustain.* **2013**, *5*, 685–695. [CrossRef]
6. Dalton, F.N. Development of Time-Domain Reflectometry for Measuring Soil Water Content and Bulk Soil Electrical Conductivity. In *Advances in Measurement of Soil Physical Properties: Bringing Theory into Practice*; Wiley: New York, NY, USA, 2012; pp. 143–167. ISBN 9780891189251.
7. Triantafilis, J.; Kerridge, B.; Journal, S.B.-A. Digital Soil-class Mapping from Proximal and Remotely Sensed Data at the Field Level. *Agron. J.* **2009**, *101*, 841–853. [CrossRef]
8. Altdorff, D.; Sadatcharam, K.; Unc, A.; Krishnapillai, M.; Galagedara, L. Comparison of Multi-Frequency and Multi-Coil Electromagnetic Induction (Emi) for Mapping Properties in Shallow Podsolic Soils. *Sensors* **2020**, *20*, 2330. [CrossRef] [PubMed]
9. Visconti, F.; Science, J.D.P.-E.J. of S. A Semi-empirical Model to Predict the EM38 Electromagnetic Induction Measurements of Soils from Basic Ground Properties. *Eur. J. Soil Sci.* **2021**, *72*, 720–738. [CrossRef]
10. Xie, W.; Yang, J.; Yao, R.; Wang, X. Article Spatial and Temporal Variability of Soil Salinity in the Yangtze River Estuary Using Electromagnetic Induction. *Remote. Sens.* **2021**, *13*, 1875. [CrossRef]
11. Corwin, D.; Analysis, J.R. soil science and plant. Establishing Soil Electrical Conductivity-Depth Relations from Electromagnetic Induction Measurements. *Commun. Soil Sci. Plant Anal.* **1990**, *21*, 861–901. [CrossRef]
12. Zare, E.; Arshad, M.; Zhao, D.; Nachimuthu, G.; Triantafilis, J. Two-Dimensional Time-Lapse Imaging of Soil Wetting and Drying Cycle Using EM38 Data across a Flood Irrigation Cotton Field. *Agric. Water Manag.* **2020**, *241*, 106383. [CrossRef]
13. Huth, N.; Research, P.P.-S. An Electromagnetic Induction Method for Monitoring Variation in Soil Moisture in Agroforestry Systems. *Soil Res.* **2007**, *45*, 63–72. [CrossRef]
14. Dunn, B.W.; Beecher, H.G. Using Electro-Magnetic Induction Technology to Identify Sampling Sites for Soil Acidity Assessment and to Determine Spatial Variability of Soil Acidity in Rice Fields. Aust. *J. Exp. Agric.* **2007**, *47*, 208–214. [CrossRef]
15. Wienhold, B.J. Apparent Electrical Conductivity for Delineating Spatial Variability in Soil Properties. In *Handbook of Agricultural Geophysics*; CRC Press, Taylor and Francis Group: Boca Raton, FL, USA; pp. 211–215. ISBN 9781420019353.
16. Van Meirvenne, M.; Islam, M.M.; De Smedt, P.; Meerschman, E.; Van De Vijver, E.; Saey, T. Key Variables for the Identification of Soil Management Classes in the Aeolian Landscapes of North-West Europe. *Geoderma* **2013**, *199*, 99–105. [CrossRef]
17. Jung, W.K.; Kitchen, N.R.; Sudduth, K.A.; Kremer, R.J.; Motavalli, P.P. Relationship of Apparent Soil Electrical Conductivity to Claypan Soil Properties. *Soil Sci. Soc. Am. J.* **2005**, *69*, 883–892. [CrossRef]
18. White, M.L.; Shaw, J.N.; Raper, R.L.; Rodekohr, D.; Wood, W. A Multivariate Approach for High-Resolution Soil Survey Development. *Soil Sci.* **2012**, *177*, 345–354. [CrossRef]
19. Cockx, L.; Van Meirvenne, M.; Vitharana, U.W.A.; Verbeke, L.P.C.; Simpson, D.; Saey, T.; Van Coillie, F.M.B. Extracting Topsoil Information from EM38DD Sensor Data Using a Neural Network Approach. *Soil Sci. Soc. Am. J.* **2009**, *73*, 2051–2058. [CrossRef]

20. Vitharana, U.W.A.; Van Meirvenne, M.; Simpson, D.; Cockx, L.; De Baerdemaeker, J. Key Soil and Topographic Properties to Delineate Potential Management Classes for Precision Agriculture in the European Loess Area. *Geoderma* **2008**, *143*, 206–215. [CrossRef]
21. Jaynes, D.B. Mapping the Areal Distribution of Soil Parameters with Geophysical Techniques. In *Applications of GIS to the Modeling of Non-Point Source Pollutants in the Vadose Zone*; Wiley: New York, NY, USA, 2015; pp. 205–216. ISBN 9780891189435.
22. Johnson, C.K.; Doran, J.W.; Duke, H.R.; Wienhold, B.J.; Eskridge, K.M.; Shanahan, J.F. Field-Scale Electrical Conductivity Mapping for Delineating Soil Condition. Soil Sci. Soc. *Am. J.* **2001**, *65*, 1829–1837. [CrossRef]
23. Martinez, G.; Vanderlinden, K.; Ordóñez, R.; Muriel, J.L. Can Apparent Electrical Conductivity Improve the Spatial Characterization of Soil Organic Carbon? *Vadose Zone J.* **2009**, *8*, 586–593. [CrossRef]
24. Doolittle, J.A.; Brevik, E.C. The use of electromagnetic induction techniques in soils studies. *Geoderma* **2014**, *223*, 33–45. [CrossRef]
25. Friedman, S.P. Soil Properties Influencing Apparent Electrical Conductivity: A Review. Comput. *Electron. Agric.* **2005**, *46*, 45–70. [CrossRef]
26. Heilig, J.; Kempenich, J.; Doolittle, J.; Brevik, E.C.; Ulmer, M. Evaluation of Electromagnetic Induction to Characterize and Map Sodium-Affected Soils in the Northern Great Plains. *Soil Horizons* **2011**, *52*, 77. [CrossRef]
27. Kachanoski, R.G.; Gregorich, E.G.; Van Wesenbeeck, I.J. Estimating Spatial Variations of Soil Water Content Using Noncontacting Electromagnetic Inductive Methods. *Can. J. Soil Sci.* **1988**, *68*, 715–722. [CrossRef]
28. Calamita, G.; Perrone, A.; Brocca, L.; Onorati, B.; Manfreda, S. Field Test of a Multi-Frequency Electromagnetic Induction Sensor for Soil Moisture Monitoring in Southern Italy Test Sites. *J. Hydrol.* **2015**, *529*, 316–329. [CrossRef]
29. Hanson, B.R.; Kaita, K. Response of Electromagnetic Conductivity Meter to Soil Salinity and Soil-Water Content. *J. Irrig. Drain. Eng.* **1997**, *123*, 141–143. [CrossRef]
30. Huang, J.; Scudiero, E.; Clary, W.; Corwin, D.L.; Triantafilis, J. Time-Lapse Monitoring of Soil Water Content Using Electromagnetic Conductivity Imaging. *Soil Use Manag.* **2017**, *33*, 191–204. [CrossRef]
31. Huang, J.; Purushothaman, R.; McBratney, A.; Bramley, H. Soil Water Extraction Monitored per Plot across a Field Experiment Using Repeated Electromagnetic Induction Surveys. *Soil Syst.* **2018**, *2*, 11. [CrossRef]
32. Hossain, M.B.; Lamb, D.W.; Lockwood, P.V.; Frazier, P. EM38 for Volumetric Soil Water Content Estimation in the Root-Zone of Deep Vertosol Soils. Comput. *Electron. Agric.* **2010**, *74*, 100–109. [CrossRef]
33. Li, X.; Shao, M.A.; Zhao, C.; Liu, T.; Jia, X.; Ma, C. Regional spatial variability of root-zone soil moisture in arid regions and the driving factors—A case study of Xinjiang, China. *Can. J. Soil Sci.* **2019**, *99*, 277–291. [CrossRef]
34. Kayacan, E.; Kayacan, E.; Ramon, H.; Saeys, W. Towards Agrobots: Identification of the Yaw Dynamics and Trajectory Tracking of an Autonomous Tractor. *Comput. Electron. Agric.* **2015**, *115*, 78–87. [CrossRef]
35. Khongnawang, T.; Zare, E.; Srihabun, P.; Khunthong, I.; Triantafilis, J. Digital soil mapping of soil salinity using EM38 and quasi-3d modelling software (EM4Soil). *Soil Use Manag.* **2022**, *38*, 277–291. [CrossRef]
36. Zarai, B.; Walter, C.; Michot, D.; Montoroi, J.P.; Hachicha, M. Integrating multiple electromagnetic data to map spatiotemporal variability of soil salinity in Kairouan region, Central Tunisia. *J. Arid. Land* **2022**, *14*, 186–202. [CrossRef]
37. Li, H.; Liu, X.; Hu, B.; Biswas, A.; Jiang, Q.; Liu, W.; Wang, N.; Peng, J. Field-Scale Characterization of Spatio-Temporal Variability of Soil Salinity in Three Dimensions. *Remote Sens.* **2020**, *12*, 4043. [CrossRef]
38. Hedley, C.B.; Yule, I.J. A Method for Spatial Prediction of Daily Soil Water Status for Precise Irrigation Scheduling. *Agric. Water Manag.* **2009**, *96*, 1737–1745. [CrossRef]

remote sensing

MDPI

Article

Estimation of Cotton Nitrogen Content Based on Multi-Angle Hyperspectral Data and Machine Learning Models

Xiaoting Zhou †, Mi Yang †, Xiangyu Chen, Lulu Ma, Caixia Yin, Shizhe Qin, Lu Wang, Xin Lv and Ze Zhang *

Xinjiang Production and Construction Crops Oasis Eco-Agriculture Key Laboratory, College of Agriculture, Shihezi University, Shihezi 832003, China
* Correspondence: zhangze1227@shzu.edu.cn
† These authors contributed equally to this work.

Abstract: For crop growth monitoring and agricultural management, it is important to use hyperspectral remote sensing techniques to estimate canopy nitrogen content in a timely and accurate manner. The traditional nadir method has limited ability to assess the nitrogen trophic state of cotton shoots, which is not conducive to high-precision nitrogen inversion, whereas the multi-angle remote sensing monitoring method can effectively extract the canopy's physicochemical information. However, multi-angle spectral information is affected by a variety of factors, which frequently causes shifts in the band associated with nitrogen uptake, and lowers the estimation accuracy. The capacity of the spectral index to estimate aerial nitrogen concentration (ANC) in cotton was therefore investigated in this work under various observation zenith angles (VZAs), and the Relief−F method was employed to select the best spectral band with weight for ANC that is insensitive to VZA. Therefore, in this study, the ability of the spectral index to estimate ANC in cotton was explored under different VZAs, and the Relief-F algorithm was used to optimize the optimal spectral band with weight for ANC that is insensitive to VZA. The angle insensitive nitrogen index (AINI) for various VZAs was calculated using the expression $(R_{530} - R_{704})/(R_{1412} + R_{704})$. The results show that the correlation between the spectral index and the ANC chosen in this study is stronger than the correlation between off-nadir observations, and the correlation coefficients between Photochemical Reflectance Index (PRI), AINI, and ANC are highest when VZA is $-20°$ and $-50°$ (r = 0.866 and 0.893, respectively). Compared with the traditional vegetation index, AINI had the best correlation with ANC under different VZAs (r > 0.84), and the performance of ANC in the backscatter direction was estimated to be better than that in the forward-scatter direction. At the same time, the ANC estimation model of the optimal indices AINI and PRI was combined with the machine learning method to achieve better accuracy, and the prediction accuracy of the random forest (RF) model was $R^2 = 0.98$ and RMSE = 0.590. This study shows that the AINI index can estimate cotton ANC under different VZAs. Simultaneously, the backscattered direction is revealed to be more conducive to cotton ANC estimation. The findings encourage the use of multi-angle observations in crop nutrient estimation, which will also help to improve the use of ground-based and satellite sensors.

Keywords: aerial nitrogen concentration; cotton; hyperspectral remote sensing; multi-angle; spectral index

1. Introduction

Nitrogen is the most important mineral nutrient element for crops, and it is also a key factor for crop growth and yield formation. Timely and accurate estimation of crop canopy nitrogen content is the key to the scientific and efficient use of nitrogen [1]. Compared with the traditional method of destructive sampling to obtain crop nitrogen status, the use of remote sensing technology can non-destructively, accurately, and quickly obtain the spectral information of crops in a large area and provide decision support for the later formulation of scientific and reasonable fertilization programs. The use of spectral reflectance to accurately monitor crop canopy nitrogen content is based mainly on the response of the biophysical characteristics of crop leaves to spectral reflectance [2]. Crop canopy spectral reflectance is affected by crop plant type, canopy structure, solar zenith angle, observation angle, and canopy coverage [3]. At the same time, the optical remote sensing observation is affected by the bidirectional reflection of the canopy, and the observation from a single angle cannot rule out the interference of many factors [3]. This directly results in a large spatiotemporal variation in the spectral reflectance of the canopy and the physiological characteristics of plants and often causes the absorption characteristic bands of the nitrogen content of the canopy to shift [4]. The vegetation index established by using methods such as normalized difference can reduce the influence of canopy structure and angle to a certain extent; for example, the optimized soil-adjusted vegetation index (OSAVI) can alleviate the structural effect to a certain extent, but it has not yet solved Canopy spectral reflectance suffers from two-way (illumination and viewing geometry) effects [5].

Multi-angle remote sensing, when compared with nadir observation, can obtain more information about the crop canopy, and this provides a method for characterizing canopy reflectance anisotropy, which is useful for effectively extracting physicochemical information [6,7]. Many studies have proposed the use of anisotropy to reduce the impact of multi-angle effects and improve exponential performance. Such as, He et al. established the angle-insensitive vegetation index (AIVI) of winter wheat to improve the estimation progress of leaf nitrogen content and the stability of the angle [4]. Some studies have also found that compared with nadir observation, non-nadir observation, and multi-angle observation can improve the estimation accuracy of crop canopy parameters [8,9], such as the estimation of leaf area index [10]. Recent studies have also shown that plant biochemical parameters can be monitored using multi-angle data. For example, Kong et al. [11] and Peter et al. [12] found that when observation is undertaken at a zenith angle of 30°, the model estimation accuracy of leaf chlorophyll content (LCC) obtained is the highest and a larger zenith angle can be used for inversion, which can obtain a more accurate estimation effect [10].

In order to improve the accuracy and stability of the model, there have been attempts to use multi-angle remote sensing data to construct new spectral indices, such as the work of Li et al. [13], which uses the modified Datt index to reduce the directional reflection effect when estimating leaf chlorophyll content, and which improves the high-precision estimation of leaf chlorophyll content in all observation directions and species. Yang et al. [14] found that the improved LAI estimation of normalized difference ratio index (NDRI) and enhanced ratio vegetation index (ERVI) for different crop geometric features achieved a higher accuracy than other spectral indices or angles at 40° viewing angles. The multi-angle index MAVI, developed by He et al. [4], combines spectral data from two observation angles to improve the stability and accuracy of the estimation of nitrogen concentration in wheat leaves; the improved right peak area index (mRPA) at $-10°$ to $10°$ can more accurately evaluate plant nitrogen status [15], and Wang et al. [16] also used 60°, 60°, and 50° to monitor leaf chlorophyll content in the upper, middle, and lower layers of winter wheat, respectively.

At present, the research mainly focuses on analyzing the performance of estimating vegetation physiological parameters under various observation zenith angles (VZAs), which limits the universality and practical value of remote sensing monitoring. The spectral characteristics of the canopy are affected by the leaf inclination, canopy structure, shadow, and soil background spectral reflection, resulting in frequent shifts in the characteristic band of nitrogen uptake [17–19]. As cotton is a crop with sunward characteristics [20], its leaf inclination angle changes with the change in the solar zenith angle under different growth periods and different times of the day, which leads to differences in canopy spectra under different VZAs, and affects the estimation accuracy of cotton aerial nitrogen concentration (ANC). In order to improve the model accuracy and stability of canopy spectral information construction under different VZAs, future research should focus on exploring how different VZA canopy spectra affect nutrient inversion accuracy and on constructing the spectral index with the lowest sensitivity to VZA but the highest ability to estimate ANC through multi-angle remote sensing data, so as to reduce the directional reflection effect when estimating ANC. In this study, the Relief-f feature selection algorithm was used to screen the optimal feature bands that can better retrieve cotton ANC under different observation angles and to construct an angle-insensitive nitrogen index (AINI). The Relief-f algorithm belongs to the classic multivariable filtering feature selection method. Compared with the encapsulation feature selection method, the Relief-f algorithm can reduce the complexity of feature search, accurately estimate the quality of strong correlation features, and detect outliers with strong robustness. Therefore, the objectives of this study were as follows: (1) to study the ability of canopy multi-angle spectra and existing spectral indices to estimate nitrogen concentration under different VZAs; (2) to find out the bands that can indicate the nitrogen content of cotton and further develop the spectral index that is most sensitive to nitrogen changes but not sensitive to VZA; and (3) construct a cotton nitrogen monitoring model based on the optimal spectral index under the best VZA to achieve rapid non-destructive monitoring of cotton nitrogen.

2. Materials and Methods

2.1. Experimental Design

The experiment was conducted in 2021 at Shihezi University's second consecutive experimental teaching field in Shihezi City, Xinjiang, China (85°59′41″E, 44°19′54″N). The location of the test site is shown in Figure 1. The altitude is 429 m, the frost-free period is 168~171 days, the annual sunshine duration is 2721~2818 h, and the active accumulated temperature of ≥10 °C is 3570~3729 °C. The soil of the test field is loam, in which the alkali-hydrolyzed nitrogen content is 60.88 mg/kg, the available potassium content is 134 mg/kg, the available phosphorus content is 17.95 mg/kg, and the organic matter content is 19.90 g/kg. The fore-rotating crop is cotton.

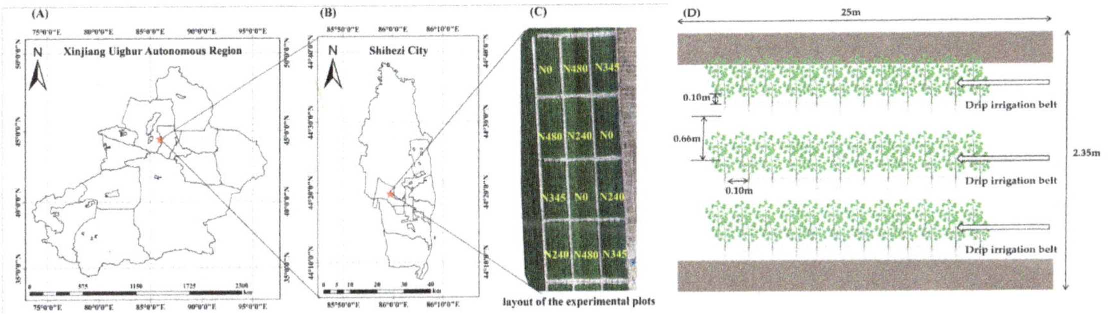

Figure 1. Overview map of study area and layout of the experimental plots. (**A**) Location of the pilot area in Xinjiang Uighur Autonomous Region, (**B**) Location of the pilot area in Shihezi City, (**C**) layout of the experimental plots, (**D**) Layout of row spacing in the test plot.

During the whole growth process of cotton, nitrogen, phosphorus, and potassium fertilizers were applied dropwise with water, including urea (N, 46%), 345 kg/ha, and potassium dihydrogen phosphate (P_2O_5, 52%; K_2O, 34%), 240 kg/ha, as the main fertilizers. There are nine periods of drip irrigation in the whole growth period. The urea application amount and proportion of each treatment are shown in Table 1. Before each fertilization, the required fertilizer is weighed in proportion and poured into the fertilizer tank for dissolution, then dropped into the plot with water.

Table 1. Time, proportion, and amount of nitrogen application for each treatment in the test plot in 2021.

Date/Dosage	Treatment/Proportion	N_0 (0 kg/ha)	N_{240} (240 kg/ha)	N_{480} (480 kg/ha)	N_{345} (345 kg/ha)
13 June	5%	0	75.16	150.32	108.04
21 June	5%	0	75.16	150.32	108.04
30 June	10%	0	150.32	300.64	216.09
6 July	15%	0	225.48	450.96	324.13
14 July	18%	0	270.58	541.16	388.96
21 July	18%	0	270.58	541.16	388.96
27 July	17%	0	255.55	511.09	367.35
5 August	8%	0	120.26	240.51	172.87
11 August	4%	0	60.13	120.26	86.43

The main cultivars in the surrounding area of Shihezi City, Xinjiang, were "Xinlu Zao No. 53" (the plant was tube-shaped, and the leaves were dark green). The submembrane drip-irrigation planting mode (66 + 10 cm) was adopted, with 1 membrane, 3 tubes, 6 rows, and a membrane width of 2.35 m. We used a fully randomized block design with 4 nitrogen application rates, namely pure nitrogen at 0, 240, 480, and 345 kg/ha (expressed as N_0, N_{240}, N_{480}, and N_{345}). Each nitrogen application treatment was repeated 3 times for a total of 12 test cells, and protection rows were set between each cell, as shown in Figure 1.

2.2. Data Acquisition

2.2.1. Measurement of Canopy Multi-Angular Hyperspectral Reflectance

Canopy spectral data were measured at the bud stage (June 24), flowering stage (July 9), flowering and boll stage (July 24), boll maturation period (August 9), and boll opening stage (August 31). Between 11.00 and 16.00 local time, an SR-3500 portable ground feature spectrometer (field of view angle of 25°, sensor sampling interval of 1 nm, and spectral detection range of 350–2500 nm) produced by SR3500 full-spectrum portable ground object spectrometer from (Spectrum Evolution, Southlake, TX, USA) was used to col

Select the spectral reflectance data of cotton canopies under different nitrogen treatments. The sensor was placed on a rotating stand of the multi-angle observation device, and the different viewing angles of the spectrum were determined according to the angle knob on the bracket (Figure 2), measured with the sensor probe at a height of about 0.7 m above the cotton canopy (completely covering the collected sample within the field of view covering a circle with a diameter of 0.31 m). During the acquisition of backscatter spectra, shadowing problems are created by sensors and devices in order to eliminate as much as possible. The multi-angle observation bracket we use uses an inclined support rod for operation, which can reduce the shadow area of the support rod while achieving precise adjustment of the observation angle. VZAs were measured from −60° to 60°, at 10° intervals, with 10 spectra per angle. The direction of solar irradiation and the opposite side of the observation direction is defined as the "forward observation direction" (+), and the same side of the solar irradiation direction and observation direction is defined as the "backward observation direction" (−). In order to reduce the influence of cloud cover and solar altitude changes on spectral reflectance, $BaSO_4$ was used for standard whiteboard correction before and after the measurement of each group of targets. The spectral data is stored by using the Personal Digital Assistant (PDA) through the CED Mobile-DAR Win compact software (Spectrum Evolution, Southlake, TX, USA) and then saved as a CSV format file by the computer's SED to CSV Converter software (Spectrum Evolution, Southlake, TX, USA) for subsequent processing.

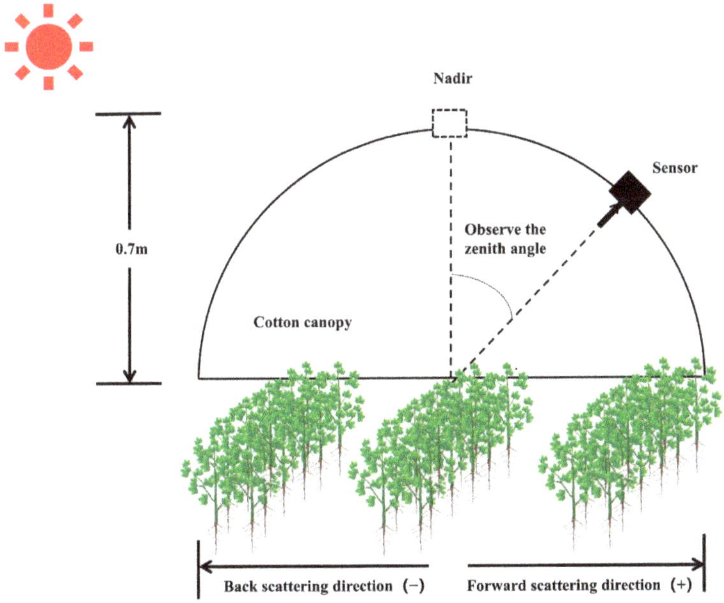

Figure 2. Schematic diagram of measurement method.

2.2.2. Determination of Aboveground N Concentrations

All cotton plants in the test were sampled from the budding stage. The sampling periods were as follows: bud stage, flowering stage, flower bell stage, full bell stage, and spit stage. Three cotton plants were selected in each test area according to stems, leaves, bud bells, and other different organs. They were high-temperature desiccation at 105 °C for 30 min, baked to constant weight at 80 °C, and the dry matter weight was determined. The nitrogen content was determined by the Dumas method, the aerial nitrogen concentration was determined by Kjeldahl−N analysis, and the aerial nitrogen concentration (g/kg) was expressed by dry weight basis [21].

2.3. Evaluation of the Spectral Index of Nitrogen Nutrition in Cotton

In this study, based on the multi-angle spectral data collected under different nitrogen treatments in the five growth stages of cotton, the precise evaluation of cotton ANC and the elimination of the angle effect of the observed spectrum were carried out. The research process consisted of three modules: feature selection, index construction, and the construction of an ANC estimation model (Figure 3). Differences among multi-angle canopy spectral data collected at five cotton growth stages were analyzed by statistical tests (Figure 4). After the normality test, the forward scatter observations (0°–60°, 36 spectra × 5 growth periods) and backscatter observations (−60°–0°, 36 spectra × 5 growth periods) of the spectral data were subjected to a nonparametric Kruskal–Wallis test, respectively. Under the analysis of the variance of multiple sample sets, all spectral bands reached extremely significant differences ($p < 0.01$), so the Kruskal–Wallis test statistic H value was used to compare the two observation directions (forward scattering and backscattering scattering). The magnitude of the difference in spectral reflectance. The larger the H value, the more statistically significant the difference between the sample medians is, so spectral bands with relatively small differences in the spectral bands under different observation angles of the two scattering directions are obtained.

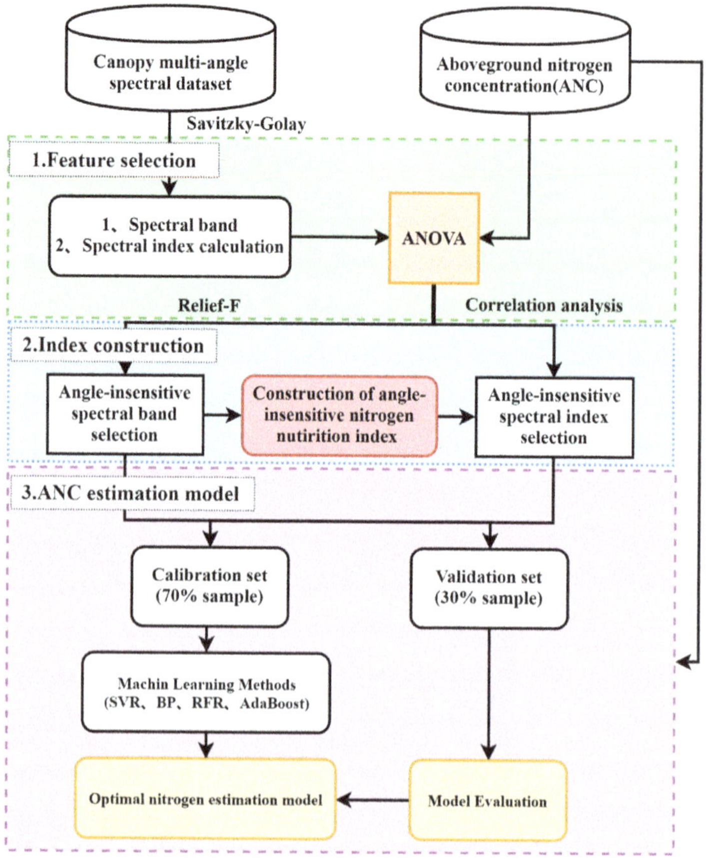

Figure 3. Schematic illustration of cotton ANC estimation based on multi-angle hyperspectral data and machine learning.

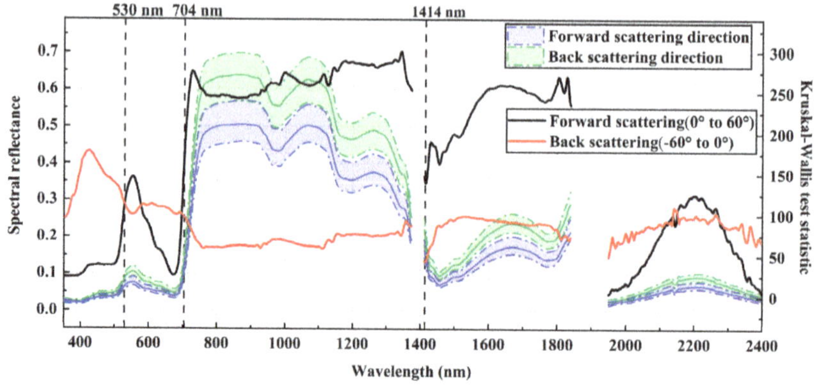

Figure 4. Cotton canopy spectral change characteristics under two-way observation angles (purple and green areas are one-quarter median and three-quarters median spectral reflectance ranges in two scattering directions (n = 2340)). Solid black and red lines are Kruskal–Wallis test statistics between different viewing angles for two scattering directions (n = 1170).

2.3.1. Construction of the Spectral Index

Based on the results of variance analysis and the theoretical basis of plant leaf radiation, scattering, and absorption, the angle insensitive nitrogen index (AINI) suitable for different VZAs was constructed using the three-band index construction method, and the nitrogen nutrient spectral index insensitive to the observation angle was normalized through three different wavelength reflective factors. The bands with good correlation with nitrogen under different VZAs were screened using the Relief-F algorithm and the exhaustive method. The Relief-F algorithm selects the optimal characteristic wavelength with a strong correlation by accumulating the weight of the relevant wavelength, and it has strong robustness to outliers. The basic idea is to first obtain a sample R from the sample set D, and then take k adjacent samples from the sample set of the same type and the sample that is different from R, and then in the feature set F; if the heterogeneous sample on a certain feature is greater than the same sample, then this feature is conducive to classification, increase its weight, repeat n times, and take the mean of all results as the final weight value of each feature [22].

$$w(F_j) \rightarrow w(F_j) - \frac{1}{ngk} \sum\nolimits_{h \in H} \left| R_j - h_j \right| + \frac{1}{ngk} \sum\nolimits_{h \in H} \left| R_j - m_j \right| \tag{1}$$

where F_j is the weight value of feature j. $\sum_{h \in H} \left| R_j - h_j \right|$ represents the sum of the distances of k homogeneous neighboring samples R on feature j; $\sum_{h \in H} \left| R_j - m_j \right|$ represents the sum of the distances of the selected k heterogeneous neighboring samples and sample R on feature j.

In order to find the best band combination, the two reference band ranges were exhaustively searched, and finally, the optimal wavelength combination was obtained, which inverted the cotton nitrogen content. The red edge (700–760 nm) is a transition region with rapid changes in leaf reflectivity caused by strong pigment absorption in the red spectrum and leaf scattering in the near-infrared spectrum, and it has been found that the red edge is sensitive to crop canopy nitrogen [23]. Nitrogen is the main raw material of chlorophyll, and nitrogen deficiency seriously affects photosynthetic utilization efficiency. The 530 nm band is considered to be a highly correlated band between the lutein cycle and the non-photochemical quenching of leaves; it can reflect the photosynthetic utilization efficiency of leaves and is an important band for monitoring nitrogen [24]. Through the Relief-F algorithm, we obtained two angle-insensitive spectral bands of 704 nm and 1412 nm, so the AINI expression is as follows:

$$AINI = \frac{R_{\lambda 1} - R_{\lambda 2}}{R_{\lambda 2} + R_{\lambda 3}} = \frac{R_{530} - R_{704}}{R_{704} + R_{1412}} \tag{2}$$

2.3.2. Classical Vegetation Index Screening

In previous studies, a number of spectral indices have been developed for estimating crop nitrogen content. In this study, 19 spectral indices were selected to evaluate their ability to estimate ANC for different cotton VZAs. The selected spectral indexes are shown in Table 2.

2.4. Model Construction and Verification

The dataset is divided into two parts: 7/10 is the training set, and 3/10 is the validation set. In this study, according to the correlation between the spectral index and aboveground nitrogen concentration, the performance of different spectral indices at different VZAs was compared to determine the most suitable observation angle for the spectral index. The two spectral (AINI, PRI) exponential model input variables were screened. The output variable is the aboveground nitrogen concentration, and Python software is used to model four machine learning algorithms based on support vector regression (SVR), BP neural network, random forest (RF), and AdaBoost, which were selected to quantify the model accuracy.

Table 2. Summary of selected spectral parameters reported in the literature.

	Spectral Index	Name	Definition or Equation	Reference
1	DVI	Difference vegetation index	DVI = R890 − R670	Jorden (1969) [25]
2	NDVI	Normalized difference vegetation index	NDVI = $(R_{890} - R_{670})/(R_{890} + R_{670})$	Rouse et al. (1974) [26]
3	SAVI	Soil-adjusted vegetation index	SAVI = $[(1 + L)(R_{890} - R_{670})]/(R_{890} + R_{670} + L)$, L = 0.5	Huete (1988) [27]
4	PRI	Photochemical reflectance index	PRI = $(R_{531} - R_{570})/(R_{531} + R_{570})$	Penuelas (1995) [28]
5	SIPI	Structure Insensitive Pigment Index	SIPI = $(R_{800} - R_{445})/(R_{800} - R_{680})$	Penuelas (1995) [29]
6	GNDVI	Green Normalized difference vegetation index	GNDVI = $(R_{750} - R_{550})/(R_{750} + R_{550})$	Gitelson et al. (1996) [30]
7	OSAVI	Optimized Soil Adjusted Vegetation Index	OSAVI = $(1 + 0.16)(R_{800} - R_{670})/(R_{800} - R_{670} + 0.16)$	Rondeaux et al. (1996) [31]
8	TCARI	Transformed chlorophyll absorption reflectance index	TCARI = $3[(R_{700} - R_{670}) - 0.2(R_{700} - R_{550})(R_{700}/R_{670})]$	Daughtry et al. (2000) [32]
9	NRI	Nitrogen reflectance index	NRI = $(R_{570} - R_{670})/(R_{570} + R_{670})$	Schleicher et al. (1998) [33]
10	TCARI/OSAVI	TCARI/OSAVI	TCARI/OSAVI = TCARI/OSAVI	Haboudane et al. (2002) [34]
11	NDCI	Double-peak canopy nitrogen index	NDCI = $(R_{762} - R_{527})/(R_{762} + R_{527})$	Marshak et al. (2000) [35]
12	NPCI	Normalized pigment chlorophyll ratio index	NPCI = $(R_{430} - R_{680})/(R_{430} + R_{680})$	Peuelas et al. (1994) [36]
13	PRIC	Photochemical reflectance index correction	PRIC = $(R_{570} - R_{539})/(R_{570} + R_{539})$	Gamon et al. (1992) [37]
14	DDNI	Novel double-peak area index	DDNI = $(R_{755} + R_{680} - 2 \times R_{705})/(R_{755} - R_{680})$	Feng et al. (2014) [38]
15	mSR705	Modified Red-edge Ratio	mSR705 = $(R_{750} - R_{445})/(R_{705} + R_{445})$	Sims et al. (2002) [39]
16	IPVI	Infrared Percentage Vegetation Index	IPVI = $R_{800}/(R_{800} + R_{670})$	Crippen et al. (1990) [40]
17	MTCI	Modified triangular vegetation index	MTCI = $(R_{754} - R_{709})/(R_{709} - R_{681})$	Dash et al. (2007) [41]
18	NPQI	Normalized Phaeophytinization Index	NPQI = $(R_{415} - R_{435})/(R_{415} + R_{435})$	Barnes et al. (1992) [42]
19	CIred-edge3	Red edge model	CIred-edge3 = $(R_{790}/R_{720}) - 1$	Gitelson et al. (2005) [43]

Support Vector Machines (SVM) is a machine learning model that uses hyperplanes to segment data, and its method of segmenting data is to find a plane (or a straight line for two-dimensional data) to classify the data and then vector to maximize the segmentation of the data. Support vector regression (SVR) is a generalized form of support vector machine (SVM), which is mainly used to solve nonlinear regression problems. It solves the nonlinear regression problem of samples by selecting kernel function ideas. This article uses the linear kernel function in SVR, whose definition is shown in Equation (3):

$$k(u,v) = u\prime v \tag{3}$$

Back Propagation (BP) artificial neural networks are the most widely used algorithms in the Artificial Neural Network (ANN) architecture and follow the basic principle of the Gradient Steepest Descent Method to iteratively minimize errors. The processing unit is the most basic component unit of the neural network, and the calculation equations for the input and output of the processing unit are shown in Equation (4):

$$f_i = f(net_i) = f\left(\sum_i W_{ij}X_i - \theta_i\right) \tag{4}$$

where f_i is the output signal of the artificial neural network processing unit; net_i is an integration function; and f is the transfer function of the artificial neural network processing unit. W_{ij} is the connection weight value between the processing units of the artificial neural network, X_i is the input vector, and θ_i is the threshold for the processing unit.

Random Forest (RF) is an ensemble learning bagging method designed for decision trees, which combines the inverse values of multiple decision trees to output the final prediction result, and each decision tree is built according to the random vector value of the random forest, and then outputs a high accuracy result.

Commonly used ensemble learning methods include bagging and boosting; this study uses the Adaboost algorithm in boosting, which is an iterative algorithm whose principle is to train different classifiers (weak classifiers) for the same training set, set these weak classifiers together to form a stronger final classifier (strong classifier), and use the voting method and vote by majority to determine the final prediction result. Among them, the base learner selected by the Adaboost algorithm in this study is Ridge Regression, which is a biased estimation regression method dedicated to collinear analysis. The structure of the Ridge Regression model is similar to the ordinary linear regression model; the difference is mainly reflected in the loss function, and the loss function calculation is shown in Equations (5) and (6).

$$J(\theta) = \frac{1}{2m}\sum_{i=1}^{m}(y_i - wx_i)^2 + \frac{\lambda}{2}\sum_{j=1}^{n}\theta_j^2 \tag{5}$$

$$\sum_{j=1}^{n}\theta_j^2 \leq \lambda \tag{6}$$

w is a vector of length n; the coefficient θ excludes the intercept term; m is the sample number; and n is the number of features. Ridge regression tends to shrink some coefficients to 0, which can alleviate the problem of multiple collinearity and overfitting.

The coefficient of determination (R^2) and the root-mean-square error (RMSE) were selected to evaluate the model. If the model R^2 is higher and the RMSE is lower, the model precision and accuracy of the predicted ANC are higher, and a 1:1 plot of the observed and estimated values can be plotted to prove the degree of model fit.

3. Results

3.1. Change in the Law of Spectral Reflectance of the Cotton Canopy under Different VZAs

In order to more clearly show the differences in spectral reflectance at different observation angles, this study conducted non-parametric tests on the spectral data of all periods

(Figure 4). The results show that after eliminating the bands affected by atmospheric noise around 1400 nm, 1920 nm, and 2400 nm, the entire spectral range (350 nm–2400 nm) shows that the backscattering reflectance is higher than the forward scattering, and the difference is extremely significant ($p < 0.01$). In the two scattering directions, the results under different observation angles show that all bands show extremely significant differences ($p < 0.001$), so the test statistic h value is used to show the spectral bands with relatively small differences. The results show that the test statistics in the visible light band (350–670 nm) show that the minimum value of the backscattering direction (0° to 60°) is in the red light band (672 nm), and the maximum value is in the green light band (555 nm); the minimum value in the forward scattering direction (−60° to 0°) is in the green light band (554 nm), and the maximum value appears in the blue light band (430 nm). It shows that the two scattering directions have different changes in the spectrum under different observation angles. The overall test statistics of the −60° to 0° observation angle are relatively stable and lower than the 0° to 60° observation angle, indicating that the cotton canopy spectrum The reflectance backscatter direction is less affected by the viewing angle than the forward scatter direction.

3.2. Nitrogen-Sensitive Spectral Band Screening of Different VZAs

The study aimed to establish the VZA-insensitive cotton canopy nitrogen nutrition spectrum index, the Relief-F algorithm was used to screen the VZA-insensitive characteristic bands, as shown in Figure 5, and the result was that the ANC of cotton had the strongest correlation with different angles at 705 nm and 1414 nm, and occupied the largest weight in all bands. At 1414 nm, VZA showed the optimal weight between −10° and 10°, 705 nm showed the optimal weight between 0° and 10°, and the rest showed a downward trend with the increase in VZA. This shows that simply using the spectral band to construct an angle-insensitive cotton nitrogen estimation model is disturbed by many external environments, and the vegetation index of the band combination can enhance a certain characteristic or detail of vegetation, which is more suitable for establishing a VZA-insensitive cotton canopy nitrogen estimation model.

3.3. Nitrogen-Sensitive Spectral Index Screening of Different VZAs

To further clarify the abilities of spectral indices to estimate ANC and whether ANC is affected by VZA, 20 spectral indices are listed in Table 3, including 19 published indices, as well as the correlation relationship between the constructed index and 180 samples of cotton ANC under different VZAs, expressed by the correlation coefficient (r); The two best-performing spectral indices (PRI and AINI) show a strong correlation ($r \geq 0.849$) in the backscattering direction, so bolded r-values greater than 0.849 are represented. It can be seen from Table 3 that the correlation between most spectral indices and ANC changes greatly with the change in VZA, such as SIPI, TCARI/OSAVI, IPVI, GNDVI, etc., and some spectral indices are not strongly correlated with ANC in different VZAs, such as DVI, SAVI, SIPI, OSAVI, NRI, NDCI, and NPCI, indicating that they are not suitable for estimating ANC. It is worth noting that the correlation coefficients of all spectral indices in the table for nadir observations are smaller than those for off-nadir observations. Among them, PRI and AINI did not differ much under each VZA, indicating that PRI and AINI were relatively stable in estimating nitrogen using multi-angle remote sensing. In addition, PRIC, DDNI, MTCI, NPQI, and mSR_{705} can also be used as spectral indices to monitor nitrogen. SIPI, DDNI, mSR705, and MTCI are the most advantageous when observing at 60°, and the correlation coefficient is above 0.63. The above results show that, compared with nadir observation, the spectral information obtained by off-nadir observation can improve the inversion accuracy of ANC.

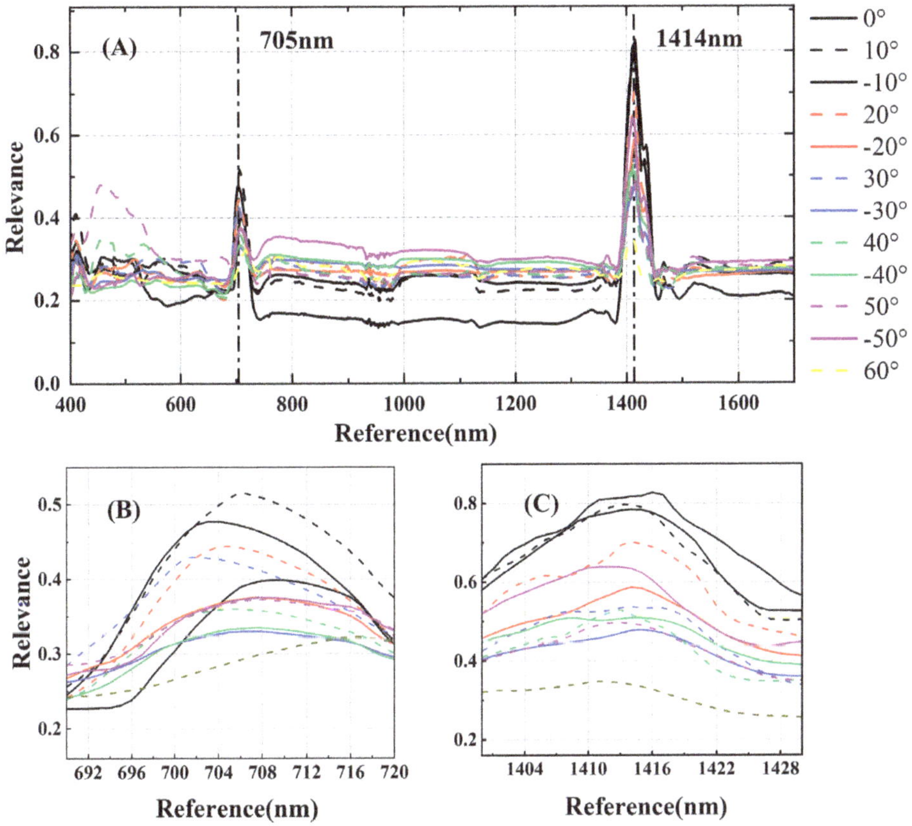

Figure 5. Based on the Relief-F algorithm, the single-wavelength weight value of ANC with cotton under different VZAs was evaluated. (**A**) Single-wavelength weight value with cotton ANC under different VZA, (**B**) Weight value of ANC near 705 nm and cotton under different VZA, (**C**) Weight value of ANC near 1414 nm and cotton under different VZA.

By comparing the relationship between spectral index and ANC, it can be seen that the change in correlation has obvious angle sensitivity. Therefore, after removing the spectral indices with no significant correlation with ANC, 14 spectral indices with good correlation with ANC were screened out, and an analysis of variance was performed on different observation angles of the two scattering directions (Figure 6). The results showed that there were no significant differences in the angles of PRI, PRIC, NPQI, and AINI in the backscattering direction ($-60°$ to $0°$), and the F value of AINI was the smallest. In the forward scattering direction ($0°$ to $60°$), only GNDVI and NPQI are not sensitive to angle differences, and the rest show statistically significant differences. Except for GNDVI and CIred-edge3, the F values of other spectral indices at $0°$ to $60°$ observation angles are higher than those at backscattering ($-60°$ to $0°$ observation angles), indicating that in the direction of backscattering, the spectral indices are affected by the angle with little effect. We found that the spectral index constructed from the near-infrared band is more affected by the observation angle, while the spectral index constructed from the visible light band range and the position of the red edge is less affected by the observation angle. The newly constructed AINI is superior to the spectral index with excellent correlation with ANC in Figure 6B in both scattering directions and can realize the estimation of cotton canopy ANC under the elimination of the influence of observation angle.

Table 3. Correlation coefficient between ANC and spectral index of cotton with different VZAs.(r) * and ** represent spectral index and ANC correlation. * represents a significant correlation of $p <$ 0.05, ** represents a very significant correlation of $p < 0.01$. values greater than 0.849 are expressed in bold.

Spectral Indices	−60°	−50°	−40°	−30°	−20°	−10°	0°	10°	20°	30°	40°	50°	60°
visible band													
PRI	0.849 **	**0.857** **	**0.853** **	**0.861** **	**0.866** **	0.849 **	0.849 **	0.848 **	0.835 **	0.836 **	0.847 **	**0.857** **	0.829 **
PRIC	−0.796 **	−0.801 **	−0.790 **	−0.804 **	−0.796 **	−0.777 **	−0.818 **	−0.832 **	−0.822 **	−0.832 **	−0.842 **	−0.842 **	−0.796 **
NPQI	−0.465 **	−0.666 **	−0.541 **	−0.563 **	−0.582 **	−0.592 **	−0.671 **	−0.702 **	−0.658 **	−0.782 **	−0.800 **	−0.746 **	−0.565 **
visible band, Red edge													
GNDVI	0.071	0.379 **	0.286 **	0.286 **	0.275 **	0.288 **	0.333 **	0.358 **	0.364 **	0.316 **	0.278 **	0.281 **	0.041
TCARI	−0.138	−0.281 **	−0.202 **	−0.192 **	−0.217 **	−0.279 **	−0.349 **	−0.386 **	−0.364 **	−0.341 **	−0.276 **	−0.286 **	−0.371 **
NRI	0.065	0.173 *	0.092	0.08	0.137	0.095	0.098	0.113	0.201 **	0.229 **	0.229 **	0.206 **	0.116
NDCI	−0.034	0.229 **	0.142	0.144	0.152 *	0.162 *	0.213 **	0.234 **	0.269 **	0.215 **	0.170 *	0.173 *	−0.036
NPCI	0.166 *	0.231 **	0.08	0.034	0.115	0.05	0.105	0.077	0.152 *	0.186 *	0.129	0.078	0.147 *
mSR705	0.676 **	0.656 **	0.629 **	0.651 **	0.658 **	0.633 **	0.656 **	0.664 **	0.637 **	0.678 **	0.709 **	0.750 **	0.790 **
AINI	**0.851** **	**0.893** **	**0.890** **	**0.880** **	**0.871** **	**0.862** **	**0.852** **	**0.857** **	0.830 **	0.827 **	0.844 **	**0.851** **	0.816 **
visible band, Red edge, NIR													
SIPI	−0.061	−0.406 **	−0.290 **	−0.326 **	−0.342 **	−0.328 **	−0.408 **	−0.368 **	−0.425 **	−0.503 **	−0.570 **	−0.562 **	−0.630 **
TCARI/OSAVI	−0.164 *	−0.328 **	−0.255 **	−0.250 **	−0.279 **	−0.342 **	−0.403 **	−0.445 **	−0.422 **	−0.408 **	−0.363 **	−0.378 **	−0.461 **
Red edge, NIR													
DVI	0.052	0.041	0.077	0.106	0.095	0.099	0.055	0.049	0.097	0.076	0.161 *	0.168 *	0.097
NDVI	0.04	0.361 **	0.260 **	0.291 **	0.300 **	0.292 **	0.363 **	0.371 **	0.408 **	0.377 **	0.361 **	0.323 **	0.021
SAVI	0.02	0.068	0.084	0.113	0.117	0.157 *	0.127	0.122	0.181 *	0.146	0.208 **	0.227 **	0.071
OSAVI	−0.007	−0.042	0.021	0.056	0.059	0.121	0.08	0.07	0.107	0.103	0.183 *	0.198 **	0.122
DDNI	0.510 **	0.619 **	0.633 **	0.656 **	0.661 **	0.649 **	0.660 **	0.663 **	0.637 **	0.642 **	0.643 **	0.687 **	0.737 **
IPVI	−0.002	0.370 **	0.276 **	0.306 **	0.314 **	0.305 **	0.376 **	0.385 **	0.423 **	0.395 **	0.380 **	0.341 **	0.031
MTCI	0.665 **	0.664 **	0.671 **	0.683 **	0.686 **	0.669 **	0.669 **	0.680 **	0.647 **	0.672 **	0.685 **	0.721 **	0.754 **
CIred-edge3	0.607 **	0.661 **	0.640 **	0.650 **	0.648 **	0.637 **	0.638 **	0.653 **	0.619 **	0.620 **	0.633 **	0.654 **	0.559 **

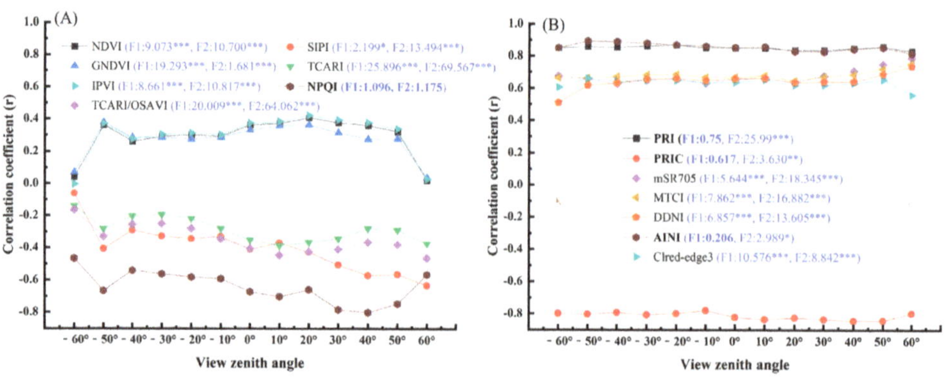

Figure 6. Correlation between spectral indices and ANC under different VZAs. (**A**) VZA sensitivity index, (**B**) VZA insensitivity index. In the brackets of the legend, F1 is the F value of variance analysis in the backscattering direction (−60° to 0°), F2 is the F value in the forward scattering direction (0° to 60°), * $p < 0.05$; ** $p < 0.01$; *** $p < 0.001$.

Through the results of variance analysis and correlation, six optimal spectral indices (PRI, NPQI, AINI, PRIC, mSR705, and MTCI) were selected, and the linear relationship with ANC was compared under the optimal VZA and nadir observation angle (Figures 7 and 8). The results show that the six indices all have higher estimation accuracy at larger observation angles. At the same time, the three indexes of AINI, PRI, and PRIC have little change in the linear model accuracy of ANC at the lowest point observation angle, and the best observation angle compared with other indexes and are less affected by the observation angle. The index with the best test accuracy is AINI, which improves the estimation accuracy R^2 by 0.13–0.29 at the best observation angle compared with other spectral indices, and at the same time, at the lowest observation angle, the estimation accuracy R^2 increases by 0.04–0.43. In summary, the AINI constructed in this study can be better used for ANC estimation and is less affected by the observation angle.

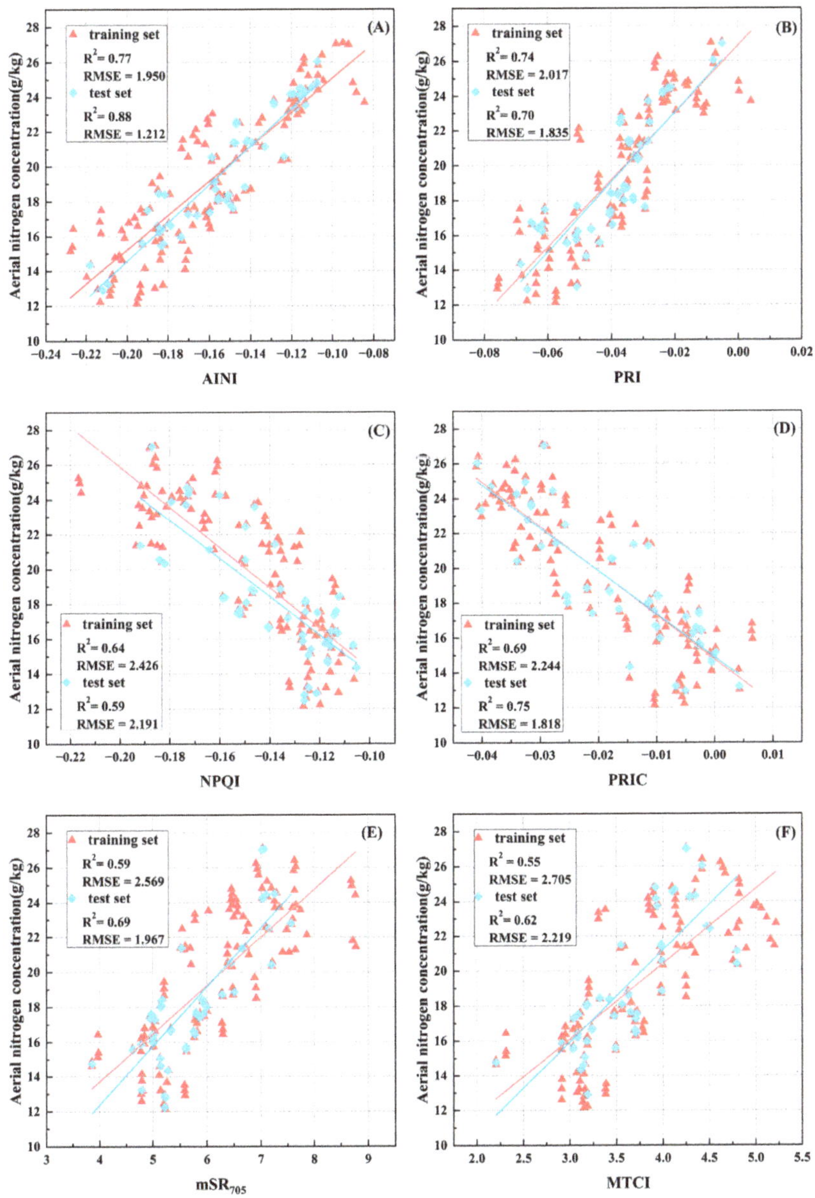

Figure 7. Linear relationship between ANC and spectral index at specific angles: (**A**) −50° PRI, (**B**) −50° AINI, (**C**) 40° NPQI, (**D**) 50° PRIC, (**E**) 60° mSR_{705}, (**F**) 60° MTCI.

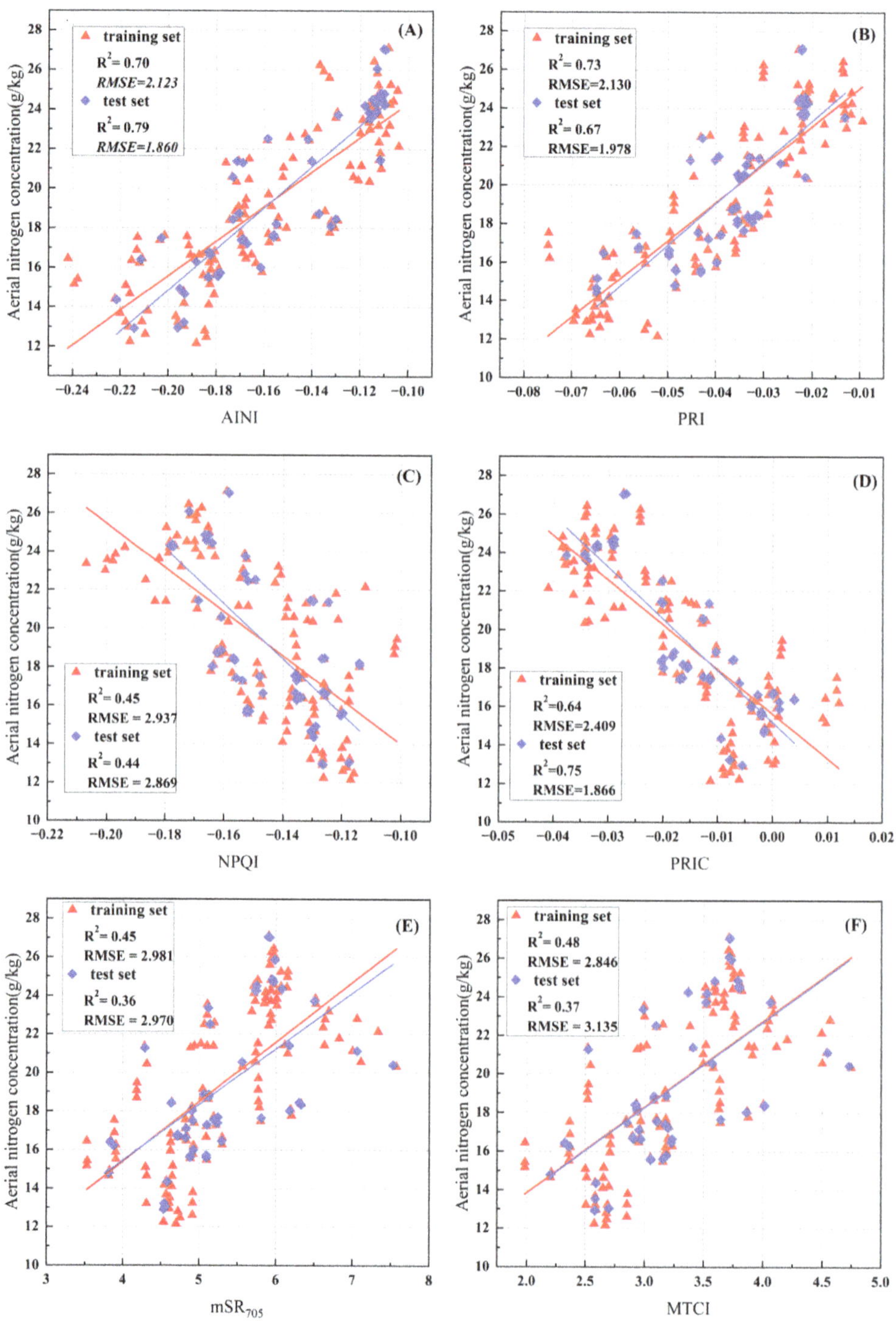

Figure 8. Linear relationship between 0° ANC and spectral index: (**A**) 0° PRI, (**B**) 0° AINI, (**C**) 0° NPQI, (**D**) 0° PRIC, (**E**) 0° mSR705, (**F**) 0° MTCI.

3.4. Cotton Nitrogen Content Estimation Model Based on Multi-Angle Spectral Data

It can be seen from Table 3 that after correlation analysis, the indices PRI and AINI are significantly correlated with ANC, and the correlation between each VZA reaches more than 0.8, so these two spectral indices were selected as the input variables for the construction of machine learning models. A total of 70% of the data volume was randomly selected as the training data set, and 30% was used as the test data set. The four models, support vector regression (SVR), BP neural network, random forest (RF), and AdaBoost, were used for training, and the Python programming language was used to implement the algorithm.

Taking the −20° PRI index and −50° AINI as the model input variables, the measured and predicted values of the four machine-learning models were compared; Figure 9 shows the two best spectral-index VZA estimation models and the combined index estimation model. As can be seen from Figure 10, the measured value and the predicted value of the model based on −20° PRI are R^2 0.76 and 0.71, and the RMSE values are 2.314 and 2.190, respectively, based on −50° AINI. The measured and predicted R^2 values of the model are greater than −20° PRI, and the RMSE is less than the −20° PRI index model. Although both the −50° AINI model and the −20° PRI model can be used for nitrogen estimation, they are based on a single VZA, and combining the two can greatly improve the accuracy of the model. Compared with SVR, BP neural network, and AdaBoost, the RF model predicts the change in cotton ANC better, with a prediction accuracy R^2 of 0.98 and an RMSE of 0.590 in the training set. The above results show that, compared with the single VZA spectral index model, the model based on the combination of the best VZA and the best spectral index can better estimate the ANC. The above results also show that the spectral index constructed in this study can improve the estimation accuracy of nitrogen.

In order to further examine the performance of the four machine learning methods, nitrogen estimation models are constructed based on spectral index PRI and AINI in the band under the optimal VZA. Figures 10–12 are based on the spectral index $AINI_{-50°}$ based on 530 nm, 704 nm, and 1412 nm band machine learning modeling, based on spectral index $PRI_{-20°}$ 531 nm, 570 nm, band machine learning modeling, based on spectral index $AINI_{-50°}$ and $PRI_{-20°}$ 530 nm, 531 nm, 570 nm, 704 nm, 1412 nm band machine learning modeling, as can be seen from Figures 10–12, The four machine learning models based on the AINI band are better than the ones based on the PRI band. Whether based on spectral index modeling or band modeling, the random forest method has the best modeling effect; the R^2 of the training set reaches more than 0.97, and the RMSE is less than 0.819; the combination of the two improves the accuracy of the model.

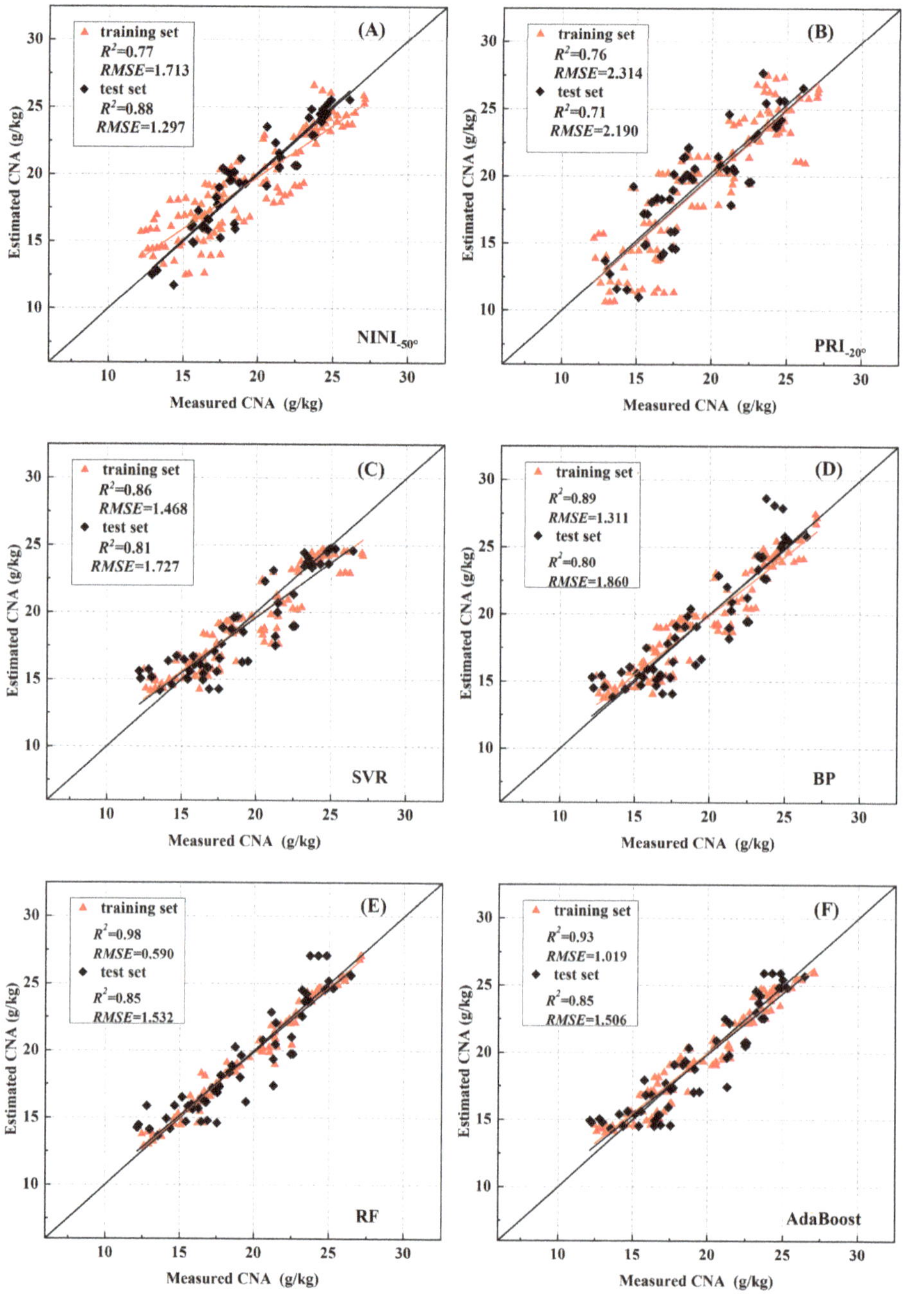

Figure 9. Comparison of predicted and measured values of nitrogen accumulation in cotton canopy based on AINI−50°, PRI−20°, and their combinations (*n* = 180, training set = 126, validation set = 54): (**A**) −50° AINI, (**B**) −20° PRI, (**C**) SVR Modeling of two spectral indices combination, (**D**) BP Modeling of two spectral indices combination, (**E**) RF Modeling of two spectral indices combination, (**F**) AdaBoost Modeling of two spectral indices combination.

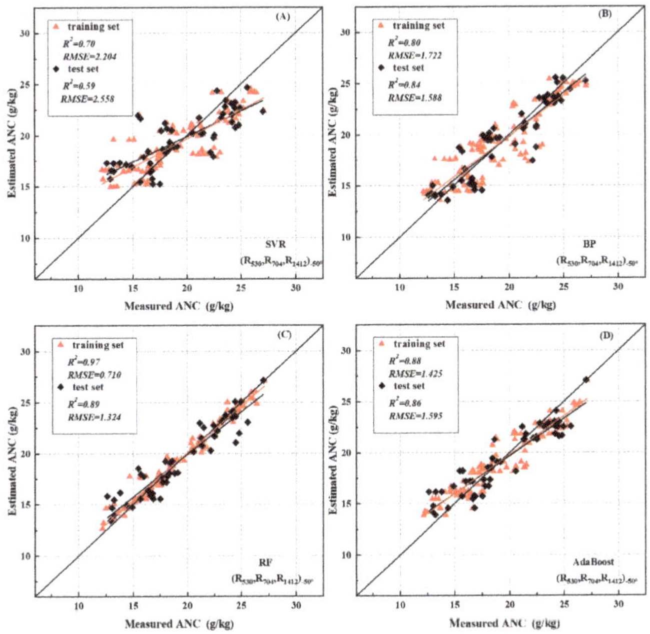

Figure 10. Machine learning modeling in the 530 nm, 704 nm, and 1412 nm bands based on spectral index $AINI_{-50^{\circ}}$ (n = 180, training set = 126, validation set = 54): (**A**) SVR, (**B**) BP, (**C**) RF, (**D**) AdaBoost.

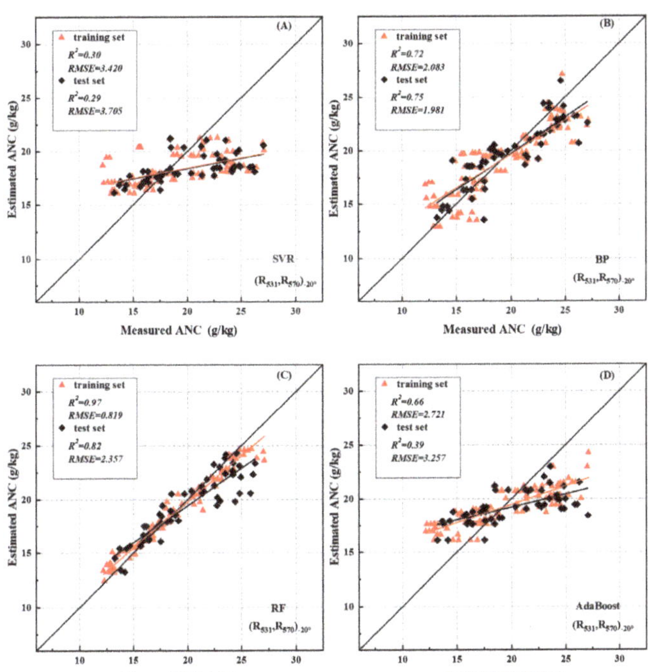

Figure 11. Machine learning modeling in the 531 nm, 570 nm bands based on spectral index $PRI_{-20^{\circ}}$ (n = 180, training set = 126, validation set = 54): (**A**) SVR, (**B**) BP, (**C**) RF, (**D**) AdaBoost.

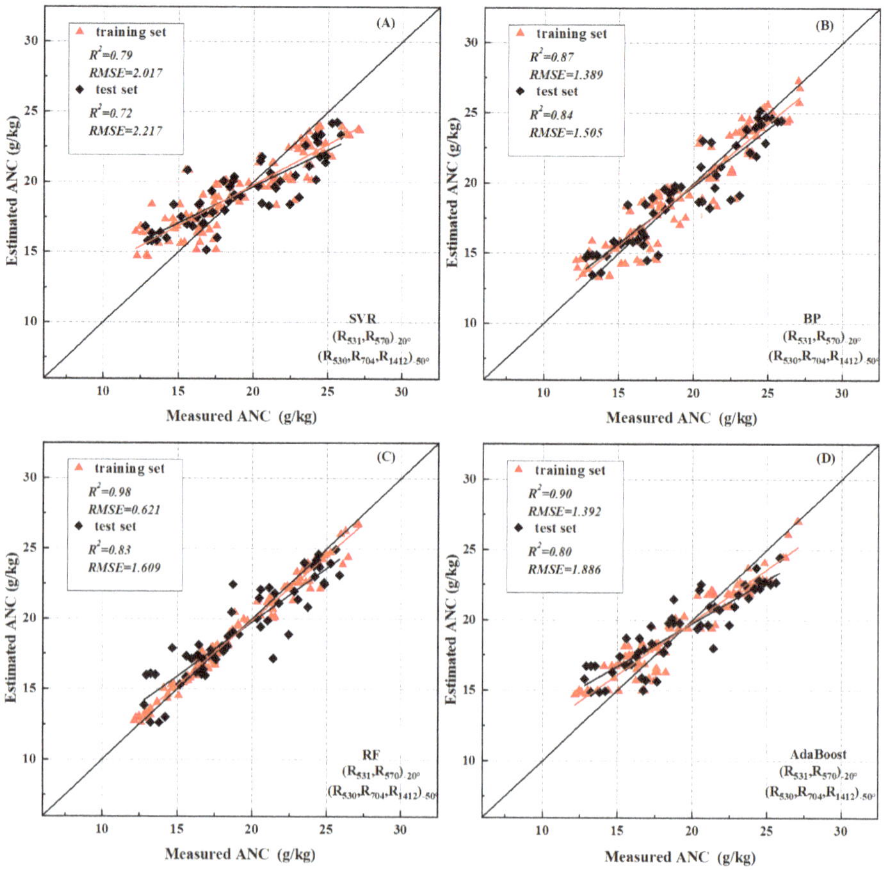

Figure 12. Machine learning modeling based on the spectral index AINI$_{-50°}$'s 530 nm, 704 nm, 1412 nm bands and PRI$_{-20°}$'s 531 nm, 570 nm bands (n = 180, training set = 126, validation set = 54): (**A**) SVR, (**B**) BP, (**C**) RF, (**D**) AdaBoost.

4. Discussion

4.1. Effect of VZA on Canopy Reflectivity

In this study, we studied the variation of spectral reflectance of cotton canopy under different VZAs and the correlation between the spectral index and cotton ANC. The results show that the spectral reflectance in the backscatter direction was greater than that in the forward-scatter direction, and the two spectral indices (AINI, PRI) screened out achieved the optimal nitrogen estimation effect in the backward observation. This is because, in the backscatter region, the spectrometer probe and the sun are on the same side, the observation field of view mainly contains the direct radiation of the sun, and the vegetation itself is brighter, so the observed observation reflectance is also larger. When the spectrometer probe and the sun are on the opposite side (that is, in the forward-scattering direction), the observation field of view will receive information about the shadow part of the canopy that is not irradiated by solar radiation, resulting in low reflectance [44]. When estimating the cotton nitrogen content, backward observations obtained better results than forward observations, possibly due to the fact that backward observations are stronger than forward [11,45].

In addition, the VZA affects the proportion of the soil background or other information captured in the observation field of view, resulting in a different canopy reflectivity in cotton, and some researchers have pointed out that the difference in the target components significantly affects crop canopy reflectance [46,47]. Compared with the visible band, the near-infrared band shows a bigger difference in reflectivity under different VZAs, which is also demonstrated by Figure 4; this is caused by spatial heterogeneity of spectral properties in the field of view [48]. The fact that pigments are strongly absorbed in the visible region and abundant in healthy vegetation leads to the fact that the reflectance spectrum of plants is generally low and less variable in the visible region relative to near-infrared wavelengths [49].

4.2. The Spectral Index Estimates the Difference in ANC

In this study, the indices AINI, PRI, and PRIC were strongly correlated with nitrogen accumulation, and the correlation coefficient reached an average of more than 0.8. The bands constituting the above spectral indices were distributed in the green band and the red edge area, which is because the green band is more sensitive to plant nitrogen status. Previous studies have shown that the degree of blue shift at the red edge of vegetation is significantly related to the physiological characteristics of the vegetation canopy [50]. Red edge (700–760 nm) is a transition region with rapid changes in leaf reflectivity caused by strong pigment absorption in the red spectrum and leaf scattering in the near-infrared spectrum, and it has been found that the red edge is sensitive to crop canopy nitrogen [23]. The previous research illustrated the reliability of spectral information in the red-edged region, and the results of this study confirm that view. The better indices (AINI, PRI, PRIC, MTCI, and mSR705) include the wavelength of green light or the red−edge region.

Under non-lowest point observation, more canopy structure information can be obtained in the detection field of view, especially for cotton as a sunflower crop. The spectral data obtained in the backscattering direction will obtain more physiological information on cotton leaves, so the estimation of nitrogen concentration is better than nadir observation in a multi-angle detection [51]. At the same time, factors such as crop canopy distribution and soil background will estimate the spectral index [52]. The larger the VZA, the larger the proportion of crop information within the sensor's field of view and the smaller the proportion of soil [10]. Therefore, AINI and PRIC have the strongest correlation with cotton ANC in larger VZAs. When making small VZA observations, the intensity and depth of light entering the crop canopy are relatively strong, the proportion of the scattering and reflection information captured increases, and the spectral index estimation ability will be improved, so the model accuracy is the highest when the index PRI is observed at $-20°$. Therefore, by selecting the appropriate spectral index, both the backward- and forward-scattering directions can obtain better estimation effects.

As PRI is an anisotropic spectral index, the canopy structure, soil background, and solar observation geometry all comprehensively affect its value [53]. The difference in nitrogen content estimated by the PRI in different VZAs is not directly driven by VZA but rather by changing the proportion of the contribution of the target components to canopy reflectance to produce indirect effects so that the PRI performance is relatively stable for different VZAs. The three-band index constructed in this study is also consistent and stable at all angles, which may be because the bands involve three relatively independent spectral regions (green light, the red edge region, and shortwave infrared), which reduces the interaction of information between bands. AINI is a spectral index that is constructed using band combination, which can enhance a certain characteristic or detail of vegetation so that the accuracy of the model is improved and its operation is relatively simple, making it more widely applicable in the monitoring of nitrogen accumulation. Although the study was conducted in the field, its estimated performance needs to be verified many times before it can be widely used. Therefore, in the next step, it is necessary to verify the different cultivation conditions of a variety of crops to prove the superior performance of multi-angle remote sensing based on the spectral index.

4.3. Future Applications and Limitations of Research

This study improves the retrieval accuracy of cotton canopy nitrogen to a certain extent and conducts multi-angle observations within a fixed time range to reduce the influence of the sun angle, effectively realizing accurate monitoring of cotton canopy nitrogen at different times of the day. Acquisition and application of multi-angle remote sensing data based on ground platforms can achieve more accurate results, but its low efficiency and limitation of measurement range limit its application in large-scale farmland [54]. UAV equipment has the advantages of high flexibility and low cost and can quickly and efficiently acquire data with higher spatial resolution [55–57]. For example, Lu et al. used the multi-angle images of UAV multi-spectral cameras, especially the multi-spectral images in the backsight direction, to help more accurately estimate the nitrogen concentration parameters of winter wheat, and the combination of multi-angle images and nadir view images also improved the estimation of nitrogen concentrations in winter wheat [48]. The rapid integration and development of various observation platforms provide data guarantees for multi-angle remote sensing. Compared with drones and satellite platforms, the VZA obtained by ground multi-angle observation equipment is more stable; the multi-angle remote sensing information of the ground, aviation, and space complement each other and can realize rapid and large-scale accurate monitoring of farmland information. As a result, the follow-up research results will be validated at the UAV scale, and large-scale accurate monitoring of cotton nitrogen can be achieved by combining the high maneuverability and flexibility of UAVs with the elimination of the influence of observation angles and sun angles.

Although the AINI-based cotton ANC estimation model has been established and has good estimation accuracy, it is limited by the low efficiency of ground remote sensing and the limitation of the measurement range, which limits its application in large-scale farmland. In addition, this study only focuses on the effect of VZA on the spectral index estimation of cotton nitrogen status and does not consider the underlying mechanisms of these influencing factors. This work only analyzed and validated AINI for cotton canopy, so additional quantitative field validation should be performed in the future to investigate the feasibility of using AINI for canopy nitrogen estimation for different crops and planting patterns to establish crop nitrogen estimation models common in different growing environments.

5. Conclusions

The timely and accurate estimation of canopy nitrogen levels is essential for crop growth monitoring and agricultural management. In this study, multi-angle remote sensing observations showed that nitrogen monitoring was sensitive to VZA and that off-nadir observation allows a more accurate estimate of cotton nitrogen content. We used the Relief−F algorithm to identify bands that are sensitive to nitrogen but not to VZA, and we created a nitrogen spectral index AINI = $(R_{530} - R_{704})/(R_{1412} + R_{704})$ suitable for different VZA to estimate cotton canopy nitrogen. We studied (i) the variation of the spectral reflectance of the cotton canopy under different VZA conditions, (ii) the ability of the existing spectral index to estimate nitrogen concentration under different VZAs, and (iii) the construction of a cotton canopy nitrogen monitoring model. The following conclusions can be drawn from this work:

(1) The spectral reflectance in the backscatter direction is greater than that in the forward scattering direction, and the constructed spectral index AINI is also better estimated by retroactive observation at -50° (Figures 4 and 7).

(2) The existing spectral indices selected in this study have obvious angular sensitivity to changes in the correlation between ANC, and the correlation coefficients in the zenith direction are smaller than those of off-nadir observations (Table 3).

(3) RF models combining the -50° AINI index and the -20° PRI index can better predict the change of ANC in cotton (test set $R^2 = 0.98$, RMSE = 0.590, validation set $R^2 = 0.85$, RMSE = 1.532) (Figure 9).

Author Contributions: Conceptualization, X.Z. and M.Y.; methodology, X.Z. and M.Y.; validation, X.Z., M.Y., and L.M.; formal analysis, X.C. and X.Z.; investigation, X.Z., and C.Y.; resources, Z.Z. and X.L.; data curation, S.Q. and X.Z.; writing—original draft preparation, X.Z. and L.W.; writing—review and editing, X.Z., M.Y., X.C., and Z.Z.; funding acquisition, Z.Z. and X.L. All authors have read and agreed to the published version of the manuscript.

Funding: The study was supported by the National Natural Science Foundation of China, China (Grant No. 42061058), the National Key R&D Program of China (Grant No. 2022YFD2002401), "Strong Youth" Scientific and Technological Innovation Backbone Talent Plan of Xinjiang Production and Construction Corps (Grant No. 2022CB002-01).

Data Availability Statement: Not applicable.

Conflicts of Interest: The authors declare that the research was conducted in the absence of any commercial or financial relationships that could be construed as a potential conflict of interest.

References

1. Zheng, J.; Song, X.; Yang, G.; Du, X.; Mei, X.; Yang, X. Remote sensing monitoring of rice and wheat canopy nitrogen: A review. *Remote Sens.* **2022**, *14*, 5712.
2. Song, L.; Wang, L.; Yang, Z.; He, L.; Feng, Z.; Duan, J.; Feng, W.; Guo, T. Comparison of algorithms for monitoring wheat powdery mildew using multi-angular remote sensing data. *Crop J.* **2022**, *10*, 1312–1322.
3. Bian, Z.; Roujean, J.L.; Fan, T.; Dong, Y.; Hu, T.; Cao, B.; Li, H.; Du, Y.; Xiao, Q.; Liu, Q. An angular normalization method for temperature vegetation dryness index (TVDI) in monitoring agricultural drought. *Remote Sens. Environ.* **2023**, *284*, 113330.
4. He, L.; Song, X.; Feng, W.; Guo, B.; Zhang, Y.; Wang, Y.; Wang, C.; Guo, T. Improved remote sensing of leaf nitrogen concentration in winter wheat using multi-angular hyperspectral data. *Remote Sens. Environ.* **2016**, *174*, 122–133.
5. Gao, F.; Jin, Y.; Schaaf, C.B.; Strahler, A.H. Bidirectional NDVI and atmospherically resistant BRDF inversion for vegetation canopy. *IEEE Trans. Geosci. Remote Sensing.* **2002**, *40*, 1269–1278.
6. Chen, J.M.; Liu, J.; Leblanc, S.G.; Lacaze, R.; Roujean, J. Multi-angular optical remote sensing for assessing vegetation structure and carbon absorption. *Remote Sens. Environ.* **2003**, *84*, 516–525.
7. Strahler, A.H.; Jupp, D.L. Modeling bidirectional reflectance of forests and woodlands using Boolean models and geometric optics. *Remote Sens. Environ.* **1990**, *34*, 153–166. [CrossRef]
8. Kennedy, B.E.; King, D.J.; Duffe, J. Retrieval of Arctic Vegetation Biophysical and Biochemical Properties from CHRIS/PROBA Multi-Angle Imagery Using Empirical and Physical Modelling. *Remote Sens.* **2021**, *13*, 1830. [CrossRef]
9. Chen, H.; Huang, W.; Li, W.; Niu, Z.; Zhang, L.; Xing, S. Estimation of LAI in winter wheat from multi-angular hyperspectral VNIR data: Effects of view angles and plant architecture. *Remote Sens.* **2018**, *10*, 1630. [CrossRef]
10. Stagakis, S.; Markos, N.; Sykioti, O.; Kyparissis, A. Monitoring canopy biophysical and biochemical parameters in ecosystem scale using satellite hyperspectral imagery: An application on a Phlomis fruticosa Mediterranean ecosystem using multiangular CHRIS/PROBA observations. *Remote Sens. Environ.* **2010**, *114*, 977–994.
11. Kong, W.; Huang, W.; Liu, J.; Chen, P.; Qin, Q.; Ye, H.; Peng, D.; Dong, Y.; Mortimer, A.H. Estimation of canopy carotenoid content of winter wheat using multi-angle hyperspectral data. *Adv. Space Res.* **2017**, *60*, 1988–2000.
12. Roosjen, P.P.; Brede, B.; Suomalainen, J.M.; Bartholomeus, H.M.; Kooistra, L.; Clevers, J.G. Improved estimation of leaf area index and leaf chlorophyll content of a potato crop using multi-angle spectral data-potential of unmanned aerial vehicle imagery. *Int. J. Appl. Earth Obs. Geoinf.* **2018**, *66*, 14–26. [CrossRef]
13. Li, W.; Sun, Z.; Lu, S.; Omasa, K. Estimation of the leaf chlorophyll content using multiangular spectral reflectance factor. *Plant Cell Environ.* **2019**, *42*, 3152–3165. [CrossRef]
14. Yang, Q.; Huang, W.; Zhao, J.; Dong, L.; Huang, L.; Zhang, D.; Liu, L.; Yang, G.; Song, X. Effect of Canopy Geometry on Estimation of Leaf Area Index in Winter Wheat Using Multi-angle Spectrum. *Int. J. Agric. Biol.* **2013**, *15*, 1187–1192.
15. Guo, B.; Zhu, Y.; Feng, W.; He, L.; Wu, Y.; Zhou, Y.; Ren, X.; Ma, Y. Remotely estimating aerial N uptake in winter wheat using red-edge area index from multi-angular hyperspectral data. *Front. Plant Sci.* **2018**, *9*, 675. [CrossRef]
16. Wang, L.; Liao, Q.; Xu, X.; Li, Z.; Zhu, H. Estimating the vertical distribution of chlorophyll in winter wheat based on multi-angle hyperspectral data. *Remote Sens. Lett.* **2020**, *11*, 1032–1041.
17. Jackson, R.D.; Teillet, P.M.; Slater, P.N.; Fedosejevs, G.; Jasinski, M.F.; Aase, J.K.; Moran, M.S. Bidirectional measurements of surface reflectance for view angle corrections of oblique imagery. *Remote Sens. Environ.* **1990**, *32*, 189–202.
18. Kimes, D.S.; Newcomb, W.W.; Tucker, C.J.; Zonneveld, I.S.; Van Wijngaarden, W.; De Leeuw, J.; Epema, G.F. Directional reflectance factor distributions for cover types of Northern Africa. *Remote Sens. Environ.* **1985**, *18*, 1–19. [CrossRef]
19. Ranjan, R.; Chopra, U.K.; Sahoo, R.N.; Singh, A.K.; Pradhan, S. Assessment of plant nitrogen stress in wheat (*Triticum aestivum* L.) through hyperspectral indices. *Int. J. Remote Sens.* **2012**, *33*, 6342–6360. [CrossRef]
20. Yao, H.; Zhang, Y.; Yi, X.; Zhang, X.; Fan, D.; Chow, W.S.; Zhang, W. Diaheliotropic leaf movement enhances leaf photosynthetic capacity and photosynthetic light and nitrogen use efficiency via optimising nitrogen partitioning among photosynthetic components in cotton (*Gossypium hirsutum* L.). *Plant Biol.* **2018**, *20*, 213–222.

21. Dumas, J. Procédés de l'analyse organique. *Ann. Chim. Phys.* **1831**, *47*, 198–205.
22. Yang, M.; Huang, C.; Kang, X.; Qin, S.; Ma, L.; Wang, J.; Zhou, X.; Lv, X.; Zhang, Z. Early Monitoring of Cotton Verticillium Wilt by Leaf Multiple "Symptom" Characteristics. *Remote Sens.* **2022**, *14*, 5241.
23. Li, F.; Miao, Y.; Feng, G.; Yuan, F.; Yue, S.; Gao, X.; Liu, Y.; Liu, B.; Ustin, S.L.; Chen, X. Improving estimation of summer maize nitrogen status with red edge-based spectral vegetation indices. *Field Crop. Res.* **2014**, *157*, 111–123.
24. Evain, S.; Flexas, J.; Moya, I. A new instrument for passive remote sensing: 2. Measurement of leaf and canopy reflectance changes at 531 nm and their relationship with photosynthesis and chlorophyll fluorescence. *Remote Sens. Environ.* **2004**, *91*, 175–185. [CrossRef]
25. Jordan, C.F. Derivation of leaf-area index from quality of light on the forest floor. *Ecology* **1969**, *50*, 663–666. [CrossRef]
26. Rouse, J.W.; Haas, R.H.; Schell, J.A.; Deering, D.W. Monitoring Vegetation Systems in the Great Plains with Erts. *NASA Spec. Publ.* **1974**, *351*, 309.
27. Huete, A.R. A soil-adjusted vegetation index (SAVI). *Remote Sens. Environ.* **1988**, *25*, 295–309. [CrossRef]
28. Peñuelas, J.; Filella, I.; Gamon, J.A. Assessment of photosynthetic radiation—Use efficiency with spectral reflectance. *New Phytol.* **1995**, *131*, 291–296.
29. Penuelas, J.; Baret, F.; Filella, I. Semi-empirical indices to assess carotenoids/chlorophyll a ratio from leaf spectral reflectance. *Photosynthetica* **1995**, *31*, 221–230.
30. Gitelson, A.A.; Kaufman, Y.J.; Merzlyak, M.N. Use of a green channel in remote sensing of global vegetation from EOS-MODIS. *Remote Sens. Environ.* **1996**, *58*, 289–298.
31. Rondeaux, G.; Steven, M.; Baret, F. Optimization of soil-adjusted vegetation indices. *Remote Sens. Environ.* **1996**, *55*, 95–107. [CrossRef]
32. Daughtry, C.S.; Walthall, C.L.; Kim, M.S.; De Colstoun, E.B.; McMurtrey Iii, J.E. Estimating corn leaf chlorophyll concentration from leaf and canopy reflectance. *Remote Sens. Environ.* **2000**, *74*, 229–239.
33. Schleicher, T.D.; Bausch, W.C.; Delgado, J.A.; Ayers, P.D. Evaluation and refinement of the nitrogen reflectance index (NRI) for site-specific fertilizer management. In Proceedings of the 2001 ASAE Annual Meeting: American Society of Agricultural and Biological Engineers, New Orleans, LA, USA, 23–27 June 1998; p. 1.
34. Haboudane, D.; Miller, J.R.; Tremblay, N.; Zarco-Tejada, P.J.; Dextraze, L. Integrated narrow-band vegetation indices for prediction of crop chlorophyll content for application to precision agriculture. *Remote Sens. Environ.* **2002**, *81*, 416–426. [CrossRef]
35. Marshak, A.; Knyazikhin, Y.; Davis, A.B.; Wiscombe, W.J.; Pilewskie, P. Cloud-vegetation interaction: Use of normalized difference cloud index for estimation of cloud optical thickness. *Geophys. Res. Lett.* **2000**, *27*, 1695–1698. [CrossRef]
36. Peñuelas, J.; Gamon, J.A.; Fredeen, A.L.; Merino, J.; Field, C.B. Reflectance indices associated with physiological changes in nitrogen-and water-limited sunflower leaves. *Remote Sens. Environ.* **1994**, *48*, 135–146. [CrossRef]
37. Gamon, J.A.; Penuelas, J.; Field, C.B. A narrow-waveband spectral index that tracks diurnal changes in photosynthetic efficiency. *Remote Sens. Environ.* **1992**, *41*, 35–44.
38. Feng, W.; Guo, B.; Wang, Z.; He, L.; Song, X.; Wang, Y.; Guo, T. Measuring leaf nitrogen concentration in winter wheat using double-peak spectral reflection remote sensing data. *Field Crop. Res.* **2014**, *159*, 43–52. [CrossRef]
39. Sims, D.A.; Gamon, J.A. Relationships between leaf pigment content and spectral reflectance across a wide range of species, leaf structures and developmental stages. *Remote Sens. Environ.* **2002**, *81*, 337–354.
40. Crippen, R.E. Calculating the vegetation index faster. *Remote Sens. Environ.* **1990**, *34*, 71–73.
41. Dash, J.; Curran, P.J. Evaluation of the MERIS terrestrial chlorophyll index (MTCI). *Adv. Space Res.* **2007**, *39*, 100–104. [CrossRef]
42. Barnes, J.D.; Balaguer, L.; Manrique, E.; Elvira, S.; Davison, A.W. A reappraisal of the use of DMSO for the extraction and determination of chlorophylls a and b in lichens and higher plants. *Environ. Exp. Bot.* **1992**, *32*, 85–100. [CrossRef]
43. Gitelson, A.A.; Viña, A.; Ciganda, V.; Rundquist, D.C.; Arkebauer, T.J. Remote estimation of canopy chlorophyll content in crops. *Geophys. Res. Lett.* **2005**, *32*. [CrossRef]
44. Kimes, D.S. Dynamics of directional reflectance factor distributions for vegetation canopies. *Appl. Optics.* **1983**, *22*, 1364–1372.
45. He, L.; Zhang, H.; Zhang, Y.; Song, X.; Feng, W.; Kang, G.; Wang, C.; Guo, T. Estimating canopy leaf nitrogen concentration in winter wheat based on multi-angular hyperspectral remote sensing. *Eur. J. Agron.* **2016**, *73*, 170–185. [CrossRef]
46. Colwell, J.E. Vegetation canopy reflectance. *Remote Sens. Environ.* **1974**, *3*, 175–183. [CrossRef]
47. Knyazikhin, Y.; Schull, M.A.; Stenberg, P.; Moettus, M.; Rautiainen, M.; Yang, Y.; Marshak, A.; Carmona, P.L.; Kaufmann, R.K.; Lewis, P. Hyperspectral remote sensing of foliar nitrogen content. *Proc. Natl. Acad. Sci. USA* **2012**, *110*, E185–E192. [CrossRef]
48. Lu, N.; Wang, W.; Zhang, Q.; Li, D.; Yao, X.; Tian, Y.; Zhu, Y.; Cao, W.; Baret, F.; Liu, S. Estimation of nitrogen nutrition status in winter wheat from unmanned aerial vehicle based multi-angular multispectral imagery. *Front. Plant Sci.* **2019**, *10*, 1601.
49. Asner, G.P. Biophysical and biochemical sources of variability in canopy reflectance. *Remote Sens. Environ.* **1998**, *64*, 234–253. [CrossRef]
50. Raper, T.B.; Varco, J.J. Canopy-scale wavelength and vegetative index sensitivities to cotton growth parameters and nitrogen status. *Precis. Agric.* **2015**, *16*, 62–76.
51. Schutt, J.B.; Kimes, D.S.; Newcomb, W.W. Effect of heliotropism on the bidirectional reflectance of irrigated cotton. *Remote Sens. Environ.* **1985**, *17*, 13–25. [CrossRef]
52. Verrelst, J.; Schaepman, M.E.; Koetz, B.; Kneubühler, M. Angular sensitivity analysis of vegetation indices derived from CHRIS/PROBA data. *Remote Sens. Environ.* **2008**, *112*, 2341–2353. [CrossRef]

53. Yang, P. Exploring the interrelated effects of soil background, canopy structure and sun-observer geometry on canopy photochemical reflectance index. *Remote Sens. Environ.* **2022**, *279*, 113133. [CrossRef]
54. Song, X.; Xu, D.; He, L.; Feng, W.; Wang, Y.; Wang, Z.; Coburn, C.A.; Guo, T. Using multi-angle hyperspectral data to monitor canopy leaf nitrogen content of wheat. *Precis. Agric.* **2016**, *17*, 721–736. [CrossRef]
55. Burkart, A.; Aasen, H.; Alonso, L.; Menz, G.; Bareth, G.; Rascher, U. Angular dependency of hyperspectral measurements over wheat characterized by a novel UAV based goniometer. *Remote Sens.* **2015**, *7*, 725–746.
56. Roosjen, P.P.; Suomalainen, J.M.; Bartholomeus, H.M.; Kooistra, L.; Clevers, J.G. Mapping reflectance anisotropy of a potato canopy using aerial images acquired with an unmanned aerial vehicle. *Remote Sens.* **2017**, *9*, 417.
57. Roosjen, P.P.; Suomalainen, J.M.; Bartholomeus, H.M.; Clevers, J.G. Hyperspectral reflectance anisotropy measurements using a pushbroom spectrometer on an unmanned aerial vehicle—Results for barley, winter wheat, and potato. *Remote Sens.* **2016**, *8*, 909. [CrossRef]

remote sensing

MDPI

Technical Note

Automated Workflow for High-Resolution 4D Vegetation Monitoring Using Stereo Vision

Martin Kobe [1,*], Melanie Elias [2], Ines Merbach [3], Martin Schädler [3,4], Jan Bumberger [1,4,5], Marion Pause [6] and Hannes Mollenhauer [1]

1 Department of Monitoring and Exploration Technologies, Helmholtz Centre for Environmental Research-UFZ, Permoserstraße 15, D-04318 Leipzig, Germany
2 Institute of Photogrammetry and Remote Sensing, Technische Universität Dresden, Helmholtzstraße 10, D-01062 Dresden, Germany
3 Department of Community Ecology, Helmholtz Centre for Environmental Research-UFZ, Theodor-Lieser-Straße 4, D-06120 Halle, Germany
4 German Centre for Integrative Biodiversity Research (iDiv) Halle-Jena-Leipzig, Puschstraße 4, D-04103 Halle-Leipzig, Germany
5 Research Data Management-RDM, Helmholtz Centre for Environmental Research-UFZ, Permoserstraße 15, D-04318 Leipzig, Germany
6 Institute for Geo-Information and Land Surveying, Anhalt University of Applied Sciences, Seminarplatz 2a, D-06846 Dessau, Germany
* Correspondence: martin.kobe@ufz.de

Abstract: Precision agriculture relies on understanding crop growth dynamics and plant responses to short-term changes in abiotic factors. In this technical note, we present and discuss a technical approach for cost-effective, non-invasive, time-lapse crop monitoring that automates the process of deriving further plant parameters, such as biomass, from 3D object information obtained via stereo images in the red, green, and blue (RGB) color space. The novelty of our approach lies in the automated workflow, which includes a reliable automated data pipeline for 3D point cloud reconstruction from dynamic scenes of RGB images with high spatio-temporal resolution. The setup is based on a permanent rigid and calibrated stereo camera installation and was tested over an entire growing season of winter barley at the Global Change Experimental Facility (GCEF) in Bad Lauchstädt, Germany. For this study, radiometrically aligned image pairs were captured several times per day from 3 November 2021 to 28 June 2022. We performed image preselection using a random forest (RF) classifier with a prediction accuracy of 94.2% to eliminate unsuitable, e.g., shadowed, images in advance and obtained 3D object information for 86 records of the time series using the 4D processing option of the Agisoft Metashape software package, achieving mean standard deviations (STDs) of 17.3–30.4 mm. Finally, we determined vegetation heights by calculating cloud-to-cloud (C2C) distances between a reference point cloud, computed at the beginning of the time-lapse observation, and the respective point clouds measured in succession with an absolute error of 24.9–35.6 mm in depth direction. The calculated growth rates derived from RGB stereo images match the corresponding reference measurements, demonstrating the adequacy of our method in monitoring geometric plant traits, such as vegetation heights and growth spurts during the stand development using automated workflows.

Keywords: stereo vision; image classification; 4D vegetation monitoring; non-invasive setup; precision agriculture

1. Introduction

The increasing demand for efficient vegetation monitoring and precise determination of crop traits under dynamic environmental conditions has driven remarkable progress in the field of precision agriculture. In particular, remote sensing-based technologies, spatially-explicit data analysis incorporating multiple data sources, and operational workflows have rapidly developed over the past few decades. These advancements have significantly enhanced our understanding and site-specific management of crop growth dynamics, optimization of resource utilization, and the adoption of sustainable agricultural practices. However, continued research and exploration are essential to fully release their potential to deal with processes related to drivers such as climate change [1]. Specifically, the dynamics of grassland and crop systems are complex due to the interaction between biotic (e.g., plant health, species type) and abiotic (e.g., soil moisture, soil temperature) system components, as well as the particular management regime. In this context, a key objective is the comprehensive monitoring of various plant traits including growth, vitality, stress, and biomass volume throughout the principal Biologische Bundesanstalt, Bundessortenamt, and Chemical Industry (BBCH) growth stages of mono- and dicotyledonous plants of an entire growing season [2], which provides information on crop response to changing environmental parameters or extreme climate conditions [3]. In turn, the BBCH classification of phenology plays a key role in the aspired standardization of remote sensing-based vegetation data products as it may link information between different scales of observation (i.e., ground truth vs. satellite scale).

Several cost-effective non-invasive monitoring strategies have been developed that are applicable to research areas encompassing plant phenotyping, agriculture, and crop modeling, e.g., [4,5]. Driven by remote sensing-based monitoring approaches (i.e., Unmanned Aerial Vehicle (UAV), airborne, or satellite), innovative ground truth methods are required that can translate BBCH parameters between scales. For that reason, imaging techniques utilizing digital photogrammetry, in combination with machine vision technologies, are promising as they enable the extraction of plant traits from camera images e.g., [6–8]. Numerous recent studies in precision agriculture are dedicated to the campaign-based assessment of geometric plant characteristics, including parameters such as growth height, biomass, leaf morphology, fruit shape, and yield estimation. Those parameters are most effectively captured by techniques that enable the extraction of spatial depth information about an object. Notable examples of such techniques are Light Detection and Ranging (LiDAR), e.g., [9,10], Structure-from-Motion (SfM), which is the three-dimensional reconstruction of structures using a series of two-dimensional RGB images captured from multiple viewpoints, e.g., [11–13], the combination of RGB cameras with depth sensors for the simultaneous capturing of color and depth information, e.g., [14,15], or the combination of several of the above-mentioned methods and carrier platforms, e.g., [16,17]. An approach that utilizes two RGB cameras installed in a stereo-capable orientation is referred to as binocular vision or stereoscopic vision, which closely resembles the depth perception of the human eye. Several studies have been conducted using this specific camera configuration, predominantly in field laboratories or pilot-scale experiments, such as isolated chambers or greenhouse tests, e.g., [18,19]. In this context, Dandrifosse et al. [20] discussed the challenges of the laboratory-to-field transition. Some studies that use stereo vision in precision agriculture focus on real-time data analysis, e.g., for camera installations on autonomous harvesters [21,22]. Within all of those applications, the determination of morphological plant features is typically conducted in a campaign-based manner, which is subject to limitations such as dependence on weather conditions and manpower availability. As a result, previously mentioned studies provide discrete snapshots of structural 3D information at specific time points.

To observe plant responses to short-term changes in abiotic factors and to understand the crop growth dynamics under climate change conditions, it is crucial to enhance the spatio-temporal resolution. This can be achieved through continuous monitoring over time and adjustments to the camera-to-object distance, on which the spatial resolution primarily depends [23]. For example, Tanaka et al. [24] attained a ground sampling distance (GSD) of 2 mm per pixel through ground-based image acquisition, while other researchers such as Zhang et al. [25], reported GSD values in the centimeter range per pixel for various flight altitudes of UAV imagery in the context of agricultural monitoring. Several studies have employed stereo vision-based approaches with rigidly installed camera configurations to monitor the morphological and geometric parameters over time [26–29]. However, current research shows limitations in terms of insufficient spatio-temporal resolution to effectively track dynamic changes in geometric plant traits, such as growth spurts, plant elasticity, or fructification. Additionally, an integrated fully-automated workflow encompassing all stages, ranging from data acquisition to 3D modeling, is missing. Such automated workflows have great potential for future remote sensing-based agricultural products but also for scientific experiments and analysis. With an interface to corresponding management apps, they provide conceivable modules for, e.g., Farm Management Information Systems.

The first objective of this study was to develop a contemporary approach for agricultural vegetation monitoring, such as canopy height and growth rate, by utilizing a permanently installed RGB stereo camera system. The system setup allows for continuous, weather-independent on-site monitoring of crop plants at a high spatio-temporal resolution. Time intervals for the acquisition of image pairs are user-defined, allowing for flexibility in capturing specific time points of interest. The stereo camera system was installed over a test field of winter barley and was tested under controlled conditions during the vegetation period from November 2021 to June 2022. We selected a sampling rate of up to twelve images per day in our study, enabling the precise observation of plant growth dynamics through 3D point cloud reconstruction and facilitating the accurate assessment of morphological plant responses to short-term changes in abiotic parameters. Our second objective was to efficiently and automatically derive primary plant traits from RGB image pairs at any given time. To achieve this, a robust and fully automated data pipeline was developed encompassing image acquisition, classification, and photogrammetric analysis. Additionally, we compared the calculated growth heights and growth rates with regularly conducted reference measurements throughout the main growing season to assess the capabilities and limitations of the system.

2. Experimental Setup

The installation of a high-resolution stereo camera system for 4D vegetation monitoring, i.e., canopy height and biomass response to changes in abiotic factors over time, requires a focus on a setup that ensures the comparability of the cameras in the system, the captured stereo images, and the computed 3D point clouds. To this end, we carefully address the following points in our workflow: (a) System calibration, i.e., respectively, determining the interior orientation and distortion parameters (IOP) and exterior orientation parameters (EOP) of both cameras; (b) Image acquisition, i.e., precise stereo image synchronization and the alignment of stereo image properties (point operations, e.g., histogram alignment) and (c) 3D point cloud generation, i.e., reasonable spatio-temporal resolution in terms of the variation to be expected and measured.

2.1. Field Site: GCEF Bad Lauchstädt

The stereo camera system is installed at the field site of the GCEF located in Bad Lauchstädt, Saxony-Anhalt, Germany (51°23′30″N, 11°52′49″E, see Figure 1). The research facility was designed to investigate the consequences of a future climate scenario for ecosystem functioning in different land-use types of farm- and grassland on several large field plots [30]. Furthermore, GCEF experimental plot data provide an excellent training database for remote sensing-based prediction models. For our study, we have chosen to monitor winter barley that is usually sown in autumn. As an essential cereal in EU agriculture, it is part of the characteristic crop rotation in the present and near-future [31]. Winter barley can develop deeper roots already during the winter months as soil moisture is usually sufficient, which increases its resistance to drought stress in the spring. This and a long growth period make it an ideal observation object to test our stereo setup under different extreme environmental and ambient light conditions.

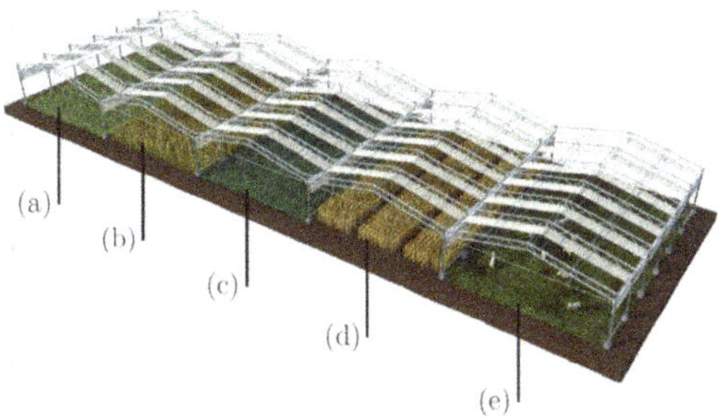

Figure 1. Overview of the field site and the crop cultivation. (**Left**): GCEF, its location in Germany, and the location of the camera setup on one of the experimental plots (red star). (**Right**): Scheme of simulated land-use forms at the facility-a: extensive grassland use (mowing), b: ecological agriculture, c: intensive grassland use, d: conventional production and e: extensive grassland use (grazing) (Illustration: Tricklabor, Marc Hermann, copyright by UFZ, 2014).

2.2. Stereo Camera Setup

Two parallel arranged RGB frame cameras of the type Mako G-319C (resolution: 2064×1544, frames per second: 37.6, pixel size: 3.45 µm; [32]) manufactured by Allied Vision were installed on the roof construction of a GCEF field plot with a camera-to-object distance of about 6.5 m (Figure 2). The cameras are fixed in a stereo-capable orientation with a baseline of about 20 cm in a waterproof hard case with protection standard IP66. Equipped with fixed lenses featuring a 16 mm focal length, they achieve a GSD of 1.45 mm per pixel. In view of the camera-to-object distance and the image overlap of 86.7%, this allows for the three-dimensional observation of a plot size of $2.16 \times 2.67\,m = 5.75\,m^2$ related to floor level without vegetation. Smaller parts of the crop plants, such as small leaves or ears of corn, can be dissolved in this arrangement. Cameras are controlled by a Pokini i2 field computer (cf. Section 2.3; [33]) and supplied by Power over Ethernet (PoE). To guarantee a stable performance, power outtakes are covered by an uninterruptible power supply (UPS).

2.3. Image Acquisition

Automatic image acquisition, see Figure 2, is part of the automated data pipeline. A key requirement for time-lapse stereo vision is the comparability of the images from the stereo cameras and of the calculated point clouds over time (cf. introduction of Section 2). For this purpose, both cameras were radiometrically adjusted for exposure and white balance using the application programming interface (API) Vimba Python v0.3.1 from Allied Vision Technologies GmbH [34] and synchronously triggered. A multi-threading approach controlled by Trigger over Ethernet (ToE) is used to simultaneously stream several frames per camera into a queue. Meanwhile, bright areas in the frames are detected, and the configuration parameters are iteratively adjusted to ensure that these areas are not saturated once the threshold for the number of frames is reached. Finally, the current frame is saved as an image in the uncompressed Tag Image File Format (TIFF). The image acquisition is controlled by a daily task scheduler. Here, variable astronomical (sunrise, noon, sunset) and constant time intervals of two hours (between 6 am and 10 pm) were chosen to ensure the comparability of point clouds both in high temporal resolution over the entire vegetation period and concerning changes in abiotic parameters.

2.4. Measurement of Reference Data

In order to evaluate the feasibility and quality of the introduced approach, manual canopy height measurements of winter barley were conducted regularly during the main growing season, starting with the principal growth stage 3 of BBCH-scale [2] in mid-

April until harvest at the end of June 2022. Plant height is determined by using an ultralight rectangular polystyrene plate, which is placed on the crop surface at a specified representative location within the overlapping area of stereo image pairs. The height is measured from the ground to the lower edge of the plate on all four sides and then averaged. Thus, the measurement method determines the mean height of a crop surface area and not the maximum height of single plants or awns. In general, canopy height is a reliable estimate of above-ground plant biomass across ecosystems and accordingly, therefore, indicates growth rates [35] and grain yield production [36]. In addition, the current developmental stage of the plants is categorized according to the general stages of the BBCH scale.

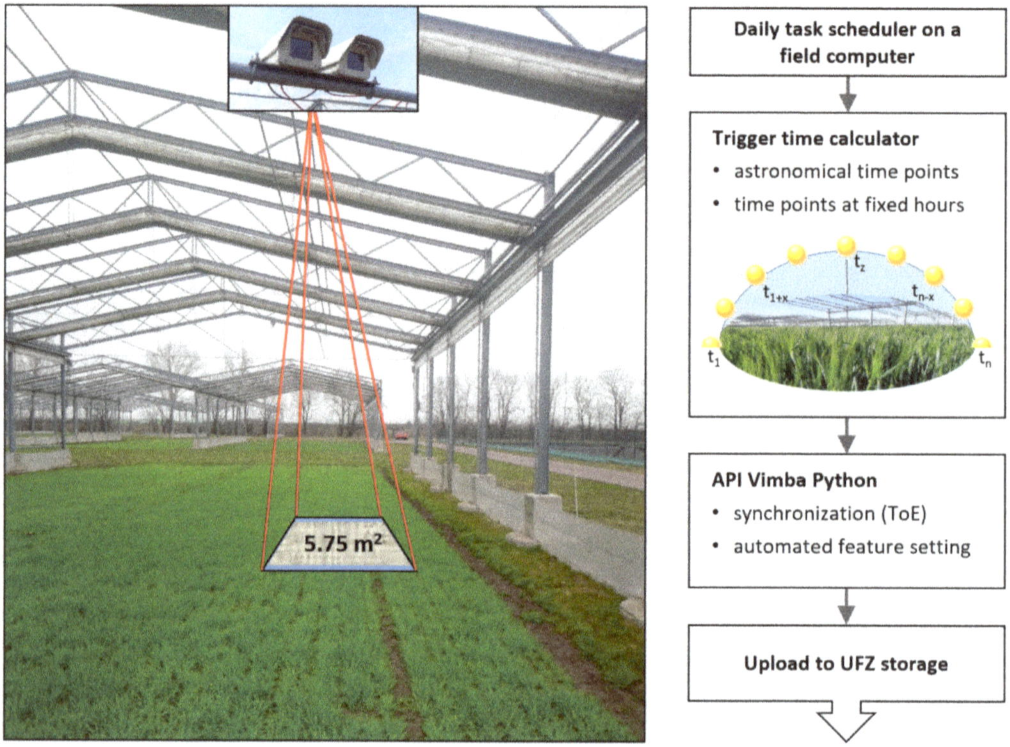

Figure 2. Left: Stereo camera system observing the corresponding vegetation plot of several square meters with an image overlap of 86.7% or 5.75 m^2. **Right**: Flowchart of the data acquisition workflow.

3. Data Processing

This chapter introduces the part of the data pipeline for generating 3D point clouds from time-lapse stereo images, which includes stereo image preselection, undistortion, and relative orientation, reconstruction of 3D point clouds, and C2C distance calculation to estimate growth heights (Figure 3). The workflow steps are realized using Python.

3.1. *Image Preselection*

The quality of the 3D reconstruction from time-lapse stereo images is dependent on their image quality (cf. Section 2). Thus, we removed images from the time-lapse series, which were impaired by over- or underexposure, blur, snowfall, snow cover, field operations, or a closed roof covering the field plot (Figure 3). To achieve this, image classification was performed by object recognition with machine learning using Scikit-learn [37]. An RF classifier [38] was chosen to separate the stereo images into two classes:

'usable' showing different growth stages of winter barley and 'not usable' which are the impaired images. The classifier was trained with 1280 images of the field plot distributed into both classes (usable: 57%, not usable: 43%) and the amount of test data was set to 400 images. Here, the best training parameter set was chosen by using grid search cross-validation over a standard parameter grid. The basis for training variables is formed by histograms of different color bands and color spaces. During classification, i.e., before class prediction, images are temporarily pre-processed by point operations using the libraries of OpenCV [39] and Scikit-image [40]. In detail, we applied histogram matching to all image pairs using a representative reference image and contrast adjustment. If an image is classified as not usable, all images of a certain time stamp are discarded. All usable images are subjected to further processing.

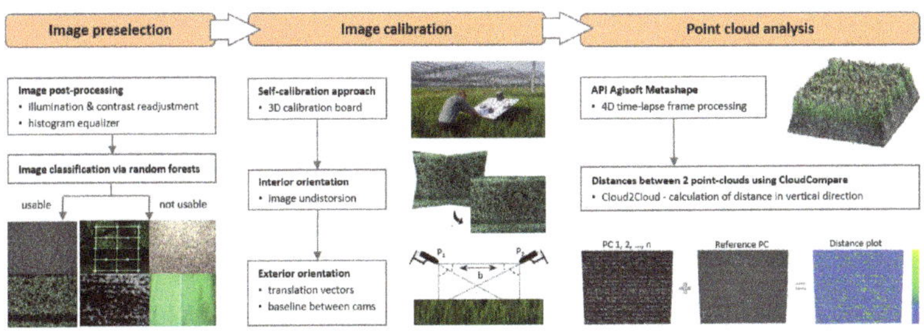

Figure 3. Flowchart of theautomated workflow for stereo image processing. (**Left**): Image preselection via RF classifier into the two classes 'usable' and 'not usable'. (**Mid**): Camera self-calibration to obtain IOP for image undistortion and the relative orientation with a known baseline between both cameras. (**Right**): 3D point cloud generation from time-lapse images and change detection by C2C distance measurement.

3.2. Camera Calibration

Deriving 3D information, i.e., canopy heights, from stereo images requires knowledge of the stereo geometry of both images, which implies the relative orientation between both images and the IOP of each image. Furthermore, a scale is required to transfer calculated 3D data from a model coordinate system into a metrically-scaled local coordinate system. Both cameras implemented in our stereo camera system use central perspective and could be described by Brown's standard camera and lens model [41]. The IOP of both cameras was simultaneously determined via camera self-calibration, implemented in *AICON 3D Studio* v12.00.10 [42]), using a 3D calibration test field that has been captured with synchronized images (see Figure 3; image measurement accuracy, given by $\hat{s}_0$, amounted to 0.56 µm). Besides the IOP of both cameras, we received the EOP for each image pair that was used in the calibration process. The pairwise determined EOP, more precisely, the translation vectors, were used to establish the baseline between both cameras, which was used to scale the 3D data in the subsequent processing. In total, translation vectors were available for 86 image pairs, resulting in a mean baseline of 198.41 mm (±11.47 mm).

The images, which have been assessed as suitable in the previous classification for further processing, were undistorted using the determined IOP via an in-house undistortion tool because the software used for relative image orientation and stereo reconstruction does not support the lens distortion model of Brown [41].

3.3. Time-Lapse Stereo Reconstruction

Calculating the relative orientation of each undistorted stereo pair of the time-lapse sequence in a shared model coordinate system was conducted in Agisoft Metashape v1.7.1 using its "Dynamic Scene (4D)" option [43]. In order to scale the 3D data, i.e., to transfer the relatively determined EOP of the stereo images into a metric coordinate system, we used the calculated baseline as a "scale bar" in Metashape (length: 198.41 mm, accuracy: 11 mm). This transforms the EOP of both cameras, which until now have only been available in an arbitrary model coordinate system, into a metric local coordinate system. When using the "Dynamic Scene (4D)" option, the local coordinate system and the EOP are determined only once for the first image pair of the time-lapse stereo sequence and applied to all subsequent stereo images that have been captured, respectively, per time stamp. The stereo camera system is assumed to be statically mounted and rigid with a stable baseline during the entire observation period. The calculation of the camera position and orientation parameters, i.e., the position of the camera's projection center and the rotation of the camera coordinate system in the object coordinate system, is conducted using the "Align Photos" option that calculates, beside the camera position and orientation parameters, a sparse 3D point cloud from homologous image points via spatial intersection. We performed bundle block adjustment ("Optimize") to, on the one hand, optimize the determined EOP and on the other hand, to calculate statistics, i.e., the 3D STD for each 3D point of the sparse cloud, whose amount is hereinafter referred to as "precision maps". Details on those precision estimates are given in James et al. [44,45].

Once the image configuration was established, we used Metashape's dense image-matching functionality to calculate a dense 3D point cloud for each time stamp. In the following, we used the reconstructed dense clouds together with the precision estimates, calculated for each time stamp and extrapolated to the dense clouds, to derive evidence about the dynamics of plant traits over time. The precision estimates allow for the estimation of the significance of any detected changes with respect to the local accuracies of the computed 3D point clouds.

Finally, to obtain depth information over time, absolute C2C distances were calculated for the entire sequence of reconstructed 3D point clouds related to a reference point cloud, in our case the date of the first plant emergence on 3 November 2021. For distance determination, the nearest neighbor distance based on a kind of Hausdorff distance algorithm, was used that is implemented in the open source software CloudCompare v.2.13 [46,47]. Furthermore, it should be noted that the error calculation performed in addition to the C2C distances calculation is based on Gaussian error propagation.

4. Results

The stereo camera system has reliably captured RGB images of a winter barley field several times a day from 3 November 2021, to 28 June 2022, and provided the database to quantify the canopy height of the winter barley test plots. In total eight to twelve stereo image pairs were captured per day, 4790 images in sum. To investigate the setup capabilities over the whole growth period we have analyzed one image pair per three days in the winter time and one image pair per two days from the end of March 2022 resulting in 86 image pairs. To ensure comparability due to ambient light conditions, we have chosen to analyze the first image pair of each day.

4.1. Image Classification Using Machine Learning

The classification of 400 test images into the two classes 'usable' and 'not usable' resulted in an accuracy score of 0.9575 for the optimal parameter configuration. The resulting 2×2 error matrix A provides insights into prediction outcomes. In the 'usable' class, which encompasses 229 images, $A_1 = [226,3]$ denotes the accurate classification of 226 usable pictures and three misclassifications. For the 'not-usable' class, comprising 171 images, $A_2 = [14,157]$ reveals 14 misclassifications and the correct classification of 157 images. The class report for 'usable' shows a precision of 0.94 and a recall of 0.99. The 'not-usable' class yielded a precision of 0.98 and a recall of 0.92, both determined from the test run. However, during the preselection of the plot image data, about 94.2% (89.6–99.8% per month) of all captured images were correctly classified. Images with impaired effects, cf. Section 3.1, were reliably removed with a prediction accuracy of 94.1%. On the other hand, several potentially usable images were falsely classified as not usable, 5.7% in sum and were, therefore, not considered further. These results fit a mean accuracy score for the classifiers' prediction of test data of 0.9425 ± 0.0275 obtained from k-fold cross-validation with 10 folds.

4.2. 3D Point Clouds: Reconstruction, Evaluation, Distances

The 3D stereo reconstruction of 86 sparse clouds was conducted within a precision of 11.4–80.6 mm in the depth direction, which, in mathematical notation, represents σ_z and is stored in precision maps (cp. Section 3.3). The calculation of the 98th percentile cut very few outliers and reduced this range to an interval of 23.1–64.5 mm. Arithmetic means of the STDs values were found to be in the range of 17.3–30.4 mm. The medians of the STDs values fell within the range of 16.9–26.9 mm.

Figure 4a displays exemplary results of the 3D stereo reconstruction, the accompanied interpolated precision maps, and the C2C distance calculation at three points in time of our measurement series. Since the stereo camera system is mounted at a slight angle to the perpendicular, the graphics show a trapezoidal shape from the top to the bottom of a single image, whose extent decreases with plant growth over time due to the fixed field of view of our stereo cameras. Additionally, we observed a decrease in point cloud density with increasing crop growth (Figure 4a; 1st column). At the same time, the point cloud precision decreased with the point cloud density (Figure 4a; second column). This effect can also be observed in Table 1(b). The intervals for STDs reveal a trend indicating an anti-correlation between the point cloud density and the maximum STD values. For example, we observed the range of STDs in the depth direction and the accompanied anti-correlated point cloud density to be 16.7–24.8 mm/5.3 M points, 19.0–40.8 mm/4.2 M points and 12.7–54.8 mm/2.9 M points with the increasing time steps in Figure 4a (see also Table 1; dates are marked with *). For these dates, the calculation of the 98th percentile reveals maximum values of 22.6 mm, 34.0 mm, 33.8 mm, respectively, and therefore, cuts the few outliers shown as dark-red dots in the precision maps. The mean/median STDs range from 19.6 mm/19.4 mm to 28.9 mm/28.8 mm. C2C distances were calculated concerning the reference date, 3 November 2021. The results map the crop surface (Figure 4a; 3rd column) and, thus, represent the current maximum vegetation height. For visualization, gaps within the calculated C2C distance maps were interpolated. At later observation times, for example, on 28 May 2022, significant height variations become evident. The distinct blue line, indicating near-zero heights, can be correlated with the track of a fertilizer vehicle (as also visible in Figure 2).

Table 1. (a) Results from C2C distance calculation for representative dates over a whole growing season and for the central cell of a 3 × 3 grid in Figure 4a. Registered reference date (3 November 2021), dates of plant height reference measurements (Figure 4b, marked with a red star), dates shown in Figure 4a (marked with * in the date column), and the harvest day (28 June 2022). Columns—h_{calc}: 99.9th percentile of height distribution; h_{ref}—hand measurement; h_{mean}/h_{median}—mean/median area height; err_{abs}—Gaussian absolute error. (b) Interpolated STD intervals for the entire observed area and accompanied point cloud density.

(a) Date	h_{calc} [cm]	h_{ref} [cm]	h_{mean} [cm]	h_{median} [cm]	err_{abs} [cm]	(b) σ_z	No. Points
2021-11-03	0.00	-	0.00	0.00	-	1.62-2.38	4.1M
2021-11-11 *	3.51	-	0.60	0.44	2.78	1.67–2.48	5.3M
2022-04-22	22.05	22	13.56	13.90	2.89	1.83–3.00	6.4M
2022-04-26 *	25.57	-	17.32	17.51	3.48	1.90–4.08	4.7M
2022-04-27	27.69	26	20.72	21.13	3.30	1.72–4.69	4.2M
2022-05-03	44.27	43	31.64	32.08	3.55	1.53–6.81	3.1M
2022-05-11	67.47	64	49.67	50.52	3.29	1.26–7.29	3.6M
2022-05-18	83.43	84	62.84	63.56	3.33	1.30–6.42	3.2M
2022-05-26	92.65	90	70.04	71.47	3.30	1.29–5.95	2.6M
2022-05-28 *	94.18	-	73.35	74.72	3.24	1.27–5.48	2.9M
2022-06-01	92.07	92	73.73	74.99	3.26	1.32–6.44	2.6M
2022-06-15	86.75	87	74.43	75.55	2.82	1.30–5.67	3.5M
2022-06-23	84.36	86	72.57	73.78	3.03	1.34–5.80	3.6M
2022-06-28	85.61	82	73.06	73.63	2.88	1.46–6.25	3.9M
2022-06-28	34.78	-	21.90	22.11	2.69	1.63–3.65	6.1M

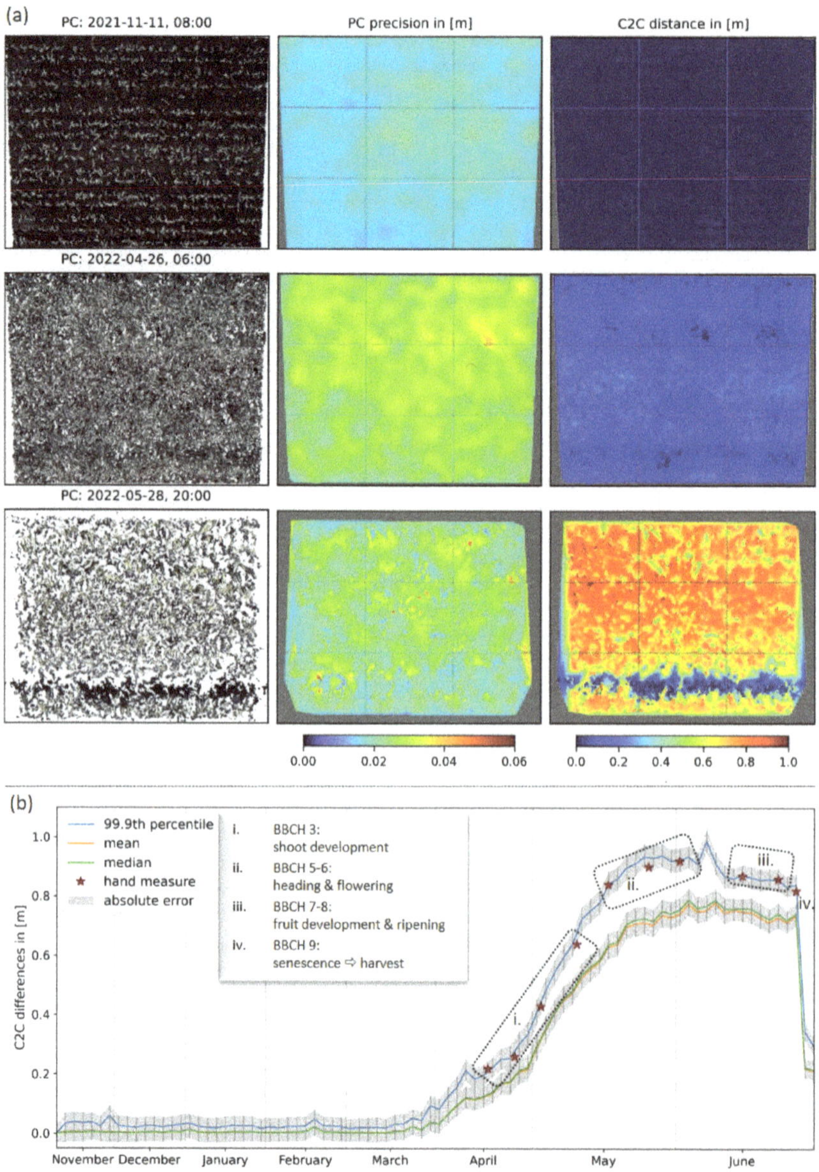

Figure 4. Results of the data processing pipeline. (**a**) First column-reconstructed 3D point clouds from top view, second column-calculated and rasterized STDs of the point clouds (called precision maps), third column-distance estimates related to the reference date 3 November 2021. (**b**) Mean, median and percentile values of C2C distances in the mid-cell of a 3 × 3 grid with respect to the reference point cloud and compared to our plant height reference measures.

Due to interpolation artifacts at the edges of the plots resulting from the C2C distance calculation steps and human-made impacts, such as vehicle tracks or footpaths, further analysis was limited to an undisturbed area, specifically the central cell of the 3 × 3 grid drawn on the images in Figure 4a. Based on this, a seasonal time-series of distance calculations is displayed in Figure 4b, and furthermore, related values for representative dates are written in Table 1(a). The resulting curves exhibit similar slopes and are enclosed by a gray ribbon representing the absolute error calculated using Gaussian error propagation. The curves of the mean (orange) and median (green) height values are almost congruent and only start to diverge with increasing plant height, which is also evident from Table 1(a). A comparison of average values for maximum growth heights (blue curve) with manual height measurements (red stars) is conducted by calculation of a 99.9th percentile for the observed rectangle. These average values take into account the temporal flattening of the surface due to the hand measurement method used (cf. Section 2.4). Both the determination of maximum height and growth dynamics according to principal BBCH stages are consistent for hand and camera measurements within error intervals (Table 1(a)). The absolute error is slightly correlated with vegetation height and ranges between 24.9 mm and 35.6 mm over the entire time series. Finally, all of the displayed curves collapsed to the swath height on 28 June 2022, due to the harvest of the field plot on this date. The observations and hypotheses described in this section are supported by the values in the last two rows of Table 1, i.e., median/mean converge, error values drop, and point cloud density increases with an abrupt decrease in vegetation height.

5. Discussion

The approach presented combines continuous vegetation monitoring using stereo-vision photogrammetry for high spatio-temporal vegetation parameter monitoring. The experiment shows proof of principle for the retrieval of canopy height within an autonomous ground truth solution. The presented automated data pipeline includes the acquisition, classification, and photogrammetric analysis of RGB image data, and thus, the automatic derivation of geometric plant traits from the 3D reconstruction of stereo image pairs. As demonstrated in this study, the sampling rate of about eight to twelve image pairs per day over a whole growing season enables the possibility to reliably and closely determine heights or growth rates, which allows for the investigation of plant response to short-term changes in abiotic environmental conditions related to plant geometry and growth.

However, long-term observation in a non-laboratory environment is a technical challenge [28], especially for a permanently installed system. A range of factors can interfere with data acquisition and affect the quality of stereo image pairs or, in the worst case, interrupt the monitoring. First, power outages due to, e.g., construction work at the field site or unexpected problems in the electricity supply caused recurring gaps in our time-series and later resulted in the installation of a UPS. Second, the quality of captured images can be affected by varying ambient light conditions during the camera configuration (cf. Section 2.3). Fast light–shadow changes due to clouds, sunlight reflection on the leaves, and also minor snow patches can lead to the wrong adjustment of white balance and exposure, resulting in overexposed images. Third, we also captured images showing snow cover or a closed construction roof. Thus, the pre-classification of image pairs was required before applying further 4D processing steps.

In this study, we used a simple supervised RF classifier to remove unsuitable stereo-image pairs from the data pipeline. The selection of 4790 stereo images into usable or not usable data using histograms succeeded in a satisfactory 94.2%. According to Millard and Richardson [48] RF is generally appropriate for RGB image classification, but better results could be achieved by adjusting the amount and selection of training data as well as strictly equalizing the training images within the number of groups. Additionally, a comprehensive test using cross-validation and grid search across a range of specific input variables can enhance accuracy by identifying the optimal variable combination for training the model. The application of further classifiers could also increase the prediction accuracy [49]. Note, for more complex classification approaches in precision agriculture, e.g., phenotyping, detecting plant diseases, observing BBCH stages, counting fruit bodies, or similar classifiers, e.g., [50,51] or a deep learning approach [52] could be more appropriate. Certainly, with regard to the extent of the applicability to various plant types and observation sites, the exploration of unsupervised learning algorithms becomes particularly relevant. In cases of generating new training datasets for distinct vegetation types with annotations, unsupervised image classifiers demonstrate clear advantages over their supervised counterparts in terms of data curation effort and processing time.

The 3D point cloud reconstruction provides reliable results. The theoretically achievable object point accuracy can be estimated separately for position s_{xy} and depth s_z by applying the error propagation law when assuming the stereo normal case (details are given in [53], p. 35), which amounts to $s_{xy} \approx 1$ mm and $s_z \approx 23$ mm concerning our setup. Note, that theoretical accuracy is a limiting factor for the observation of geometric parameters, and therefore, must be included in the considerations of an appropriate setup. In our study, the determined STDs of the reconstructed 3D points range in the same order of magnitude (Metashape: 11.4–80.6 mm; 98th percentile: 11.4–64.5 mm), as is the range of the STDs mean and median values of 17.3–30.4 mm and 16.9–26.9 mm, respectively, and the range of the absolute error of 24.9–35.6 mm obtained by C2C calculation. Image measurement and matching of homologous points in the stereo image pair are significant factors impacting the accuracy of the object points to be reconstructed. With increasing vegetation height, the detection of homologous points becomes more and more difficult due to varying perspectives and the probability of mismatches increases, e.g., both images capture different sides of upright leaves, awns, and fruits. Any gaps in the point clouds are due to superimposed vegetation causing mutual occlusions (Figure 4a). Furthermore, Table 1(b) demonstrates a clear trend of an inverse relationship between point cloud density and the STDs achieved. This is primarily a result of the increased presence of outliers, which have a more pronounced impact on the mean than on the median, leading to an increasing divergence between the mean and median height curves (cp. Figure 4b and Table 1(a)). Any discontinuities in the marginal areas of the plots shown in Figure 4a result from interpolation errors due to a greatly reduced point density in the marginal area covered by high vegetation. Consequently, the elevation values presented at the margins of the observed study area should be viewed with caution. Anyway, the accuracy of 3D point cloud reconstruction as well as the point cloud density can be increased by using additional cameras within the setup, as stereo image matching would detect more homologous points due to a higher number of ray intersections, e.g., to better deal with occlusions. However, a reasonable cost-benefit calculation in terms of, e.g., the number of cameras, available mounting stations, etc., is necessary for a field application of our approach on a farm.

A critical aspect of our approach is the geometric stability of the camera setup. Currently, we assume that both the IOP and EOP of both cameras remain stable over the entire observation period. The camera setup was designed for outdoor use, installed in robust, waterproof housings, and firmly mounted to the steel structure above the plot. Elias et al. [54], however, demonstrated that based on low-cost cameras the accumulation of waste heat, which is to be expected as a result of the housing construction, likely has an impact on the physical integrity of the camera. Furthermore, they show that the temporal stability of the calibration parameters is influenced by environmental factors, e.g., sunlight and cold. In particular, changes in the principal point and principal distance are to be expected, which in turn, are directly correlated with the depth measurement. Consequently, it is recommended that the calibration, i.e., the IOP, of both cameras is inspected regularly and updated if required. The same applies to the EOP of both cameras, respectively, and their relative orientation. Even if the installation is most stable, weather impacts on the temporal stability of the position and orientation of the involved cameras cannot be excluded. Accordingly, the EOP should likewise regularly be verified and, if necessary, updated. For both, on-the-job calibration using a sufficient number of ground control points in the field of view should be considered.

The data pipeline for plant monitoring with a stereo camera system can be improved concerning the aspects previously discussed. Transferability to other practical agricultural applications is conceivable since the pipeline is automated, starting with the high-resolution data acquisition. As the data analysis consists of modules, it can be supplemented by further methods of photogrammetric data analysis or computer vision. In summary, this is a promising application for service companies in precision farming and a promising tool for fundamental research on vegetation dynamics under global change.

6. Conclusions and Outlook

We presented a robust, cost-effective, non-invasive system for potential long-term crop monitoring and associated automated analysis of geometric plant traits for precise agricultural applications, such as biomass, canopy height, or Leaf Area Index (LAI). The high spatio-temporal resolution allows for the correlation of stereo vision-based 3D depth information to abiotic parameters in terms of, e.g., growth spurts, plant elasticity, or fructification. A unique feature compared to the current use of drones is the potential of weather-independent continuous monitoring with a suitable, automated, and expendable processing pipeline. In principle, the workflow is transferable to drone applications in precision agriculture.

One point to note about the overall workflow package, however, is that the camera calibration procedure is not fully automated, i.e., it is advisable to calibrate the system regularly to control the stability of the IOP. A critical point of the data pipeline concerns the compilation of an appropriate RF training data set for each specific installation site. In this state, an agronomic service is still required.

Considering the workflow as a sequential arrangement, it is conceivable to augment the data analysis with supplementary methodologies, such as detecting geometrical objects using machine learning, once the 3D point clouds have been reconstructed. Perpendicular porosity of the vertical foliage walls, plant geometry under changing sunlight or wind conditions, or observation of BBCH stages correlated to climatic events are influencing environmental effects, which should be the subject of future observations in order to improve the workflows' validity of results. For example, our study will be extended to another non-greenhouse field plot at the GCEF for evaluation reasons and to examine crop growth with respect to abiotic parameters by comparing a manipulated and a non-manipulated plot. Furthermore, the implementation of the presented or similar workflows may be conducted by using sophisticated open-source software like COLMAP v3.9.1 [55] in the future.

Further potential for use cases in agriculture lies in the processing of the color information of the recorded images. These data can be used to determine the optimal timing for the harvest of crops from images, e.g., utilizing machine learning for detecting flowering [56]. In situ stereo-vision camera data may provide ground truth information for UAV or satellite-based color mapping for this purpose. Additionally, the detection of diseases, deficiencies, and stress symptoms in plants is enabled by the color information. This can be conducted, among other things, using spectral vegetation indices. In the setup described here with RGB images, e.g., the application of the Visible Atmospherically Resistant Index may be appropriate, which is designed to estimate vegetation fraction in the visible portion of the spectrum [57]. Using color information to differentiate between weeds and crops enables the precise application of herbicides for weed control while at the same time protecting the crops. Therefore, several weed detection methods based on computer vision [58] involve color information to improve crop productivity. Furthermore, stereo vision-based geometric plant data could be extended by further remote sensing-based observations, e.g., of the near-infrared (NIR), short-wave infrared (SWIR), and thermal infrared (TIR) spectral bands. Especially, the combined analysis of plant geometric data and thermal emissivity may support research and parameter retrieval for evapotranspiration and plant health scenarios under changing environmental conditions [59,60].

In conclusion, there is potential for further investigation regarding the camera setup and the data pipeline. Higher accuracy and density of the reconstructed 3D point clouds could be achieved by using multi-image techniques, as a larger number of cameras can capture the object with multiple convergent images to reduce stereo reconstruction ambiguities and occlusions, e.g., [61]. Here, RGB and thermal oblique camera solutions [62] provide innovative observations and may be coupled to the 3D point cloud reconstruction. Experiments using UAV-based data acquisition at various spatial scales also provide a cost-efficient method to study scaling effects in point cloud reconstruction quality. However, one significant added value of the described actual setup lies in the utilization of established, passive, non-invasive measurement techniques, resulting in minimal costs and substantial gains, even if it entails accepting certain trade-offs, e.g., decreasing accuracy measures or point cloud density with increasing plant height. Building upon the presented data pipeline and included processes, the potential for enhancing output quality and expanding applicability to diverse vegetation types and observation sites is evident through the incorporation of additional methods in data curation, analysis, and error estimation.

Author Contributions: Conceptualization, J.B. and H.M.; methodology, J.B. and H.M.; setup, H.M. and M.K.; data pipeline & software & validation, M.K. and M.E.; reference measurement, I.M.; site management, M.S.; writing—original draft preparation, M.K., M.E., H.M. and M.P.; visualization, M.K.; supervision, H.M.; project administration, H.M.; funding acquisition, H.M. All authors have read and agreed to the published version of the manuscript.

Funding: This research was funded by the Federal Ministry of Food and Agriculture, grant number 28DE102B18.

Data Availability Statement: The data presented in this study are available upon request from the corresponding author. The data are not publicly available due to personal data protection laws for imaging data.

Acknowledgments: This study is part of the EXPRESS project which addresses the above key issues and supports farmers with the development of modern monitoring strategies in the selection of suitable crops, their cultivation and maintenance. The GCEF is funded by the Federal Ministry of Education and Research, the State Ministry for Science and Economy of Saxony-Anhalt and the State Ministry for Higher Education, Research, and the Arts of Saxony. Additional thanks to Konrad Kirsch and Ines Merbach for their excellent fieldwork and support. Furthermore, we gratefully thank Frank Liebold for providing a tool for image undistortion using Brown's camera and lens model.

Conflicts of Interest: The authors declare that they have no known competing financial interests or personal relationships that could have appeared to influence the work reported in this paper.

References

1. Mulla, D.J. Twenty five years of remote sensing in precision agriculture: Key advances and remaining knowledge gaps. *Biosyst. Eng.* **2013**, *114*, 358–371. [CrossRef]
2. Meier, U. *Growth Stages of Mono- and Dicotyledonous Plants: BBCH Monograph*; Open Agrar Repositorium: Quedlinburg, Germany, 2018; p. 204. [CrossRef]
3. Morison, J.I.; Morecroft, M.D. *Plant Growth and Climate Change*; John Wiley & Sons: Hoboken, NJ, USA, 2008.
4. Vázquez-Arellano, M.; Griepentrog, H.W.; Reiser, D.; Paraforos, D.S. 3-D imaging systems for agricultural applications—A review. *Sensors* **2016**, *16*, 618. [CrossRef]
5. Li, L.; Zhang, Q.; Huang, D. A review of imaging techniques for plant phenotyping. *Sensors* **2014**, *14*, 20078–20111. [CrossRef] [PubMed]
6. Wakchaure, M.; Patle, B.; Mahindrakar, A. Application of AI Techniques and Robotics in Agriculture: A Review. *Artif. Intell. Life Sci.* **2023**, *3* , 100057. [CrossRef]
7. Kolhar, S.; Jagtap, J. Plant trait estimation and classification studies in plant phenotyping using machine vision–A review. *Inf. Process. Agric.* **2021**, *10*, 114–135. [CrossRef]
8. Li, Z.; Guo, R.; Li, M.; Chen, Y.; Li, G. A review of computer vision technologies for plant phenotyping. *Comput. Electron. Agric.* **2020**, *176*, 105672. [CrossRef]
9. Blanquart, J.E.; Sirignano, E.; Lenaerts, B.; Saeys, W. Online crop height and density estimation in grain fields using LiDAR. *Biosyst. Eng.* **2020**, *198*, 1–14. [CrossRef]
10. Schirrmann, M.; Hamdorf, A.; Garz, A.; Ustyuzhanin, A.; Dammer, K.H. Estimating wheat biomass by combining image clustering with crop height. *Comput. Electron. Agric.* **2016**, *121*, 374–384. [CrossRef]
11. Ji, Y.; Chen, Z.; Cheng, Q.; Liu, R.; Li, M.; Yan, X.; Li, G.; Wang, D.; Fu, L.; Ma, Y.; et al. Estimation of plant height and yield based on UAV imagery in faba bean (Vicia faba L.). *Plant Methods* **2022**, *18*, 1–13. [CrossRef]
12. Volpato, L.; Pinto, F.; González-Pérez, L.; Thompson, I.G.; Borém, A.; Reynolds, M.; Gérard, B.; Molero, G.; Rodrigues, F.A., Jr. High throughput field phenotyping for plant height using UAV-based RGB imagery in wheat breeding lines: Feasibility and validation. *Front. Plant Sci.* **2021**, *12*, 591587. [CrossRef]

13. Kröhnert, M.; Anderson, R.; Bumberger, J.; Dietrich, P.; Harpole, W.S.; Maas, H.G. Watching grass grow-a pilot study on the suitability of photogrammetric techniques for quantifying change in aboveground biomass in grassland experiments. *ISPRS Int. Arch. Photogramm. Remote Sens. Spat. Inf. Sci* **2018**, *42*, 539–542. [CrossRef]
14. Rueda-Ayala, V.P.; Peña, J.M.; Höglind, M.; Bengochea-Guevara, J.M.; Andújar, D. Comparing UAV-based technologies and RGB-D reconstruction methods for plant height and biomass monitoring on grass ley. *Sensors* **2019**, *19*, 535. [CrossRef] [PubMed]
15. Vit, A.; Shani, G. Comparing RGB-D sensors for close range outdoor agricultural phenotyping. *Sensors* **2018**, *18*, 4413. [CrossRef]
16. Jimenez-Berni, J.A.; Deery, D.M.; Rozas-Larraondo, P.; Condon, A.T.G.; Rebetzke, G.J.; James, R.A.; Bovill, W.D.; Furbank, R.T.; Sirault, X.R. High throughput determination of plant height, ground cover, and above-ground biomass in wheat with LiDAR. *Front. Plant Sci.* **2018**, *9*, 237. [CrossRef]
17. Wang, X.; Singh, D.; Marla, S.; Morris, G.; Poland, J. Field-based high-throughput phenotyping of plant height in sorghum using different sensing technologies. *Plant Methods* **2018**, *14*, 1–16. [CrossRef]
18. Bernotas, G.; Scorza, L.C.; Hansen, M.F.; Hales, I.J.; Halliday, K.J.; Smith, L.N.; Smith, M.L.; McCormick, A.J. A photometric stereo-based 3D imaging system using computer vision and deep learning for tracking plant growth. *GigaScience* **2019**, *8*, giz056. [CrossRef]
19. Tilneac, M.; Dolga, V.; Grigorescu, S.; Bitea, M. 3D stereo vision measurements for weed-crop discrimination. *Elektron. Elektrotechnika* **2012**, *123*, 9–12. [CrossRef]
20. Dandrifosse, S.; Bouvry, A.; Leemans, V.; Dumont, B.; Mercatoris, B. Imaging wheat canopy through stereo vision: Overcoming the challenges of the laboratory to field transition for morphological features extraction. *Front. Plant Sci.* **2020**, *11*, 96. [CrossRef]
21. Wen, J.; Yin, Y.; Zhang, Y.; Pan, Z.; Fan, Y. Detection of Wheat Lodging by Binocular Cameras during Harvesting Operation. *Agriculture* **2022**, *13*, 120. [CrossRef]
22. Bao, Y.; Tang, L. Field-based robotic phenotyping for sorghum biomass yield component traits characterization using stereo vision. *IFAC-PapersOnLine* **2016**, *49*, 265–270. [CrossRef]
23. Eltner, A.; Hoffmeister, D.; Kaiser, A.; Karrasch, P.; Klingbeil, L.; Stöcker, C.; Rovere, A. *UAVs for the Environmental Sciences: Methods and Applications*; wbg Academic in Wissenschaftliche Buchgesellschaft (WBG): Darmstadt, Germany, 2022; Chapter 1.5.1.2.
24. Tanaka, Y.; Watanabe, T.; Katsura, K.; Tsujimoto, Y.; Takai, T.; Tanaka, T.S.T.; Kawamura, K.; Saito, H.; Homma, K.; Mairoua, S.G.; et al. Deep learning enables instant and versatile estimation of rice yield using ground-based RGB images. *Plant Phenomics* **2023**, *5*, 0073. [CrossRef]
25. Zhang, J.; Wang, C.; Yang, C.; Xie, T.; Jiang, Z.; Hu, T.; Luo, Z.; Zhou, G.; Xie, J. Assessing the effect of real spatial resolution of in situ UAV multispectral images on seedling rapeseed growth monitoring. *Remote Sens.* **2020**, *12*, 1207. [CrossRef]
26. Zaji, A.; Liu, Z.; Xiao, G.; Bhowmik, P.; Sangha, J.S.; Ruan, Y. Wheat Spikes Height Estimation Using Stereo Cameras. *IEEE Trans. Agrifood Electron.* **2023**, *1*, 15–28. [CrossRef]
27. Cai, J.; Kumar, P.; Chopin, J.; Miklavcic, S.J. Land-based crop phenotyping by image analysis: Accurate estimation of canopy height distributions using stereo images. *PLoS ONE* **2018**, *13*, e0196671. [CrossRef]
28. Brocks, S.; Bareth, G. Estimating barley biomass with crop surface models from oblique RGB imagery. *Remote Sens.* **2018**, *10*, 268. [CrossRef]
29. Schima, R.; Mollenhauer, H.; Grenzdörffer, G.; Merbach, I.; Lausch, A.; Dietrich, P.; Bumberger, J. Imagine all the plants: Evaluation of a light-field camera for on-site crop growth monitoring. *Remote Sens.* **2016**, *8*, 823. [CrossRef]
30. Schädler, M.; Buscot, F.; Klotz, S.; Reitz, T.; Durka, W.; Bumberger, J.; Merbach, I.; Michalski, S.G.; Kirsch, K.; Remmler, P.; et al. Investigating the consequences of climate change under different land-use regimes: A novel experimental infrastructure. *Ecosphere* **2019**, *10*, e02635. [CrossRef]
31. Ballot, R.; Guilpart, N.; Jeuffroy, M.-H. The first map of crop sequence types in Europe over 2012–2018. *Earth Syst. Sci. Data* **2023**, *15*, 5651–5666. [CrossRef]
32. Allied Vision Technologies GmbH. Mako Technical Manual. 2023. Available online: https://cdn.alliedvision.com/fileadmin/content/documents/products/cameras/Mako/techman/Mako_TechMan_en.pdf (accessed on 18 January 2024).
33. EXTRA Computer GmbH. Pokini i2 Data Sheet. 2023. Available online: https://os.extracomputer.de/b10256/devpokini/wp-content/uploads/2020/07/Pokini-I2_Datenblatt_DE_V1-2_02-2020_web.pdf (accessed on 18 January 2024).
34. Allied Vision Technologies GmbH. About. 2023. Available online: https://www.alliedvision.com/ (accessed on 18 January 2024).
35. Proulx, R. On the general relationship between plant height and aboveground biomass of vegetation stands in contrasted ecosystems. *PLoS ONE* **2021**, *16*, e0252080. [CrossRef] [PubMed]
36. Walter, J.D.; Edwards, J.; McDonald, G.; Kuchel, H. Estimating biomass and canopy height with LiDAR for field crop breeding. *Front. Plant Sci.* **2019**, *10*, 1145. [CrossRef]
37. Van der Walt, S.; Schönberger, J.L.; Nunez-Iglesias, J.; Boulogne, F.; Warner, J.D.; Yager, N.; Gouillart, E.; Yu, T. scikit-image: Image processing in Python. *PeerJ* **2014**, *2*, e453. [CrossRef]
38. Breiman, L. Random forests. *Mach. Learn.* **2001**, *45*, 5–32. [CrossRef]
39. Bradski, G. The openCV library. *Dr. Dobb's J. Softw. Tools Prof. Program.* **2000**, *25*, 120–123.
40. Pedregosa, F.; Varoquaux, G.; Gramfort, A.; Michel, V.; Thirion, B.; Grisel, O.; Blondel, M.; Prettenhofer, P.; Weiss, R.; Dubourg, V.; et al. Scikit-learn: Machine learning in Python. *J. Mach. Learn.* **2011**, *12*, 2825–2830.
41. Brown, D.C. Close-range camera calibration. *Photogramm. Eng* **1971**, *37*, 855–866.

42. Godding, R. Camera Calibration. In *Handbook of Machine and Computer Vision*; John Wiley & Sons, Ltd.: Hoboken, NJ, USA, 2017; Chapter 5, pp. 291–316. [CrossRef]
43. Agisoft Helpdesk Portal. 4D Processing. 2022. Available online: https://agisoft.freshdesk.com/support/solutions/articles/31000155179-4d-processing (accessed on 18 January 2024).
44. James, M.R.; Antoniazza, G.; Robson, S.; Lane, S.N. Mitigating systematic error in topographic models for geomorphic change detection: Accuracy, precision and considerations beyond off-nadir imagery. *Earth Surf. Process. Landf.* **2020**, *45*, 2251–2271. [CrossRef]
45. James, M.R.; Robson, S.; Smith, M.W. 3-D uncertainty-based topographic change detection with structure-from-motion photogrammetry: Precision maps for ground control and directly georeferenced surveys. *Earth Surf. Process. Landf.* **2017**, *42*, 1769–1788. [CrossRef]
46. Girardeau-Montaut, D. CloudCompare. *Fr. EDF R&D Telecom ParisTech* **2016**, *11*, 5.
47. Huttenlocher, D.P.; Klanderman, G.A.; Rucklidge, W.J. Comparing images using the Hausdorff distance. *IEEE Trans. Pattern Anal. Mach. Intell.* **1993**, *15*, 850–863. . [CrossRef]
48. Millard, K.; Richardson, M. On the importance of training data sample selection in random forest image classification: A case study in peatland ecosystem mapping. *Remote Sens.* **2015**, *7*, 8489–8515. [CrossRef]
49. Sheykhmousa, M.; Mahdianpari, M.; Ghanbari, H.; Mohammadimanesh, F.; Ghamisi, P.; Homayouni, S. Support Vector Machine Versus Random Forest for Remote Sensing Image Classification: A Meta-Analysis and Systematic Review. *IEEE J. Sel. Top. Appl. Earth Obs. Remote Sens.* **2020**, *13*, 6308–6325. [CrossRef]
50. Peña, J.M.; Gutiérrez, P.A.; Hervás-Martínez, C.; Six, J.; Plant, R.E.; López-Granados, F. Object-based image classification of summer crops with machine learning methods. *Remote Sens.* **2014**, *6*, 5019–5041. [CrossRef]
51. Kumar, S.; Kaur, R. Plant disease detection using image processing—A review. *Int. J. Comput. Appl.* **2015**, *124*. [CrossRef]
52. Zhou, C.L.; Ge, L.M.; Guo, Y.B.; Zhou, D.M.; Cun, Y.P. A comprehensive comparison on current deep learning approaches for plant image classification. In *Proceedings of the Journal of Physics: Conference Series*; IOP Publishing: Bristol, UK, 2021; Volume 1873, p. 012002. [CrossRef]
53. Kraus, K. *Photogrammetry*, 2nd ed.; DE GRUYTER: Berlin, Germany, 2007. [CrossRef]
54. Elias, M.; Eltner, A.; Liebold, F.; Maas, H.G. Assessing the Influence of Temperature Changes on the Geometric Stability of Smartphone- and Raspberry Pi Cameras. *Sensors* **2020**, *20*, 643. [CrossRef] [PubMed]
55. Schoenberger, J.L. COLMAP. 2023. Available online: https://colmap.github.io/index.html (accessed on 18 January 2024).
56. Kim, T.K.; Kim, S.; Won, M.; Lim, J.H.; Yoon, S.; Jang, K.; Lee, K.H.; Park, Y.D.; Kim, H.S. Utilizing machine learning for detecting flowering in mid-range digital repeat photography. *Ecol. Model.* **2021**, *440*, 109419. [CrossRef]
57. Gitelson, A.A.; Kaufman, Y.J.; Stark, R.; Rundquist, D. Novel algorithms for remote estimation of vegetation fraction. *Remote Sens. Environ.* **2002**, *80*, 76–87. [CrossRef]
58. Wu, Z.; Chen, Y.; Zhao, B.; Kang, X.; Ding, Y. Review of weed detection methods based on computer vision. *Sensors* **2021**, *21*, 3647. [CrossRef] [PubMed]
59. Gerhards, M.; Rock, G.; Schlerf, M.; Udelhoven, T. Water stress detection in potato plants using leaf temperature, emissivity, and reflectance. *Int. J. Appl. Earth Obs. Geoinf.* **2016**, *53*, 27–39. [CrossRef]
60. Sobrino, J.A.; Del Frate, F.; Drusch, M.; Jiménez-Muñoz, J.C.; Manunta, P.; Regan, A. Review of thermal infrared applications and requirements for future high-resolution sensors. *IEEE Trans. Geosci. Remote Sens.* **2016**, *54*, 2963–2972. [CrossRef]
61. Maas, H.G. Mehrbildtechniken in der Digitalen Photogrammetrie. Habilitation Thesis, ETH Zurich, Zürich, Switzerland, 1997. [CrossRef]
62. Lin, D.; Bannehr, L.; Ulrich, C.; Maas, H.G. Evaluating thermal attribute mapping strategies for oblique airborne photogrammetric system AOS-Tx8. *Remote Sens.* **2019**, *12*, 112. [CrossRef]

MDPI AG
Grosspeteranlage 5
4052 Basel
Switzerland
Tel.: +41 61 683 77 34

Remote Sensing Editorial Office
E-mail: remotesensing@mdpi.com
www.mdpi.com/journal/remotesensing

www.ingramcontent.com/pod-product-compliance
Lightning Source LLC
Chambersburg PA
CBHW040744250926
51850CB00007BB/1400
* 9 7 8 3 7 2 5 8 5 8 6 9 9 *